YOUR
G

OH, WHAT A CIRCUS

Tim Rice

The Autobiography

1944–1978

coronet

CORONET BOOKS
Hodder & Stoughton

First published in Great Britain in 1999 by Hodder and Stoughton
First published in paperback in 2000 by Hodder and Stoughton
A division of Hodder Headline

A Coronet Paperback

10 9 8 7 6 5 4 3 2 1

A CIP catalogue record for this title is available
from the British Library

ISBN 0 340 65459 7

Typeset by Palimpsest Book Production Limited,
Polmont, Stirlingshire
Printed and bound in Australia by
Griffin Press Pty Ltd, Netley, South Australia

Hodder and Stoughton
A division of Hodder Headline
338 Euston Road
London NW1 3BH

For my mother and father

For Jo and Andy

For Jane, Eva and Donald

Acknowledgements

My thanks to Rowena Webb and Laura Brockbank at Hodder & Stoughton; to Eileen Heinink, John Fingleton and Stephanie Darnill for checking things; and to around 85 per cent of the people mentioned in the text.

While every effort has been made to obtain permission from the photographers and copyright holders of the pictures used in this book, the author and publishers apologise to anyone who has not been contacted in advance or credited.

Prologue

On 21 April 1965, I wrote a short letter to a young man I had never met. His name had been given to me by a book publisher but I was hopeful that we would write some songs together. The following day he phoned me at the office at which I was pursuing a half-hearted attempt to become a lawyer and a day or two later I went to his parents' flat in South Kensington to say hello.

The boy who greeted me proved to be the acme of paradox. He oozed contradiction. Aspects of this were instantly apparent; he seemed at once awkward and confident; sophisticated and naïve; mature and childlike. Later I discovered that he was also humorous and portentous; innovative and derivative; loyal and cavalier; generous and self-centred; all these characteristics to the extreme.

I was ushered into his room, a drawing room, a salon even, an oasis of cultured sanity surrounded by what appeared to be a quite shambolic cluster of rooms in which the less enterprising members of the family operated. Moving from the kitchen to his parlour was an upgrade from economy to business class. Here was the largest collection of records I had ever seen, the first stereo record player and tuner I had come across and the astonishing evidence that a teenager existed who had spent money on Georgian wine glasses, pictures and furniture.

His name was Andrew Lloyd Webber and he was just seventeen (you know what I mean). He had won a scholarship to Magdalen

College, Oxford, to read history, and he had nine months to kill before going up, during which time he intended to kill to become England's Richard Rodgers.

My own ambitions were just as insane; I wanted to be a pop star, for all the healthy reasons – women, money and fame. It seemed to me that plenty of other blokes around my age (twenty) and not overburdened with talent were making it and I wished to be of their number. There were even guys from my home town (Donovan, the Zombies) and from public school (Peter and Gordon) in the charts – surely I had the qualifications. The difference between Andrew and myself was that my dreams were never life or death to me, though it's easy to say that now. They might have become so had I failed.

Consequently when Andrew suggested a completely new insane ambition for me, i.e. to become the Hammerstein to his Rodgers, I had no qualms about giving it a go. This was partly because within ten minutes of our introduction, he was at the piano and had played me three or four tunes he had composed – I could tell that he was good. Very good. I was reminded of many of the best show albums from my parents' LP collection as he confidently bashed out selections from some of the many shows he had written and produced at school. He needed a new lyricist for the outside world.

I had very little to impress him with in return, other than instant praise for his music and a bona fide, actually released, seven-inch single of a song I had written (both words and music) with which an unknown pop group had dealt the final blow to their moribund career by recording three months previously. Actually many years later Cameron Mackintosh (not always the most reliable source of gossip) told me that Andrew had admitted being bowled over by my looks and general demeanour. This is hard to believe thirty years on but I suppose, with hindsight, that I was a reasonably striking youth in 1965. The pity is I never realised what I had in that department until it had more or less departed.

We parted, promising to meet again and to write something together. I was still more interested in the charts than in the West End, but told myself on the bus back to my flat in Gunter Grove that I had just met somebody of rare ability and determination and I would be mad to miss out on being a sidekick to a chap who was clearly going to take the musical theatre by storm, probably by next week.

Furthermore, he did have the largest private collection of pop records I had ever seen (what was more, mainly LPs) and if Lionel Bart was not successfully challenged, then we could try to knock the Beatles and Stones off their perches later in the summer. The Everly Brothers had just made a comeback and would clearly be in need of some new material.

Back at my articled clerk's desk the next day the brief certainty I had enjoyed of a life in show business with Andrew Lloyd Webber had faded somewhat. I would of course continue to keep an eye on the small ads in *Melody Maker* for groups needing a vocalist, and would turn out a few more three-chord songs tailored not to expose the limitations of my voice, but it was still odds-on that eventually I would stagger through my exams and wind up a respectable lawyer by the time I was twenty-five. Make that twenty-six, as I had already fallen at the first examination hurdle twice. By then I would have surely grown out of pop music as my father had confidently predicted I would by the time I was twenty-one. This was worrying – if he was right I only had a few more months of enjoying it.

But in the meantime I felt I had nothing to lose by seeing Andrew again. It would be fun to go and see a musical with him, to write words that aped Alan Jay Lerner or Michael Flanders rather than Bob Dylan or Ray Davies. And Andrew was a fascinating individual who talked of *Good Food Guides* and Victorian architecture, besides supporting Leyton Orient. I wasn't convinced by the idea for a musical that he had been working on for the past year, but in 1965 I was very rarely convinced about anything. His talent was beyond question and he claimed to have all the contacts. I was soon back in his drawing room.

The idea was the life of Dr Thomas Barnardo, the nineteenth-century philanthropist who founded the orphanages that bear his name. His story was a worthy one indeed, but not one that truly fired my imagination. The hero was too squeaky clean, at least in Andrew's version of his life, and the enterprise was unoriginal in both conception and execution. It owed far too much to Lionel Bart's *Oliver*, the biggest and best British musical of the decade. Like *Oliver*, our show, *The Likes Of Us*, was set in Victorian London with Cockney children, well-meaning aristocrats and loose women with hearts of gold all over the shop. On the other hand, Andrew's conviction of his score's precocious brilliance was infectious and not totally unjustified. What did I know about musicals? As David Land, later to be my agent for over a quarter of a century, memorably (and repeatedly) said, if there's a demand for one hamburger bar on the block, there was room for two. We could be the second hamburger joint.

I set to work with enormous enthusiasm, in particular for those songs that were intended to be funny. Andrew outlined the plot, played me the tunes and in many instances gave me the title as well, most of which had presumably been thought up by his ex-wordsmith school pal who had already had a go. I often wonder if he would have sued me had any of my songs with his titles become a hit ('where there's a hit, there's a writ' – David Land). My first ever effort for Andrew was a number entitled 'Going, Going, Gone', an auction set to music, during which the oh so noble Barnardo buys the Edinburgh Castle gin palace to house the first of the many children he has pulled in from the squalor of the London streets. An anonymous auctioneer sang the first ever Lloyd Webber/Rice couplet:

> Here I have a lovely parrot sound in wind and limb
> I can guarantee that there is nothing wrong with him

At least it was a pure rhyme which is more than can be said for many others in *The Likes Of Us*.

I skipped a day at the solicitors' office, faking illness, to write my first batch of theatrical lyrics. I did not know it that day but I had changed careers.

Chapter One

The route that led me to a lawyers' office in 1963 was conventional and in most respects I was a conventional child. I had every opportunity to break away from the herd in that I ran up some remarkable academic achievements from a very early age, but time and time again I got bored when things got too easy. I spotted far too soon that out and out rebellion rarely produced the desired result and, even more alarming, often felt my parents were by and large right about most things, which they were. From day one I seemed to have a very detached view of my own place in the world. I reckoned most of my failings and enthusiasms were just a phase I was going through, which meant I could enjoy them wholeheartedly until I became part of an older generation which would probably be perfectly satisfactory judging by the fist my parents had made of it. I was happy to be programmed to be all right on the night.

I remember numbers most of all. I loved them, the bigger the better. When my mother was twenty-eight, in August 1947, I recall spending hours designing a birthday card which featured every number from one to twenty-eight in loving sequence. The first conversation I can recall with my father had me asking what the number 1947 on the kitchen calendar and at the top of *The Times* meant. By the time I was five I was writing out endless strings of multiplication tables. My father had a wonderful book about the Solar System, *The Conquest Of Space* by Chesley Bonestell and Willy Ley, which led me into even more unimaginable lists of figures and in turn into an obsession with the planets, moons and asteroids. I learned their names and statistics off by heart, beginning to enjoy romantic words as much as beautiful numbers. The (then) nine moons of Saturn: Mimas, Enceladus, Tethys, Dione, Rhea, Titan, Hyperion, Iapetus and Phoebe. I recite it still.

Astronomy earned me my first newspaper cutting and an early realisation that you always get misquoted by the press. In 1951 I was taken to the Festival of Britain on London's South Bank, a marvellous celebration of Britain's past achievements and of its certain domination of the future. Science and architecture were strikingly combined. Post-war austerity was surely finished and this impressive exhibition, in part a commemoration of the centenary of Prince Albert's Crystal Palace extravaganza of 1851, included futuristic constructions such as the Skylon and the Dome of Discovery as well as a huge funfair. Inside the Dome of Discovery was housed a working scale model of the Solar System. The nine planets rolled silently around the sun and the satellites in turn scuttled around the planets. I fought my way to the front of the crowd and stared for hours at this hypnotic contraption. My mother's desperate appeals that we should visit other parts of the exhibition were countered by a squeaky plea to stay for one more Jupiter lap, or at least one more from Mars. We did get out long enough on one occasion to buy ice-creams from a cheerful girl under a sign which read 'See you all again in 2051!' I determined then and there to keep the date as I would only be 106 and to this day have a crazy feeling I might – I'm half way there already.

Later that year I read with horror that the Solar System model was to be dismantled after the Festival closed. What a waste! I rushed off a letter to the organisers of the exhibition and asked if I could have the model as it was clearly not needed by anybody else. I enclosed my own map of the Solar System as proof of my astronomical credentials but even this did not persuade the authorities, who wrote me a polite letter of regret. They also tipped off the London *Evening News* and a photographer turned up a few days later to take a picture of this embryo Einstein. A reporter interviewed me on the phone and asked me various questions about the planets. I gave him a few facts and on 1 October 1951 I made my national (well, London and the South-East) press début:

COSMOLOGY IS FUN TO SIX-YEAR-OLD TIMOTHY
Evening News Reporter

Surrounded by hefty encyclopedias and other bulky volumes dealing with the science of astronomy and the conquest of space, he sits there in his den poring over curious, self-drawn planetary charts and diagrams and scribbling down arithmetical equations.

Suddenly he calls out: 'Saturn is 75,000 miles in diameter, and the atmosphere of the planet is largely ammoniacal.'

Let me explain that this authoritative statement is uttered not by a bearded professor but by a shrill-voiced little boy of six.

For everybody who lives around his home at Popesfield Farm, Smallford, Near St Albans, knows that fair-haired young Timothy Rice has hitched his hobby-wagon to the stars.

You can't tempt him with trains or aeroplanes any more – not since his father left a book on star-gazing lying around the house.

That was eighteen months ago, when Timothy was 4½. Since then he has read and re-read every book on the subject he can get his hands on.

He has even widened his studies to include cosmology, and his brain for figures finds it comparatively easy to calculate planetary distances.

Of course brothers Jonathan, aged four, and eighteen-month-old Andrew, haven't the faintest idea what Timothy is talking about when he expounds his technical knowledge.

Frankly, I was amazed at the sloppy report. Well might the *News* man have remained anonymous. Apart from the mis-spelling of Popefield Farm, and the fact that my brother Jo knew almost as much about the planets as I did because he had to listen to me going on about it all day, I never said what he claimed I did about Saturn's atmosphere. Nor did I know what cosmology was. No one lived near enough to our home to know about my hobby-wagon, whatever a hobby-wagon might be; we lived in a farmhouse with no neighbours. But I never wrote to complain – a wise move and something I wish I had stuck to more often since.

My mother told me recently that as she had nothing to compare me with she was never proud, or for that matter worried, that they had sired a prodigy. She did however wonder if it was entirely natural for a five-year-old to write out multiplication tables up to and even beyond a hundred on rolls of unwanted wallpaper, but if that was the nearest I came to being a problem child, she could live with it. But I never recall any attempt to push me into further precocious ventures, and they never dreamed of cashing in on my mini-brush with fame, commercially or socially. Which was just as well, as I was soon to relapse into more down-market obsessions derived from my love of numbers such as cricket and the pop charts – not to mention girls' school stories by Enid Blyton, and the *Eagle*.

My father, Hugh Gordon Rice, was born in London in 1917. Towards the end of his life (he died in 1988) he spent considerable time investigating the Rice family tree and although one of my great-aunts was convinced until her dying day that my father was only a couple of heartbeats removed from the Dukedom of Buccleuch, he never uncovered much evidence to support this claim. (Aunt Nettie did however share the family name Scott with His Grace.)

Hugh's family was Scottish. His great-grandfather William McPherson Rice, who was born in 1796, was a painter of some achievement and a naval architect. A striking oil by William McPherson entitled 'Ships At Bay' is about the closest we come to a family heirloom. His son Michael, born in 1843, was a doctor in Edinburgh and it was he who shifted the clan south of the border, to Lincolnshire. Michael's son Frank, my paternal grandfather, was born in 1877, and my father arrived in 1917, by which time the family were in Surrey. Frank was never able to marry my father's mother, Edith Cole. His first wife, Beatrice, by whom he had a son and daughter, had disappeared rather abruptly from her family's life, denying Frank any opportunity of divorce.

Beatrice eventually wound up in America, as (much later) did her children, my father's half-brother and sister. I was unaware of, or had forgotten about, this fact when I first achieved a modicum of notoriety in the United States in 1970. Consequently, when I received one or two letters from Rices in America, claiming to be relatives of the young English chap who had just written *Jesus Christ Superstar*, I am afraid I dismissed them as obvious fakes. Some undoubtedly were, notably the alleged cousins who wanted a loan, but I now realise I may have unfairly dismissed some of those with whom I shared a gene or two – perhaps if they read this, they may try to establish contact a second time, when I can assure them they will not be treated in such a cavalier fashion.

Both my father's parents died young: Frank, a wallpaper designer, suffered from rheumatoid arthritis which led to a fatal heart attack in 1923, and two years later, when Hugh was not quite eight, Edith succumbed to cancer. He went to live with Frank's eldest sister, the socially confident Aunt Nettie in Wallington, Surrey, and her husband Bindon Scott, a civil servant based in the City of London. Nettie, with no children of her own, had already nobly brought up Beatrice's abandoned offspring.

Soon after being orphaned, Hugh was sent to Christ's Hospital, the public school near Horsham, known to this day not only for its excellent educational reputation, but for the uniform of cassock, yellow socks and buckled shoes which have remained unchanged since its foundation in the sixteenth century. Then as now, it was a school that took first the sons of clergy and those who had lost one or both parents, enabling it through trusts to ease the burden of high fees on these generally disadvantaged boys. Both at school and at home Hugh's upbringing was strict and instilled into him a fairly inflexible code of behaviour, the ordered middle-class values of the times by which he lived throughout his life. These were good values which, allied to his great personal charm and perfect manners, served him, and those he looked after, well. Six foot five, dark, handsome and (at least when I first knew him) slim, his attributes ensured him great popularity which he treated with modest good humour. He lacked, indeed deliberately rejected, the killer instinct to bring him ultimate financial and business success – being a good guy will only get you so far. But his wit and intelligence, not to mention his great capacity for having a good time, and the love of his family were the foundation of a happy life (lived permanently just above his means).

His sons inherited, and my mother shared, his inefficiency as far as making money is concerned, which may sound ludicrous coming from a son who has on occasion appeared in the Top 500 Richest People in Britain lists. These lists are often little more than desperate guesswork on the part of their compilers, but if I had been blessed with cash know-how I would have by now clocked into the Top Twenty. I was simply lucky enough to succeed in a career that overpays its winners to the extent that even the most drug-crazed earl would have trouble mislaying it all. My parents were on more than one occasion bailed out of trouble by my maternal grandmother, not a woman of enormous wealth, but one who kept a tighter rein on the readies than her descendants. My brothers and I never had any inkling of this at the time, beyond the endless demand, economic, not environmental, for energy conservation – switch off every light and close every window in the winter. To this day I feel uneasy if a video stand-by light is winking at me.

Upon leaving Christ's Hospital in 1935, Hugh joined the Orient Line as a shipping clerk, working in the City, with the occasional working cruise thrown in. He joined the Honourable Artillery Company as a volunteer, which gave him a head start when call-up and war loomed in 1939. His passion was aeroplanes, fired by endless hours of plane-spotting at Croydon Aerodrome as a boy, but good opportunities with the RAF were limited and his size would have weighed against any attempt to become a pilot. His army war service began at Aldershot, whence he was posted overseas to India, took part in the Liberation of Iraq and arrived in Egypt in early 1942 as an Air Liaison officer.

The highlight of his war was imminent. On a photographic reconnaissance course he met my mother, Joan Odette Bawden, a lively redhead just a foot shorter than he, a section officer with the Women's Auxiliary Air Force, based in Egypt as a photographic interpreter. He was twenty-five, she was twenty-three and a whirl-wind, or at least Khamsin*, romance led to a wedding in Cairo on 27 December of that year.

Guests at their wedding were few and in the main friends whom they only knew briefly as part of the transient rushed chaos of war

---

* A strong flow of warm desert air from the south, a North African weather regular.

in foreign countries. Many years later my father ran into one of his former wartime colleagues in the Strand and over a beer they caught up with the past. 'Well, for a start, I've been married for over ten years,' my father revealed. 'I know,' said his friend. 'I was your best man.'

Joan was the elder daughter of George Dountain Bawden and Florence Mabel Raison. George (Grandpa), who died in 1949, and of whom I have only one or two hazy memories, was an erratic businessman, husband and father, one year a high-rolling spender, the next down to his last penny. On more than one occasion during Joan's childhood, the family had to make a hurried move from substantial house to ramshackle lodgings as fortunes waned, only to return to the luxury of servants and more comfortable surroundings as his next scheme took off for a while.

George dabbled in many things but hit the jackpot most often in the rag trade. A heart condition prevented first World War service and those terrible years saw him establish a thriving blouse business in Watford. My grandmother, Florrie, or Ray (for Raison) as she was known in her working circles, born in 1890, enjoyed a long career in fashion, not retiring fully until the 1960s, and was among other things a model in her twenties. Family archives do not reveal a great deal about George's first wife, still in tow when he embarked upon his affair with Ray, nearly twenty years his junior. My mother was born in 1919, before George and Ray married, thus completing a family illegitimacy double that neither of my parents knew about until well into their fifties. Joan's sister Pamela followed in 1921.

Ray, a remarkable woman who played nearly as important a role in my life as that of my parents, and who died in 1986 at the age of ninety-five, was one of five children. Her father, John Raison, was for a time Alfred Lord Tennyson's valet, and later kept a coffee shop at 321 Portobello Road, Notting Hill. His wife Eliza's maiden name was Wedlock, singularly inappropriate in view of subsequent events. John died in 1912, in his mid-fifties.

My mother and her father were never that close. It was difficult for Joan to come to terms with the way he reacted to the serious illness of her sister Pamela. At thirteen years of age, Pamela contracted rheumatic fever. Today she would have undoubtedly survived, and might have done so in 1935 but for my grand-father's involvement at the time with Christian Science. Instead of medical attention Pamela was sent to the seaside to stay with Ray's sister and brother-in-law, the delightful Auntie Gertie and Uncle Arthur (a butcher), at St Leonards-on-Sea in Sussex. Gertie summoned the doctor for Pamela, but the illness was too far advanced and the little girl died, in hospital too late, in March 1935.

Joan's first school was a very repressive convent in Finchley but when cash became tight she was moved to Paddington and Maida Vale High School of which she has nothing but good memories. She left at seventeen with a fistful of matriculation successes and after a secretarial course joined Shell in the City, working at the Aseatic Petroleum Company branch of the company. She had ambitions to be a writer and sent off a string of 'long sad stories and heartrending plays' to publishers and newspapers. Her first break into print came with a funny poem, published in *Eve's Journal*, for which she was paid 10/6d (52½p). The war put a stop to her literary activities but they were to resume very productively many years later.

In 1939 she volunteered for the WAAF almost on the spur of the moment in one lunch hour and, after eighteen months at RAF Hendon, was posted to Medmenham in Oxfordshire, qualified as a photographic interpreter and eventually achieved her ambition to go abroad when chosen for a posting to Singapore. What could have been a fatal move for her was aborted when Singapore fell to the Japanese and instead she sailed around the Cape to Egypt, where she took up her duties as photographic reconnaissance officer.

After the marriage my father fought with the Eighth Army in North Africa (El Alamein) and in Sicily and Italy. Major Rice returned to England in early 1944 in preparation for the D-Day operations and shortly afterwards my mother, on her first home leave after over two years abroad, became pregnant. On the morning of 10 November 1944, Joan was admitted to the temporary nursing home established at Shardeloes, a beautiful country house just outside Amersham in Buckinghamshire. Hugh, having survived the Second Front campaign and the aftermath of

D-Day, was back in England training young officers locally, and visited her in the afternoon where he noted she

> was having a very rough time – however it had only started just before and we didn't expect junior to appear for ages. I left her, rather apprehensively, at 5.30 and drove back to the college and had some beer while wondering how to pass the time. At 9 o'clock, after dinner, I rang up to see how she was. To my astonishment, I heard that Timothy had arrived 15 minutes after I left, and that they were both flourishing!

My father met me for the first time at eleven the following morning and described Joan as 'like a dog with two tails', me as 'fine and hearty but I was a bit apprehensive of something so small and of such an odd colour. He weighed 8lbs 6 oz and had a little wispy hair.' Not the best, but certainly not the worst, review I was to get in my life.

Chapter Two

My mother and I remained within the stately confines of Shardeloes for a few days while my father's diary records that he wrestled with my grandmother, an extraordinary succession of flat tyres and 'the opening phases of the very sinister coastal convoy exercise which goes on all this week', the first two items causing him more immediate problems than the third. A relationship was temporarily strained on the domestic front as Hugh confidently placed his mother-in-law plus several suitcases on a bus to Windsor instead of on the bus to see her daughter and new grandson in Amersham. Another would have been had I understood English then as my father's next diary reference to his son and heir on 14 November describes him as the 'heaviest and greediest baby in the world'.

However I was not the only individual to suffer therein. The lecturers at Hugh's staff college all received detailed critiques of their performances, for both content and delivery, many praised, but some, like Sir Archibald Sinclair – 'a pompous patronising ass who can't speak and seems to be far too clueless to be a Secretary of State' – thought of less highly. On 29 November Sir Stafford Cripps (then Minister of Aircraft Production) talked on 'officially, post-war reconstruction, but actually, on post-war socialisation. I didn't agree with a word he said and he was so ridiculously Russia-is-always-right and equally ridiculously the-worker-is-more-important-than-the-management. Nonetheless he was so patently sincere that one felt rather an outsider trying to shoot him down, which we all attempted.'

On 27 November my heavy and greedy frame was finally shipped out of Shardeloes to my first home at Greenriggs, a small house in Gerrard's Cross which my mother had rented for a year with her best friend, my godmother, Barbara Howroyd. Barbie too was the mother of an extremely young but hefty infant, Michael, who never knew his father. Barbie's husband David, a bomber pilot, was killed in action after seeing his only child just once.

Although my father's diary entries of his spell in England at the end of 1944 are often very funny and give the impression of a spirited class and generation determined to make the most of life, there is no doubt that the shadow of war, albeit a war nearly won, was a sobering presence, as Barbie's loss must have continuously emphasised to my parents. My father was still to see a good deal more active service, primarily in Germany, in 1945. He had the good fortune to survive the six years of war almost unscathed, but too many of his pages noted the deaths of friends and colleagues, just as many others record truly exciting and inspiring moments. The first part of my parents' adult lives was played out against a background of urgency and uncertainty that my generation, and my children's generation, can only wonder at. Had I kept a diary in my twenties as detailed as my father's, it could not have reflected a fraction of the challenge and excitement, of the highs and the lows, of Hugh's early adulthood, or of those of so many of his contemporaries, so many to die so young.

Nonetheless, a record of my twenties is in part what is coming up. Well before that, however, I moved to my second semi-permament home in Combe Bissett, Wiltshire. After the end of the war in Europe and the General Election of July 1945 – 'the completely overwhelming and completely unexpected socialist victory has astounded everyone, and most of the officers were pretty gloomy' – my father's final posting was to another staff college, in Old Sarum. He had long decided not to stay in the army after the war and began searching earnestly for a civilian job. He reverted to his first love – aeroplanes – and among his applications was an approach to the de Havilland Aircraft Company, based in Hatfield, Hertfordshire. An excellent writer (and lecturer), he had a few articles published in aviation magazines around this time.

My father eventually received a letter from Martin Sharp, the boss of de Havilland's public relations, and on 1 December, went to Hatfield where he was offered £650 p.a. and a £50 cost of living bonus, to start by 1 February 1946. This important step in his life was matched by my first four days later: 'Tim took one step – and fell flat. But he can stand for nearly a minute at a time.' My second Christmas was spent at Walmer, Kent, with my great-aunts Nettie, Lizzie and Pat, the first the grand lady who had raised my father, the second her sister, and the last a cousin who was also the grandmother of the then as-minuscule-as-me future cricket writer and authority (and friend), Christopher Martin-Jenkins.

Hugh's first position at de Havilland, under Martin Sharp, was as editor of the *De Havilland Gazette*, a very glossy, especially for the time, in-house magazine, that put many wider-circulation publications to shame. Mint copies of issues are very valuable today. The *Gazette* covered many aspects of the aviation world beyond the far from narrow confines of the internationally-famous aeroplane manufacturer's Hertfordshire HQ. Martin Sharp, his wife Barbara, and daughters became very close and life-long friends of the Rices. Christabel and Rosalind Sharp, respectively two years and four months older than me, are my oldest friends, have played an important part in many aspects of my life and we remain in close touch to this day. They were the sisters I never had, I suppose, although that phrase sounds faintly rude (and if so, not totally accurate).

House-hunting had to be renewed and my parents moved to temporary digs in London and then to Watford, while searching for a more fixed abode nearer Hatfield. Eventually they were able to rent a house in Croxley Green, near Watford, that was the subject of a probate dispute for the best part of a year, while lawyers of different sides of the testator's family slugged it out. My earliest memories are of that home in Croxley Green – the incredibly cold winter of early 1947, and the arrival of a young lady named Edna Webdale as a lodger-cum-nanny. Edna too is still very much a part of our lives, even though she emigrated to Australia in 1956, as Mrs George McKaige. Every time I go to Melbourne in connection with some show or, more probably, to watch a Test Match, I go to see, and sometimes stay with, Edna and George, in order to sample 1947 again.

In February 1947 my brother Jonathan was born and Edna became his godmother. If I ever held a position of prime attention in the family I do not recall Jo (as he soon became known) ever threatening it – if anything he was even heftier and greedier than I was during his early days and easily as laid back. Two contented children moved at the end of that year to my parents' first owned home (mortgaged to the gills) at 29 Cross Path, Radlett, only a few miles from de Havilland at Hatfield.

I was always a pretty healthy child. The only remotely serious health cock-up (literally) I suffered before 1960 was the highly embarrassing one of prepuce problems. I was unable to pee without intense pain and eventually my father had to abandon his anti-circumcision position. I have a hazy recollection of a short stay in hospital, just before we moved to Radlett, but fortunately no recall of the actual operation that converted me irrevocably to the Roundhead cause. The operation was further justified in later years as Roundheads always won the dormitory fights against the Cavaliers at all the educational establishments I subsequently attended.

I occasionally drive through Radlett today and usually make a diversion away from the main street to potter down Cross Path. Although Radlett has expanded a great deal since the late Forties, the road itself seems to be much as I have always known it, although for some reason, doubtless inspired by a manic local bureaucracy, the road is now called 'The Cross Path'. Humps in the road can only be a meeting away. Number 29 was and is a modest semi-detached, which in our day had a small lawn and vegetable plot at the back. I recall that we also had a chicken or two, which in the strictly rationed post-war grocery scene, made a vital contribution to variety at breakfast.

Funnily enough, although I have a long-running antipathy towards 'sleeping policemen' or humps in the road, it is just possible that they would have done me a favour in 1948, as I have a vivid memory of our dog, a poodle named Suzie, being hit by a car in Cross Path, inciting me to brief hysteria. Both dog and child survived their respective traumata.

This is not a desperate bid to establish credentials as a deprived or abused child, but I do recall an England when very few luxuries were available and where at the most basic level, that of food and of household services such as heat and light, every measure had to be carefully considered. Extravagances such as entertainment and travel were rare indeed – and we were a comfortable middle-class family. On the other hand, there appeared to be a unifying spirit within the country that we were all in this together and a confidence that things would only get better. The phrase 'before the war' was constantly used by all but the very young and one had a sense of emerging bloody but unbowed from a cataclysmic slice of history, even if one had no idea what had been going on at the time, concerned only with cot and pot.

I was pretty quickly into reading and writing, encouraged enormously by both parents who today would probably be hauled before a social worker to explain their stress-creating force-feeding of letters and numbers to a child who should be allowed to develop at his own pace. My father was a newspaperholic, as I have become. As he spread out his *Times* every morning he spread his enthusiasm for current affairs and for every feature of the paper in my direction. Before I was four I knew my way around *The Times* and the *Daily Graphic*, thanks to him; easier than it would be for a child today as the papers (more rationing) were so much thinner than they are now. I cannot claim to have been reading the political or business columns with enormous interest in 1948–9, but I was an avid fan of less cerebral corners such as the strip cartoons (Pop and Blondie my favourites) and weather forecasts (anything with a map appealed) and I believe to this day a paper that gets those areas right is bound to hook the reader for the rest. I used to enjoy watching my father do *The Times* crossword – I doubt if I ever solved a clue for him but I understood one or two of his explanations. He used to construct less taxing crosswords for me.

Most of my number-mania came from my mother, who always claimed that mathematics had been her weak link at school. Nonetheless, spotting my love of counting, she raced me through the first five or six years of the average prep-school elementary maths syllabus by the time I was five. This was never done formally but for fun. I learned about angles and degrees, even a bit of basic algebra. We played lots of card and board games too and I was as happy as a sandboy writing out multiplication tables. I had a surprising lack of interest in anything mechanical and soon demonstrated what was to be a life-long inability to do anything practical with my hands.

Both my parents were literary rather than musical; in fact both were more or less tone deaf. They did however read prodigiously, fact and fiction, ancient and modern, heavy and light. The house was full of books, mainly sixpenny Penguins, and magazines, when a fraction of the number published today existed. There are still many cubic feet of *Punch* and *The Aeroplane* in my mother's attic. They loved the radio and the *Radio Times* became one of my favourite journals, a magical cornucopia of dates, times, numbers, people and places. And it really was the radio times that mattered – the television listings were a tiny footnote to those of the Light Programme, Home Service and Third Programme, and having no television, we had no need of them anyway. My father's general knowledge was voluminous. Every car journey was like an up-market game show with quizzes and facts and figures about every subject under the sun. I am still unbeatable on British cars from 1946–56 – a foreign car was a major event and about a one in 200 shot on the English country lanes back then. I still like to be asked to name all fifty US States in under two minutes.

The young Rice family stayed at Cross Path until September 1950, by which time I knew exactly where, who and when I was. Most of my recollections are general, rather than specific – of embarking upon half a century (to date) of being a nauseatingly fussy eater with a particular aversion to rabbit, served up regularly for Sunday lunch, of sums and a sandpit in the garden, of misbehaving with David and Susan who lived at Number 33, of my father's Ford Anglia (KNK 289) and of Mrs Knight's kindergarten down the road. My mother says she hoped that Mrs Knight's academy would have the effect of stopping me devoting so much time to mathematics and other cerebral antics, presumably the complete opposite of the ambition of every other parent.

I believed that my family was typical and perfect. My parents were loving, father quite naturally stricter than mother, both fine-looking and even nicer than other people's parents. Granny was super-generous, smoked and was only a tiny bit older than my mother (she claimed to be forty when I first enquired about her age). The first time it dawned on me that not every family set-up was exactly the same was when a wee lad at Mrs Knight's claimed to have two grandmothers; I disputed this obvious lie vigorously in the playground but when thinking about it later – of course . . .

Edna moved on to a photographic job at de Havilland, and the first of a string of foreign au pair girls took her place as mother's help. The French one often ate the dog's horsemeat (which despite post-war austerity was, I am glad to say, never intended for the family) with gay abandon. Denmark and Germany were also represented during our Radlett years.

There are also a few specific events that I remember well from that time: the birth of my second brother, Andy, at home, one night in March 1950. My parents were not progressive enough (thank God) to let me and Jo witness the birth but I recall being mildly intrigued by the new member of our family the following morning before returning to the more pressing matter of Tiger Tim, hero of the *Rainbow* comic. A couple of weeks later a far more exciting event took place when my father brought home the first issue of a brand new comic – the *Eagle*. Hugh had the incredible foresight to spot that this was no ordinary publication and made sure that the clumsy hands of his offspring never damaged a single copy. He kept every issue in pristine condition and I have every one of the first fifteen years of *Eagle* in my study today. The influence of *Eagle* upon almost every middle-class British child growing up in the Fifties cannot be underestimated – it was a truly remarkable, mould-breaking enterprise, a creation of genius, the genius being the Reverend Marcus Morris. Many years later I interviewed Marcus Morris for Capital Radio and I still derive enormous pleasure from re-reading the adventures of Dan Dare, PC 49, Harris Tweed and, for that matter, real life back page stars St Paul and St Patrick. On more than one occasion those old *Eagles* have helped me in my story-telling efforts many years on.

Hugh was a success at de Havilland and it was obvious to the powers there that he had potential beyond editing the firm's magazine. De Havilland's vast headquarters bestrode the Great North Road at Hatfield and dominated the employment of the fast-expanding New Town there. Their planes were all tested at de Havilland's adjacent aerodrome. Within the boundaries of this massive field was Popefield Farm. Several employees had been successively offered the ancient farmhouse, accessible from the main Hatfield–St Albans road, a mile or two from HQ, as a company house at the remarkable rent of £3 a week, with a couple of barns and a substantial garden thrown in, but there had been no takers for the rambling, somewhat run-down residence, in part because of the infernal noise made daily by DH aircraft going through their paces a few hundred yards away.

In 1950 however my father boldly decided that Popefield was an opportunity too good to miss – it could be a home of a size and character that his means and salary could never otherwise achieve. It could be a wonderful place for three boys to grow up in. He had expectations of worldwide travel on de Havilland's behalf in the very near future and he wanted to feel that his wife and children would have DH close at hand, at Joan's call if the need arose. The downside was the fact that there would be no prospect of Hugh owning his own home for years, but his decision proved to be a superb one. Joan took some convincing but it was not more than a few days after the move from suburban Radlett to countrified if noisy Hatfield that all five Rices were happily settled at a house they all grew to love intensely and lived in for nineteen years.

Chapter Three

My father was dead right: Popefield Farm, parts of which dated back to Elizabethan times, was a wonderful childhood home for his three boys. My mother soon came around to a similar view and within a few months loved the eccentric property as much as any other member of the family. Although the land that belonged to the house covered barely an acre, our garden and yard seemed vast, even when the latter was occasionally occupied by de Havilland cows. In any event as the farmhouse backed on to literally hundreds of acres of airfield plus adjoining fields, woods and barns we felt as if our estate matched that of Hatfield House, the stately pile of the Salisbury family on the other side of town. De Havilland did farm the land around their runways, but primarily grew crops as livestock and aeroplane noise were not a perfect match. This meant that every summer and autumn there were huge piles of hay bales to play in and my brothers and I probably spent as much time in the seventeenth- and eighteenth-century barns as we did in our bedrooms, at least until Auntie Gertie gave us a gramophone.

We provided our own animals. Other than the odd rat, a psychopath of a barn cat and the few cows that were drafted in for a season or two, Popefield was a fauna-free farm. Our garden became the HQ for chickens, tame cats, hamsters, white rabbits and above all a boxer dog, imaginatively named Prince, though we spelled it Prinz in deference to the breed's German origins. Both the acquisition of this adorable hound and several

23

of the au pair girls who were part of our household in the Fifties demonstrated that my parents were free of any post-war anti-Teutonic hangover. Prinz was like all boxers, beset with wind and drool problems, maniacally affectionate, rather dim, extremely handsome and unceasingly tolerant of small children clambering over him night and day, fingering his orifices and mauling his most intimate areas, in which he was incidentally under-equipped having, like Hitler, only one ball. This never prevented him leading a full love life in various parts of Hatfield, many of his nocturnal escapades ending with my father collecting him from the local police cell. Prinz was never in danger of being thrown off the payroll, for his social deficiencies were outweighed by his efficiency as a guard dog. He would raise hell if anyone other than a Rice came to the door, a vital attribute during the long dark winter nights when mother and children were often alone in a comparatively remote house. I have been besotted with boxers ever since and never had more than a year or two without one in my life.

Would that I could say the same about au pair girls but just when things were getting really interesting the supply dried up. The last of a great line left when I was fourteen and I had anyway just started at boarding school. My mother simply didn't need the extra help any more – at least that was the official reason for the cutback. Few stayed more than a year – some got homesick or broke an ankle in their first week and only lasted days, but a young French lady named Simone and a Finnish girl named Tui remain etched in my memory as delightful members of the family rather than the glorified nannies they really were. Simone taught us quite a bit of basic French, so that by the age of six I could and did bore guests by counting to 1000 in two languages.

In the same month that we moved to Popefield I started at prep school. Aldwickbury, six miles away in Harpenden, had been in existence for less than three years, a partnership between Kenneth Castle, then in his forties, and Brian Chidell, in his early thirties. Castle had run a prep school at Lea House in Harpenden since before the war and in 1948 invited the younger man to be co-headmaster if they were able to purchase Aldwickbury, a fifty-room Victorian mansion set in twenty acres of beautiful ground in what was then the outskirts of Harpenden. They succeeded in obtaining the property (for £12,750) and had already built up a fine local reputation by September 1950, when I began there. There were around a hundred boys in the senior school, between seven and thirteen, and half that number again in the lower school, where I was deposited, within minutes behaving extremely feebly.

I have very clear memories of my first day at Aldwickbury, of being driven the few miles to school by my father in his Morris Ten, BVM 661, thrilled with my purple cap adorned with a golden wheat sheaf, yellow and purple striped tie and purple topped long socks. Short trousers of course – I can't recall wearing anything long, formal or informal, until 1956 when jeans first broke into Hatfield middle-class consciousness, as my scarred knees testify to this day. But as soon as we cruised up the impressive school drive I turned into a snivelling wreck who fought like a tiger to avoid leaving the womb of BVM 661. I was literally dragged into form 1A where to the amusement of my fellow inductees I screamed blue murder for the best part of an hour, oblivious to bribes, threats or sympathy. My father was eventually hustled away and in due course I took my tear-stained place at a double desk next to a delightfully friendly six-year-old named Robert Blyth. By lunchtime I was totally relaxed and, all embarrassment forgotten, never worried about schooldays for another minute of my life.

Aldwickbury was a very traditional English prep school, run superbly, though on a shoestring, by Messrs. Castle and Chidell. Despite the economic restraints that still dominated virtually every aspect of life in Britain in 1950, the co-heads managed to provide an astonishingly wide range of facilities for their pupils. Sport of course: the school had extensive football, rugby and cricket fixtures, plus an extremely imaginatively organised athletic programme and sports day every summer term. No swimming pool in my time, but weekly trips to Luton baths. There was a Wolf Cub (and Scout) troop to which I signed up. There were carpentry classes to which I did not.

Arts, in particular music, were given high priority. Brian Chidell, in addition to being an outstanding maths teacher, was a gifted musician who regularly drove batches of boys up to London to attend concerts and plays. Brian's Saturday morning music classes were a highlight of the week and although I appeared to have a very unmusical ear at that time, I loved taking part in lusty renditions of such terrific warhorses as 'Men Of Harlech', 'Marching Through Georgia' and 'The Lincolnshire Poacher'. I must have known the lyrics (and in most cases had a reasonable handle on the tune) to about a hundred traditional English songs and hymns by the time I was seven. Brian was also a Gilbert and Sullivan fanatic and I adored the brilliance of such arias as 'My Name is John Wellington Wells' and 'I am the Very Model of a Modern Major-General', and dozens more, primarily but not exclusively because of the words.

Brian Chidell was a terrific patriot and often told us as we were about to launch into 'Rule Britannia' that he felt this, rather than 'God Save The Queen', should be the national anthem. The death of King George VI on 6 February 1952 made a great impression upon me because it clearly mattered so much to all the adults at Aldwickbury. One of Brian's leading articles in the school magazine stated, 'It is in our schools that true qualities must be nurtured, and we should guard them jealously if we are to serve our Queen and Country.' There was no doubt that we believed ours to be the greatest nation in the world and that we were lucky indeed to be British.

This was not a view that was held with arrogance but with a typically British understated confidence. Such a philosophy would of course be laughed out of the classroom today but (a) I still believe it and (b) I do not feel it is incompatible with respect for other nations and cultures, many of which instil the equivalent belief in their own worth, often forcibly, into their own younger generations today. Thanks in part to my father's lifetime of travel and connections with friends and business partners from all over the world, already well established in the early Fifties, there was never much danger of his children becoming Little Englanders, had they ever given the matter any thought.

During my six years at Aldwickbury, there was in fact quite a lot of evidence to support the theory that being British was hard to beat. No one in my parents' circle was extravagantly wealthy, but most were getting by in comfort, if only because their demands were not high. However, expectations were. There was a feeling as the war slowly receded into history that everything was going to improve. Clothes and cars became more colourful. Television moved in. Rationing was gradually phased out, sweet rationing one of the last to go, inspiring one of my earliest lyrics submitted to (and failing to make) the *Aldwickbury Magazine* of 1953:

> When sweets came off the ration
> Crowds hurried to the shops
> Just like the pre-war fashion
> To buy their lollipops

I greatly enjoyed writing as an extra-curricular activity by the time I was eight or nine; in part because I was obsessed by my mother's typewriter, which held me in greater thrall than any toy as I raced away at thirty words per minute. I used to turn out magazines and even books for my parents' birthdays, always preferring fact to fiction. If my mother or father was ever bewildered to be presented with a list of the world's capital cities or longest rivers as an attachment to a birthday card, they never showed it. In any event, an attempt at something more creative would never have produced anything memorable. I might have been a slight freak as far as my assimilation of facts and figures was concerned, but a literary child prodigy – never.

In fact such creatures do not seem to exist; music, mathematics, chess – these are areas in which an extraordinarily young genius can match the achievements of a mature one, but no novelist, poet or lyricist has ever written anything worthwhile until all but adult. Why is this? Command of number or intellectual game requires no command of emotion or experience of life; the beauty and emotion conveyed in music is as often in the ear and mind of the listener as in those of the composer – else how could a nightingale move Keats? It is possible for a listener to a piece of music to be moved in ways unintended by, and even incomprehensible to, the composer. Words are too specific, too clear, to give the receiver any significant variation of interpretation, so they must be well-crafted, knowing, mature.

I am painting a picture of a near-idyllic childhood, and that is what it was. I probably did not appreciate sufficiently every aspect of the good life at the time, but I tended to assume that it was universal. We posh prep-school boys were aware of the rougher element at the state school down the road and tried to avoid too many confrontations at the bus stop, but all in all we led a happy, sheltered existence. The national news that filtered through to me seemed to be all good – Everest climbed, a new, young Queen, Roger Bannister and the first four-minute mile. We young Elizabethans were part of it and this was our heritage.

My academic record at Aldwickbury was at first phenomenally successful. In my first year in the Upper School, 1951–2, aged seven, the youngest in the form, I came top of the class in every fortnightly order for the entire year. Even more nauseatingly, I loved exams and romped away at the top of the table there as well. My reports were, not surprisingly, pretty good. I don't think I attached much importance to this and have no recollection of working particularly hard or of wanting to be in pole position – it just happened, thanks largely no doubt to my parents' informal home tuition.

As a result of my clean sweep in every ranking going, I jumped a year. I arrived on the first day of the winter term 1952, expecting automatic promotion with all my chums to the third form, only to find that I had been elevated to the fourth, making me the youngest in my class by an even greater margin. I was initially very upset about this and after the first day's morning assembly slunk into the third form classroom in the vain hope that the authorities would forget that I should have been in Form IV. I was gently removed. I knew resistance was useless from my experience on my first ever Aldwickbury day.

This is beginning to sound extremely unpalatable, but the truth must be told – by my second term in my new year I was coming top again. I don't think I was a swot, but I must have enjoyed nearly every subject, by now including Latin and French. In the latter subject my chats to the au pairs paid off. Not only that, brother Jo was by now doing just as well two forms down the ladder. He even won a prize for an essay entered by the school in a national competition. My mother and father were, to put it mildly, happy with their sons' scholastic records. In my case, however, a decline of sorts was soon to set in.

Sports-wise I loved nearly every game I played, without showing any great natural ability. I did not become a gangling giant until I was about seventeen, but I was never very co-ordinated in the presence of a ball. I never got near to selection for any of the Aldwickbury cricket or football teams other than on one occasion when a flu epidemic forced the selectors to spread their net to desperate lengths and I made right half for the under-eleven side. I thought I played out of my skin but I was back in D game a week later. I was however extremely fit and in a sport at which nothing other than stamina counted, such as cross-country running, I was as good as most.

Cricket was my favourite. I loved the numbers and statistics involved and at an extremely modest level played with huge enthusiasm. I was hooked for life after the Oval Test of 1953. My parents, like millions of others, had finally given in to the mistrusted medium of television because of the Coronation in June that year. I'm afraid the Coronation hoopla rather bored me – I was severely castigated by my old man for not wanting to sit through the entire ceremony as portrayed on our new nine-inch set (with special magnifying screen attachment that increased the apparent size to at least eleven inches) but I could not be dragged away from the screen when the final Test was televised two months later. I became a cricket junkie and absorbed the facts and figures, characters and culture of this great game with the thoroughness and fanaticism with which I had taken up astronomy three years earlier. When Michael Dunning brought a copy of the 1954 *Wisden* to school the following spring I felt as Keats did on first reading Chapman's *Homer*. I was one up on Keats in that even if he had lived he would never have had a new Chapman to enjoy every April, as I have had *Wisden* ever since.

Cricket pushed all other interests into the sidelines, even astronomy (but I remember being thrilled by the summer 1954 eclipse of the sun), even stamp collecting (my first introduction to a pretty lady called Eva Peron who was on all the Argentine stamps), even bus ticket collecting – a craze of monster proportions at Aldwickbury in the days when bus tickets were solid mini-works of coloured art. My brothers and I played endless Test Matches at Popefield throughout the summer, and indeed throughout most of the winter as well. Then, as now, Jo had considerably more natural ability than I, although I still relive with pride my 208 against his bowling in 1956.

One of the strangest crazes, that Jo and I actually launched at Aldwickbury, was the deaf and dumb alphabet which we were taught by a profoundly deaf and dumb old lady, a companion of my father's aunt Daisy. What we ingrates had expected to be a dreary family duty day out turned out to be an unforgettable occasion when this delightful ancient, unable to speak to us directly or to hear any noise we made, enthralled two small boys for hours, teaching them a skill that has on more than one occasion been vitally useful decades after Aunt Daisy and her two friends faded away.

Friends loved coming to Popefield. My two closest Aldwickbury friends were David Robbins and John Fossett and they seemed to be coming round to play almost every day – barns to climb in, huge spaces for bike races, a lawn big enough for a decent football or cricket match, were irresistible attractions. The fact that my parents didn't own their wonderful residence might have caused Hugh and Joan a few headaches later on, but I know they never regretted the eventual financial drawbacks of providing near-perfect surroundings for our childhood.

Best friends come and best friends go, but after losing touch with David Robbins for many years, I was delighted to meet up with him again in 1996. He is now a prosperous solicitor in Surrey and when we had our first sandwich together for over thirty years the old cliché about it seeming as if we had last met only yesterday held true. John, sad to say, had a troubled life. He was a talented sportsman, good looking, funny and a popular child, if not academically gifted. He never came to grips with the adult world and after a series of debilitating illnesses, died in his early forties. I remember him and his family with lasting affection.

By 1954 my golden era of scholarship was definitely on the skids, albeit not drastically. The days of coming top without effort were over. Other boys were catching up. Variations of the dreaded phrase 'could do better' began to dominate my reports. I was not an intellectual. By six or seven I had read a lot of children's classics, such as *Alice In Wonderland*, *Treasure Island* and the wonderful works of E.Nesbit – and I loved the nonsense poetry of Edward Lear – but in the mid-Fifties my tastes went downmarket. My favourite reading around this time, apart from the *Eagle*, the newspapers and *Wisden*, were the Enid Blyton stories of the girls of St Clare's. I could not get enough of the adventures of the O'Sullivan twins, firm but fair head-girl Hilary Wentworth and madcap Doris. I don't know whether my parents were at all worried about this quirky development in my literary interests, fearing that I might not be as other boys, but they really had nothing to worry about, at least in that regard. I secretly fancied Carlotta the circus girl and Claudine the exotic French pupil. Funnily enough I never showed any inclination to get into Mallory Towers,* Miss Blyton's other great girls' school series. It wasn't all St Clare's though – I loved the Billy Bunter books, the genius of Nigel Molesworth as per Geoffrey Willans and Ronald Searle, Richmal Crompton's peerless William stories and of course comics. The *Eagle* held sway with the children of the Fifties.

By the time I was ten I was fascinated by the cinema, by animation in particular. I saw nearly all of the Disney classic full-length features such as *Peter Pan* and *Dumbo* several times. I loved Tom and Jerry, Bugs Bunny, Tweety and Sylvester – indeed almost anything in cartoon form – a love that stood me in good stead nearly forty years on when I first worked for the Disney Studios on *The Lion King* and *Aladdin*. The first adult movie I saw was *Genevieve*, the brilliant Henry Cornelius comedy about the London–Brighton vintage car run, starring Kenneth More, John Gregson, Kay Kendall and Dinah Sheridan. Those four actors, three long since passed away, still hold a special place in my heart. I have been lucky enough however to have met Dinah Sheridan and to be able to tell her how much her greatest film meant to me. Ditto the magnificent Norman Wisdom whose string of brilliant comedies such as *Trouble In Store* made him one of the most famous and loved stars of my lifetime.

Television in the early Fifties meant far less to me than the cinema. Of course there wasn't very much of it; one channel,

---

* When my daughter Eva's book *Who's Who In Enid Blyton* was published in 1997 (Richard Cohen Books) she presented me with a Mallory Towers book to fill this serious gap in my literary experience. Not bad, but not a patch on St Clare's.

just one hour a day for children, much of it drearily educational. Only the antics of 'HL' – Humphrey Lestocq – and his sidekick, a vegetable on strings, a marionette named Mr Turnip, on the Saturday variety showcase *Whirlygig*, leave a glowing small screen impression nearly fifty years on.

I hardly ever went to the theatre as a child, other than on school trips to local productions of Gilbert and Sullivan. I performed in a few Aldwickbury school plays, without distinction and indeed without lines in most cases. My grandmother took me to see my first West End show in 1954, *Salad Days*, the show which fired the young Cameron Mackintosh to pursue a career in musical theatre. Maybe Cameron was the noisy little pest in front of me who kept jumping up out of his seat. I loved *Salad Days*, once again being impressed by the words as much as by the music. I thought the night club song about ptolerating Ptolemy and the line 'Any old pia – No!' quite superb but strangely I was not inspired to rush to see another musical. The show was just a great part of a London weekend with Granny, which was always an exciting event. She lived near Regent's Park and organised boat rides, trips to the zoo, rides on double-decker buses and on the underground whenever any of her grandchildren came up to stay from distant Hertfordshire. Her husband, George, the grandpa I just remember, had died in 1949, and she was still, at sixty-four, a remarkably glamorous and active woman. I never knew at the time how much her close friend of these years, whom we called Uncle Harry, would have agreed with this assessment.

My father's career was on an upward curve at de Havilland. In 1952 he had been appointed Far East representative, which meant that he was away for long periods of time, mainly in Japan, Hong Kong and Singapore. The DH Comet was the new star performer and Hugh's job was to sell it. It was tough for my mother to be abandoned for quite long spells, as quick flips to the other end of the globe were totally out of the question in those days. Hugh even missed one Christmas, which went down like a Mexican Wave at a funeral. Phone calls were only possible when booked long in advance, and even if a connection was made, the conversation had to be brief and the line was so crackly, speech was almost inaudible. When he was asked to go to Japan for a full six months in 1955, to restore the Far Eastern buyers' confidence in the troubled Comet, I am sure he would have resigned if he had not been able to take his family with him.

Chapter Four

In January 1955, none of the three Rice children had set foot outside England, not even in Scotland or Wales. Family holidays had only extended as far as Southsea, Exmouth or Yarmouth, one summer to Cornwall, many summers to Auntie Gertie and Uncle Arthur in St Leonards. Of course foreign travel was much much rarer in 1955 than it is today. Even a trip to France was never a serious consideration for most British middle-class holidays and a jaunt to Disneyland (which opened in 1955) or even to New York an impossible dream, millions of British tourists in shellsuits an impossible nightmare.

When we heard that we were all off to Japan for six months my response, having lived second-hand with my father's globetrotting for three years, was not one of the excitement and anticipation it might have been. I was just ten, but I was already very fond of England and a little uncertain about a move to a country without cricket and my pals. My brothers, at seven and four, probably failed to register that any change at all was afoot until we set off in the wintry gloom for Southampton. My main concern was that we were unable to take Prinz and I remember arguing that there would be room for him on the boat, I would walk him on board every day, the quarantine laws wouldn't stop him getting into Japan and if we were going to have six months without him anyway, better that these should be when he was down the road in kennels than 10,000 miles away. This argument did not wash and a temporary home in England was found for the boxer I loved. I snivelled most of the way to Southampton.

I might well have showed even more emotion had I known that my presence on the trip was in doubt until the last minute. Being well advanced in my schooling, a mere three years away from the all-important Common Entrance exam to public school (and my parents were unwisely banking on a scholarship), long discussions took place between parents and teachers as to whether I should opt out of the English system for the best part of an academic year. Aldwickbury had good boarding facilities, which I had already sampled and survived for the odd term as a weekly boarder. My still way above average academic record and my mother's insistence that this was a once in a lifetime opportunity saved me. Both parents felt that I could survive two terms out of the English treadmill without imperilling my chances of subsequent acceptance at Lancing College, the public school they already had in mind. Mercifully I was unaware of this debate and had no inkling as we set off to Japan that I was a last-minute selection.

The boat trip to Japan was a fabulous experience and even at the age of ten I appreciated it as such. The ship was the *Bayernstein*, a German vessel on its maiden voyage. Many of the passengers were English and and there was a fair smattering of children on board, though for the first time in my life I found I was the oldest in my group. One of the boys was Stephen Morse, who coincidentally turned up in my house at Lancing five years later. The Bay of Biscay was lethally rough and our entire party save my mother retired hurt, including our current au pair, Tui the Finn, whose father had agreed to fork out for her passage. Tui, one of the most delightful, efficient (while in England) and attractive girls ever to be in my mother's employ, did not always justify her presence on our Oriental trip, for once she recovered from seasickness she spent most of her time on board in the company of a young *Bayernstein* officer,* leaving Joan to monitor the whereabouts of her offspring, whose absence

---

* Tui was never short of male admirers throughout our months in Japan. A close friend of my father's proposed marriage and a lifetime in Tokyo. In the end, Helsinki triumphed for she returned tearfully to Europe with her charges, who also thought she was terrific.

for more than five minutes set child overboard worries into overdrive.

There was only one class of passenger on the *Bayernstein*'s maiden voyage and to the eyes of a ten-year-old it seemed pretty luxurious. It probably was. Our party had two fair-sized cabins with we three children sharing with Tui. Any lack of space was more than compensated for by my first regular sightings of an attractive young woman in various stages of undress – on a good night, total. Just about as important (at the time) was my first taste of Coca-Cola. It bore no relation to any drink I had ever consumed in England and I absolutely adored it. I have switched feebly to Diet Coke forty years on but I still see a fleeting image of the *Bayernstein* every time I·take a swig.

Two other educational pluses of the six weeks at sea were learning to swim and learning about foreign currency. All transactions on the boat were in marks and pfennigs and for the only time in my life I was an advocate of decimalisation. When I left England I could barely do more than a few strokes of doggy-paddle. I spent so much time in the minuscule *Bayernstein* pool and even more time during the Tokyo summer that followed in the vast American Club pool, that by the time I got back to Aldwickbury I was the best swimmer in the school.

My father was not present for the first half of our trip east – he flew out to join us at Colombo, having stayed in the UK for three weeks after our departure to be fully briefed for his latest task. The year before, two serious accidents, eventually shown to be a result of metal fatigue, had led to the grounding of the de Havilland Comet. The Japanese and other Far Eastern buyers were naturally reluctant to fulfil their orders and Hugh was a key de Havilland player in the quest to renew their confidence in the Comet and other aeroplanes. The Comet eventually flew again in 1955 and was reintroduced to commercial service in the autumn of 1958.

Our first stop was Genoa. I shall always associate this Italian port with one of the most shameful moves of my life. I had done a deal with Jo that if he let me be the first to board the *Bayernstein* in Southampton (which he did) I would allow him to be the first Rice of his generation to set foot on foreign soil. When we docked at Genoa, before the passengers were allowed ashore, I could not resist nipping illegally down the gangplank. I raced down the wobbly ramp, ran around in a tiny circle and raced up to the boat again before even the most alert German border guard spotted me. Jo has never held this against me – in fact he probably never remembered our Southampton pact – but it troubles my conscience still and I would like to take this opportunity to apologise publicly.

We had a day in Genoa during which Joan was ripped off by a couple of Italian conmen who convinced her that they could change her English pounds at a better rate than any bank. I was one hundred per cent behind these guys, assuring my mum that they were honest brokers. When their used lira notes were later presented at a restaurant, we were informed that this particular folding stuff had been illegal tender since Mussolini's time. It is of course possible that the restaurant owner was the conman but in any event it was an eye-opener to this young innocent that not all grown-ups played by the rules.

Stop Number Two was Port Said where we were enthralled by the Gully Gully men who swarmed around the *Bayernstein* in their tiny bobbing boats, offering passengers trips ashore and conjuring tricks that involved the removal of chickens from a handbag and snakes from a fez. Unfortunately it would not always be a chicken that was removed from the handbag but the Genoa experience had made our entire party most wary of overseas negotiations and we emerged unscathed from our second encounter with the wily foreigner. We visited the famous department store Simon Artz, where we bought a cricket bat.

The Suez Canal was quite extraordinary, regular and white-banked, just over a year away from its crisis that brought the world to the brink of another war. My brothers and I played ping-pong throughout its 101 unturbulent miles and for most of the voyage after that – my competence at the game still in evidence at the 1996 Heartaches table tennis championship in which I emerged victorious. At Aden I was ecstatic to find a copy of the *Daily Mirror* less than a week old which told me that despite Neil Harvey's gallant 92 not out, England had won the Second Test at Sydney.

Next stop was Colombo where we were reunited with my father.

We drove the magical route from Colombo up to Kandy and I suspect that it was about now that I realised I was incredibly lucky to be enjoying such a privileged holiday. We rode elephants and marvelled at tropical gardens. We swam in the ocean off the beach of the Mount Lavinia Hotel. I wrote to David Robbins back at Aldwickbury, rating each new country with marks out of one hundred, beginning to understand that this was the geography lesson of a lifetime. In theory I was not on holiday, as Messrs. Castle and Chidell had given my father text books for us to study in parallel with the classmates back home, and my father did his best, but it was hard for Kennedy's *Latin Primer* to hold sway over the exotic thrills of Ceylon, as it then was.

Then came Singapore, Hong Kong, Manila and finally Yokohama. Hong Kong made a special impact on me. The walk around the Peak is a pilgrimage I have made on every subsequent visit, no matter how tourist-afflicted (and on subsequent visits I have of course been a tourist), simply because I loved the first circuit I made there in February 1955 with my father pointing out every highlight of the city, frantic even then, and of the islands and seas far below. We watched cricket at the old Hong Kong CC ground, long since moved off the actual island, forced to give way to admittedly impressive skyscrapers of banks and hotels. We travelled back and forth from Hong Kong to Kowloon on the Star Ferry (no tunnel then) and had full English teas at the Peninsula Hotel.

Finally, after six weeks at sea, we arrived in Japan. The family home provided for us was in the Shibuya district of Tokyo. The house was an interesting amalgam of Western and Japanese, with our staff of three Japanese ladies installed in an Oriental wing, all paper walls and rush matting. The three women wore only traditional Japanese kimonos and tended to every need of the British family in the traditionally European half of the house, furnished very much as Popefield was back in England. One item in Tokyo that we had never possessed back home was a piano at which I spent hours bashing out one-fingered versions of the songs I had learned at Aldwickbury. I had no clue about chords or keys, technique or rhythm, and had always been considered a worthy inheritor of the Rice total lack of musical ability, but these fumblings indicated that I might not be tone deaf. A momentous decision was therefore taken to enrol me for piano lessons with a French lady down the road, if only to lessen the agony my stints at the piano must have given my parents.

Our garden was nothing like as big as the lawns of Popefield but still large enough for us to play cricket and it was a great day when my father finally managed to obtain some stumps for our Test Matches, commissioned from a mystified local carpenter who had been given the dimensions from *Wisden* 1954, which naturally had been the star item in my luggage. The weather that summer in Japan was consistently extraordinarily hot, even by local standards, and Hutton and Lindwall in the persona of Rice one and Rice two had plenty of time to resume their endless struggles in unfamiliar surroundings. Annoyingly, it was here that Rice minor began to show signs of being considerably more adept at the game than his elder brother, who at least could still score freely off Rice minimus, less enthusiastic and only five years old.

In 1955, Japan was still occupied by US forces, and one of the centres of American social activity in Tokyo was the American Club, a complex that included a massive swimming pool and a wondrous, unheard-of distraction – a ten-pin bowling alley! American allies seemed to qualify for membership too, and we spent many long days sampling, and loving, our first experience of Americana. US comic books were a special treat, unlike any British children's comic, and the slogan we absorbed on opening every copy – 'Dell Comics are Good Comics is our only credo and constant goal' – had my total commercial and emotional support. American characters who had never impinged on British consciousness, such as Little Lulu, Howdy Doody and Caspar the Friendly Ghost, not to mention Blondie and Dagwood and the entire host of Disney and Warner Brothers' heroes, became as important to us as Dan Dare and Lord Snooty.

I found that my early knowledge of American children's comic books was another useful string to my bow decades later when I worked at Walt Disney; there were very few references to US childhood icons of whom I had not heard. Spending two terms at an international school run on American lines taught me a great deal about the United States. Throw in frequent visits to new school friends at Washington Heights, a microcosm of a middle-America town slap in the middle of Tokyo and it is easy to see how Jo and I probably absorbed more of America than of our host country during our six months in Japan. Another factor here was my father's subscription to the *Saturday Evening Post*. This great US news magazine was then in fine fettle and inspired in me a lasting appreciation of the magnificent work of Norman Rockwell, whose art graced many of its covers.

Not that we were cut off from England. My grandmother nobly sent packets of English magazines and comics out east (sea-mail) and although we were six weeks behind our English chums, we never missed a beat of every *Eagle* hero's continuing fight for all that was decent and fair and British. We pored over the airmail copies of *The Times*, in this lagging only three or four days behind readers at home – the 1955 English cricket season is as vivid in my memory as any other and I never saw a ball of it bowled. We were rather annoyed that the summer in England was also unusually hot; my letters to David Robbins bragging about the heat in Tokyo cut little ice, if that is an appropriate metaphor.

The school we attended in Japan was St Mary's International. The staff were a bunch of rather aggressive Canadian monks, whose order, the Brothers of Christian Instruction, clearly regarded corporal punishment as an essential stop en route to heaven. I was placed in what was then the highest form, the Third Grade, which matched my age (ten) but was way behind my academic status. Subjects that I had already studied for three years at Aldwickbury, such as Latin, French, algebra and geometry were nowhere on the St Mary's syllabus, although baseball (which I loved), excessive Catholicism and American history were. My parents made a reasonable attempt to keep me up to par with my ex-schoolmates in England but it was a struggle for them and for me to wade through French irregular verbs and congruent triangles after hours; eventually an unspoken truce was called and my education in the summer of 1955 became merely an extremely comfortable cruise through stuff I had mastered ages before. Parental consciences were salved by the hope that I was bright enough to catch up when I got home and that my brothers and I were learning far more about the world than we could possibly have during two more terms at Aldwickbury.

They were certainly right on the second count. At St Mary's I may not have got myself any closer to a public school scholarship, but my view of the world was hugely broadened. There were maybe twenty-five or thirty boys in my class, of which the majority were sons of American servicemen (some with Japanese mothers) stationed in Tokyo. There were a couple of fellow Brits and even a Spanish child, but our class was essentially exactly like thousands of Third Grade classes all over the United States. To put it mildly, St Mary's was long on religion. Only about half the pupils were Catholic but we were all subjected to indoctrination. There was a vague feeling among non-Catholics that we were perhaps not as important to God as the rest, but discrimination only occurred as far as chapel was concerned. Non-Catholics didn't go, which was fine by me.

Every other lesson seemed to be Divinity and at the slightest opportunity Brother Andrew or Brother Michael would divert the progress of any other subject into a sermon. Most of the boys had rosaries and Hail Marys were recited first thing every morning, more often than not between lessons too. Any student's slight fall from grace was an excuse for a beating and/or prayer. The Brother in charge of our form usually found three or four excuses to lay into a boy per day, administering whacks with a cane on the bottom or with a ruler on the hands. The latter was far more painful. The victim's colleagues watched with a combination of ghoulish fascination and apprehension as the punishment was delivered. No child ever seemed particularly disturbed by the experience (though I may simply have been unobservant, or insensitive to long-term reactions) and I doubt very much if any parent ever complained.

I was only ever beaten once, for some wisecrack. It was a ludicrous reaction on the part of whichever Brother it was, to beat me for making the class laugh, but it didn't really hurt and I enjoyed the brief notoriety. What worried me most was that my parents found out – today most victims would have been instructing their parents to instruct a lawyer. In view of the high thrashing count, I must have been rather wet to have only suffered once, but I suspect the monks did not really formulate their sentencing policy to fit the crime. One poor boy named Gregory Jones seemed to be permanently bending over or holding out his hands, often as a result of others sneaking on him, which struck me as being desperately unfair. The Brothers of Christian Instruction seemed to encourage ratting on your mates, presumably justified because this gave the sinner a chance to repent that he might otherwise not have had. And yet it seemed to be a happy school. The monks pursued their overall mission to educate with unflagging, if not unflogging, enthusiasm and generally good humour.

I often wonder what happened to my American schoolmates. Did Gregory Jones and the guy next to him, the exotically named Briggs Ekrem, go to Vietnam? This possibility only struck me, and forcibly, after watching the film *American Graffiti* in the early Seventies. None of my contemporaries from all the other schools I attended would have faced such a grim assignment – I hope Gregory and Briggs did not.

I suppose I became slightly religious as a result of the Brothers' force-feeding. I used to recite the occasional Hail Mary out of school and became fascinated with the words of the Lord's Prayer, for language reasons as well as for religious ones. I said my prayers every night, asking God to forgive me and bless all my family and friends. But I was pretty low-key about it. My parents had never been regular churchgoers and even at ten I reckoned they wouldn't go wild about a son who had seen the light. On top of that I wasn't really converted, more intrigued, keeping all options open – but my interest in Bible stories and the language of Christianity never waned.

Perhaps of all the influences that I first absorbed in 1955, that of American pop music became the most significant. Before living in Japan, my interest in the hits of the day was pretty half-hearted. Sometimes a hugely popular song such as 'Doggie In The Window' or 'Happy Wanderer' sunk in, but I had no awareness of the record charts, or rather the hit parade. Not that many other people in Britain had. Radio, or rather wireless, had been important to me only for early morning news while Daddy was shaving, cricket commentary or for comedy, such as *Educating Archie*, *Take It From Here* or *Life With the Lyons*. Our family possessed no gramophone and, not surprisingly, no records. American Forces Radio in Japan was a staggering ear-opener.

For starters, the music was all good. I had never heard of any of the artists or songs and indeed, looking back, I would not say the last pre-rock'n'roll year was a particularly distinguished one for music. Nonetheless every record I heard was infinitely more appealing than the soporific stuff served up sporadically on the BBC and was linked by an excited and exciting voice I soon discovered to be that of a 'disc-jockey' – in turn leading me to the revelation that gramophone records could be known as 'discs' or even 'platters'. Best of all, the records were arranged in a new order each week which was right up a statistic freak's alley. I was hooked after just one Top Twenty run-down on the triple whammy of radio, pop records and the charts. The three biggest hits of our months in Japan were 'Unchained Melody', 'Cherry Pink and Apple Blossom White' and 'Rock Around The Clock' – only the last in any way a clue to the music revolution around the corner, but all three, together with the many other hits of the day, a whole new treasure trove, a whole new source of entertainment in a young boy's life.

Of course, besides our American diversions, we saw a good deal of the real Japan. We picked up a smattering of the language (my parents actually took a course) and were able to make ourselves understood just a little in shops and on the streets. We thought in yen, not shillings, nor for that matter, marks. We were forever purchasing goldfish at the nearest Shibuya department store which I think was our intention, not because the Japanese for 'goldfish' sounds rather like the Japanese for 'hello'. These fish kept dying but even had any lived for more than a week or two there was never a danger of their replacing Prinz in my affections. We played in Meiji Park and flew paper carp on Boys' Day. We were often followed around in the street by crowds of schoolchildren giggling at the strange *gaijin* (foreigners), inquisitive, never threatening. We learned to play *jan ken pon* (scissors, paper, stone) and my brothers and I still settle the odd dispute this way. We went on a family holiday to Lake Chuzenji, then a two hour drive out of Tokyo into the mountains, where we spent a week on the lakeside in a fairly primitive house, home to some extremely weird insects, where we had the biggest of several earth tremors we experienced during the summer. Shamefully, the dreary younger generation of Rices made no attempt whatsoever to contemplate trying Japanese food.

In early September, after what had seemed like an endless summer, we began the trek home. We were to go by plane. I was delighted by this prospect, having been thrilled by my first flight, from our back yard – the de Havilland runway – to an airshow in Kent in a DH Dove two years before. Our return from Japan was scheduled to take the best part of a month. This was not only because aeroplanes were much slower than they are today, and were not capable of anything like the long non-stop journeys of the modern airliner. My father had various meetings in different Asian cities on the way home and consequently we were able to add several new countries to our already impressive list of places visited – Burma, India, Thailand, Pakistan. I tended to judge each place by the quality of its swimming pools, but, as had been the case during the whole fantastic nine months, I was just about old and aware enough to know that this could be as good as it gets.

I arrived home dying to see Granny and the dog (I trust in that order), not remotely sharing my parents' concern whether their two eldest sons, particularly me, had lost too much educational ground. I remember reading a newspaper item about the death of an actor I had never heard of, James Dean, within hours of our return. For no reason that I can explain the story made a big impact upon me.

Chapter Five

We were soon back in the old routine. Although both grandmother and dog were overcome with emotion on our return, few of my friends were very interested in our travels and I slipped back into Aldwickbury life almost as if our great journey had never happened. However, the headmasters did not take the view that I could perform at my old level and, to my parents' chagrin, I was not moved up to the Sixth (the top) Form, but placed back with the classmates I had unwillingly left behind three years earlier. Jo did not suffer similar lack of promotion. The decision in my case may well have been in part because of my age – even staying down in the Remove I was still the youngest in the form. I had three full years to go before the public school exam, and two of these in the Sixth Form should have been enough to secure me the vital scholarship to Lancing in summer 1958.

I shall never know whether I would have won a scholarship because I never took it. Those were the days of the eleven-plus, an exam taken by every state school child in the country to determine the level of his or her subsequent education: grammar school for the bright ones, secondary modern for the less able. Entire educational futures hung on a few tests at the tender age of eleven – often rough justice although few can honestly claim its abolition has resulted in a higher standard of national scholastic achievement. Quite the opposite, in fact. The private schools, the fee-paying preparatory schools, ignored the eleven-plus; the nationwide exam had no bearing on their pupils' entrance to secondary education which was determined at thirteen by exams set by each individual public school. Aldwickbury had no wish to see any of its potential scholarship or common entrance stars deserting at eleven even to go to a fine grammar school and made no attempt whatsoever to gear their syllabus to the demands of the eleven-plus. Of course independently educated boys were still entitled to take it and a few did – I was one.

In our area, St Albans School, a thousand years old and with the famous Abbey as its next door neighbour and school chapel, was part of the state system, even though it was primarily a fee-paying public school. In terms of educational standards it was right up there with the best in the land. It was not surprising that many Hertfordshire parents of boys, not just the financially strapped, took the decision to take their offspring away from prep school two years early, if their son won a free or assisted place at St Albans via the eleven-plus. My father certainly had money in mind when he decided I should take the eleven-plus, but I know he would have ignored this consideration if St Albans had not easily matched Lancing academically. I didn't mind. I liked exams, had a day off routine school work and found the whole thing to be rather like a glorified IQ test or newspaper quiz game.

Along with one or two other Aldwickbury boys I passed and was offered a free place (for the next seven years) at St Albans. My father was faced with a difficult decision. He had always wanted me to go to a boarding school and visits to Lancing had convinced him that if I went there I would be happy and well-taught at the school in Sussex by the sea, the county where he had boarded as an orphan at Christ's Hospital. But I suspect the financial question settled the issue between two excellent establishments and after just three post-Japan terms I left Aldwickbury, creating a process that Jo was to go through the next year. I fear Jo might have suffered a little in consequence during his last year at Aldwickbury; unintentionally or not, some staff and boys reacted a little less warmly to someone whom they knew would not be around for the full stretch.

Mr Castle was particularly miffed by the decision of any parent to take a boy away early and refused to let those leaving at eleven become members of the Old Boys' Association, a move rescinded by Brian Chidell after his partner's death in 1960. This may not have seemed a particularly important act of revenge on Mr Castle's part, but under Brian's quite phenomenal aegis, the AOBA has become a most fascinating network of former childhood friends. To this day Brian Chidell is in touch with over eighty per cent of the boys who had passed through his school during his hundred terms (exactly) as headmaster and I am not alone in benefiting from the renewed friendships and contacts that his devotion to his former pupils has instigated. Just to read about some of the lives of men I have not seen for forty years is great fun and I am very grateful for the belated offer of membership that I accepted in 1960.

My two years at St Albans were happy ones, but very undistinguished. It was a huge place, with a hundred boys arriving every year and there was little likelihood of a junior making any sort of mark, at least outside his own level. However, I did start coming top again and thus got moved up a year after just one term, along with my runner-up, an ex-Aldwickbury chum, John Gott, who became my new best friend. Having been a weekly boarder at the end of my Aldwickbury career, I was back in day-boy mode, which involved bus journeys between Hatfield and St Albans. Sharing our daily travels were many pupils from other schools, including girls from St Albans High School, and led by the precocious charm of another close friend of mine, Bruce Campbell, several of us Abbey boys used to chat up the local lovelies. Innocence was too strong a word; nothing remotely exciting happened even though I became infatuated with a girl named Jan who always fancied Bruce much more than me anyway. By my second year on the buses we would often hang around for ages outside the High School, whose pupils seemed to go home later than us, in the hope of a second fix of feminine companionship each day; the most sensational event being when one young lady, all of thirteen, revealed her vital statistics to Bruce – just the numbers, not the actual bodily parts – which soon became information known to all of Form 2a.

I may have been displaying an early interest in the opposite sex but in most other ways (and indeed even in my dealings with women) remained staggeringly immature. The days of effortless success in the classroom were gone; this time I did not or could not take a year's jump in my stride and I found myself often in the relegation zone, although I always managed to hang on to my place in the top stream – and I was a year younger than most of the class. My interest in most sports was still great. In the summer of 1957 I very briefly looked as if I might be a competent cricketer, finding I could bowl quite accurate slow left-arm *à la* Johnny Wardle. I both batted and bowled left-handed, which was strange as I never did anything else in life that way round. I was made captain of the first-year team to universal amazement and for a few short weeks I saw myself as Pip, the eponymous hero of Ian Hay's magnificent 1915 novel, which tells the story of a young sportsman from kindergarten to engagement.

In his first year at public school Pip discovers that he is actually a left-handed cricketer, not a right-handed one as he had believed, and as soon as he makes the change he is unplayable. I was unplayable, meaning unselectable, after just two games as skipper, losing all form and demonstrating quite absymal leadership. I was dropped from the side, affecting not to care and spent most of my sports time in the swimming pool. But following first-class cricket remained a passion; my father had taken Jo and me to our first county match (Middlesex v. Sussex at Lord's) and to our first Test Match (England v. Australia at the Oval) in 1956, the summer before I began at St Albans. My mother was a chum of Jessie Edrich, then married to the famous Bill, still playing for Middlesex. The Edriches lived on the other side of Hatfield so I actually met the great player – naturally he and Denis Compton became my favourite cricketers. I discovered E.W. (Jim) Swanton in the pages of the *Daily Telegraph*. I also discovered Elvis Presley at around the same time and ever since have thought of E.W. and E.P. as a joint deity.

Pop music was taking a greater hold on me. On our return from Japan, Auntie Gertie gave the family her old wind-up gramophone and a pile of pre-war seventy-eight r.p.m. records. My brothers and I worked our way through her eclectic collection, ranging from 'Barnacle Bill The Sailor' to classical symphonies spread over several discs, loving many of the Thirties pops but soon wanting to buy our own favourites. My father despaired as Tommy Steele ('Singing The Blues' was the first record I ever bought) and then even more vulgar singers such as Frankie Vaughan and inevitably Elvis were cranked out incessantly on Auntie Gertie's decrepit machine. Perhaps hoping to elevate our musical standards they eventually purchased their own gramophone, a Trixette record player, which could cope with new-fangled LPs and forty-five r.p.m. singles, on which they played Gilbert and Sullivan and original cast recordings of the great Rodgers and Hammerstein shows. This new hardware didn't stop us buying rock'n'roll whenever pocket money or secret contributions from Granny permitted – in fact it encouraged us – but I did become almost as keen on many of the songs from shows and movies as I was on the music loved by all sane teenagers of the time.

The popular recordings my father wanted me to like – and I did – were the likes of *Oklahoma!*, *Kiss Me Kate*, *High Society* and *The King And I*. Above all, *My Fair Lady*. The last remains my favourite musical score of all time. The show exploded on to the New York stage in 1956 but did not arrive in England until two years later. The album was therefore not issued in England until 1958, and paranoid copyright rulings of the day prevented any radio broadcasts of the score or advance release of any of the songs in any form. However, every household in England that had any connection with anyone who went to the States between 1956 and 1958 seemed to own a copy of the peerless LP, and my father had the good fortune to go on an American business trip shortly after *My Fair Lady* opened there. He brought the album home and I soon knew every one of Alan Jay Lerner's magnificent lyrics by heart. I did not understand anything like all the subtle nuances of his words but this did not matter. In fact it was a plus, as for many years afterwards I was still discovering new meanings and fresh wit in his lines. When, many years later, I included words and phrases such as '*quid pro quo*' (*The Lion King*) and 'fratricide' (*Joseph*) in those of my own efforts that were written primarily for young children, I never worried about whether or not they would understand every syllable at the time. As long as they enjoyed the whole, the extra fun of enjoying some of the details could easily be postponed for a while.

I had the pleasure of meeting Alan Jay Lerner on several occasions towards the end of his life, when he was married to

Liz Robertson and based in England. He was always charmingly enthusiastic about the work of others and it was quite something to get the odd note of congratulation from him – especially generous if the show in question had been a disaster. He was indirectly responsible for my winning a trip to Luxembourg in 1970, just before my initial success as a writer with the album of *Jesus Christ Superstar*.

I entered a competition that summer in the *Sun* (it must have been a friend's copy) in which contestants were invited to prophesy the Top Ten a month hence. Lee Marvin had just released a single of the wonderful Lerner/Loewe song from *Paint Your Wagon*, 'Wand'rin' Star', which at the time of the competition was lurking at around number 49 in the charts. I had a hunch that it might be a surprise smash and put it down to be Number One four weeks later. This duly happened and as I was presumably the only person to have made this wild forecast I won first prize – fifteen minutes as a disc-jockey on Radio Luxembourg. Having announced my win and splashed my photo in the paper ('Top Ten Tim wins chance of radio fame with the *Sun*') the contest organisers showed a distinct lack of interest in actually delivering the prize. After hearing nothing for several weeks I called the paper only to be asked 'Oh – do you really want to go?' to which they received a curt, affirmative answer. The gardening correspondent drew the short straw to be my date for a weekend in the Grand Duchy and once on the air I shamelessly plugged the forthcoming *Superstar* album. I recounted this tale at Alan's memorial service many years later and as a result was invited to sing 'Wand'rin' Star' at a Drury Lane tribute concert to the great wordsmith. I would not have accepted had the song been one made famous by Rex Harrison or Julie Andrews, but even I can sing better than Lee Marvin. With the vital help of the brilliant vocal quartet Cantabile, I was one of the hits of the night and our version was even released as a single – sad to say, failing to establish me as a middle-aged idol. I still await my chart début as a vocalist.

Curiously, much as I loved all the show and film LPs in my parents' collection, I never had any great urge to see the productions from which they came. I was truly a vinyl freak. But I did enjoy the family trip to see *My Fair Lady* (starring Rex

Harrison and Julie Andrews) when it finally got to the West End. The production and cast lived up to the show I had seen a thousand times in my imagination – something that has rarely happened for me since, even as far as my own work is concerned.

It was during my two years at St Albans that rock'n'roll really took hold of teenage Britain. For the first time music divided the generations and it was to remain that way for a quarter of a century. In the Nineties, as rock itself has become middle-aged, parents and children often have surprisingly similar tastes, but in 1956 it was inconceivable that anyone over the age of twenty-one would have expressed anything but disgust for Elvis, Little Richard, Jerry Lee and Co. This of course made the new music even more attractive to my generation and my friends and I found new heroes by the week – wonderful, unattainable Americans such as Buddy Holly and the Crickets, the Everly Brothers and Eddie Cochran; home-grown imitators (but not necessarily untalented) such as Tommy Steele, Billy Fury, Marty Wilde and Cliff Richard and the Shadows.* It was not that easy to hear teenage music – the BBC, the nation's sole radio network, gave rock a thin time, and Radio Luxembourg, cheerfully and commercially playing a non-stop hit parade every night (plus the odd religious tirade), assumed enormous importance. The generally appalling reception of the station on 208 metres somehow added to the excitement and the feeling that its listeners were a persecuted, enlightened band, united and strengthened by the disapproval of the majority.

Our pocket money was modest (until I was twelve, an old penny per week per year of my life) but somehow Jo and I pretty speedily managed to build up a collection of singles – by now nearly all in the amazing new forty-five r.p.m. format. Pop music still got so little attention from the BBC that buying a single became a major event. A trip to a record shop was an excuse to spend as long as the shop would allow in the listening booth, usually with ten pals crammed inside, pretending that we had not made up our minds which hit we wanted. The B-sides were a crucial factor when we discussed in which of half a dozen desperately desired hits to invest

---

* Originally Cliff Richard and the Drifters.

our 6/3d (roughly 31p), which is where Buddy Holly always scored. Television belatedly recognised the power of this musical revolution and shows such as *6–5 Special* and later *Oh Boy* became unmissable Saturday events. Nothing else mattered in my life at this time as much as pop music, a state of affairs that did not thrill my parents. Pocket money was for saving (for what?) and only our purchase of 'Mary's Boy Child' by Harry Belafonte received a modicum of approval.

I guess a few other distractions occupied my last two years as a non-boarding student, but school activities took up a relatively small part. The junior forms at St Albans were caught up in a bike culture (drop handlebars mattered) and I briefly flirted with the almost universal train-spotting craze. Fortunately my heart was never really in it. I became almost as keen on soccer as cricket, supporting Sunderland because I liked the name, but once I realised the Roker Park lads were not on the local bus route, went to watch Sid Owen and the lads at Kenilworth Road, Luton (but to this day, follow Sunderland, hopefully, loyally, and too often at a distance). The Munich air disaster of February 1958 which destroyed Matt Busby's Manchester United team was perhaps the first national news story that really broke into my sheltered world; every afternoon on the way home I would buy (sometimes all three) the evening papers for my parents – '*Star, News, Standard*' was the rallying cry in St Peter's Street – and the bus home was quiet for once on the chilly grey afternoon that my papers reported the death of Duncan Edwards.

I learned that there was an England north of Luton on a couple of school-organised Lake District holidays, whence my most vivid memory is of my first investment in the joys of a juke-box, in a coffee bar (another first) in Keswick. In my final summer holiday from St Albans, years two and three ventured to St Malo, following which I got a severe talking to from my mother for sending an allegedly indecent post card to Rosalind Sharp – I deny the charge but by now I certainly appreciated charms in Rosalind that were not sisterly ones. Again, she preferred a more mature bloke (not difficult to find), all of fifteen and on a heftier weekly allowance. The bastard.

I continued to be a cheerful, relaxed (too relaxed in the view of both parents and teachers) student at St Albans but neither the school nor I made a great impact upon each other – hardly surprising in view of the fact that I moved on again before getting anywhere near the top. My father had forgotten to tell Lancing College that I was now not going to sign on at the age of thirteen and my mother was thus startled to receive a call from the Headmaster in the summer of 1958, enquiring if I was still on the ticket. Joan, sure that they could not really afford the fees (all of £300 p.a.), yet knowing how much my father had always wanted me to go to a boarding school (not because he didn't like me), wrestled with her conscience for some time before passing the problem on to Hugh. I was just as startled when my parents turned up in the middle of a scout camp week to inform the patrol leader of the Peewits that the Lancing option was still on the table. I had missed both the Common Entrance and scholarship exam dates, but apparently the school might be willing to take me purely on an interview. Lancing had obviously made this offer based on my Aldwickbury track record, rather than on my St Albans one.

Loitering within tent, the family summit agreed we should go down to Lancing to meet the Headmaster. I have no recollection of worrying about another dramatic move, adopting an attitude I have never really shaken off throughout my life of assuming nothing will happen until it does. I don't think I was indifferent to the prospect of losing close touch with friends or of being away from home for long spells, simply capable of living from day to day, most of which were extremely comfortable. I had no real concept of my parents' financial concerns, even though they explained their dilemma. I assumed they'd get it right. They did.

My parents and I drove to Lancing where I met John Dancy, the Headmaster, a tall, imposing man, not yet forty, with an interesting limp – a legacy of polio. Dancy had been at Lancing for five years – one generation of boy turnover – and had been quite a mover and a shaker, reflecting and responding to the turbulent social changes of the time, which were still some years away from their Sixties apogee. On the way down in the car my father did his best to prepare me for the interview with various general knowledge questions, although the odds of any of his tips materialising in the Headmaster's study must have been remote.

But at least I felt more confident armed with the name of the then Prime Minister of Canada (Diefenbaker, if I remember correctly). In the event the only subject I was questioned on was myself, a topic I knew quite a bit about – perhaps too much, for a few days later we were informed that Mr Dancy felt my performance did not justify a scholarship. However there was an offer of a place for me starting next term, with a £30 p.a. exhibition (roughly a ten per cent discount) thrown in. My parents bit the financial bullet and, with my acquiescence, St Albans were informed that they had lost Form 3a's twenty-fifth most sparkling student (out of thirty-three).

So for the second time I left a school without having got anywhere near the top. I most surely benefited from my two years at St Albans, primarily because I had made friends with boys from different backgrounds – not all from the sometimes narrow confines of the middle class. But it had not been anything like the golden run I had enjoyed for most of my Aldwickbury days, and I am sure that my comparative academic failure at St Albans was a factor in my parents being in favour of the move. A fresh start might be the thing to get the boy wonder back on track. Of course, one of the reasons for my less than glittering record was that academic standards at St Albans were then extremely high – one of the very best in the country.

Fellow pupils had included Rod Argent and Hugh Grundy, later of the Zombies beat group, and Tony Hendra, a prefect in my time, who resurfaced in my life in Los Angeles many years later in the most unlikely guise – editor of *National Lampoon* magazine and manager of Spinal Tap in the hilarious movie. Perhaps my closest friend from St Albans was a lad named Tony Watkins who for years almost lived at Popefield Farm during the holidays; of all the childhood chums who have got in touch with me since I became a minor celebrity (and I am usually glad when they do) he is one that has never done so – and I wish he would. Maybe he'll read this and give me a call.

Chapter Six

In December 1962, the day before I left Lancing College (motto: *Beati Mundo Corde* – Blessed Are The Pure in Heart) Sir William Gladstone, headmaster and direct descendant of the former Prime Minister, gave a talk to those of his charges leaving the womb of a cushy public school for the chill of the real world. He informed us that the only advice he got upon leaving Eton from his headmaster was never to wear your Old Etonian tie in a brothel. He would however give us a little more instruction than that, proceeding to inform us that, by the time we were all thirty, one of us would be an alcoholic, another might be in prison and another might not even be still of this world. Fortunately he did not specify who. It was up to us to make sure we avoided these perils out there, while yet making the most of all the undoubted advantages our education had given us in order to lead a worthwhile and enjoyable life. All good stuff, but it did seem a little over-dramatic.

Willy Gladstone rather optimistically also put forward the prognosis that all those of us who had dabbled with homosexual activity during our years at Lancing (about ninety-nine per cent) would discover that this was just a phase, to be discarded forever once we cruised down the drive for the last time. He also stressed the importance of showing great respect for the opposite sex, and here I was right behind him – if that's the appropriate phrase. I had been trying desperately to get close enough to women in order to have the chance of showing some respect ever since I took over the organisation of the dancing classes in my fourth year.

Despite the fact Willy had brought girls into his speech I would not have described his audience as gripped; there was little post-match analysis as we trooped off for our last supper. I couldn't help feeling that his headmaster at Eton had been more on the button, and I have certainly followed (metaphorically, of course) the advice given to the adolescent Willy. But I suspect I have taken in quite a few of the adult Gladstone's words too.

I was at Lancing College for just over four years – thirteen terms. Apart from my last term, at the end of 1962, I was very happy there – on the face of it, appalling material for an autobiography. All schools have ups and downs and I believe I was lucky to be there during a Lancing up, which I naturally failed to appreciate at the time. By the standards of the day, the school was very liberal; indeed even by today's standards it was more like a country club than Tom Brown's Rugby. I cannot recall any unduly warped or even incompetent members of staff, and my fellow inmates were a lively, intelligent bunch. Beating was still in force for the most heinous crimes (which nearly always meant smoking), though during my time the right of senior boys to beat juniors was discreetly phased out. Bullying existed but was not rife and it was hard in some cases not to feel that the victim asked for it. The uniform was no hardship to wear, the principal feature being a rather natty grey herringbone jacket. No cap.

Few public schools have such a splendid setting as Lancing. Perched on a hill on the South Downs, the austere group of solid flint buildings, dominated by the ninety-foot-high chapel, built of Sussex sandstone, is a monument to both Victorian confidence and to the boundless ambitions of the Founder (Nathaniel Woodard, in 1848), who was not content with leaving it at Lancing, establishing a whole company of fiercely Christian Woodard Schools primarily in the South of England, including Hurstpierpoint and Ardingly.

In winter the atmosphere could be bleak but I have always liked cold weather, particularly when viewed from the inside of a warm study with Elvis on the record player. In the summer Lancing was England at its beautiful best. The view from the top of the College drive was spectacular: the River Adur, Shoreham town and airport, and the Channel. Brighton, a magnet to all boys on half-holidays, was a few miles east, Worthing, less exotic, a few miles to the west.

Even less racy than Worthing (quite an accolade) was Steyning to the north. The chance of being granted permission to visit any local town was inversely proportional to the desire one had to go there. A bike was essential at Lancing, not only because the bike-sheds were the base for numerous illegal activities.

Chapel dominated Lancing's architecture and timetable – a gargantuan nineteenth-century Gothic Revival masterpiece in which we had eight compulsory services a week. Lancing was about as High Church as it is possible to be without actually being Catholic. Most prayers were sung, there were banners, robes, processions and, on Saints' Days, incense. If one has to go to church that often, it was at least a good show, rather like a musical being saved by its set. There were half-holidays on major Saints' Days, which many regarded as the only plus to emerge from the Christian convictions of the Founder. Ascension Day was the real bonanza – we were let loose from 9a.m. to 9p.m. The Chapel during my time was in a permanent state of near-completion; every term a larger builders' hut appeared while the Chapel remained stubbornly unfinished. When I arrived £50,000 was needed to finish the job; by the time I left five years later the shortfall had risen to £250,000.

Nearly every issue of the *Lancing College Magazine* kicked off with an editorial along the lines of 'we must remember that Lancing is not a microcosm of the real world', written by a boy in his last year who was doubtless beginning to feel a combination of guilt and panic about his imminent transfer to it. Once school had been left behind, it was pretty clear that this assessment was wildly inaccurate – Lancing and places like it were little societies that in many respects were phenomenally like the real world. Great importance was attached to rank and custom; the best-lookers tended to be more popular than the uglies; in order to pursue one's own predilections and vices it was wiser to appear to go with the flow of the system than to flail manically against it. But no one had to go to the wall unless they made the effort to do so. Few boys seemed unable to cope.

While ninety-five per cent of the electorate was slap in the middle of the middle class, a good variety of companion was assured by the fact that in the late Fifties geography played a relatively minor part in boarding school selection. Public schools today are to all intents and purposes weekly boarding schools and the Nineties' parents who send their offspring to board more than half an hour away are condemning themselves to years of stress behind the wheel. We only saw our parents once or twice a term and whether they came to us or we staggered home, it was an event to look forward to that even a 500-mile round trip could not spoil. My round trip was a little under 200 miles, but three of my closest friends at Lancing lived in Cornwall, Solihull and Yorkshire. A boy at Lancing today would only have pals from West Sussex (or from the Far East, but that's a separate development).

Why Lancing? I suppose the comparative proximity to Christ's Hospital influenced my father, but really the deciding factor was the word of the vicar of Sandridge, the Rev. Handford, whose son Richard, a pal of mine at Aldwickbury though two years older, had been so polite and charming every time he came round to play at Popefield that whatever school he was down for had to be on the Rice shortlist. It was Lancing, so that's where a place was booked for me, subject of course to Common Entrance or scholarship results (this was all fixed before the St Albans saga sidetracked me for two years). Richard was almost halfway up the school when I arrived and for someone so senior to mix with new men would have been infra dig and/or given rise to gossip, so ironically I saw less of him once we were at school together than I had for some time, even though we were both in Second's House.

Nonetheless Richard often went (discreetly) out of his way to help me, his one mistake being to propose me for the Debating Society three weeks in. When he generously announced 'I would like to propose Mr Rice', the only response came from a lout at the back who shouted 'I bet you would!' to loud laughter all round. I subsequently discovered that I had made it on to some Top Twenty chart of pretty new boys (annoyingly, only at about Number Eighteen) and Richard's kindness had been misconstrued. I was never sure to the end of my Lancing career whether I had actually been elected to the Debating Society or not. Richard went on to become Head Boy – incidentally, an extremely lax one, leaving it rather late to rebel against the system. After he left I barely saw him for thirty years until I ran into him at

Yorkshire TV – he was producing *Emmerdale Farm* and I was on *Countdown*.

Life was not very tough for new boys (or 'new men' as they were known). Having to walk around with all three buttons of your jacket done up was one of the greater hardships. I only recall one during my time who failed to last the course and who was whisked away before he had even seen out the new men's three-week punishment immunity period. All the same, it was not the done thing for even the most junior old hands to mix too enthusiastically with the incoming squirts, so my first close friends were my three fellow Second's House virgins, Geoff Strong, Ian Huish and Jason Neal. I have not seen Jason for thirty-five years, but I am still in touch with the others, notably Geoff. Geoff was not a fit child; he had missed whole terms at prep school because of serious bouts with asthma. Unable to participate fully in most sports, and inevitably struggling to keep up with the pack academically, he on many occasions suffered grossly unfair teasing at the hands of the more fortunate; I know that more than once I would feebly follow the mob and not give him the support he deserved, but these lapses were mercifully rare and I became, and remain, a great admirer of the way he coped with his problems. Geoff was tiny and I was lanky – we formed a strange Pete 'n' Dud type duo and our friendship is still going strong.

My sporting life at Lancing was erratic. Everything was on offer and I was entranced by new games such as squash, fencing and Eton Fives. The most important sport of all was soccer. Thanks to the superb coaching of Ken Shearwood, the First XI was for a decade undoubtedly one of the very best in the country. There was genuinely enthusiastic support on the touchlines from most of the College (home and away). A maverick of immense charm, Ken brought both Tottenham and Aston Villa down to the school to play the first team. It is one of my great regrets that I barely got to know him while I was at Lancing, but I was neither good at soccer nor in his house. Nor, surprisingly, did he teach me at any point – perhaps he never taught anybody. A wartime naval officer who won the DSC, he played in two amateur cup finals at Wembley, some first-class cricket, wrote several books including one about his time as a Cornish off-shore fisherman and at one point threw the academic world into confusion by applying for the headmastership of Eton, for which he was foolishly passed over. I am glad to say that in recent years I have seen a good deal of Ken, who only finally left Lancing in 1996.

My soccer was restricted to humble house matches but I did make a bit of an impact in other sports. Every winter term two great cross-country events took place, the three-mile for under-sixteens and the five-mile for the seniors. Both were hilly courses around the Downs, at the end of which were a series of flooded dykes, some three or four feet deep. Taking part was compulsory unless medical excuses could be found. Thus within a month of my arrival I lined up with 150 others to take part in the three-mile, normally won by a hairy lad in his third year. To this day I am not sure how I managed it, but I came fifth, and would have been third but for an unseemly scramble out of the final dyke in which the superior weight of the other two in there with me paid off. I was very fit, but above all totally confident, under no pressure to achieve anything. I was miles ahead of the next new man and instantly hailed as a great prospect. Invited to join the under-sixteen running squad, I never produced that form again. Once again in my life, a golden start and a quick decline. Being expected to be good wrecked me and I lost nerve and interest. In my second year I came a wretched twenty-eighth, in my third a more respectable tenth – but I should have won it both times.

Still a fanatical follower of cricket (though the England performance in Australia in 1958/9 severely tested my loyalty) I played as much as possible in the summer, but once again I was restricted through lack of skill to minor games. I played a lot of squash, which was immensely popular, and although I was nowhere near a school team, the overall standard at Lancing was so high (at one point in the Sixties Lancing Old Boys made up almost an entire England team) that I found I was quite capable of holding my own on a social level in later life. Boxing was still on the agenda. This was one sport I was not keen to get into. My feeble frame was quite heavy for my age, but only because of my height, and I was bound to get matched weight-wise with an over-developed violent brute, small in stature but with a grudge about his lack of inches and a piledriver of a left hook. I fought just one bout – with enormous reluctance – in which I displayed remarkable backward running technique.

Swimming was the one sport at which I retained some semblance of ability. I walked, or rather swam, into the house team and was generally on the fringe of school team selection, usually for backstroke. The Lancing bath in those days was very small – just twenty yards long – and indoor although, bewilderingly, it was never used in the winter terms. All boys swam stark naked, the official excuse being that fluff from trunks would block up the filter, which I hope was the real reason. School team members were allowed the privilege of trunks and once this was achieved it was a great feeling to be able to leap into the pool honeypot style without undue risk to your scrotum.

In November 1960, at the start of my third year, just before half-term and just after my competent tenth place in the three-mile, running up from the tuck-shop, I felt a twinge in my left side, exact location hard to pin down, but somewhere between groin and hip. There was no pain but I suddenly found it impossible to walk without a slight limp. For a few days I was treated in the sanatorium for a pulled muscle but no amount of rubbing ointment into my inner thigh seemed to make any difference. At home a few days later for the half-term mini-break, my mother became very concerned about my inability to walk properly. I assured her it would clear up, but she insisted that I should have an X-ray if nothing changed within a week or so. Nothing did, so I was sent to Shoreham hospital where it was revealed that the ball and socket joint in my hip had become dislocated.

I was immediately banned from putting any weight on to my left leg and rushed up to London to see a specialist. I missed the last three weeks of term, being operated on by Mr Ivor Robertson of Harley Street at the University College Hospital in the first week of December. Mr Robertson pinned the wayward bones back into position and I was then told I couldn't walk for at least six months. This meant crutches until after Christmas and a caliper, or 'iron leg', fitted just in time for my return to Lancing. This gadget, which necessitated special shoes, adding another unwanted two inches to my height, took the weight off my left side and enabled me to walk stiff-legged at a reasonable, if awkward, pace. There was a lock that could be released to enable me to bend the leg when I sat down and of course at night I was able to dispense with the contraption altogether, which was just as well as the leather tube that was clamped around my thigh all day smelled pretty grim by bedtime. All games, except swimming, were out, although I was able to ride a bike, taking care not to lean to the left when stopping. Needless to say I became quite cavalier about the whole thing and after a couple of months had even played squash and fives again, seeing myself as a poor man's Douglas Bader. Naturally I got the sympathy vote from staff and fellow students alike, even winning a prize for hard work after my first term as a cripple, when I had put no more nor less effort into my studies than in previous terms, in other words not very much.

It was however very easy to appear brave as I was never in the slightest pain from start to finish. In fact there were quite a few advantages to my condition: I was allowed to sit in comfort at the back at Chapel, received official immunity from the crime of being late, and was invalided out of the school Corps. I had been totally fit again for over a year before anyone rumbled that I hadn't re-enlisted. Races in the dormitories on my crutches (kept as emergency backup should the iron leg succumb to metal fatigue) became a Second's House social highlight. Not yet being a hypochondriac, I never had the slightest doubt that I would make a full recovery as promised. I was encouraged to swim as much as possible, to prevent my left leg withering away, and found that I was as fast as before. Thus it was I came to hold an all-time Lancing record in that I represented the school at a sport while being unable to walk. I gained minor representative honours swimming backstroke. I couldn't dive, but backstroke didn't need a dive.

Despite my almost permanent residence in the pool during the summer of 1961, it was amazing how much thinner my left leg was than my right when I returned to Mr Robertson's knife for the removal of the pins. The bones had now ossified together and I was told to throw away my crutches, walking normally almost instantly, although I was a little apprehensive before my first cured step. I was informed that I might have some stiffness in my hip in my fifties which seemed ludicrously distant to contemplate. However, touch wood, so far so good, although I still tend to take weight on my right leg when, say, jumping out of windows.

I cannot be sure what caused my hip to give way – it is possible that it was nothing more than rapid teenage growth – but a candidate for the blame must be a motorcycle accident I had had the previous summer holiday while staying with a Lancing chum, Adam Diment. His parents owned a farm at Battle and Adam owned a lethally unroadworthy track bike which I ploughed into a post. At the time, bruised and dazed, I thought I had been merely bruised and dazed.

Adam was one of the most important influences of my early life. Though in my house, he was a couple of years senior to me and I did not really get to know him until I was half way up the school. He was a bit of a loner, rarely hunting in the gangs that so many adolescents favour. Nonetheless he was popular, highly entertaining and appeared worldly wise beyond his years. He wore a natty leather flying jacket and jeans whenever possible (not always easy then at public school) and had a bit of the James Dean about him, not so much in looks (he was attractive rather than handsome) but in attitude. He appeared to know a great deal about most aspects of popular culture and current affairs without actually showing any enormous interest in them – he seemed aloof from the common herd while simultaneously affecting a studied working-class persona. He was also a highly talented cartoonist who drew witty portraits of staff and fellow pupils.

One of the first things I ever heard him say (addressed to a casual house-room gathering at which I stood in awe of F.A. Diment and other senior philosophers) was the spot-on observation that I still take comfort from today: 'Everyone thinks they're different; but they're wrong – we're all the same'. At fourteen that struck me as pretty original thinking; forty years on I still have to remind myself from time to time how right he was. Adam had ambitions to be a writer which seemed at odds with his modest academic achievements. In 1967 he sold as many novels in Britain as any other popular writer.

In my third year six of us formed a pop group, the Aardvarks. I sang and played a dinky little instrument called the Melodica. My co-vocalist was close pal Henry Speer*, who bought a bass guitar on the never-never, and Geoff Strong doubled as rhythm guitar and

---

* Henry Speer's sister Janet married my brother Jo in 1970. Henry is now a senior partner of an East Anglian law conglomerate.

manager (his greater gift was for management). The one with talent (there's usually one and only one) was Pete Romyn (lead guitar) who could actually play quite a few Hank B. Marvin licks. On drums (or rather drum) was Mike Saunders. Pete Rawlings had an amplifier so he could do what he wanted if we could all plug in. We were seriously frowned upon by authority, as indeed was anything to do with pop music. And not just by authority; the really cool guys preferred modern jazz to the crassness of Elvis and Cliff – Mulligan, Monk and Miles ruled in many studies. We were informed we had the taste of peasants, which thank goodness we did.

From truly dire beginnings the Aardvarks (so called in order to guarantee top billing on any alphabetically arranged poster) wound up just about good enough to play at various school dances in our final year, having to wait for our turn in the spotlight until the previous year's combo, a trad jazz band, had all departed. Our heroes were Cliff Richard and the Shadows and our repertoire limited, but we won a following of sorts if only because we were the first to introduce electric instruments into school life. Two years after the Aardvarks had gone their separate ways, there were half a dozen rock groups in the school, all equipped to the gills with flash hardware.

Having been notably unmusical for the first fifteen years of my life, it was really rather strange that I was able to make a reasonable fist of singing rock – or perhaps it's not so strange. I was so obsessed by pop music, living from one *New Musical Express* chart to the next, listening to the current hits over and over again (they were rarely on the radio, but every Top Ten record could usually be found in someone's dive or study), that against all the odds I picked up the rudiments of singing in tune and even such subtleties as harmony (thank you, the Everly Brothers). I had a natural flair for presentation, i.e. for showing off, and with a truly fine guitarist in Pete Romyn behind me, got by. I am still liable to leap up on stage at parties when a Sixties band is playing and let rip with songs I first manhandled with the Aardvarks.

Ropey though they were, the Aardvarks were Number One in a field of one at Lancing and were unchallenged performers at the school dances and concerts. Young ladies from nearby schools were bussed in for dances and, although heavily chaperoned from the moment of arrival until the last waltz, tended to be more interested in Aardvarks than prefects or First XI footballers. In any event I usually managed to ensure that one particular girl, whether or not her school was the scheduled opposition, came to every dance at which we played. Her name was Joanna Killpack and she was the first great love of my life.

I met Joanna at the school ballroom dancing classes. As secretary of the classes I was responsible each week for meeting and greeting Mrs Allbright and her three young female charges who demonstrated the waltz, quickstep and foxtrot to around three dozen spotty social climbers. Joanna was nearly sixteen, slim and dark; I was seventeen and besotted. Nevertheless I was hopelessly inadequate when it came to making the first move and by the time I got around to writing her a letter (at her suggestion) I was about the fifth foxtrotter to have done so. However, once contact had been established there was no holding us and my rivals were swept aside. Our innocent but all-consuming affair lasted for nine months, from just before Christmas 1961 until the middle of the following summer. I was obsessed – literally dozens of letters, sometimes more than one a day, and long long telephone calls from the one pay phone that served the entire school. This intensely annoyed people at both ends – Joanna's father, a doctor of whom I was fairly terrified, and chaps in the queue for the call-box.

Teenage passion was fuelled by the fact that we didn't really see an awful lot of each other, even during the holidays. Joanna's family lived in Haywards Heath, a long way from Hatfield, and I only ever spent two or three nights there. In the term it was possible to sneak off to Haywards Heath, sometimes legally, for an afternoon of bridled lust, but in the main I passed the blissful months of my first true love affair counting the days to our next moment together. I was a ghastly bore about Joanna to all and sundry; several of my friends, and no doubt my parents, despaired for my sanity as I could think and talk of little else. In the end Joanna began to doubt my sanity too and I was gently given the brush-off via her best friend who was having a similarly torrid time with another Lancing dancer. I was absolutely devastated (a situation in which the Nineties cliché seems for once appropriate) and spent hours locked in my study tearfully playing 'I Can't Stop Loving You' by Ray Charles over and over again. I wrote lovesick poems about her for the school magazine, mostly dire but one impressive in structure if not in content in that it was a villanelle.

But she really was beautiful and on several occasions later in life I have met her again. Her mother, Mona, is a distinguished painter who still lives and works in Haywards Heath. One of her striking pictures of Manhattan hangs in my office and to this day I keep in touch.

The Aardvarks actually made a record, but one that they paid for themselves, recorded in a classroom with the biggest echo we could find. It was a six-track EP featuring recent hits such as 'Michael Row The Boat', 'Save The Last Dance For Me' and my big solo 'Travellin' Light'. We managed to flog most of the fifty copies we ordered and almost covered our costs. We also entered a talent competition in Brighton, getting nowhere but earning ourselves a write-up in the local press in which I was called Jim Price. Our final performance was at the end-of-term concert in December 1962, which was hampered by the previous act putting his foot through our rhythm section's amplifier seconds before we went on stage, but the vocal mikes and Pete's guitar worked and we went down a storm. We were reviewed by a youth in Field's House, David Hare:

> As always we had our full share of 'pop'. Fortunately it was of a very high standard: nothing could have given a show such a brilliant start as Munro-Wilson's* dance routine. At the end there were the Aardvarks, the Lancing singing group, who performed their songs with great gusto. When Rice sang 'I've been cheated, been mistreated' he really looked as if he meant it, although I did feel they were digging for encores and earned them rather too easily. This held up the flow of things considerably. Nevertheless it was talented performance.

* Broderick Munro-Wilson is a highly cheerful and exuberant fellow who many years later had the distinction of being labelled a cad by a High Court judge during a legal spat with a girl friend. He brilliantly cashed in on this notoriety, becoming a media personality advising on social etiquette for the self-respecting cad.

We earned our encores, mate!

There were coincidentally two future outstanding British play-wrights at Lancing when I was there, the unfair reviewer David Hare and Christopher Hampton. I'm inclined to feel that the fact that there were three people who went on to make a mark in the theatre at the same school at the same time was merely a coincidence. I knew Christopher better, as he was in my house. Christopher wrote at least one novel while still in Second's House and David a stream of plays and even films. David (now Sir David) was by far the most conventionally successful of the three of us at Lancing, rising to be second head of school. Other Lancing Old Boys of my time who have made their public mark include Charles Anson, sometime press officer to the Queen (during Her Majesty's *annus horribilis*, among others) and Chris Meyer now, as Sir Christopher, our man in Washington, who was at one time John Major's press officer at Number 10. For a year or two Lancing simultaneously controlled the PR of both head of state and head of government – and had an Elton John single in the charts.

Apart from the Aardvarks, my contribution to the Arts side of the school was limited. I did appear as Lorenzo, having been demoted from Bassanio after one rehearsal, in Donald Bancroft's production of *The Merchant of Venice*. Donald however was quite right around a quarter of a century on, to reveal to the *Brighton Evening Argus* that my performance had been 'terrible'. That production was fun, though, because Donald brought in real live girls, including his daughter Sally, with whom half the school was infatuated, to play the female roles. Playing opposite me as Jessica was Jane Gibson, recently the choreographer of Emma Thompson's *Sense And Sensibility*, whose line, 'Catch this casket', was accompanied every performance by an Olympian throw that Lorenzo struggled manfully and not always successfully to prevent crashing noisily and painfully on to his metal codpiece.

Pre-and post-Joanna my social life at home consisted of a series of frighteningly respectable parties, at some of which the Aardvarks plugged in. Many were hosted by local cosmetics millionaire Bertie Holloway and his family. Jan, Bertie's eldest daughter, fell in love with Henry Speer and/or his guitar and they became engaged while both were still at school. I wished that Joanna and I could have done the same, though by the time Henry and Jan got married three years later my views on early commitment had changed considerably. My father, by now a director of one of the Hawker Siddeley companies that had taken over de Havilland, was fond of pointing out that Bertie sold combs and could afford to buy an aeroplane while he sold aeroplanes and could afford to buy a comb.

My brother Jo had followed me to Lancing, Andy was scheduled to do the same. Throughout the Sixties my mother had a string of articles and short stories published in a wide range of magazines, including the then highly considered *Punch* and *The Times*. She appeared several times on the BBC's *Women's Hour*, generally using her family as inspiration for humour. One broadcast was a very funny assessment of the Aardvarks' capabilities and the impossibility of her son making it in the pop world.

It never crossed my mind at the time to write any songs for our group – we were just determined to copy each new Cliff single note for note. I was however generally writing (or typing) something. Jo and I used to write regularly to pop papers under a host of pseudonyms in an attempt to win LPs. At this, as Adam Golightly, Cranston F. Cranston, Gerrard Portslade and others, we were remarkably successful. We both created our own music magazines, parodies of the *Melody Maker* and the *New Musical Express* in which a host of fictitious pop singers shot up and down imaginary charts. Sixty copies of 'Spin' – The Top Disc Mag' are locked in my files today. I read non-fiction voraciously and fiction hardly at all. I could not get enough of newspapers and *Playboys* mounted up under my bed. Life at Popefield Farm or on family holidays continued its untroubled way with only the death of our beloved boxer disturbing the idyll.

My headmaster and housemaster when I started at Lancing were John Dancy and Donald Parsons respectively; when I left they were Willy Gladstone and Bernard Fielding. The only one of the four men I knew other than fleetingly was Bernard and I am afraid that for much of our time together in Second's House our relationship was a strained one. I was a bolshie adolescent; he was perhaps rather inflexible and less in tune with what was then the modern youth than he might have been. But inevitably I have matured and he has mellowed – it is always a pleasure to see him these days. In any event I was nothing like his biggest problem; I was never a serious lawbreaker, just maddeningly indolent. Even though the form of punishment was on the wane I am still surprised I was never beaten once at Lancing – but more than once dead scared that I would be, which had the desired effect.

I have found during this recollection of my days at Lancing that I remember my life there through my very naïve eyes of the time; I have barely mentioned the academic side of things, embarrassingly revealing the lack of importance I attached to it. I passed all the required O and A levels (History and French) without ever regarding learning as anything more than an obligation. My reports were usually just about adequate. My father's only angry reaction was to a history master's statement that my greatest achievement of the term had been the introduction of a tame jackdaw into class. The master genuinely meant this as a compliment but it was interpreted as a comment upon my trivial approach to just about everything. I had found the bird in question outside my study one afternoon and it sat on my desk or shoulder for two weeks of the summer term before it outwore its welcome and I handed it on to a birdlover in another house.

To the great disappointment of my mother and father, I had no desire to go on to university. To this day I'm not sure why; although my life might not have taken such a fortunate course if I had done, it was basically a feeble non-decision, taken through laziness. Yet I was not rebellious, or brave enough to buck the system completely and mollified my parents during my final term by announcing that I would take up the law. There did not seem to have been any discussion at home or at school about the possibility of my trying for a job in the one area I was passionate about – pop music.

I had little idea what doing law actually entailed but this option at least covered my elders' insistence that a 'qualification' was vital. Several contemporaries, no doubt having given it rather more thought than I had, were law-bound and it seemed like a good idea at the time. So instead of guiding me towards Oxford or Cambridge, which both parents, having missed out on university themselves, would have loved to have done, my father began to do the rounds of finding a solicitors' office that would take me on. I am glad to say both my brothers made up for my aversion to higher education by going to Cambridge.

While dithering over my future I stayed on for one term beyond A levels. The most exciting events of my final term were the Aardvarks' farewell performance and the Cuban Missile Crisis. We reckoned a bomb on London would probably not wipe out Lancing. I rose to the not very dizzy heights of house prefect (a rank hard to avoid if one lurched into a fifth year) but otherwise the term was rather a waste of time – and my father's money. But the reliving of the other four years has been a pleasure; I think the ethos, the liberal spirit of the school, the fact that even insensitive souls such as myself dimly realised that there was more to education than exams and discipline, was a good basis for life. Of course it was privileged, of course it was a bubble of security, but when I return now, it's impossible to feel that my time there was wasted. I am still lying on a bank in the sun in 1961, half-watching the cricket XI, half-listening to Del Shannon's 'Runaway'.

There is an informal photograph in a school magazine of that year's soccer side which I often look at; a dozen or so of my friends, young, unspoiled, not quite innocent but still beautiful, and it's all too apparent that every story, every life is only about one thing – growing old.

Chapter Seven

My immediate post-Lancing future was naturally a major topic of discussion around the Rice breakfast table during the Christmas holidays of 1962. My parents were more interested in these conversations than I was and my contribution to the 1963 game plan was negligible. However I had no objections to the scenario that emerged – my father would continue his quest to find an unsuspecting firm of London solicitors to take me on as an articled clerk, but in the meantime I would go to the University of Paris, La Sorbonne, for a few months. This would allegedly enable me to brush up my A level French and give me just a taste of the university life that I had so carelessly rejected. Before that I would attempt to earn some money and cease to be a drain on the rocky family finances.

My father fixed me a temporary job at de Havilland up the road where I was given £10 a week for sorting out orders for parts of aeroplanes. I never had a clue what either the parts or the aeroplanes they fitted looked like, but rather enjoyed my first taste of office life, 'working' alongside jolly companions of sex, age and social backgrounds unlike my own in a large open-plan office. I was mildly shocked and pleased to discover that engaged women were even more flirtatious than single girls and shudder to think what might have happened had I been there for longer than four weeks. Nothing much happened but what did was (a) not my idea and (b) very enjoyable.

During my brief career in the aircraft industry, Britain was plunged into one of the coldest winters on record – the Big Freeze of 1962/63. Even the Home Counties ground to a halt. I had just passed my driving test and this was not the ideal time for a novice to venture on to the roads but I wanted to visit my pals at Lancing as a sophisticated Old Boy. Our family owned a 1934 Austin Ten, which my father had bought for £40 in 1956 and I boldly set off in this magnificent machine, loaded with supplies for my brother, some four or five days after the first term without me began. It took so long to get there that I was worried that term would end before I arrived, but AYU 594 eventually made it. Some of the pleasure of showing off my new independent status in the world was dented when a master hauled me up for not wearing a school tie. He eventually accepted my story that I had left, but this embarrassing incident made me realise how little impact my departure had made and that the school could run perfectly well without me.

At the beginning of February I set off by train and boat to Paris in the company of my childhood chum Rosalind Sharp, who had already been at the Sorbonne for three months before Christmas and whose enthusiasm for the *Cours de Civilisation Française* had given my parents the idea of sending me there. The course was designed purely for foreign students and consisted of the study of half a dozen different aspects of French language, history and culture. There was to be an exam at the end and it was impressed upon me how important it was for me to justify the expense and parental sacrifice with a pass certificate in June.

My first impressions of Paris are those I have of the city today – alluring, chaotic, beautiful, with a lot of rude and some very attractive locals; murder to get around in, but just the ticket for a short burst of culture or depravity if you aren't in a hurry. It was the first time in my life I was truly living on my own, albeit still surviving on an allowance from my parents. The weather was as bleak as it had been in England. I spent my first night there in a one-star (at most) hotel on the Boulevard Raspail, with orders to find an even cheaper place as soon as possible. I had made no progress whatsoever in this task when after three days I ran into a fellow Lancing alumnus, Chris Brooker, walking as aimlessly I was, but in the opposite direction, down the Boulevard St Michel.

Neither of us had any idea that the other was on the *Cours de Civilisation Française*. We had not been close friends at school simply because we had been in different houses, but in this foreign environment we bonded for life within minutes.

Chris was filling in time before he went up to Cambridge as a choral exhibitioner and had somehow wangled a grant from his college to support his stint in Paris. He had already located an hotel that more than qualified as the ultimate in economy price-wise (and comfort-wise) and within an hour of our meeting I was checking my bags into the Hôtel de Verneuil, 29 Rue de Verneuil, in a fairly bohemian section on the Left Bank, just across the river from the Louvre. A long-time resident there, who had, sadly for us, just checked out, had been the famous black American author James Baldwin, whose *Giovanni's Room* had been largely inspired by his stretch at what we came to call the Château de Verneuil.

The Château was a five-storey edifice with around twenty rooms, in the main occupied by long-term residents. It hovered Pisa-like on the corner of two streets with its two lavatories a striking feature of the view from the outside and an extraordinarily primitive feature of the view from the inside. Occupants could not actually be seen in action from the street but the two tiny rooms jutted out conspicuously from the front of the building, apparently supported by little more than one wooden beam each. The second-floor box we named the Dwarfs, as only a person under five foot tall could have done anything without adopting a foetal position, and the third-floor equivalent was known as the Giants as even Magic Johnson would not have needed to stoop to conquer. Neither had any plumbing features beyond a hole in the floor, but both were supplied with back numbers of the Paris telephone directory. At the start of my stay there we were doing what had to be done with Armand et Fils; by the time we left we had worked our way through to Vichy. Every trip to *Géants* or *Nains* was tinged with the excitement of wondering if this would be the visit that proved one ablution too many for the fragile beam.

But enough of the *toilettes*. The Château holds many other vivid and more romantic memories for me. The hotel was run by the family Dumont. Monsieur and Madame Dumont lived on the ground floor and their three teenage children shifted around various rooms in the upper regions fitting in with the comings and goings of the paying guests. *Les parents Dumont* were a marvellously strong couple, Madame in particular, terrorising their offspring and occupants with aggressive affection and were more French than anyone my most cliché-ridden school textbooks ever portrayed. Both were quite understandably virulently anti-German, having lived through the occupation of Paris, and no student from Munich or Vienna had a hope in hell of getting past the front door, let alone checking in. We British were much more gratefully received and before long had the privilege of being invited to join the occasional family supper. Madame's cooking was simple yet outstanding and her eldest daughter, Solange, sixteen and devastatingly beautiful.

Needless to say I fell for Solange in a big way, and needless to say was too incompetent to do much about it. However, at one of the dinners *en famille*, while *maman* was knocking up another basic masterpiece in the *cuisine*, Solange confided that she and her brother and sister often used to nip out at night after her parents had gone to bed and suggested that Brooker and I might come along too. This developed into a fairly regular routine and there were a few moments of wonderful innocuous romance alongside the banks of the Seine. Solange spoke very little English, which would have pleased my parents from the improving my French point of view, but deep and meaningful conversation was beyond me and unnecessary. It should not be thought that C. Brooker was a mere wallflower – he revealed a year or two later, when such things did not matter so much, that he had actually lost his virginity to an American lady in the hotel, putting my soirées with Solange into guileless perspective. Only a real friend would not brag about being first to the finishing post – but there again I never met the lady.

Christopher's grant kept us afloat. He generously adopted the attitude that I was as entitled to his share of the British taxpayer's money as he was and from about Wednesday each week I lived on Christ's College, Cambridge until the following Monday when the bank received both his sufficient grant and my paltrier allowance. Not that my parents were mean, but we were spending quite a lot on the cinema, jazz clubs and records, having long since abandoned the struggle to attend lectures, or to eat cheap in the only dining room in Paris that served truly disgusting food – the Sorbonne's. Lectures began far too early in the morning and because of a chronic seat shortage, about which more dedicated students staged several revolts in subsequent years, anyone arriving less than an hour before the lecture started had to stand, even making doing the *Daily Telegraph* crossword an unpleasurable experience.

Once we discovered that English language films opened in Paris in English with French sub-titles, we spent most of our days in the cinema. Whenever a movie from the first half of 1963 is shown on television, I know I have seen it. Cambridge University also eased our passage into several dives on the Left Bank, plus more salubrious venues such as L'Olympia. We saw many contemporary jazz greats, including Chet Baker,* Ray Charles, Freddie Hubbard and Art Blakey. My first love was still pop music, but few of the current stars seemed to venture into Paris during our time there, despite, or because of, the fact that the Beatles-led music revolution was taking place back home. I was by now genuinely interested in modern jazz, the preferred music of the hip at school. I found it quite possible to enjoy both pop and jazz, and later relished the irony that rock music was eventually lumbered with much of the pretentious analysis that was so beloved of jazzers. I also became rather keen on French pop music which was as charmingly naff then as now; Johnny Hallyday was about a year into his still booming career which has never penetrated a centimetre beyond French-speaking borders, Richard Anthony and Sheila were the bees' *genoux* and Françoise Hardy was simply perfection.

We also spent a packet on pinball machines, the centrepiece of nearly every Parisian bar, virtually unknown in England at that time outside piers and dodgy amusement arcades. Once or twice we forked out a comparative fortune for a strip club but in general our innocent sexual fantasies were more economically dealt with via the Olympia Press. This long-established Paris-based publishing house selflessly published pornographic literature in

---

* Baker really was the highlight of our Parisian musical education. We saw him as part of a very small crowd at the Chat Qui Peche, a Left Bank jazz dive-cum-shrine. He seemed seriously unaware of his surroundings but played trumpet like a man possessed, which he certainly was – by smack. He signed one of his LPs for Christopher.

English, shocking then but now barely worthy of the bottom shelf of the most conservative UK newsagent.

To a certain extent we corrupted Rosalind, luring her away from most Sorbonne meals and some of the lectures, but she worked hard and it was no surprise when she romped through her exams in June with distinction. What was a surprise was that I also managed to do so, albeit without the distinction. Although the only new French word I had mastered in four months was '*soutien-gorge*' (bra), I recalled quite a lot from my A level syllabus and managed to write more or less the same essay on Flaubert three times for three different examiners. Chris made no attempt to bluff his way through the exam, or indeed to turn up for it. I thoughtfully purloined a certificate of merit awarded to an entrant in a vegetable show that was taking place at the Sorbonne at the time. Chris' parents and doubtless those who paid his grant seemed quite happy with a certificate with a good deal of French, the names of the Sorbonne and C.M.F. Brooker on it (only the last inserted by me).

Having achieved our initial Parisian objective in passing these rigorous examinations, we spent the last two weeks before Christopher's grant finally petered out hitch-hiking to Corsica and back. Tearful goodbyes to the Dumonts, promises to return (especially to Solange) and back to England for a few months of freedom before starting in the law.

Return I have many times, the first time being just three months later. When I went to Paris in 1972 for the opening of the French production of *Jesus Christ Superstar* I stayed again at the Château, rather than in the slightly more upmarket hotels quite reasonably chosen by Andrew Lloyd Webber, David Land and Robert Stigwood. It was there that I met the beautiful Solange again, by now in an unhappy marriage. We renewed our affair on a less immature basis and she came over to England several times in the next year or so. Perhaps I was no more mature, for it didn't work out.

The last time I visited the Château was in 1988 when Christopher, the Sharp sisters and I went on a twenty-fifth anniversary trip, revisiting as many of the old haunts as possible. We would have stayed in the Château but I was a little wary of raking up the complex past with Solange, although the residence we chose was of comparative status in all but emotional content. The Hôtel de Verneuil was anyway on its last legs in 1988 in that M. Dumont had passed away and Mme was getting on a bit, to the extent that she did not even recognise me, although that may well have been because I was also getting on a bit. Solange, she said, was married again and as beautiful as ever. But she had had no children. I would love to see her once more to say I'm sorry but I never will.

Meanwhile, back on the home front, progress had been made towards getting my legal career airborne. Shortly after my return from Paris I went off to be interviewed by two London firms of solicitors, one fairly grand outfit in Lincoln's Inn Fields and one smaller concern, Pettit and Westlake, on the fourth floor above a post office in Baker Street. Both seemed mildly keen to take me on (perhaps my Sorbonne certificate was the clincher) and for no other reason than an English sports fan's love of the underdog I went for Pettit and Westlake. My starting date was fixed for the end of September, which meant I had one last full summer of irresponsibility to enjoy. Unfortunately for the first time I would have to work through it.

I had on occasion during school holidays clocked in for a few days' work as a petrol pump attendant at Waters, the massive garage that straddled both sides of the A1 (the Great North Road) at Hatfield, less than two miles from Popefield Farm. I had mastered the basic skills, and the hourly pay rate and, above all, tips were good. The garage was happy to take me back on a more permanent basis, i.e. two consecutive months, and throughout July and August I looked like an oil slick as I put in extremely long hours, as much overtime as possible, for the first time in my life being a net contributor to the Rice family budget.

In those days, self-service at petrol stations did not exist – indeed any driver attempting to stick a nozzle into his tank got extremely short shrift from us guardians of the pumps. Neither could you buy petrol by the pound – it was only possible to purchase to the nearest half-gallon. In 1963 most brands of petrol sold at just under 5/- (25p) to the gallon with the 4/9½ (24p) the most popular. Consequently the vast majority of motorists would hand over a pound for four gallons, and in many cases leave the change as a tip. These tenpences or whatever mounted up during a long day at a very busy garage and I was able to bank my weekly cheque (around £15) and live off tips alone, which on a good shift would amount to £2/10/- or more. Lunch and tea at Gerry's Café across the road (where I developed a lifetime's craving for bacon sandwiches) were rarely more than 4/- between them, even allowing for 3d a breaktime for the jukebox.

I became as oily inside as out as I obsequiously grovelled to the more prosperous-looking drivers, emphasising the public school accent as I cleaned their windscreens and offered to check their tyres. When rough-looking scrap metal lorries or gypsy trailers lurched in I affected a rougher demeanour. No approach would have got me a tip from these plain-speaking members of society but I had no wish to test their tolerance of middle-class *mores*. My fellow pump-men were probably closer to the scrap metal than to the Rover three-litre end of the spectrum but were by and large a genial bunch. I did my best to fit in, looks and accent-wise at least, although conversationally I did find the insertion of four-letter expletives between every other word, or even between every other syllable, a struggle. My father did suggest one morning as he surveyed his inadequately Swarfega-ed son that my appearance was really rather a disgrace and that I should attempt to be an officer among men, setting an example with clean boilersuit and a tie(!) but I felt this would not have gone down a bundle with the forecourt's other ranks.

The turnover in the other ranks was so quick that by the time I began my last week's work at Waters I was, in length of service terms at least, the senior nozzle man on the east side of the A1. Blokes came and went with bewildering speed, often in rather murky circumstances; I remember being somewhat shocked at the universal approval given by my colleagues to the Great Train Robbers whose criminal coup in August was but one feature of a year of news sensations. I was even offered promotion to shift supervisor with the prospect of becoming a car salesman within a year. Frankly, it was tempting – the cash was so good and I knew that when I started at Pettit and Westlake I was going to be back on the breadline and dependent upon my parents' support once more. I also rather enjoyed being a petrol pump attendant. But I was never seriously going to take such a radical step and turned down all offers. I had about £200 in the bank – I bought a Hacker radio and blew the rest on ten days in Paris.

Chapter Eight

1963, ushered in with that freak freeze, was a most remarkable year in Britain. Something shifted and the shackles of post-war austerity and respect for authority trickled away. The Conservative government spent all year in Profumo Affair damage limitation; Harold Macmillan fell and Christine Keeler and Mandy Rice-Davies (no relation) became household names. The Great Train Robbery thrilled millions besides my former garage pals. The Beatles rose and rose to a fame and acclamation that pop groups of the Nineties such as Oasis could barely dream about; 'satire' boomed via *That Was The Week That Was* and *Private Eye*, and every headline was dwarfed in late November by the assassination of President Kennedy. And I lost my virginity on Christmas Eve to the strains of the Singing Nun on the radio.

Everyone around at the time remembers where they were when they heard that news about JFK – it's become a cliché – but where was I? It was a Friday evening and I was heading out of Popefield Farm's drive in my mother's Mini, going to one of the first black-tie parties I had ever been invited to, just as my father drove in. He looked extremely grim – had he been fired?

'Where are you off to?' enquired the old man.

'A party,' I perkily responded.

'Hasn't it been cancelled?'

'No – why?' Had something happened to the hostess? Had the band pulled out?

'President Kennedy's been assassinated.'

I was truly shocked. JFK was the first and only politician I and many of my age found inspirational. I never wasted a moment worrying about nuclear war which seemed to concern some of my generation (but not half as many as the Left believed) but Kennedy was a political being who grabbed me. It was of course mainly his youth and stunning good looks, but what he had said seemed full of decency and hope, what he had done seemed strong and courageous, e.g. re the Cuban Missile Crisis. Now we know better, unfortunately.

There were two schools of thought at the unwisely uncancelled dance: one, by and large older, that couldn't care less about the President and seemed to regard it as a minor news item from a country of nutters, and one that felt we shouldn't be trying to have a good time after such a shattering event. I was part of the latter, and scored no points at all by spending a good deal of the night outside in the car park with some male chums listening to the radio. Two girls on my table stormed off into the night in a huff, and I received a major bollocking from one of the lady organisers for my disgraceful breach of social etiquette, which was not even redeemed by my later interpretation of 'How Do You Do It' and 'Please Please Me' with the band, in a desperate attempt to prove I was the life and soul.

To an eighteen-year-old newspaper fanatic, the events of 1963 were as manna from heaven. My interest in current affairs was probably my principal claim to be considered a near-adult, although in most matters cultural I was still somewhat on the unsophisticated side. Or perhaps I was actually ahead of the game as the thing I liked most, pop music, was before long to be to be taken up as a seriously intellectual pursuit by many old enough not to know better. The Beatles were simply phenomenally good at their job, and though it took me a month or two to realise just how good they were, it was clear at the time that what was happening in British rock music that year was exceptional.

My literary pursuits beyond newspapers and *Wisden* (and the Olympia Press in Paris) were still minimal, although I had liked the obligatory *Catcher In The Rye*. My vow to take an interest in theatre petered out after one trip to the Royal Court – I forget the name of the offending play. I still loved the cinema and kept a meticulous card index record of everything I saw, awarding each film a rating and compiling my end-of-year Oscars. I was a huge admirer of the best radio comedy: Frank Muir and Denis Norden (*Take It From Here*), Barry Took and Marty Feldman (*Beyond Our Ken* and *Round The Horne*). Sportswise, by now I participated in virtually nothing organised but began a life of regular attendance at the Lord's Test Match – and the 1963 England v. West Indies Test was one of the greatest ever played, Colin Cowdrey with a broken arm enabling England to hang in for a draw.

It was a pretty innocent young man who began his London life on 30 September at the compact offices of Pettit and Westlake. I had emerged from a most conventional middle-class upbringing with a combination of gratitude and indifference. I was polite; I was very good at adapting my attitude, manners and even accent to suit the occasion (a creep anxious to be liked?); I was witty (if sometimes childishly so) and had a great love of word-play. I so often found myself listening to conversations in two ways; interpreting them the way the speaker intends and at the same time in a literal way, analysing and playing with the speakers' words to set them spinning off into unintended meaning and complication. I had not a clue about finance – I had been permanently broke at school, always owing some pal half a crown, always looking for some item to flog. I was a non-smoking, barely-drinking virgin, for whom the idea of drugs was as remote as the likelihood of a trip to Saturn. This would have been true for almost all of my Lancing contemporaries. When I left I very much doubt if more than two boys in the entire school had been all the way with a girl, and it was not very high on my list of priorities – primarily because I assumed I'd never get an offer. Luckily, I was wrong there.

Perched on the top floor at 111 Baker Street, the family firm of P & W, with three Pettits as partners (I never did discover what happened to Westlake), had a total staff of four qualified solicitors, including the three family members, an accountant and assistant, half a dozen girls in the typing pool who doubled as secretaries, a male telephone operator, an imposing lady called Mrs Norman who sat in reception, and a junior or two. Plus of course the articled clerks, of which I was the third on the day I joined. The whole shooting match was housed in a pretty confined area which was really one largish room divided by very impermanent-looking walls and doors. There was always talk that the firm would move to grander premises within a year or two, but it was certainly still at 111 at the start of the Nineties.

We articled clerks (referred to wittily as 'articled particles') were the lawyers of the future, on £5 a week plus luncheon vouchers. It would take five years for us to qualify, during which time we had to take two sets of examinations, and presumably spend nigh on 1500 luncheon vouchers. (Had I read law at a university and got a degree, that would have been a substitute for two years and Part I of the exams.) 1968 seemed aeons away. My fellows in articles when I started were a chap named Paul Buckley, six months ahead of me, and an older (at least twenty-three) woman named Angela who was mysterious and graceful. Paul and I were articled to Morwen Pettit, the daughter of the senior partner, to whom Angela was signed.

It was highly unusual back in 1963 to be articled to a female solicitor. Morwen (and we called her by her first name) was only about ten years older than Paul and I, but the gulf in age and experience was vast. Most of the office staff were rather frightened of her. I certainly was but before I was completely entrusted to her command I was put on to the office phones for a week, not only to master the plug and socket switchboard, which every member of staff had to be able to operate, but also to learn everyone's name and extension.

Despite my innate lack of skill with things mechanical I grasped the essence of both switchboard and personnel by the end of my first Tuesday. I had no objection to serving out the rest of Week One in this humble capacity, but was slightly surprised to be informed on Friday that I was to have another week at the controls. When a third week was suggested I protested, having realised that the reason for my record-breaking stint was not electronic dyslexia but that the regular operator had become rather attached to his latest recruit and had recommended further coaching for me. Perhaps it was his portfolio of pictures of young boys that he began to show me in Week Two that made me twig, or his recommendation that I should read Alec Waugh's *Loom Of Youth*, a famous homosexually-tinged novel which he happened to have in his briefcase.

Transferred to a small desk outside Morwen's prefabricated wall, doubtless considered as thick as a post by all those who had passed the phone test in one week, I soon entered the regular ebb and flow of office life. This meant a bit of the most primitive legal work, such as checking documents and delivering writs, but primarily meant listening to the exploits of the typing pool. The ladies there were all engaged, or worse, engaged to be engaged and the ups and downs of their relationships with fiancés and department stores (they were each slowly accumulating fixtures and fittings for a betrothal scheduled for 1967 at the earliest) provided better entertainment than any soap opera of the day. Even the junior girls, the only people in the office younger than I was, were avidly anticipating wedlock and had no thought of their time in a lawyer's office being anything other than a stepping stone to a bottom drawer full of pillowcases and saucepans. Their men were children allowed off the leash to the pub one night a week, constantly misbehaving in unimportant ways but with hearts in the right places. At least that was how their women saw them. The build-up to ring purchase or to engagement party was intense; the typing pool throbbed with emotion at each blip on each pre-destined relationship. These were women of the 1963 world, friendly and blinkered, and though they were as virginal as I, treated me as an innocent who had a long way to go. I rather liked them.

There were of course exceptions – my boss for one who was as career-minded as any feminist today, and Marion Brown. Marion too was engaged, but she was different. Very bright, funny and curvaceous, she seemed to be a true woman of the world. Her co-workers did not look down their noses at her, but occasionally one sensed a frisson of disapproval. Mere males in the office were naturally attracted. There were not that many spare males in the office. Before long Marion was more often than not my lunch-hour companion round the corner at Joe's or the Quality Inn and the Christmas Eve office party in the Barley Mow sealed my delirious fate. Paul Buckley and I, together with my old school pal Adam Diment, had recently moved into a basement flat in Wimpole Street and after three hours in the pub Marion and I recovered horizontally below ground level – the strains of 'Dominique' by the Singing Nun happened to be on the radio at the crucial moment. Naturally I fell in love. For the perfect description of my reaction, listen to the Four Seasons hit of 1976 'December 1963 (Oh What A Night)' which recounts my Christmas Eve experience with uncanny accuracy both as far as emotions and date are concerned. Was Frankie Valli ever an articled clerk at Pettit and Westlake?

We were flung out of our flat shortly after arriving back noisy and late once too often for our landlady. The final straw was our return from New Year celebrations when Adam, Christabel Sharp and I made it to the top of the fountains in Trafalgar Square where we had had a Scotch and a lot of water with a very nice pin-striped accountant. This was the first time in my life that I got drunk, almost totally on Watney's Red Barrel. Somehow the New Year revels in those days were totally friendly occasions, without no-go areas, riot squads or punch-ups. And we had to be back at work on 1 January. We were delighted to see ourselves on the news the next day, gallivanting in the fountains, relieved to be unidentified.

My television début had thus been anonymous, but I was to follow it up with a second appearance a mere two days later on the hugely popular Friday night television pop programme *Ready Steady Go*. Every week the show featured a lookalike spot in which four contestants mimed to a hit of the day. I had turned up on the Tuesday before with about sixty other would-be Billy J. Kramers to audition for the honour of lip-synching 'I'll Keep You Satisfied' on national TV that Friday, and after what seemed to me to be a very slapdash procedure in which all sixty of us jerked around simultaneously in a large room to the strains of Billy J. on a Dansette record player, I made it to the finals. I therefore had to fake illness on the great day itself in order to skip work and attend rehearsals.

My day at Associated-Rediffusion's studios in Holborn was absolutely thrilling. My co-stars included the Ronettes, Dave Berry, Georgie Fame, Chris Sandford of *Coronation Street* and the Tony Meehan Combo. Not perhaps the most stellar line-up that excellent programme ever signed, but by miles the closest I had ever got to the evermore glamorous world of British pop, with which I was evermore obsessed. Again I recalled my father's words

Above The wedding of Hugh Rice and Joan Bawden, Cairo, Egypt, 27 December 1942.

Left My grandmother, Florence Mabel 'Ray' Bawden, around the age of twenty-four, just before the Great War.

Below Timothy Miles Bindon Rice, aged three. Bindon after my great-uncle whom I never knew; other choices seemed like a good idea at the time.

Popefield Porch Pose – Tim (nin Jo (seven) and Andy (four) with Prinz (five); lifetime infatuation with boxers well underway.

Popefield Farm, near St Albans, Herts. The happiest of homes from 1950 to 1969; love of mowing lawns established here.

My father inside an unfinished de Havilland aircraft in the early Fifties, which was clearly not being built for passengers his size.

Lancing College Chapel, dominating the first XI cricket pitch, on which I was never asked to play.

A 'terrible' Lorenzo in *The Merchant of Venice*, Lancing College, 1961. Real girls, though.

The Aardvarks, 1961, top of every bill (alphabetically); *left to right*: Henry Speer, Geoff Str Pete Rawlings, Pete Romyn, Mike Saunders, TR.

Joanna, Lancing Founder's Day, 1962.

The shot I would have used for my first alb I recorded it in 1962.

Rosalind (*left*) and Christabel Sharp, my two oldest friends, well before they became Mrs Cliff and Mrs Butler respectively.

Alas, regardless of their doom
The little victims play!
No sense have they of ills to come
Nor care beyond today

See end of Chapter Six. The Lancing College First XI with Joe Mercer, 1962. I never got near the 4th XI. Lines from Thomas Gray's 'Ode On A Distant Prospect of Eton College' which my favourite modern English author, Simon Raven, publishes in full in his memoir *The Old School*.

Left Solange in her room at her paren hotel. L'Hôtel de Verneuil, Paris 7ème early 1963, when Chris Brooker and had just moved in.

Below My Paris soul-mate Chris Brooker, aged eighteen, looking as cc as it is possible to be in a photo-boo in 1963. He looks younger now.

The hutch held in place by a modest beam was the rather frightening third floor toilette at L'Hôtel de Verneuil in which excessive movement was unwise.

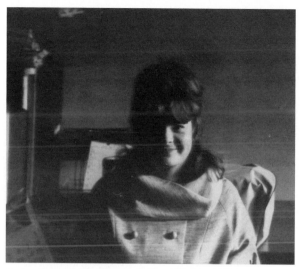

Marion, the star of the typing pool, Pettit and Westlake, 1963–5.

...iet Simpkins and I took some Pettit and Westlake paperwork to Devon for a weekend in 1965; ...hin a few months we had both abandoned the law.

Two ex-Aardvarks (Geoff Strong and TR) demonstrate the one chord they know between them, near the end of the Popefield era.

that I would grow out of it all by the time I was twenty-one, so I had to grab chances like *Ready, Steady, Go* pretty sharpish.

At the run-through, host Keith Fordyce chose me as the winner, emphasising to my three surly rivals that this would have no bearing whatsoever on the result when it came to the actual show (which of course went out live). However I felt sure that this premature taste of glory doomed me to failure in the real final and sure enough Chris Sandford cruelly ignored my subtle interpretation of Mr Kramer's idiosyncrasies. In recent years many vintage episodes of *Ready Steady Go* have been issued on video, and clips have often been broadcast, but never my show and I fear it must have been wiped, which is a tragedy if only because the Ronettes were sensational.

Performing their second (and last) great hit 'Baby I Love You', the three black girls from New York were quite simply the most exotic ladies I had ever seen. Obtaining their autographs was an experience to match my encounter that the Singing Nun had unwittingly accompanied and the day after the show I wrote Ronnie, Nedra and Estelle a letter inviting them to dinner any night they wanted during their tour. Amazing to relate, they wrote back, but regretted that they simply did not have any spare time. It was a bitter pill to swallow when I saw pictures of them in the *New Musical Express* out on the town with the Rolling Stones.

In the end though, I did get back together with Ronnie Spector. In the early Nineties I translated the hit French musical *Starmania* into English, which became the album *Tycoon*, featuring a number of distinguished rock and pop singers, including the by now legendary Ronnie. Her song was entitled 'Farewell To A Sex Symbol' and I spent a couple of days in a New York recording studio working with her. She is a charming woman, voice still thrilling, but, strange to relate, she had no recollection of my 1964 fan letter. She did remember Mick Jagger and Brian Jones.*

Adam and Christabel were now an item and they and I shifted

---

* Another character I had met at *Ready Steady Go* was Andrew Loog Oldham, then manager of the Rolling Stones. The next day I sent him a copy of my Aardvarks single and a photo. I never heard back. In 1994, he called me about a film idea. I told him I had been waiting thirty years for a reaction to my single. He asked me if he could have another two weeks.

from Wimpole Street to an even more upmarket address just behind Sloane Square tube station, in Bourne Street. Marion (still engaged) more or less moved in with us from Monday to Thursday and I never enquired about her weekends. It was a terrific arrangement. Adam, selling space for an advertising agency, and I both had wild ambitions – he was going to write a best-selling novel and I was going to have a hit record. We set about this primarily by going to a pub and/or movie every night.

We soon realised we were part of a rather murky scam operated by our alleged landlord, a Mr Taylor, who simultaneously rented several moderately smart houses around town and illegally sub-let them to an eclectic bunch of tenants. Rent was cheap, even by 1964 standards. We were paying £15 a week for three rooms on the first-floor in SW1 but occupiers had to be prepared for the occasional wholesale removal of furniture and indeed of fellow tenants as goods and guests were shifted from property to property one jump ahead of creditors. Fixtures and fittings were of pretty good quality, presumably having only recently been obtained on the never-never, but it was a mistake to get too attached to a red sofa when after a day at the office one was liable to come home to a green one. We were often visited by Hire Purchase heavies who had come to remove goods not paid for, but in the absence of those goods and of Mr Taylor, failed to achieve their aims. When Mr Taylor did appear (usually at dead of night) he would occasionally offer us a job cleaning out one of his new homes, or shifting wardrobes from A to B, offers worth taking as he paid a fiver a day – Pettit and Westlake still gave me just a fiver a week. Eventually it looked as if the net was closing in as policemen began to make frequent visits and, after a bonus three weeks when Mr Taylor disappeared completely without even collecting rent, we decided on a moonlight flit. We moved a little downmarket from the edge of Belgravia to Gunter Grove in Fulham, where our landlord was a pillar of rectitude, a man who had achieved Adam's primary ambition of becoming a best-selling author, James Leasor.*

---

* *Passport To Oblivion* was then Leasor's most recent best-seller. He has written over fifty books, novels and non-fiction, much military history.

During the latter part of 1964 I found myself having less and less of a satisfactory time at work (other than close encounters with Marion) and enjoying every other aspect of London life more and more. There was the odd interesting case at P and W, such as the firm's efforts to defend a struggling rock'n'roller from accusations that he was passing himself off as Gene Vincent (which he undoubtedly was doing); and I once visited the St John's Wood home of the painter Dame Laura Knight, perhaps our most distinguished client; but in the main I was uninterested, uninspired and achieving nothing for Pettit, Westlake or myself.

I was secretly harbouring thoughts of post-Aardvarks pop fame, but beyond answering a few ads in *Melody Maker* and very occasionally being asked to audition with a band, I had no opportunity to demonstrate my abilities one way or the other and really did not make any great effort to create an opportunity. Subconsciously I still listened to the voice of adult disapproval that pop music was something not to be taken seriously. I treated the law rather as I had treated school, assuming that after five years I would have drifted through the exams and moved along the conveyor belt to life's next stage. Fortunately for British rock music, many far more dedicated (and talented) performers did not adopt this appallingly slack approach to ambition. They were springing up everywhere, young, gifted and arrogant; the swinging Sixties were just beginning and I was on the fourth floor checking wills or in the pub.

I did not drift through my law exams. I eventually took Part One three times. First time around I passed the requisite minimum number of subjects (three out of six) but failed the lot as my overall score was not high enough. Second time around I only passed one subject and after my third disastrous stretch at Law School in Lancaster Gate I decided after half an hour of the first paper that it was a nice day outside. For the first time in my life I had been unable to get away with bone idleness and by the time of my third failure (towards the end of 1965 and my twenty-first birthday) it even began to dawn on me that I was going down the wrong road. The tasks given to me by an exasperated Morwen were becoming more menial, not less. I was sent around London on trivial errands and searched for spelling mistakes in endless conveyancing documents. I did learn a bit about accountancy under the eye of a dynamic Canadian lady, Alannah Campbell, who had once been dated by Conway Twitty and, better even than that, had flown the Channel standing on the back of a bi-plane, but in truth office life had gone pear-shaped. A rare plus there was the arrival of a large new articled clerk, Les Green, still a chum, who is now a larger and highly successful solicitor in Yorkshire with a stranglehold on all fruit machine disputes north of Watford.

I rather wished I had gone to university – was it too late to do so? I had visited several Lancing pals at both Oxford and Cambridge and they seemed to have got it right. But even that belated re-think was only a half-hearted desire to return to the womb of youth and I never got beyond sending off for some university application forms which I could not bring myself to fill in. At least I finally summoned up the courage to tell my parents that I was desperately unhappy, which was hardly a surprise to them. They were worried too, but totally on my side and to my delight and amazement talked about looking for a career in the one walk of life I had shown enthusiasm for – the music business.

I had in fact made some progress towards achievement in music during my last twelve months at Pettit and Westlake. I had bought myself a guitar and had written a few songs, all three-chord efforts in sub-Bob Dylan mode, not because I felt I could be a great composer, but because I needed to construct tunes that would show off my voice to best advantage, i.e. tunes without too much range. In early 1965, I wrote to Tony Hall, who was not only a well-known disc-jockey on Radio Luxembourg and head of pop promotion at Decca Records, but had been at Lancing College – some years before my time, but the old school tie link worked. Tony invited me up to his office, gave me a Jackie Wilson Greatest Hits LP, and rang one of the company's top record producers, Noel Walker (then in the charts with the Fortunes) to fix an audition for this promising young singer-songwriter. There was another hopeful loitering around Tony's office, with far more confidence than I had, named Jonathan King, who had been to Charterhouse and was currently up at Cambridge. He had just made his first record for Decca, entitled 'Everyone's Gone To The Moon'. Jonathan played it to me and it sounded like a hit. He played it again and it still did. He played it several more times and then he took me out for a Chinese dinner. A few weeks later he was number three in the charts.

My own first visit to a recording studio, at ten o'clock in the morning, was supervised by Noel Walker who had booked the arranger and pianist Arthur Greenslade, famous leader of the Gee Men who had graced countless BBC radio pop shows, to back me and my guitar on my début session. We recorded three songs in an hour, all with words and music by me. The total number of chords involved was four and Arthur did not seem to have too much trouble with them. I was given a reel-to-reel copy of the tape and told, as one is, that Noel would let me know.

A few days later I got a call at Pettit and Westlake from Noel Walker. He gave me the bad news first – he didn't really think I had a future as a singer. Before I could reel from the blow, he softened it considerably by saying that he had played my tape to a few music publishers and one in particular felt that the songs had a shot. I was to ring Cyril Gee of Mills Music. Cyril was great – very friendly and I was fascinated to be inside a music publisher's HQ in the world-famous Tin Pan Alley, Denmark Street.* Cyril signed all three of my songs to Mills. For an advance of one shilling, I gave away the copyright in 'Who Needs Love', 'Another Girl, Another Town' and 'That's My Story', in return for a royalty that Cyril seemed confident would materialise. This was still a time when songs and singers were as often as not separate entities (though the Beatles were changing that for ever and fast) and Cyril said he felt that he could place one of my numbers at least – 'That's My Story' – with a contemporary pop group as a potential A side of a single. Who would this lucky group be? I ran through the possibilities as I nipped back along Oxford Street to P and W. Herman's Hermits? The Animals? The Fortunes? Maybe some of the biggest names of all who normally write their own stuff had dried up and needed outside inspiration – the Kinks, the Stones, the Who?

It tuned out to be an act on Piccadilly Records, part of the Pye empire, who had the Kinks, Donovan and Petula Clark on their

---

* Where I was immediately impressed to meet two of Britain's greatest songwriters, Roger Greenaway and Roger Cook, then near the beginning of their huge run of hits with 'You've Got Your Troubles' by the Fortunes.

books. The group was the Nightshift and my song turned out to be their entire career. I had written 'That's My Story' as a folk-rock song but these boys beefed it up considerably and, grateful though I was and am for their support for my song, I don't think it emerged as quite the delicate study of introspection I had envisaged. It died a death and though Cyril printed up some sheet music of the song and even managed to obtain a Mexican cover version in Spanish by Los Six Kings, I barely repaid the minuscule advance he gave me. 'That's My Story' actually earns around £100 a year these days, because I tend to feature it during radio interviews wherever possible and have even sung it myself on TV with Hank B. Marvin on guitar. So in the end I did get a star name to perform it. The first verse of the first Tim Rice lyric ever to be commercially recorded went as follows:

> Well I know you are leaving, but that's just what I expected
> For I know you never cared that much for me
> But don't start thinking that I'll worry for I can live without you
> I'm sure I'll feel much better now I'm free
> There's a tear in my eye but it's not because I love you
> There's an ache in my heart but it's not because of you
> Go away for I don't want you, I'll be better off without you
> That's my story but oh Lord it isn't true

There were two further verses, which the Nightshift decided not to bother with. I have no idea what became of the group (I never met them) and have always been slightly surprised that none of them has ever revealed themselves to me as the years have rolled by. I feel I owe them a beer at least. No one ever recorded 'Who Needs Love' or 'Another Girl, Another Town', hard though Cyril Gee and his then partner Tony Hiller (who became a major songwriter ten years later with Brotherhood of Man and others) tried.

I made a serious mistake in writing a rude letter to Pye Records once it became clear that the single had gone down the tubes, questioning their wisdom, and indeed their sanity, in releasing a single that they clearly had made no effort to promote. I got a stinker back from a gent named Les Cocks who pointed out in words of one syllable that they had pushed it as much as possible and it was obviously a lousy song. Furthermore, said Les, he would make sure that no Pye artist ever recorded one of my songs again. I felt this was rather an extreme reaction to a naïve complaint but was nonetheless devastated to feel that I had blown my songwriting career before I had even got off the blocks. What if Les told his pals at EMI and Decca about this ingrate named T. Rice? My father helped me construct a suitably grovelling reply and six years later Pye star Petula Clark recorded 'I Don't Know How To Love Him' from *Jesus Christ Superstar*.

I made other efforts to break into music during my twilight years in the law. Answering yet another music paper ad, I applied to join a vocal outfit being set up by two of the top songwriters and record producers of the day, Mike Leander and Geoff Stephens. Their wheeze was a semi-permanent pop choir who would be automatically booked on any of their sessions as back-up singers. In return for this virtual guarantee of work, Mike and Geoff would take agents' commission from the statutory (Musicians' Union) fees we would each be paid, but would also coach the choir – a much-needed aspect of the venture, as it turned out. Down the road they envisaged the choir becoming an act in its own right. As Mike and Geoff were involved in producing such hot acts as Marianne Faithfull, Billy Fury and Donovan, this seemed a very attractive proposition. I was confident I could fit the choir work into my ever-less demanding legal schedule (less demanding because I was ever-less dedicated) and of course it would give me invaluable contacts for my newly-discovered songwriting ambitions. I passed the surprisingly undemanding audition and soon found myself in a backing singers' vocal booth at a session by the less than hot Decca act Catherine Parr. For this I was paid seven guineas less ten per cent and oohed and aahed in the company of Paul Raven, the future Gary Glitter, and George Bellamy, the former Tornado (of 'Telstar' fame).

Sad to say our contribution to Ms Parr's 'He's My Guy' was not a major feature of the finished recording. In fact we were so feeble that we were all but mixed out of the final version, though I did buy a copy (almost the only person who did) and could just about discern a weak groan from three clueless males in the chorus. The impetus for the scheme faded there and then and though I was £6.61 (in today's money) up on the deal, I decided to look elsewhere for music business recognition. At least I was by now firing on all cylinders, genuinely trying to break into the magical profession in which British artists and writers were now leading the world. I managed to get myself a part-time job in a Paddington record shop one evening a week.

My next scheme was a treatise on the pop charts. Back in 1965, outside the pop magazines there were very few articles and virtually no books about rock music – it had simply not been around long enough to have a history. Serious discussion and criticism did not exist and intellectual appropriation of the art form had not yet taken place. No one, not even those making the music, would have considered it an art form anyway. It was just fun, although Bob Dylan was breaking through – I had been knocked sideways by his first Albert Hall acoustic concert the year before.

I sent my idea for a detailed and statistical analysis of the Top Twenty since charts began in England in 1952 to various publishers but even those who replied to my letter showed no interest. However my mother, still placing plenty of articles and stories in all kinds of journals, had recently met a young independent publisher named Desmond Elliott, when he had spoken to the Society of Women Journalists. She suggested I contact his one-man-band imprint, Arlington Books, and Desmond agreed to meet me. He showed no interest whatsoever in my learned thesis on the hit parade, saying that it was hard enough to sell books about what Mick Jagger ate for breakfast so how could he flog a book about pop without glamour photos and consisting of little more than lists? My point was that it was precisely because my work would not be a sycophantic fan book that it had great potential, but this did not wash. By the mid-Nineties, this exact idea, under the title of *The Guinness Book of British Hit Singles*, compiled by Paul Gambaccini, Mike Read, my brother Jo and me, had sold over one million copies in ten editions, with another twenty-one related books of ours selling a further half-million.

Luckily Desmond asked me what else I did and I whipped out the copy of 'That's My Story' that I carried with me everywhere, pointing out the very lower case 'T. Rice' in brackets beneath the song title. Desmond didn't like the song much either but did say that he was representing a young songwriter named Andrew Lloyd Webber and perhaps it would be a good idea for us to meet up. He gave me a phone number and address.

> 11 Gunter Grove
> London, S.W. 10
> April 21 1965

Dear Andrew,

I have been given your address by Desmond Elliott of Arlington Books, who I believe has also told you of my existence. Mr Elliott told me that you were looking for a 'with-it' writer of lyrics for your songs, and as I have been writing pop songs for a short while now and particularly enjoy writing the lyrics I wondered if you consider it worth your while meeting me. I may fall far short of your requirements, but anyway it would be interesting to meet up – I hope! Would you be able to get in touch with me shortly, either at FLA 1622 in the evenings, or at WEL 2261 in the daytime (Pettit and Westlake, solicitors are the owners of the latter number).

Hoping to hear from you,
Yours,
Tim Rice

Within days Andrew and I were beavering away at *The Likes Of Us*, a project that for over two years we were convinced would be a long-running hit in the West End and on Broadway. Desmond became my agent as well as Andrew's and through his good offices we obtained a music publishing deal with Bob Kingston's Southern Music, on the opposite side of Tin Pan Alley to Cyril Gee. We were each paid the staggering sum of £100 in exchange for the publishing rights and Southern also paid for demo recordings of the work. We were introduced to another successful book publisher, Ernest Hecht of Souvenir Books, and signed a very impressive document with Desmond and Ernest as theatrical producers for our show, including clauses that promised us first-class air fares to New York for the Broadway opening. Desmond told the world about us, or at least the *Daily Express*, whose William Hickey column of 22 January 1966 announced with uncharacteristic accuracy (apart from the hyphens between Lloyd and Webber) and prescience:

> After Rodgers and Hammerstein, Lloyd-Webber and Rice? A long-distance forecast which could be right. Andrew Lloyd-Webber, seventeen-year-old Oxford undergraduate son of William Lloyd Webber, fifty-one, director of the London College of Music, has collaborated on a full-scale musical with his friend Timothy Rice, twenty-one. Andrew has been given time off by his college, Magdalen, to complete the fourteen songs for the show, which is set in the nineteenth century.

Soon most of my extra-curricular activities during my final year at Pettit and Westlake involved Andrew. He and I hit it off spectacularly well; the three years' difference in our ages never mattered. In some ways – culturally, academically – he was far more advanced in the ways of the world than I was, in others – socially – the reverse was indubitably true.

My affair with the lovely Marion lasted a lot longer than the typing pool had predicted. However for several reasons – not least her impending marriage – it was doomed to end. I was young, irresponsible and broke. When we finally finished I was far more upset than I thought I would be. I remember coming over all weepy hearing for the first time Matt Monro's 'Walk Away', a big hit at the end of 1964. The lyric 'we should have met some years ago', summed up my feelings perfectly – for she would have been free. But then I would have been about twelve. This song was the first hit for a marvellous lyricist who was to become a good friend of mine – Don Black.

But my resilient young heart soon recovered. In my new status as experienced lover I was not averse to adding to that experience when the opportunity presented itself and there were encounters after parties and with a French au pair – at last my years of research into both the language and the species finally paid off.

All my rather tame exploits were however kicked into touch when another irresistible lady came to Pettit and Westlake – Juliet Simpkins. Over thirty years on she remains one of my closest friends and as attractive as she was the first day I saw her in the office. She looked remarkably like Julie Christie; if anything better. What she was doing in the typing pool I have no idea for she was clearly officer material; indeed she did not stay there all that long, moving on to an executive position at Madame Tussaud's. I barely spoke to her at all until her last day when I asked her out – a combination of crafty tactics and sheer funk.

My father said he knew a man who knew a man at EMI Records, then the country's, if not the world's, leading record company. In the meantime my status at Pettit and Westlake slumped to a new low when I was ordered by Morwen to tear up a pile of old documents on her desk. The firm had no shredding machine (such gadgets may well not have existed then) and all destruction of legal documents was a hand job – about the only task for which I was by then considered capable. Needless to say I ripped up the wrong pile, manually converting twenty or thirty brand new wills and title deeds into confetti. Just as shredding machines did not exist, neither did word processors nor photocopiers. The originals had to be reassembled. All other work in the office was suspended for a fortnight as every secretary, clerk and junior, all highly amused, set about sticking the pieces together again. This gigantic jigsaw puzzle was eventually completed but long before that I bit the bullet and handed in my notice, minutes before I would have anyway been shown the door.

My cloud and I left Pettit and Westlake in May 1966 after two and a half years of staggeringly incompetent service. My father had come up trumps in fixing an interview for me at EMI Records in Manchester Square (just a few hundred yards from Pettit and Westlake) and a day or two after I was lost to the law I heard that EMI were to accept me as a management trainee at the stratospheric wage of £16 a week. I bought a new suit (£4 down and £4 a month for a year) and resolved that I had turned the corner.

Chapter Nine

So on 6 June 1966, I entered the music business full time – the trade I should have taken up two or three years before. Management trainee was a rather nebulous term at EMI Records, one assigned to promising young men in suits who would probably be despatched to head up EMI's operation in Mexico City or Auckland five years down the road. In the meantime they were shifted around the departments.

My first duties were vague in the extreme; I was assigned to half a desk in a huge open-plan office and sat by a phone which seemed to be the line for disgruntled fans. My first call, at approximately 9.30, came from an official of the Dean Martin Appreciation Society who wanted a complete list of Dino's releases on EMI's Capitol label. I confidently assured him I would get this information to him within minutes and then spent the next few days failing to do so. There appeared to be little or no official archival material at EMI House which surprised me as in the days before I began my new career I had imagined myself whiling away many happy hours examining the label of a copy of every disc EMI had ever issued, which they obviously would have filed in their vaults. I soon discovered that the best source of historical information came from the private research of record buffs within the company. One of these, Alan Warner, became a lifelong friend.

My second call, at about 10.15, came from Andrew asking whether I had yet found any artists wanting songs. He too received an unsatisfactory answer. Although I thoroughly enjoyed being a record company man from the very first minute, it soon became clear this was not quite the non-stop riot of glamour and hobnobbing with the stars I had envisaged. After a fortnight I did have a pee next to Peter Noone of Herman's Hermits and spent a good forty-five seconds in the lift with a massive American singer named Solomon King who eventually had one huge Engelbert Humperdinck type hit entitled 'She Wears My Ring', but with neither personality did I feel the time or place quite right to open negotiations about a Webber-Rice song.

Obviously life outside office hours was a good deal more closely related to my new job than it had been to my old one, but most of my evenings and weekends were spent in furthering my own prospects rather than those of The Greatest Recording Organisation In The World as EMI labelled themselves. For starters, Andrew and I grew ever closer, as Adam and I began to drift apart. Andrew abandoned Oxford after one term, always claiming later because now that he had met me, he could and should devote all his time to writing musicals. Adam and I left Gunter Grove and after a short spell back at Popefield with my parents, I moved in to the Lloyd Webber menagerie in Harrington Court, South Kensington. This was quite an eye-opener.

The Lloyd Webbers lived in two adjacent flats, connected by a narrow balcony, at the top of a smartish block just round the corner from South Kensington tube station. Andrew, his younger brother Julian and his parents, Billy and Jean, lived in No. 10, with Jean's mother Molly and Jean's protégé, the pianist John Lill, living next door in 2a. I moved into the spare room in 2a, which meant that my new flatmates were Andrew's granny and a classical musician. Andrew's room in No. 10 was a home within a home, its elegant décor, banks of sound equipment and neat files of record albums in stark contrast to the cheerful Bohemia in which the rest of his family resided. Far from returning to the kind of well-ordered home rule of my childhood I had envisaged, I was part of a free-range if not deranged set-up with a fascinatingly wacky cast of enchanting characters. This suited me fine.

Andrew seemed to rule the roost, with an ability to summon almost any other member of the family to his bidding, mainly his devoted gran. Now and then I caught a hint of the odd flare-up from a distance but was usually able to lie low until the all-clear was sounded. I never had any clashes with Andrew myself. Andrew's father, Dr William Lloyd Webber, a highly gifted but under-achieving romantic classical composer, was the director of the London College of Music. A sensitive and undemonstrative man, he presided over his family with a world-weary affability, always friendly, clearly interested and proud of his sons' successes, albeit reticently so. Jean, Andrew's mother, taught piano to a huge number of children in all parts of London, regarding her work as much a social crusade as an educational endeavour. Her great discovery was John Lill, from an impoverished East End family, who had been virtually adopted by Jean two years before, and whose move into the Lloyd Webber household as a talent to be nurtured caused more than a few family ructions. John had made his concert début in 1963 at the Royal Festival Hall, playing Beethoven's Emperor – seven years later he was to win the Tchaikovsky International Competition in Moscow.

Andrew's brother Julian, younger by three years, was a day pupil at University College School in North London and already an outstanding cellist. Of the three phenomenally talented young musicians in those Harrington Court flats, Andrew, who yearned to be a theatrical composer, was the one whose path seemed to have moved away from Lloyd Webber traditions. Molly Johnstone, who completed the line-up I became a part of, was like my own grandmother in that she was the only member of the household with any money, and again in common with my elderly relative, not much at that. She subscribed to the laissez-faire ambience of the household, seeming far less shocked than I was by the four-letter words, and by the total lack of respect for things held sacred in my parents' home, such as school reports, table manners and parents themselves. Yet the chaos engendered, at least as far as I could tell, a happy, as well as an extraordinarily noisy, atmosphere.

While John pounded and Julian scraped, while Molly watched television at deafening volume, while Bill played the organ and while Jean taught an endless succession of would-be Lills, while Siamese and Burmese cats yowled and prowled, Andrew and I pursued our assault on the musical theatre. With Desmond Elliott, we went to see a host of rival shows, emerging from nearly every one with the arrogant and erroneous view that *The Likes Of Us* was miles better and that if this was the kind of competition we were up against our prospects were good indeed. In fact we were right in that many of the musicals we saw were pretty ropey, but utterly wrong in believing our work to be better.

Our deal with Southern Music entitled us to make a demo recording of our show, to play to potential investors and directors. We spent many happy hours in the music publishers' basement studio, a cupboard-size sanctum where nevertheless several smash hits of the Sixties were recorded – 'Winchester Cathedral' by the New Vaudeville Band and 'Let's Go To San Francisco' by the Flowerpot Men among them. Economics necessitated that we take most of the singing roles ourselves, which gave me the chance to do my Rex Harrison, my Anthony Newley and my Peter Cook in Harold Macmillan mode. Proper singers were booked for the ballads, Danny Street and Jackie Lee, king and queen of session singing at the time, becoming the most distinguished names yet to sing a Webber/Rice song. Desmond also persuaded one of his new authors to write the book for *The Likes Of Us*, appropriately a former Barnardo boy who had just published what was to be the first of a never-ending line of hugely popular novels, *The Virgin Soldiers*. His name was Leslie Thomas.

I have never been accused of allowing my work to dominate my life, even during the heady first few months of my full-time employment in music. My principal extra-curricular activity in 1965 and 1966 was undoubtedly Juliet, and our affair flourished, perhaps helped by the surrogate glamour I had acquired (a) by my position on a humble rung of the record business, which certainly cut more ice than articled clerkdom, and (b) by my father's permanent loan of AYU 594, the 1934 Austin Ten which even then caused heads to turn (although Juliet in the passenger seat might have been an even bigger draw). AYU, now driven more often by my son Donald than me, did sterling service thirty years ago. On occasion its glamour wore thin after one breakdown too many, and in the depths of winter parked outside Juliet's parents' house it was not the ideal passion-wagon, but it and we survived several long journeys on mini-holidays around the country.

Juliet's family lived in Ruislip* and as she was the eldest of three extremely attractive sisters there could be quite a line-up of parked cars in their street at night. Coincidentally Juliet's mother had been at the same school as my mother. Joan Rice remembered Joan Simpkins as Joan Payne, one of twins who had been school tennis champs, and both Joans must have contemplated a permanent old girls' reunion as their offspring seemed to be very serious about each other. Indeed we were, but after two years in which the thought of marriage crossed my mind on many nights (only to be shiftily cast aside in the cold light of day when my financial and artistic prospects suddenly seemed less rosy than they had in the pub eight hours before), the point of all the passion, if not the passion itself, almost imperceptibly cooled. An AYU seize-up which caused me to miss her father's funeral was not one of my greatest moments. I don't believe Juliet was ever daft enough to have seriously contemplated marrying me at that time, but as we have remained the most affectionate of friends ever since it might not have been as daft an idea as all that.

One of the unexpected spin-offs from my association with Desmond Elliott was that Adam became a star. My former flatmate had continued to pound away at his novels and as I had such close contact with a young, dynamic publisher, he asked me to show Desmond his manuscripts. I thought little more about it until Desmond mentioned at the end of another lengthy telephone conversation about how he was just about to sign Harry Secombe for the lead in *The Likes Of Us* that he was very impressed by Adam's work, and even more so by Adam.

Desmond may have been struggling to unload our musical in the theatre world but he knew his onions in the book world and almost overnight turned Adam Diment into a publishing sensation. Adam had written a very funny novel about a pot-smoking, cowardly spy named Philip McAlpine, *The Dolly Dolly Spy*. McAlpine was a kind of antithesis to James Bond, though too original to be dismissed as a spoof. Adam's hero captured the Swinging London

---

* Her phone number was RUIslip 2433 which unfortunately spelled SUICIDE. The house was occasionally called by tragic individuals about to do away with themselves, under the impression they had called the suicide helpline. Extreme tact was required when informing a caller in those circumstances that they had the wrong number.

mood perfectly and, as he later said, it was almost inevitable that after the English pop cultural revolution which had taken place in rock, fashion and movies, someone had to be the first dopehead novelist and he was lucky it happened to be him. Desmond flogged six McAlpine novels to the leading publishers Michael Joseph for a small fortune, and an announcement inevitably followed that a film was about to go into production, starring David Hemmings.

Adam grew his hair, began to dress like a man in a Brian Jones lookalike contest, acquired an Aston Martin and groupies, and seemed permanently stoned. Desmond marketed him brilliantly. Adam's slightly zonked countenance stared out from posters on buses and tubes, complete with slogan 'If you can't read Adam Diment, love him'. I watched in amazement as he turned up on TV chat shows and drew crowds at book stores. All this tended to obscure the fact that the books were rather good, and they sold very well. The follow-ups to *The Dolly, Dolly Spy* had equally intriguing titles: *The Great Spy Race*, *The Bang Bang Birds* and *Think, Inc.* Numbers five and six (and the movie) never appeared. Adam soon became totally disillusioned with the books (wrongly) and his success (more understandably), pulled out halfway through a promotional tour of the United States and left England.

Adam did not surface again in my life for many years until well after Andrew and I had made it with *Jesus Christ Superstar*. Few people remember his books today. I find it sad, probably sadder than he does, that his talent did not bring him more lasting success but his attitude to the trivial circus of acclaim was too honest for him to keep going – he felt too manufactured. He admitted to being green with envy at our stupendous international success in the early Seventies, but when I see him now he combines a genuine interest and enthusiasm for what I am up to with a healthy cynicism for celebrity and public esteem which was what attracted me to him in the first place. Someone should republish his books.

Adam's meteoric rise to fame, thanks in part to me, did not go down a storm with Andrew. He felt that Desmond had abandoned us in favour of a vastly inferior artist. No doubt he felt I had betrayed our partnership. Not much was said about this at the time, although Andrew did explode once in Desmond's office about the attention being paid to Adam. I was annoyingly (from Andrew's point of view) laid back, feeling less threatened and convinced that anything that boosted Desmond's clout in any field could only help, but none of Adam's good fortune trickled down to us. It did not cross our minds that our product could be at fault.*

The Likes Of Us failed because it was unoriginal and dated, even thirty years ago. Furthermore we, or rather Desmond, made the great mistake of aiming too high. We were never going to leap straight into the West End with such a conventional show and even the skills of Leslie Thomas were unable to make it anything other than standard fodder. (We couldn't even break straight into the West End some years later with *Superstar*, a truly original piece, and had to get there via a hit record.) Had we concentrated on mounting a production of our Barnardo show at Oxford University or with some minor repertory company, we would have seen it on stage, been far more aware of the work's limitations, learned a lot more, and started something new sooner. As it was, *The Likes Of Us* never got beyond our demo disc, and its progress towards a brick wall rather than towards a glittering first night gradually led to a parting of the ways with Desmond.

Nevertheless, our first work was not that bad. It showed us that our different abilities complemented each other well and encouraged us to think that if we had a better idea we might yet write the hit musical we (or at least Andrew) craved. The music was definitely more sophisticated than the words, although in some of the humorous songs I held my own. Many of the tunes have re-emerged in other Lloyd Webber works, notably in Andrew's *Variations* album of 1978, with the amusing (to me) consequence that I now receive the odd royalty cheque from Southern Music. The company finally twigged that it owned some of the music in *Variations* but under titles from *The Likes Of Us*, in which I have a writer's interest even if the words are not used.

The title song, one of the *Variations* selections, was sung by the

---

* Perhaps in an attempt to calm us down, Desmond commissioned us for £50 each to write a half-witted annual entitled *Top Twenty* under the joint pseudonym 'Philip Buckle', in which we recycled pop stars' publicity handouts. This was Desmond's idea of a commercial pop music book, and might have been, as it was actually published two years running. We got no royalties.

orphans on a London roof and the plaintive melody just about propped up my sugary lyric:

> Have you seen my brother Johnny? Not since yesterday
> Is it gonna rain tonight? It's kind of hard to say
> We don't want to cause no problems, we won't make a fuss
> This is what we know is proper for the likes of us

Stronger were my words for the Victorian aristocrats who show cruel indifference to the social ills of the time in a tribute to Queen and Empire, 'Lion Hearted Land':

> Englishmen have style and flair to cope with all their needs
> Little things accomplished well will lead to greater deeds
> It's because we have the taste to know a good cigar
> Half the map is coloured red and we are where we are
>
> I must comment on this wine, its character is strong
> Its impudence is striking and its flavour lingers long
> We can spot these subtleties, in this we stand alone
> Foreigners are merely there to see the grapes get grown
>
> The workers in our factories all recognise their place
> We'd love to entertain them but we haven't got the space
> We know that they are splendid chaps beneath the dust and grime
> We'd love to mingle with them but we haven't got the time
>
> Why does England rule the world?
> Queen and Empire understand
> Oh England, valiant rock of splendour
> Lion Hearted Land

My comic lyrics were by and large much more successful than the serious ones. I was strongly influenced by the brilliance of lyricist Michael Flanders, who with the composer Donald Swann had featured prominently in my parents' record collection. Flanders' and Swann's greatest hit was probably 'The Hippopotamus Song' ('mud, mud, glorious mud . . .') just one of a stunning selection of witty songs that had turned the pair into West End musical stars, as performers as well as writers. Paddy Roberts ('The Ballad Of Bethnal Green') was another writer operating in the same vein whom I admired.

Naturally there were a slew of dramatic ballads in *The Likes Of Us*. 'Where Am I Going?', banging on about 'dreams of dust' and 'dreams that I can trust', was a poor man's 'What Kind Of Fool Am I' and 'Strange and Lovely Song' did not quite live up to its title, to the second part of it at least. 'You Can Never Make It Alone' was a dying man's 'My Favourite Things'. One or two of the numbers, such as 'Love Is Here', a perky Cockney duet, and the auctioneer's song 'Going Going Gone', our first ever collaboration, had more than a spark of individuality and there is no question that anyone sitting through the entire demonstration record would have encouraged its writers to keep at it, but maybe at something else.

No one actually put it that way to us, but slowly the message got through. We would have to try something else and surely with my new contacts at EMI we could at least get a pop song recorded? I had after all managed that as a law student, on my own, tune and all, with 'That's My Story'.

We tried writing a few one-off songs, something that neither of us has ever found very easy. Nearly all of the hit songs I have been involved with over the years have been part of a larger work and would never have been written out of the blue. Who would ever contemplate 'Don't Cry For Me Argentina' as a title for a song, let alone a hit single, unless they were writing a two-hour musical about Eva Peron? When working with specific characters in a dramatic situation it is far easier to produce an original way to say things such as 'I love you' which have been said so well by so many before. Either part of 'I Know Him So Well' from *Chess** is a relatively straightforward love lyric, but the fact that the song is really two lyrics in one, sung simultaneously by women each with a perspective of the man diametrically opposed to the other's, makes it unusual and only came about because of the needs of the show. But such erudite thoughts about songwriting were far from our minds as we attempted our assault on The Greatest Recording Organisation In The World.

---

* My 1984 show with Bjorn Ulvaeus and Benny Andersson.

Chapter Ten

EMI was quite justified in 1966 to print that slogan 'The Greatest Recording Organisation In The World' on its record sleeves and in its advertisements. Under the energetic and imaginative leadership of Sir Joseph Lockwood it had become a powerful force in virtually every aspect of the music business. In its own studios EMI recorded the sounds that went on to shellac and later vinyl; it owned factories that actually manufactured the discs and the gramophones on which they were played; it owned shops where they were sold and the copyrights of vast numbers of songs recorded by both themselves and their rivals. Its three major British pop labels were Columbia, Parlophone and His Master's Voice; it also owned the US-based Capitol records and acted as UK licenser for many other American companies, notably the Tamla Motown labels. It had many classical music and non-music interests too, but to ninety-nine per cent of the outside world, EMI meant pop. The only companies of remotely similar stature were Decca, Philips and Pye. EMI House (since pulled down), then a new addition to the hitherto delicate Manchester Square, was a mildly hideous but practical six-storey building almost totally devoted to the music side of the company's business.

Management trainee chaps (no women) were really glorified office boys. We all seemed to be public school products. We wore suits and ties and clocked in by nine a.m. whether or not we had been out late the night before at a concert or club, allegedly working or talent-spotting.

The music business then was still extremely conservative, at least within the empires of the major record companies, despite the fact that the Swinging Sixties were well under way. All this was changing fast, as independent record producers were beginning to finance recordings which they then leased or sold to the major companies, replacing the system of in-house producers of whom EMI had had a distinguished roster. George Martin and several others, rightly miffed at the paltry incomes they received for producing huge hit records from the Beatles downwards, had recently broken away from EMI to form their own company, enabling them to earn more than a fixed salary from their creative efforts. Even so, in 1966 great recording managers such as Norrie Paramor and Wally Ridley were still operating from offices within EMI House.

I thus joined a company in a state of some flux, but still just about the world's Number One. This was thanks primarily to the Beatles, whose run of staggering success since late 1962 showed no signs whatsoever of decline. In fact they were getting bigger all the time; as journalist Maureen Cleave put it so wisely, the world was divided into two groups, the Beatles and everybody else. But the Beatles were nothing like EMI's only strength; a myriad of merely mortal acts, some only a little less potent in terms of record sales, such as the Beach Boys, the Hollies and several Tamla Motown stars, kept the company in the charts between Beatle releases, although it was amazing how the entire workforce seemed to measure time by the weeks since or until the next record by the Fab Four.

My inaugural management training was interrupted on my first morning by the summons of the entire staff (over two hundred) to a pep talk in the company's conference room. The meeting was called by the MD, Geoff Bridge, the friend of the friend of my father, through whom I had sneaked into the empire. Pointing out that the date was 6–6–66, Mr Bridge urged us all to double our efforts to keep the firm in pole position. A date like this with all its digits the same only occurs nine times in a century, he stated. Let us use this numerical oddity to inspire us to higher things. I felt like pointing out that such a combination of figures occurred twelve times in a century, not nine, as in 1911 1 January, 11 January and 11 November qualified, and in 1922 both 2 and 22 February, but reckoned this exposure of my new MD's ignorance not the best move after less than two hours in the business.

Geoff Bridge was obviously concerned about the fact that since the Beatles' last Number One, at the end of 1965 ('We Can Work It Out'/'Day Tripper') only Manfred Mann, who were about to lose their charismatic lead singer Paul Jones and defect to Fontana, had taken EMI to the top of the singles chart. Frank Sinatra, of all people, was the current Number One, which must have had a lot of the more ancient executives wondering if they were right all along and should unload the odd beat group. Bob Dylan (CBS) and the Rolling Stones (Decca) were running the Beatles extremely close in sales and cultural impact. We were exhorted to find new talent, whatever our department.

I wasn't even sure what my department was. After a week or two in the main zoo I requested a more specific role and to my delight I was posted to the A and R department. This was winning the pools – I could have been sent to the postroom, or to the classical floor. The Artistes and Repertoire division was where hit records were actually conceived, where stars came to discuss their next sessions. The king of the department was Norrie Paramor.

Although the A and R offices had been not long before depleted by the joint exit of producers George Martin, John Burgess and Ron Richards, which took away much of EMI's control over such major acts as the Beatles, Hollies and Manfred Mann, the reputation and track record of Norrie Paramor ensured that there was still significant power left within the department. As producer, arranger and composer, Norrie had been a vital factor in the careers of dozens of singers, many of them major stars. It was true that he never participated in any massive success in the post-Beatles boom, but his greatest stars, Cliff Richard and the Shadows, were still among EMI's most vital assets, and Norrie, who enjoyed important executive as well as creative status within the company, still spent many profitable hours in its studios in Abbey Road, St John's Wood.

Norrie had joined EMI after extensive work as pianist and leader of touring and broadcasting bands in the Forties and Fifties. He and fellow bandleader Ray Martin revitalised EMI's Columbia label in the early Fifties. In addition to Cliff and the Shadows, stars he had discovered and recorded included Helen Shapiro, Frank Ifield, Ruby Murray, Michael Holliday, Eddie Calvert and the Mudlarks. He had twenty-seven British Number Ones as a producer, a total only surpassed by George Martin (in 1997). He worked as musical director with many great visiting American singers such as Judy Garland and enjoyed considerable success as an artist in his own right, fronting the Norrie Paramor Orchestra and creating outfits such as the Big Ben Banjo Band. He wrote several film scores, and hit songs such as 'Once Upon A Dream' for Billy Fury and 'Voice In The Wilderness' for Cliff, but his greatest talent was in providing the best possible support to more glamorous personalities as producer, arranger or friend. He was a quiet man, unassuming in both appearance and manner, but forthright, with an experience in the British music business which in 1966 was virtually unmatched.

Norrie's corridor in summer 1966 consisted of about half-a-dozen record producers. Other than himself and Wally Ridley they were young and barely known outside the building. I was placed in an office with another management trainee named Sean Blake and Norrie's nephew David who was our immediate boss. Our main job was to wade through the huge pile of unsolicited tapes and discs that piled up every day at EMI, then as now, except that this was the pre-cassette era. Most of the hopeful singers and songwriters sent in reel-to-reel tape recordings of abysmal quality both technically and artistically. Some had forked out for demonstration discs, easier to play but generally just as grim to the ear. Sean and I were full of enthusiasm on day one, expecting to find, if not the next Beatles, the next Brian Poole and the Tremeloes, but we soon realised why we had been lumbered with the task. It was stupefyingly unimportant. Norrie told us that not one artist had ever been signed as a result of sending in a home-made recording, but someone had to monitor the flood just in case. I thought of my own tape of 'That's My Story' doing these hopeless rounds a year before.

At least I got to go to a real recording session, at EMI's Abbey Road studios, although they were not yet known by that title, the Beatles album which gave the building immortality still three years in the future. The first recording session that I ever went to was produced by Bob Barratt. The artists were the G.U.S. Footwear Band who laid down a whole album's worth of military stomp in around three hours. This was not really an album I would take home and play to impress friends that I was a major figure at the heart of the music world, but I was captivated by the atmosphere of the studios (though bewildered by most of the technical procedure), and loitered in corridors, lavatories and the canteen in the hope of bumping into a *bona fide* pop star. None materialised.

Just days later, I met a fairly famous group without recourse to subterfuge, when I attended my first contemporary pop recording. It turned out to be a huge hit, 'Got To Get You Into My Life' by Cliff Bennett and the Rebel Rousers. This was produced by David Paramor and was a song from the forthcoming Beatles album *Revolver*. EMI obviously had the inside track as far as forthcoming Beatles albums were concerned and usually managed to beat other companies in the race to cover new Lennon-McCartney songs. I was also allowed to sit in on one or two of Norrie's meetings and sessions, often in a coffee-serving capacity, which of course meant that I met Cliff Richard. The fact that on our second meeting Cliff remembered my name impressed me even more than his consummate professionalism in the studio.

After a few weeks I was given the opportunity to make some creative contributions of my own. I was urged by Norrie and the staff to get out and about searching for new talent. Discovery of same could lead to my being allowed to produce a recording – an audition session at least. My EMI card got me into a lot of London clubs that would not normally have admitted nonentities. I generally had a great time gawping at established stars but unearthed no new ones.

We were encouraged to go further afield and as I had always wanted to see Sunderland play at home I wangled an expenses-paid trip to Newcastle where I failed to recognise the potential of Bryan Ferry. My advance planning was dire – Sunderland FC were away that Saturday. The best group I saw during my brief north-eastern tour was one that EMI already had by the short and curlies, the marvellous Hollies, in a Sunderland Working Men's Club. The act I invited down to London for a recording test in preference to Bryan Ferry's group were called the Sect. I asked them to record the Left Banke US hit 'Walk Away Renée' and the Dylan classic 'It's All Over Now Baby Blue' which they did, very well, in three hours at Abbey Road. I produced the session, in as much as I sat there while the engineer masterminded everything. Convinced that 'Renée' could be a big hit in Britain (the Left Banke's version had flopped) and that the Sect were the act to have that hit, I was very disappointed that no one higher up than me in EMI (i.e. almost everybody) shared my enthusiasm. The Sect went back North to obscurity and the Four Tops had a huge hit with the song a few months later.

The first recordings I produced that actually got released were by a group originally called the Marvin Lois Enterprise. They were Tamla Motown obsessives who hailed from the Southend area and first came to my attention via the hitherto impossible route of a home-produced demo disc. I travelled down to the depths of Essex to witness them in action and apart from their ghastly name and their determination only to perform Motown songs they had quite a bit going for them. I re-christened them the Shell, after the name of a class in the Billy Bunter books, and found them an original song to sing (not one of mine, unfortunately) as they had little hope of impressing the company that put out Temptations singles with a Temptations cover.

The song, entitled 'Goodbye Little Girl' was published by EMI, which doubtless helped the Shell's cause when the executives listened to their demo. Every so often, junior staff from EMI's publishing arm, Ardmore and Beechwood, did the rounds of the A & R department hoping to persuade producers to record their copyrights and I am sure Graham Nolder of Ardmore was staggered when I offered to record 'Goodbye Little Girl' with the Shell. It was a fairly inane pop song but catchy in a nagging way and my new discoveries certainly attacked it with vim. They were less enthusiastic about their new name, having built up a fair local following under their former moniker, but beggars couldn't be choosers.

At least the group had their name on the label, even if it wasn't the one they wanted. In accordance with the EMI policy of not giving any of their employees any more credit than they had to, mine wasn't. Although I received no producer's credit I did get a mention in the music trade paper *Record Retailer*:

> First production by 'new boy' Tim Rice and a strong
> contender for the Fifty. Catchy, fast-paced tune, teen-
> slanted lyrics, and a violently pounded piano. Good
> beater for young tastes.

The single flopped completely and as far as I am aware that was the end of the Shell's recording career. At least they could say that the Marvin Lois Enterprise had never failed on record.

My next assignment was to produce a single by a young man named Murray Head. He had already made a couple of records for EMI, under Norrie's direction, but neither had succeeded despite strong record company support. Norrie and his department had now lost faith in Murray and the good-looking singer was finding it difficult even to get a meeting with his producer, despite the fact that he had had a three-singles deal and EMI was therefore obliged to cut one more with him. I got to know Murray quite well as he hung around our offices hoping vainly for a friendly word from above and I dug out his two previous efforts from the EMI library. One in particular, 'Alberta', struck me as an undeserved failure – Murray clearly had a terrific voice. When a harassed Norrie eventually asked, no, told, me to supervise Murray's third and final single, I was delighted, though instructed not to exceed a budget of £400.

Murray had actually got a job with an insurance company, so deflated was he by his lack of progress, but shortly after I was foisted on to him he won a good part in a movie, the Boulting Brothers' *The Family Way*, starring James Mason and Hayley Mills. Not only that, he had been asked to provide a song for the soundtrack which was in the main to be written by Paul McCartney. He produced a demo of a song he had written called 'Some Day Soon', a jazzy Georgie Fame-type number that he had recorded with a soul-tinged group called the Blue Monks, with whom he often performed live. I thought the song was great and all the elements of a hit seemed to be effortlessly falling into place – a film, a Beatles connection, a great group who already knew the song . . . EMI would regret handing this sure-fire smash to such a humble member of their staff. I would even have change from the £400.

Needless to say, it didn't quite work out like that. The session went well enough, but although EMI more or less had to release it, if only to get Murray's contract off their backs, they gave it virtually no promotion priority. The song was featured so fleetingly in the film that the average-length rustle of a popcorn bag would have obscured it totally. There would be no champagne reception with Paul McCartney as we launched our joint soundtrack album.

I had one last crack with Murray. Just before EMI dropped him from their roster I heard an advance copy of a superb American pop single entitled 'Happy Together' by the Turtles. The Turtles were all but unknown in Britain (a previous US hit single had flopped) and I felt that a great British version of what was obviously a hit song would have every chance of outselling the US original in the UK, if only because the UK artist would be around to promote it in the flesh. Quick action was essential in order to beat the Turtles to the starting gate. I had no difficulty in convincing various EMI executives or Murray that the song was a certain smash and the EMI machine swung into action to prepare a major recording session (orchestra, choir, the works) at unusually short notice. It looked good, even though I was not to be entrusted with anything more than an assistant producer role – this big one was handed over to Tony Palmer (not the film director), one of the in-house producers.

What no EMI bigwig mentioned until the last minute was that the vocalist on 'Happy Together' was not to be Murray Head but another EMI underachiever called Graham Bonney. Bonney had had one minor hit, 'Supergirl', a year before and had even progressed to making an LP, but EMI had lost considerably more on him than they had on Murray Head. Bonney was a good singer (though not in Murray's class) and made a fair fist of the song, but in the end the Turtles' superior version was the UK hit. I can't say I was sorry about that, and I doubt if Murray would have done any better than Graham Bonney, but it would have got him some useful new exposure on radio, TV and in the press which could in turn have led to a Rice/Head hit later in 1967. After 'Happy Together' Murray wouldn't have stayed at EMI even if they wanted him – the song title was wonderfully inappropriate for the two parties.

I kept in touch with Murray, however, and even sang a couple of songs at Blue Monks gigs on odd occasions over the following year or two. One of the band members was the tenor saxophonist Chris Mercer and, as was to be the case with Murray, our paths would cross in recording studios again.

By the beginning of 1967 – the year of the Summer of Love – Norrie (who had played no part in the 'Happy Together' saga), seemed to be taking less interest in the day-to-day workings of his department and I was now personal assistant to Bob Barratt, a producer who spent a lot of time recording middle-of-the-road acts that ranged from military bands to Vince Hill. Vince and Bob had a massive and totally unexpected hit in early 1967 with a revival of 'Edelweiss' from *The Sound Of Music* and many of the orchestral and novelty albums Bob supervised were extremely profitable; however it wasn't the kind of material that inspired me, nor did I feel I could make anything other than a perfunctory contribution to much of Bob's work.

The event of EMI's year in 1967 was of course the release of *Sergeant Pepper*. It was the event of the entire music world's year. I sought any excuse to go to Abbey Road where the gods resided. I kept quiet to friends about the sessions I was officially attending and bragged instead (truthfully) of being in the Abbey Road canteen when all four Beatles came in wearing their Sergeant Pepper uniforms. I sneaked into Studio One and watched the massive orchestra rehearsing the long crescendo that is the magnificent climax to 'A Day In The Life'. John Lennon spoke to me in what seemed like fluent Spanish as we passed on the stairs once; I suspect now it might have been stoned Jabberwockian. So near, yet . . .

With our Dr Barnardo musical looking more and more like a non-starter, I was beginning to get serious pressure from Andrew about the total failure of my EMI contacts to help our songwriting ambitions in any way whatsoever. Even he was beginning to doubt its chances of making the West End and new avenues had to be explored. Having abandoned Oxford to concentrate on his partnership with me in general and *The Likes Of Us* in particular, his frustration was understandable. He had hoped for more from my official entry into the music business – the odd free LP and the occasional meal or late night in a club on EMI expenses was not enough. Worse, I had written a couple of (admittedly mediocre) songs with David Paramor under my childhood pseudonym of Gerrard Portslade (one of the many characters I had created for writing letters to music papers) for B-sides of singles by the Nocturnes, a six-piece vocal group David was producing. My loyalty to our collaboration was in question.

Andrew had enrolled at the Guildhall School of Music and subsequently at the Royal College of Music to study aspects of orchestration and composition, but he fairly reasonably felt he was already equipped to conquer the world. Theatrical producers didn't want to know us – how were we going to get our work performed or published now? EMI had to be the answer and I had to deliver.

I couldn't see any current EMI artists, even the unsuccessful ones, being interested in songs by two totally unknown and unproven writers. I would still dearly have loved to have made a record myself, or even with Andrew as a double act, but reluctantly recognised that even if the market was ready to support another Peter and Gordon or Chad and Jeremy type duo, we were not it. We had to find our own tame artist.

One evening, over a beer in a pub just off Abbey Road, I spotted just what we were looking for. Not in the flesh, but in the columns of the *Evening Standard*. In those glorious pre-sexist days the paper ran an annual promotion entitled The Evening Standard Girl Of The Year. Friends and relatives of attractive young things were invited to submit them as candidates for this fluffy honour. From the hundreds who wrote in six finalists were chosen. Judging solely from a few paragraphs of biography and a photograph or two, readers were then invited to vote. The winning girl would be carted around to various *Standard* promotions during the year, receive a bundle of prizes and outings along the way and generally brighten up the paper's feature pages every now and then during the rest of 1967. A voting form appeared in the paper every day for about a week before and readers were expressly told that they were not restricted to one vote. As long as every vote came on a separate form, readers could vote as many times as they liked – the more votes, the more papers sold. Or so they thought.

I must admit that my initial thoughts about all six were less than subtle. But on studying the page more closely carnal thoughts took a back seat when I read that one of them, Ross Hannaman, was a singer. I immediately rang the newspaper and, explaining that I was a top EMI A & R man, asked whether Ross Hannaman (funny name) was (a) singing anywhere in the near future and (b) had a recording contract. The answers were those I wished to hear, viz. 'Yes' and 'No', and later that night Andrew and I went down to a club somewhere in the East End to hear Miss Hannaman sing. She was by no means bad; she sang tunefully in a rather pedestrian folk style, but she was certainly very attractive and were she to win the competition would be an ideal platform for our songwriting ambitions. Her real name was Rosalind and she was from Cambridge. She was warm and friendly, unfortunately accompanied by two male managers, at least one of whom seemed to have more than a business interest in his client. I fancied her myself but art had to come first – just.

Ross and her managers were definitely interested in a recording deal and she was flattered that we wanted both to produce and write for her. However we explained that even with my enormous clout at EMI it was essential that she win the *Evening Standard* competition, otherwise my company would not be prepared to take a punt on her. The closing time for votes was only just over twenty-four hours away, which gave us no chance of any kind of campaign, even if we knew where and how to mount one. The alternative was to rig the vote. We all agreed this was the course of action to take.

But first I had to check with EMI that they would sign Ross if she won the competition. At nine the next morning I obtained that assurance from the new MD of the record division, Ken East. Next we shot down to Fleet Street to get hold of as many copies of the paper as possible. We managed to find several thousand copies of the previous night's issue waiting to be pulped and removed the lot. All day and all of the night in one of the managers' flats, the five of us tore out and filled in nearly 5000 forms with Ross's name. We were also required to state the reason for choosing her, which got briefer as the hours passed. 'A sparkling personality, striking good looks and a unique vocal dexterity' became 'wow!' by midnight and by four a.m. just an exclamation mark. At seven a.m. we dumped a bag full of voting slips on the desk of Angus McGill, the *Standard* writer who ran the competition. (No security precautions in newspaper headquarters then.) To save him the bother of counting we attached a note, explaining who we were and stating that he just had to add approximately 4700 votes to Ross's tally, though he was welcome to check every slip if he wished.

To this day Angus McGill is a good friend* but this distinguished journalist was not wildly impressed by our first contact with him. We had clearly infringed the spirit of the competition though not the regulations; the paper had specifically stated that there was no limit to the number of times any one person could vote, provided that they used a separate form each time. Angus's problem was that our bag of slips did indeed alter the result. Without our help, Ross would genuinely have been second to another swinging chick, named Jenny; with our unsporting 4700 votes she romped into first place. Yet we had not actually broken the rules. Angus's solution was to announce a tie and for 1967 the *Evening Standard* proclaimed two Girls of the Year. Ross was signed to EMI.

Ross's personal and business life was pretty shambolic and before long we found ourselves more or less managing her. We were of course primarily concerned with writing for her and came up pretty quickly with a slightly gloomy pop ballad called 'Down Thru Summer' and a ludicrous novelty entitled 'I'll Give All My Love To Southend'. They became the first ever Lloyd Webber-Rice compositions to be released commercially. Just as I was not allowed to be a solo producer of the recording (Bob Barratt took charge), no one at EMI felt that Andrew could be entrusted with the musical arrangements (a ludicrous view) but we felt we were fortunate in getting Mike Leander to write the parts and wave the baton. Mike had gone from strength to strength since I had last seen him in 1965 during my failed backing vocalist days. Most recently he had

---

* I am now a regular judge on Angus' *Evening Standard* Pub of the Year panel, a more politically correct successor to the Girl of the Year.

arranged and conducted 'She's Leaving Home' for the Beatles and written two big hits for Paul Jones.

The recordings took place at Olympic Studios in Barnes as the Abbey Road studios were full and EMI wanted to strike while Ross's iron was hot. Thus we had our first glimpse of one of the most celebrated independent studios of the next three decades (at least) in which we were soon to record *Jesus Christ Superstar* and *Evita*. Angus McGill and a *Standard* photographer turned out to record the event in words and pictures. The day went as well as we could have hoped, although Andrew was not over complimentary (in private) about Mike Leander's arrangement, pointing out that it was a re-hash of his work on Paul Jones's 'I've Been A Bad Bad Boy' and too bombastic for our gentler ballad. He was probably right.

'Down Thru' Summer' had a very pretty tune, parts of which surfaced as the bridge of 'Buenos Aires' in *Evita* nearly ten years later, and glum words that were really rather dumb:

> Sadness now, but my life goes on
> The night and the morning gone
> Lost in the air
> Now I wait for the afternoon
> Why does it come so soon?
> Life isn't fair . . .

And so on. I cannot recall why I chose a title that did not really make sense. There were a few tolerable couplets however, and the overall effect was quite touching even if the backing did go on a bit. Ross sang very well, with no trace of nerves. The more uptempo flip side was extremely rushed and rather a mess, not best suited to a female soloist. A beat group approach would have got more out of the number, but not much. The *Standard* gave the release a good deal of attention (including a generous review from their new arts writer just down from Liverpool, Ray Connolly) and EMI pushed it a little on their Radio Luxembourg programmes, but the world out there didn't care.

'Thru' the summer of 1967 Andrew and I tagged along with Ross (and Jenny) as Angus and the *Evening Standard* squeezed every ounce of publicity out of their bubbly representatives. We went to Royal Ascot, the Chelsea Flower Show and numerous other terminally unhip functions, while most sensible pop wannabees were getting stoned in the Ad Lib or Scotch of St James's. This social round may have done things for the paper's circulation, but Ross's regular appearances therein did nothing for her singing career. Later in the year we tried again with a markedly more interesting single entitled '1969'. The tune was a straight lift from Beethoven's 'Für Elise' and the flip side, 'Probably On Thursday', leaned heavily on the best-known melody from Dvorak's *New World Symphony*. '1969' was a gloomy glimpse into the future but although the lyrics tottered along the knife-edge of pretentiousness, they were by far the most interesting and original I had yet delivered:

> And then I heard the songs they sung
> A hundred tongues
> Began to shout
> And then a panic in the hall
> I heard them call
> We can't get out
> The world had died
> They meant it to
> And no one cried
> For no one knew
> I took a photo of the night
> In black and white
> In colours too
> Hey I hate the picture 1969
> Lord I hate the picture 1969

A wildly inaccurate forecast but plenty of established songwriters from Dylan down had expressed similarly apocalyptic views with equal inaccuracy. In any event, I did not remotely believe that the world was going to end or even come to minor grief. I simply enjoyed putting myself in the position of one who did believe it. A lyric does not have to be based on personal experience to work, although the older one gets the more likely one is to draw on the events of one's own life. In 1967 I would soon have run out of real-life personal experiences to write about.

The words of the flip, 'Probably On Thursday', were also a considerable improvement on the likes of 'Down Thru' Summer' and *The Likes Of Us*. There was one ghastly verse that nodded to the contemporary hippy obsession with flowers, but the bulk of the lyric and the title made for a strangely affecting loss-of-love song:

> You're going to leave me, possibly on Wednesday—
> probably on Thursday

I never questioned why Andrew relied so heavily on the classics for quite a few of his tunes at the time. But there had been plenty of original efforts too* and it would be a brave popular composer who could put his hand on his royalty statements and claim he had never borrowed from the deceased. In fact it is annoying that it is virtually impossible for lyricists to do the same – one has to wait fifty years after a writer's death before being able to appropriate his work without penalty and words date far more quickly than tunes.

In any event, we saw the recordings with Ross Hannaman as only a means to an end – the end being to get our names known via a hit. Sophistication and originality had never been an automatic passport to a chart single. Anything would do until we got our ball rolling. Both sides of Ross' second single were officially orchestrated by the former Shadows drummer Tony Meehan and both officially produced by Bob Barratt and myself, but in reality Andrew and I called all the shots. '1969' had a striking harpsichord-dominated backing and could almost be classified as a rock song; the highlight of the arrangement of 'Probably On Thursday' was a horn rendition of the phrase (not Dvorak's) that eventually became 'Give me my coloured coat, my amazing coloured coat' in *Joseph* a few months later.

Our songs with Ross were not our only EMI-based activity. A young postboy at EMI named Martin Wilcox, who had embraced the Summer of Love culture with unbridled enthusiasm, had been continually pestering me with stories of two brilliant pop groups

* When Andrew deservedly won a plagiarism suit brought against him by an unknown composer in America in 1998, a spiteful journalist in the London *Observer* wrote a piece attacking Andrew for *not* stealing more from the greats!

based in his home town of Potters Bar. He had in fact become rather well-known for his pestering in all corners of EMI House as he delivered (extremely slowly) tapes, discs and mail, with the result that I was almost the only employee who would even give him the time of day. At my ripe old age of twenty-two, the sixteen-year-old Martin did not at first endear himself to me with what I considered his rather over-matey approach, but I soon realised that, beneath the Fabulous Furry Freak Brothers' haircut and the pongy combination of incense and dope, resided a likeable and musically intelligent kid who just might have something to contribute to the struggling Rice-Webber record world domination plans. I was still supposed to be looking for new talent and a certain disgruntlement had grown in senior EMI corridors that I was working more for myself than for the Greatest Recording Organisation In The World. So although doubting that the Potters Bar Sound had quite the ring of Merseybeat about it, I went north of Barnet with Martin to see the two acts – the Tales of Justine and the Mixed Bag.

The Tales of Justine were a three-piece band led by a precociously talented fifteen-year-old named David Daltrey, allegedly a distant cousin of Roger of the Who. David sang, played lead guitar and wrote all the songs, nearly all psychedelic laments of spaced-out anguish. They were a far cry (with the possible exception of '1969') from the kind of stuff Andrew and I had been writing, except in one respect – strong tunes. Backed by Paul Myerson on keyboards and Bruce Hurford on drums, David's material had surprising power. It was bang up-to-date, influenced in part by the early Pink Floyd and Jimi Hendrix, but for every ethereal 'Aurora' or 'Sitting On A Blunestone' there was a light-hearted pop song such as 'Albert The Sunflower' or 'Something Special'. David had a great voice and played seriously good guitar. I was sure that he could be a major star and Andrew agreed. We would probably not be able to write anything for him, but we could produce and orchestrate for him. A few hits as backroom boys and we would attract others who would need our songs.

The Mixed Bag were a very different outfit. They were a four-piece who primarily performed the hits of the day, and very well too. Led by vocalists Malcolm Parry (bass) and Terry

Saunders (lead guitar), they were the perfect group to hire for a party, reproducing every current smash with thumping precision. Their keyboards man, John Cook, eventually joined Mungo Jerry. Bryan Watson (drums) completed the line-up. They also wrote the odd song, but here surely was a band we could write for.

With *The Likes Of Us* almost dead and buried, it seemed by the end of 1967 that the joint ambitions of Andrew and me had switched from stage to pop. We had visions of success as record producers, pop songwriters and even as managers – we had by now formed Antim Management (i.e. had some writing paper printed), to which insolvent enterprise we had already signed Ross Hannaman, her previous managers having lost their grip – or their interest.

By now I was probably the least popular employee in EMI's A and R department. Attempts at personal aggrandisement, however unsuccessful, were not smiled upon. Just as we managed to convince EMI that David Daltrey's band were worth a recording contract, I was brutally reminded that I was still technically a management trainee and had no right to permanent residence in the most glamorous department. I was suddenly booted sideways into the classical division, although I was given leave to continue work on the projects I had already started, i.e. the Tales of Justine and Ross Hannaman. However, further progress with the latter was suddenly cut off when Ross unilaterally broke away from Antim's clutches.

Andrew and I, if not the EMI hierarchy, were just beginning to think about a third single for our female star when she announced that she was going to record with, and marry, the producer and writer of 'Excerpt From A Teenage Opera', one of the biggest hits of 1967, better remembered as 'Grocer Jack'. The gent in question, a superstar at EMI compared with Webber and Rice, was Mark Wirtz. We were somewhat put out by Ross's business decision but I was quietly rather relieved at her personal one, having embarked on a rather reckless affair with her at some point between her first and second flops, and having just fallen extremely heavily for one of her flatmates. Mark announced (in the *Evening Standard*, rubbing salt into the wound) that the 'world would now hear a new Ross Hannaman'. Technically it did. The new one was even less successful than the old – every Mark Wirtz-Ross Hannaman platter sank without trace.

We recorded about a dozen songs with David Daltrey. Most were his own compositions, a few were revivals of former hits that we felt had the commercial potential to score again; nearly all turned out very well. Andrew, for once allowed full orchestral rein by EMI, wrote some marvellous arrangements for David's songs. I still enjoy playing them today, but thirty years ago, hardly anyone in power at EMI did. We only secured one actual release, a single of two of David's lighter, almost bubblegum, numbers, 'Albert' and 'Monday Morning'. Needless to say, the single, despite the full weight of Antim's promotion behind it, was a complete failure. It seemed to have escaped, rather than to have been released. There was a happy ending of sorts when, in 1997, Tenth Planet, a record label devoted to really obscure vintage rock recordings, issued virtually everything we had recorded with David and the Tales three decades before. It got excellent reviews a mere thirty years too late to keep David in the music business.

Another recording we made around this time sounds far from good these days. It didn't sound too hot then. This was an EP (four songs) performed by a French starlet named Danièle Noël. Daniele was beautiful and had had tiny roles in a couple of movies. We met her and her husband/manager at a party at which he was somehow convinced that we had only to say the word and she could become an EMI recording star. EMI did not remotely agree with this and rejected Danièle's demo tapes with brutal alacrity; her old man however had a few bob of his own and commissioned us to make a record anyway, for which he would pay, and guarantee release in France. From my point of view this was not the most enticing of prospects as the record would have to be in French. We wrote two new songs in English and handed them with 'I'll Give All My Love To Southend', the first Ross Hannaman flipside, to a French lyricist. The fourth song for the EP, 'Danièle', I wrote in French myself, determined to have at least some of my original work on the finished platter. We recorded all four numbers on the cheap, the very cheap, in the studios where we had made the Barnardo demos. It was issued in France but we shouldn't have bothered.

With our pop careers looking about as promising as our theatre careers, the Summer of Love, the high point of the Swinging Sixties, seemed to have passed us by. For the first time I began to wonder if I was still in touch with contemporary music – perhaps my father's prophesy that I would grow out of pop music was about to come true. Much as I was sure I still loved the music, I had ignominiously failed to make my mark, and many of the trappings of pop culture such as drugs and the hippy ethos of peace and love had never remotely taken hold. Not even a smoker of cigarettes, my occasional attempts at smoking a joint were unenthusiastic and laughable – or not laughable, as they seemed to produce no effect whatsoever. I almost believe Bill Clinton when he said he never inhaled. I attended a love-in at Alexandra Palace where I smoked half a banana and had my wallet stolen. I had a ghastly suspicion that Swinging London was just four guys having a great time with everyone else running around trying to find them.

Not only was I haunted by the fear that I was out of touch, I was all but out of a job. I was informed that after my stint in the Siberia of filing Bach and Beethoven albums I was unlikely to grace any other department at Manchester Square. But I was saved by Norrie Paramor. The great man had become totally disillusioned with EMI, convinced that he had received scant reward for the huge successes he had brought them over the years. Following, perhaps a little too late, in the footsteps of George Martin and colleagues, he suddenly announced that he was setting up his own recording and music publishing organisation. Perhaps the only man in the building convinced that I had something to contribute to the recording industry of the late Sixties, Norrie asked me to leave with him, to be his personal assistant. Amazed that the one man in the A and R department who was on my side was the most important man, I accepted with alacrity, staggered by my good fortune and the fact that my new salary would take me over the £1,000 p.a. mark.

I had no intention of deserting Andrew. I attempted to convince him that my new post would give us even more opportunities to make it; we could still work with acts such as the Tales of Justine, and Norrie had several big-name acts, led of course by Cliff and the Shadows, who might one day record our songs. I think Andrew went along with this, but he had been approached by a music teacher called Alan Doggett to write something for the schoolboys of Colet Court preparatory school, and Andrew hoped I might have time to write the words. I thought I might.

Chapter Eleven

I regarded my new job with the fledgling Norrie Paramor Organisation as my most likely route to security and prosperity, if not fame and fortune, and my schemes with Andrew as a good back-up – Plan B. Of course I did not put it this way to Andrew at the time, which was just as well for before too long Plan B became Plan A.

Alan Doggett had been the choirmaster at Westminster Underschool (the prep school division of the school both Lloyd Webber boys had attended) and through Julian's membership of the choir had come to know the Lloyd Webber family. He had helped out with one or two of the demo recordings of *The Likes Of Us*. I thoroughly enjoyed the company of this extremely camp teacher, who was some ten years older than I was. By late 1967 he was established as head of music at Colet Court, a prep school then based in Hammersmith, the junior branch of St Paul's – the entire establishment is now located south of the river in Barnes. Alan was a talented music master, though a less talented composer, always on the lookout for a new way of instilling enthusiasm for music into his young charges (aged eight to thirteen). Being completely bald he qualified for comparison with a coot on two counts, a correlation he never objected to, indeed relished. Alan spent many amusing evenings at Harrington Court with me and the Lloyd Webber menagerie.

Impressed by *The Likes Of Us* (a minority view), Alan suggested that Andrew and I write something for his boys to perform at a school concert. A cantata would be ideal – a story told entirely through song. As our last work together had been created for the West End and Broadway, we were clearly being asked to set our sights a little lower. There would be no payment, no theatre, no professional performers. The only carrot was the chance that some educational music concern would publish the work, which meant that other schools might in turn perform it. We would then have the prospect of a modest income from sales of the sheet music – it was a bit like being offered an outside chance of writing a hit Latin text book. The only definite plus (and how big a plus we did not at the time appreciate) was that whatever we came up with was certain to be performed, at least once.

Alan gave us *carte blanche* over subject matter, beyond pointing out the obvious: it had to appeal both to the juveniles who were to perform it and to the teachers who would have to teach it. Our first thoughts were to write a mini-musical about a James Bond type – no doubt influenced by Adam Diment's success – but we realised that this might easily become dated very quickly. We needed to be more traditional and choose a timeless topic, which in practice came down to English history or the Bible. Alan had introduced us to two Bible-based cantatas that he had already produced with his choir, *The Daniel Jazz* by Herbert Chappell and *Jonah Man Jazz* by Michael Hurd. These were enjoyable pieces but seemed to me a little old-fashioned, lacking the out and out fun, particularly as far as the words were concerned, that I had experienced way back in 1952 when Brian Chidell had first exposed me to Gilbert and Sullivan at Aldwickbury School.

My favourite Bible story had always been Joseph and his coat of many colours. Alan and Andrew both thought this was an excellent subject. We set to work with an alacrity that I would be in raptures to achieve now. The first two tunes Andrew produced were the opening numbers that eventually became 'Jacob and Sons' and 'The Coat of Many Colours'. Both were bouncy melodies, devoid of any classical influence, ideally suited to narrative and to humour. I reckoned that the best way to a child's heart was through laughter and set out from the word go to make the songs funny. My principal source text was *The Wonder Book Of Bible Stories* (which contained the line about the first recorded rationing in history), rather than the Bible itself and my inspirations (whether wittingly or not) Michael Flanders and Paddy Roberts.

Funnily enough (or perhaps not), I had a little trouble convincing Andrew that my style of language was right for the project. I remember a long discussion about the phrase 'multi-coloured coat'. Andrew felt 'many coloured' more appropriate and he also felt uneasy about 'took the biscuit' and one or two other anachronisms. But the first time we played the opening five minutes to Alan, he was enchanted and we both realised we had hit upon a form, both musically and lyrically, that would be perfect for the Colet Court choir. Alan couldn't wait to play the first two songs to his boys and when their reaction was just as glowing, we positively raced ahead with the rest of the twenty-minute work. The long list of colours at the end of the song about Joseph's coat was actually put together by Alan's class. Our song originally ended simply 'red and yellow and green and brown and blue', but Alan and the Colet Court boys added a further twenty-four. A few years later this joyful string of hues won me great praise from none other than B.A. Young, the famous theatre critic in the *Financial Times* – 'This, to my mind, is pure poetry', waxed B.A. specifically about the twenty-nine colours – the only problem being that I only came up with five of them.

Without being aware of it, Andrew and I obeyed several vital rules for musical success when we embarked on *Joseph*, none of which we had followed with *The Likes Of Us*. First and foremost we picked a good story. There is a famous quote in theatrical circles which has been attributed to nearly every musical writer and producer over the years: the three most important things to get right when embarking upon a musical are 'book, book and book', the book being the storyline. Our Barnardo story was not a very dramatic tale, even though Leslie Thomas had done his considerable best with it. When all the returns were in, *The Likes Of Us* was simply about a nice but rather unexciting bloke who helps deprived children, and clashes with blinkered aristocracy and the evil influence of drink among the lower orders, while conducting an untorrid love affair with a virginal young lady.

Contrast the story of Joseph and his brothers: cocksure young man drives his brothers to near-murder when he arrogantly informs them that his dreams have told him he is special, 'born for higher things than you'. Worse, Joseph is their father Jacob's favourite, having been given a coat of many colours by his besotted parent. At the last minute the murder is called off but only because the brothers spot a chance to make a quick buck by selling Joseph into slavery. Thus our hero is deported from Canaan to Egypt. In Egypt Joseph rises to the very top, becoming 'Pharaoh's Number Two', but only after an escapade with the sex-starved wife of his wealthy employer which had unfairly landed him in prison. He gets out of jail through his remarkable ability to interpret dreams. His brilliant explanation that Pharaoh's dream about seven fat and seven thin cows foretells years of plenty and years of famine for Egypt wins him the post of right-hand man to the king. Thanks to Joseph, Egypt is well-prepared to cope with the famine when it duly arrives, in stark contrast to his family back in Canaan. His brothers are eventually driven in desperation to Egypt to beg for food, completely unaware that the man to whom they are grovelling is their own brother, missing presumed dead. Joseph at first makes no attempt to identify himself, instead testing the brothers' integrity by falsely accusing the youngest, Benjamin, of theft. The brothers pass the test with flying colours and Joseph, now free of the arrogance that helped to destroy the family in the first place, reveals all. A joyous reunion is the climax of the story, with Jacob coming to Egypt to meet the beloved son he thought he would never see again.

This great tale has everything – plausible, sympathetic characters, a flawed hero and redeemed villains. The figures of power can be portrayed comically yet they retain their potency and even their dignity. The storyline is both original (perhaps not surprising as it is one of the first ever told) and unpredictable, yet moves with unerring force towards a happy conclusion. It is a symbolic, spiritual, religious and human story – even in our light-hearted re-telling of it the presence of God is inescapable. The props, coat and goat, and locations, bleak (Canaan) and extravagant (Egypt), are magnificent. It is a story of triumph against the odds, of love and hate, of forgiveness and optimism. As with all great stories, the teller has no need to spell out the messages if he tells the tale well. Perhaps risking comparisons with the youthful Joseph's lack of modesty, I believe Andrew and I told the story very well indeed.

I am not sure how much of all this we appreciated at the time, but we had certainly obeyed rule number one in choosing a good storyline. Rule number two for musical success is orginality of style. This is easier said than done but because we were free from the ludicrous belief that we were writing for West End critics and Broadway butchers, we made no attempt to ape any previous theatrical hit. We thought only of entertaining our immediate clients – Alan and his schoolboys – and ourselves. Had we been invited to write a show for even the humblest of adult or professional companies, we would have undoubtedly been long-winded and far more serious. We would probably have included spoken dialogue which would have been fatal. We would never have captured the essence of the story as we did through humour in both words and music.

Once it became clear that Colet Court loved the irreverence of the opening numbers, we became more daring and as a result stumbled upon a unique style. Of course we were influenced and inspired by other writers, of course there were many obvious echoes of other composers and lyricists, but the final product was not quite like anything else. That is why *Joseph*, entirely under its own steam, gradually and irresistibly progressed from tiny school concert to world-wide commercial acclaim, remaining one of the most popular musicals in the world thirty years after its creation. That and the fact that almost everybody who heard it loved it – until it became so big that eventually it attracted the loathing of success-haters, determined to believe the whole enterprise was a cynical commercial venture from day one.

Rule Number Three for those wishing to break into musical theatre is get your work performed, no matter how humble the level of performance. Another mistake we had made with our Barnardo epic was to aim for the heights of the West End. The show was simply not good enough to get there, and as a result was never seen anywhere. Had we mounted a school or amateur production, which would have been achievable, we would have realised much sooner that we were flogging a dead horse, or at best an extremely knackered one, and we would have learned far more about musicals in general and our limitations in particular. Only with a real audience reaction can you begin to judge your show's potential – tapes and demo recordings are virtually useless on their own.

There are plenty of other useful tips which the success of *Joseph* has retrospectively taught me, many of which I have ignored to my cost in subsequent shows. Keep your shows short and if the subject allows, make it funny. Even if the subject doesn't allow, make it funny somewhere, or find another subject. This is particularly important for first-time musical writers. Big ballads and deeply meaningful thoughts take time to sink in and most producers don't have the time. Good gags allied to a catchy tune will grab the attention of a jaded impresario who will also know that angst-ridden tragedies cost more than comic shows. Serious stuff needs greater musical and production forces. When you have made your name, then you can wallow in doom and gloom to your heart's content, secure in the knowledge that a producer will back your expensive misery to the hilt. But in the early days, keep it light.

However, any sophisticated analysis of our chosen form of artistic expression was far from the minds of Andrew and me as we raced to complete *Joseph* in time for its world première on Friday, 1 March 1968, at two thirty p.m. in the Assembly Hall of Colet Court School. As I was occupied all day with Norrie, and as Andrew was still studying at the Royal College of Music, evenings and weekends were our times of productivity, but I have no recollection of any great pressure caused by the deadline, which seems almost inconceivable to me whenever I write now.

We had no initial intention of making the work a retirement home for various styles of pop – the only pastiche in the original twenty-minute version of *Joseph* was the Elvis Presley parody for Pharaoh. I really cannot remember how we came up with that particular idea, but once we had decided to include a tribute to the King of rock 'n' roll the song almost wrote itself. There were connections between Elvis and Pharaoh which we did not even notice. During a recording of the Broadway cast album of *Joseph* in 1982, I suggested to the actor playing Pharaoh, Tom Carder, that perhaps he should not include an ad-lib line about Memphis in 'Song of the King' – an anachronism too far. Tom quite rightly pointed out to the dumb lyric writer that the line referred to Memphis, Egypt, not Memphis, Tennessee – the coincidence that Elvis and Pharaoh had operated in cities with the same name had never dawned on me.

From the first rehearsal it was clear that 'Song of the King' would be a show-stopper, the only problem being that none of Alan's unbroken voices were ideal Presley impersonators. Consequently my vocal demonstration of the song to the boys won me the part for 1 March, with the choir given an equally crucial role during the number – the bup-bup-shoo-waddy-wahs. As the work gathered momentum in choir practice, it was clear to us that we could and should add a little glitzy support to the proceedings. My appearance as Elvis/Pharaoh would be one aspect of this, the addition of some electric backing to beef up Andrew's piano, another. We called in our tame pop musicians – the Mixed Bag and David Daltrey.

The Mixed Bag were the perfect outfit for *Joseph* in that their forté was the note-perfect rendition of others' material. They added a great deal to the piece with their reliable beat and instrumental flourishes. As the structure of the oratorio took shape, certain lead vocal lines were given to Malcolm and Terry of the group to lend variety to the non-stop narrative flow. However devoted parents are, however tuneful the offspring, twenty consecutive minutes of treble warbling is a lot to take. Besides, the kids were always required to ooh and aah behind the broken voices. We asked David Daltrey to lead the singing of the two principal solo numbers for Joseph himself. Again, the boys participated fully in both 'Close Every Door' and 'Any Dream Will Do', but the strength of the choir was in its ensemble singing and we knew that the whole show would be better served if these two major numbers were in the hands, or rather the larynx, of a confident and mature (albeit only sixteen) vocalist. I am sure that neither David nor the Mixed Bag had expected a prep school concert to be the first concrete (and unpaid) offer of work found for them by Antim Management, but they bit the bullet bravely. They were at least in at the very start of a little bit of theatre history.

Although we had thus, mainly for musical reasons, introduced a few solo voices, *Joseph* had been commissioned as a work for a choir, and the majority of the lyrics were written from a narrator's point of view – the entire choir being the narrators. Joseph's brothers had no lines of their own at all other than as part of reported speech. It was written to be performed as a concert, not as a musical play. Little did Andrew and I know that by not trying to do what we had teamed up for in the first place, we were on the threshold of writing a very fine dramatic musical comedy.

Writing the words was great fun, all the more so because every tune that came off the ALW conveyor belt sounded like a winner. There are several examples of bad rhyming throughout *Joseph*, but while purists (and I now count myself as one) would shudder, no one was anything but delighted with the couplets as they flowed from my portable typewriter. 'Biscuit' and 'district' always hit the button laugh-wise, but is of course an inaccurate rhyme. Elsewhere we find 'mean' and 'dream', 'fine' and 'time' and plenty of other solecisms that would have me railing against a lyricist who tried them in theatre today (pure rhymes and rock are almost mutually exclusive). In my defence I point out that we had no inkling that the work would even survive for a second performance and that telling the tale entertainingly for children was almost all that mattered. Furthermore, when I have tried to correct rhymes for subsequent professional productions, the directors and singers involved always refused to accept the changes, saying they had always loved the original. I am stuck with 'biscuit' and 'district'.

The question I have been asked most since around 1970 is, 'Which is written first, the words or the music?' With Andrew (and I have primarily worked this way with nearly all of my collaborators with the notable exception of Elton John) it was always the music, but before the tune comes the plot. Both partners should be fully aware of and completely happy with the structure and storyline (book) of the entire show, ideally before a single song is contemplated. Writing the book of a musical is generally a job in its own right, the job Leslie Thomas had manfully tackled for *The Likes Of Us*, and generally involves a good deal of spoken dialogue. However, *Joseph* had a story already written by some Old Testament sage and was an oratorio, the tale told entirely through song. My initial task was simply to suggest to Andrew what aspect of the story each musical scene should convey. He then produced a tune to fit the mood and plot of each scene, and I added the words.

The very first lines, to a most cheerful uptempo melody, set the mood of the entire work:

> Way, way back many centuries ago,
>> not long after the Bible began
> Jacob lived in the Land of Canaan,
>> a fine example of a family man
> Jacob, Jacob and Sons,
>> depended on farming to earn their keep
> Jacob, Jacob and Sons
>> spent all of their day in the fields with sheep

I would defy any child under thirteen, hearing that for the first time, not to want to know what happened next. And somehow we managed to keep up the standard of that dynamic start for the telling of the entire story.

'Joseph's Coat' was one of the easiest lyrics to write. Simple humorous couplets describing Joseph's sartorial splendour seemed to flow effortlessly.

> And when Joseph tried it on
> He knew his sheepskin days were gone

And:

> He looked handsome, he looked smart
> He was a walking work of art

hit the bull's-eye straightaway with Alan's class. Once Andrew was convinced that the slang-tinged approach worked, and once Alan and the boys had unilaterally extended the list of colours, we were certain we had found the formula to communicate.

'Joseph's Coat' contained my first dodgy rhyme, but

His astounding clothing took the biscuit
Quite the smoothest person in the district

has been so well-received by audiences it has survived thirty years of criticism.

After two bouncy numbers, the pace was slowed with 'Joseph's Dreams'. Next up was the only mildly memorable 'Poor Poor Joseph' which scored with its original singers primarily because of a reference to Ishmaelites as 'a hairy crew'. This possibly should have been 'an hairy crew'. With no Potiphar song yet written, the plot cut straight to Joseph in prison where he sings 'Close Every Door', one of the few serious scenes, in which I attempted to make a parallel between Joseph's fortunes and that of Israel itself. When accused, ridiculously, of anti-Semitism in *Jesus Christ Superstar* some years later, I often quoted 'Close Every Door' as proof of our pro-Israel credentials. It has never been one of my favourite songs, but for dramatic impact and welcome change of mood, has always worked wonderfully in all *Joseph* productions, large or small.

After the sombre 'Close Every Door' the twenty-minute version cut straight to Pharaoh's problems which 'pinned him to his sheets with fright'. Here we were on a winning streak. Andrew's brief but superbly menacing melody before Pharaoh launches into his Elvis tribute ('chained and bound, afraid, alone'), set up the 'Tempo 1957 Rock' (as it was described in all official versions of the printed score) perfectly. The original 'Song of the King' was a mere single verse, and evoked Elvis's greatest period in style alone, but by the time the show-stopper was expanded to two verses and a middle section, I managed to fling in direct references to several Presley hits, including 'All Shook Up', 'Don't Be Cruel', 'Treat Me Nice', 'I Beg Of You' and even 'That's When Your Heartaches Begin', the final title destined to become an even more significant part of my life as the inspiration behind the name of my personal business company, and thence my cricket team, Heartaches C.C.

But tax-avoidance schemes and directorships were on another planet as we hastened to complete *Joseph*. This we did by following Pharaoh's big moment with a consistently tuneful and funny sequence incorporating a reprise of the 'Joseph's Coat' melody and some lines that I still immodestly smile at today:

All these things you saw in your pyjamas
Are a long-range forecast for your farmers

And:

Pharaoh thought, 'Well stone the crows, this Joseph is a clever kid
Who'd have thought that fourteen cows could mean the things he
    said they did?'

A pity that the former pairing was followed soon afterwards by a clumsy 'famine/planning' rhyme.

A chirpy hand-clapper entitled 'Back in Canaan' told us of the all-but-forgotten brothers' food shortages and of their trip to Egypt to beg for supplies. Joseph's framing of Benjamin when the golden cup is stolen leads to a happy, tear-jerking reunion, reprising the delightful 'Joseph's Dream' melody, and then into the finale, 'Any Dream Will Do'.

'Any Dream Will Do' is by far the best song in *Joseph* and one of the best four or five Andrew and I ever wrote together.* It combines a rather sad, resigned lyric with a very sweet and catchy tune – a paradoxical mix that usually proves very powerful. Not that I believe many people see 'Any Dream Will Do' as a pessimistic song, so jauntily and enthusiastically does it climax the show. But its message, expressed in deliberately obscure terms (I must have been listening to Paul Simon rather than to Michael Flanders that day) is that most of us would rather dream about anything at all than face reality. The coat is the dream and the singer is only truly happy when he is asleep, when he can 'draw back the curtain' and see colours that are 'wonderful and new'. When he awakes he only wants to 'return to the beginning' of his dream – and how annoyed I am now that I rhymed 'beginning' with 'dimming'. Still even Paul Simon rhymed 'friend' with 'again' in 'Sounds of Silence'.

So *Joseph* ends with a plea – 'Give me my coloured coat' – but any doubts or unhappiness in that thought have always been swept aside by the triumphant music. *Joseph* is, after all, an optimistic

---

* Andrew had come up with the tune a year or two earlier when we decided to write a pop song for Herman's Hermits (after my meeting with Herman in the EMI lavatories). My first lyric for the melody was entitled 'I Fancy You', now mercifully missing from my archives.

piece. It still works best when performed by the kind of people for whom it was first written (not the actual people, who are nearly all now balding and/or bearded family men themselves) – children learning about music and language – and maybe about God too. However polished some of the gigantic commercial productions have been, it is versions similar to the spirit and size of the world première at Colet Court School on 1 March 1968 that I enjoy most, and it is those performances that make *Joseph* the work of mine (and maybe of Andrew's too) most likely to survive into the twenty-second century.

Chapter Twelve

Colet Court's Assembly Hall was pretty full for the first ever *Joseph* concert, although I doubt whether this was because the one hundred or so parents expected an afternoon of musical enlightenment or even entertainment. They were amazed to find they were sitting through something they really enjoyed, and at just over twenty minutes, mercifully short. With Alan Doggett's baton brisk and firm, the strange aggregation of choir boys, pop group, David Daltrey and me, plus Andrew thumping on piano, gripped the assembly from first note to last. The audience got all the jokes as I had wisely dished out complete lyric sheets beforehand, and loved all the tunes. Elvis went down an absolute storm and everyone, young and extremely young, sung their hearts out. We had to perform most of the piece again, unwittingly foreshadowing a feature of even the most sophisticated productions of *Joseph* down the years.

The headmaster, Henry Collis, was ecstatic. There were plenty of requests from parents for the show to be repeated, at a time when fathers, somewhat under-represented at the première, would be unable to plead the office as an excuse for non-attendance. Andrew and I, confident now that we had written something with a future, felt that we should stage the reprise at a more public venue. Not even educational music publishers had yet shown an interest, but a larger production with a little publicity might get that particular ball rolling. Andrew's father, who had witnessed the Colet Court show and loved it, then chipped in with the perfect suggestion. Bill Lloyd Webber was the organist at the Methodist Central Hall, Westminster, and proposed that we use that mighty building for the oratorio's public début. The evening of Sunday, 12 May, was duly booked. The show was scheduled to follow the regular Sunday evening service so we hoped that a good number of the Methodist worshippers would hang on in there for *Joseph* – there were 3000 seats to fill. Maybe some of the more senior members of the congregation wouldn't even notice that the service had ended.

With Alan and Bill's help, we managed to get a little publicity for the show – both Radio Four and the *Daily Express* gave us a plug – and we printed some posters and leaflets. We announced optimistically that proceeds from the concert would be given to the Westminster International Centre's drug addiction section. I fear that, as is so often the case when good causes and pop music come together, our prime concern was not to help the druggies but to flog tickets. There was never any serious chance of selling 3000 seats, even at the giveaway price of 2/6d, but we were hopeful that we could fill most of the stalls and some of the balcony of this most impressive arena. We had a built-in following of parents and friends of Colet Court, and by involving the entire school, rather than just the choir, in the show, we automatically increased the overall parental enthusiasm.

The Mixed Bag and David Daltrey were signed to repeat their triumphs, and their instrumentation was boosted not only by the Colet Court school orchestra but by Dr W.S. Lloyd Webber himself on the Hall's organ. Not only that, Bill and other distinguished Harrington Court inmates – Julian and John Lill – agreed to help fill the evening out with organ, cello and piano turns. Joseph was, after all, only twenty-two minutes long. We invited journalists, the BBC, Novello and Co., the music publishers, and my boss Norrie Paramor. We invited friends and families (most of Andrew's were already part of the show). We also tried to invite a few celebrities but our clout in this area was limited – the only one who turned up was Peter Asher, like Andrew an old boy of Westminster School, who had enjoyed a couple of years of significant record success as half of the pop duo Peter and Gordon.

We eventually herded around a thousand souls into the Central

Hall and Andrew and I nervously sat through forty-five minutes of Bill, Julian and John. A brief interval – and then we were hoping lightning would strike twice. Had we over-egged the pudding? Was *Joseph* just a tiny gem that really had no place attempting to venture beyond prep schools into the public arena? Did it even have a future with prep schools? Was the Novello rep in the audience?

For the second time the audience went wild. For the second time we had to do great chunks of the show again – but we were not besieged by any agents, publishers or record producers immediately afterwards. An artistic success we felt, but probably not a commercial one. We were relieved, thrilled, but a little deflated. In the week that followed we had no indication from any source that our exercise in self-promotion had got us anywhere at all. We had lots of congratulatory letters and telephone calls from delighted parents and others who had been in the audience, but nothing from anyone who mattered. At work Norrie was very complimentary – and genuinely so – it was hard to imagine this gracious man ever saying anything insincere, but he seemed to regard the forthcoming Cliff Richard season at the Talk of the Town as his most pressing assignment that week.

The following Friday night I went away for a wildly unoriginal break – a weekend in Brighton. My companion was Sara Bennett-Levy, a young lady, a sultry brunette, with whom I was overcome with love and devotion. Ross Hannaman had briefly been her flatmate in Adams Row, a posh mews tucked away behind Grosvenor Square. Sara's flat was coincidentally right next door to one occupied by the pop agent, record producer and impresario Robert Stigwood, before long to play a hugely important part in my life, and we spent many an hour staring out of the window hoping to spot a Bee Gee (we often did).

Sara had definitely moved a bit downmarket by becoming involved with me – in financial terms at least. My rivals, not all of whom I was confident of having shaken off, seemed to be without exception loaded, the owners of exotic phallic symbols masquerading as Aston Martins (with gadgets that played those new-fangled cassettes, Sara informed me), and older. I was nearly a whole year younger than Sara and had no car at all – brief ownership of a 1950s Austin Cambridge which had cost me, or rather my grandmother, £90, had recently ended in tears and a deceased big end on the A1. But I was hanging in there and scraped together enough for a weekend in a seafront hotel, down the road from my old school. We went by train.

The first half of the weekend was a great success but ruined from a romantic point of view on the second morning by the arrival of the *Sunday Times* with our breakfast tray. I had no intention of wasting more than a few minutes of Sara-time in our exotic location, but I did wish to have a quick squint at the music reviews to see what their distinguished critic had thought of Cliff Richard at the Talk of the Town. To my amazement Derek Jewell's weekly column was headed 'Pop Goes Joseph' and nine-tenths of his space was taken up with a rave review of our Central Hall concert:

'Give us food', the brothers said, 'dieting is for the birds'
Joseph gave them all they wanted, second helpings, even thirds . . .

Even on paper the happy bounce of lyrics like these comes through. They are exactly right for singing by several hundred boys' voices. With two organs, guitars, drums and a large orchestra the effect is irresistible.

The quicksilver vitality of *Joseph And His Amazing Technicolor Dreamcoat*, the new pop oratorio heard at Central Hall, Westminster, last Sunday, is attractive indeed. On this evidence the pop idiom – beat rhythms and Bacharachian melodies – is most enjoyably capable of being used in extended form.

Musically, *Joseph* is not all gold. It needs more light and shade. A very beautiful melody 'Close Every Door To Me', is one of the few points where the hectic pace slows down. The snap and crackle of the rest of the work tends to be too insistent, masking the impact of the words, which unlike many in pop, are important.

But such reservations seem pedantic when matched against *Joseph*'s infectious overall character. Throughout its twenty-minute duration it bristles with wonderfully

singable tunes. It entertains. It communicates instantly,
as all good pop should. And it is a considerable piece
of barrier-breaking by its creators, two men in their early
twenties – Tim Rice, the lyricist and Andrew Lloyd Webber,
who wrote the music.

The performers last Sunday were the choir, school and
orchestra of Colet Court, the St Paul's junior school, with
three solo singers and a pop group called the Mixed Bag.
It was an adventurous experiment for a school, yet Alan
Doggett, who conducted, produced a crisp, exciting and
undraggy performance which emphasized the rich expan-
siveness of pop rather than the limitations of its frontiers.

Poor old Cliff was reviewed in somewhat less glowing terms, not
rudely but not a rave, tucked away at the foot of Jewell's column.
I was on the telephone to Andrew in a flash – he had already seen
the review but had been unable to contact me as I hadn't told
him, or indeed anyone, where I was that weekend. What now?
We arranged to meet that very evening; somehow I managed to
persuade Sara that we should catch an earlier train back to town.
I don't think I paid full attention to her allure for the remainder of
our time in Brighton – I was too excited by Derek Jewell's article.
I cannot imagine allowing a *Sunday Times* review to curtail any
romantic tryst these days.

It is ironic that the first ever lyrics of mine quoted in a national
newspaper were lines that did not long survive in the official
version of the work. Derek was even more generous to me than
he was to Andrew, but I can honestly say that I did not even
notice this at the time. I suspect Andrew might have done but as
far as we were both concerned this was a hugely important boost
for our partnership, which helped us equally and which we had
earned equally.

The rave review had an immediate effect – we did not even
have to think about what to do next. I was slightly wary about
facing Norrie on Monday morning in case he felt that my out of
office work had cut the column inches given to his top star, but
Norrie was delighted and simply said that he felt we should make
an album of *Joseph* as soon as possible. He wanted to record it

with any major record company other than EMI, and he was sure Decca would be interested. Novello, the music publishers, suddenly popped up out of nowhere and said that after much consideration they now thought that this could be a work with potential across the educational spectrum. Our contact with Desmond Elliott had been under slight strain since the failure of 'The Likes Of Us' had grown ever more obvious, but we asked him to field these and any other *Joseph* enquiries.

One of the first of these was a brusque note from Technicolor asking us to desist from using their name in the title of our work. The title itself had been largely Andrew's idea, adapted and expanded from the unimaginative 'Joseph And His Coat Of Many Colours', which was my first, uninteresting thought. On the way we came up with 'Pal Joseph' and 'How To Succeed In Egypt Without Really Trying' but fortunately these smart-ass gags were rejected in favour of the title that has become a nightmare for poster designers ever since – not 'His' but 'The' 'Amazing Technicolor Dreamcoat', so Derek Jewell got the title slightly wrong. Desmond brilliantly told Technicolor that we would be more than happy to change the word to 'Eastmancolor' or 'Color-by-Deluxe', and their protest faded away.

He also negotiated an advance of £100 for each of us from Novello for the rights to publish the work, signing away our ownership of the piece in return for a royalty on all printed or recorded versions of all or any of the songs. In due course a further deal was done between Novello and the music publishing arm of the Norrie Paramor Organisation. Norrie wanted a slice of the copyright action as it was thanks to his reputation and desire to make a commercial LP of *Joseph* that there was to be any prospect of serious income. He had quickly concluded an agreement with Decca to make the *Joseph* album, and I was to be allowed production credit with Norrie. Andrew would write all the orchestrations and the hit team of Alan Doggett, the Mixed Bag and David Daltrey would repeat their roles, as would the Colet Court choir and W.S. Lloyd Webber on organ – and I would get to do my Elvis impersonation as Pharaoh for posterity.

By this time, the summer of 1968, I had been with Norrie for six months. Despite my activity with Andrew and *Joseph*, I still felt that the comparatively conventional career of music executive was where my future lay. My parents were pretty happy with my new position – I was just about able to support myself and clearly working for one of the most respected and successful men in my chosen business. In fact my parents have often been far less conservative than I when considering important decisions in my life. They acknowledged that the law was a loser long before I faced up to it and much later when my marriage was in difficulties tried to make me realise that any decision was better than no decision.

Norrie's empire at worker level initially consisted of me and his elder daughter Carolyn. His formidable wife Joan was a director and took an invaluable interest in the proceedings. The NP Organisation began operations at the Paramor home in 'Millionaire's Row' – The Bishop's Avenue in Hampstead – but after a few weeks both family and business moved to a large flat in Harley House, near Regent's Park, W1. One of my duties, which I thoroughly enjoyed, was to walk the Paramors' boxer bitch, Psyche. More relevant to my ambitions was my work as studio dogsbody when Norrie was recording his stars such as Cliff and the Shadows. I made the coffee, labelled the tape boxes and placed the music on the musicians' stands. Cliff, then as now about as famous and successful as you could get in the UK recording world, was in early 1968 involved for the first time in his career in the annual bedlam of artistic incorrectness that is the Eurovision Song Contest.

The first Cliff Richard session I ever attended was his re-recording of one of his recent hits 'All My Love' in German, the second his commitment to wax of all six of the songs competing for the honour of representing Britain in the Eurovision Final. Two of the six were arranged and conducted by John Paul Jones, barely a year away from becoming the bassist for Led Zeppelin. He kept pretty quiet about his Eurovision involvement during his time with that hedonistic quartet and in the long run must have been relieved that neither of his numbers with Cliff won. They never had a chance against the thumping inane brilliance of the Bill Martin-Phil Coulter creation, 'Congratulations', arranged and conducted by Norrie Paramor, who could spot a hit from fifty paces.

I volunteered to write the sleeve note for Cliff's Eurovision

EP which featured all six finalists and, following that literary triumph, was asked by Norrie to write commentaries for most of the albums in the NP catalogue. Norrie had for a long time recorded instrumental albums under a variety of names such as the Big Ben Banjo Band and I (or sometimes my old *alter ego* Gerrard Portslade) enthused about the sounds within the covers with what I hope was a glimmering of originality.

Besides the great Cliff, whose professionalism, good manners and vocal dexterity were a wonder to behold, and his longtime henchmen, the Shadows (at this point consisting of Hank B. Marvin, Bruce Welch, John Rostill and Brian Bennett), Norrie had deals to record the French idol Sacha Distel, the half of Peter and Gordon who had not come to see *Joseph* at the Westminster Central Hall, Gordon Waller, and the English comedy-pop trio, the Scaffold. Distel, musician and crooner, had for many years been a sex symbol in France, boosted by his highly-publicised affair with Brigitte Bardot (it would have been difficult to have had an unpublicised affair with BB in the Sixties) which had somewhat obscured his genuine musical talent as jazz guitar player and composer. He had written a song called 'The Good Life', already a standard by 1968 thanks to recordings by Tony Bennett among others. The plan in England was to launch him as a middle-of-the-road sexpot.

Gordon was a superb pop singer, vocally on a par with Scott Walker, who on his own never repeated the international success he had enjoyed with Peter. Norrie cut some excellent tracks with him, including one outstanding Jim Webb ballad, 'Rosecrans Boulevard' but nothing took off.* The Scaffold, Mike McGear (Paul McCartney's brother), Roger McGough (the distinguished poet, now OBE) and John Gorman (a lugubrious comedian) had broken through in 1967 with the novelty single 'Thank U Very Much' and were keen to maintain a high profile through pop singles while pursuing their more ambitious performance work which combined rock music, poetry and comedy. They were a class act.

* In 1972 Gordon played Pharaoh in the first ever professional production of *Joseph* at the Edinburgh Festival. His Elvis impersonation was uncannily accurate. I financed and produced some Gordon Waller recordings myself in the mid-Seventies, but once again without commercial success – not the fault of the vocalist.

Norrie commissioned me to write some lyrics for Sacha, English versions of quite ghastly French songs that I could not even imagine the hopelessly primæval French record buyers liking. However I was not in a position to reject any writing work and dutifully adapted four or five rock solid flops, wondering when I would be offered a Cliff lyric. These grisly Sacha efforts were recorded but none, quite rightly, was considered good enough to be included in his début English album. However a completely new song by me and Andrew was: a eulogy to Solange, my Parisian love, with music by Webber and Mendelssohn. Fortunately Felix was not around to collect his share of the (miniscule) royalties – or any of the credit. Solange was not mentioned by name in the lyric and to my distress Sacha objected to the title 'Song for Solange' as Solange was also the name of his apparently less than desirable cleaning lady. Consequently the title was changed to the anodyne 'Believe Me I Will' and the inspiration for the lyric never knew of the tribute. It hardly mattered as Sacha's album was a complete stiff.

The Scaffold wrote all of their own material, offering no opportunities for ambitious young songwriters, but provided me with far greater artistic satisfaction than the French heart-throb did. Their first single under Norrie's supervision was a delightful song entitled 'Do You Remember' which was a minor hit, and the NP recording of the group live at the Royal Festival Hall was quite outstanding. I did quite a bit more than set up the music stands and plug in the amplifiers, relishing the work both at Abbey Road studios and at the South Bank concert venue. Both Norrie and the Scaffold appreciated comments and suggestions and my occasional contributions to aspects of the music and sound were not always ignored. In time I was even able to chip in with the odd idea from the back of the control room when Cliff and the Shadows were recording – their new joint project was an album (I wrote the sleeve notes) entitled *Established 1958*, celebrating their ten years at the top, which seemed a staggering achievement. It was – but not as amazing as Cliff's current forty-plus years as a star.

On top of all this Norrie activity I was in charge of listening to all the unsolicited tapes that rolled in – nothing like as many as hit the EMI doormat, but still a considerable flow. Norrie was desperate to discover a new, young act and felt that my youthful ear was as likely to latch on to a winner as his. Sad to say, the one tape that I thought promising was rejected out of hand by my boss. An ex-Uppingham public schoolboy called Bill Heath sent in some demos of two or three strange songs he had written and performed with a band called The Lost. Their songs were not unlike some of the Scaffold's weirder creations which may have been why Norrie was not that keen, feeling that one Scaffold-type act was enough and that the Scaffold themselves were the best of that type. However I asked Bill to come to the office and, since Norrie would not agree to his group joining our enterprise, I joined Bill's.

On free non-Andrew or non-Norrie evenings I often nipped down to Walton-on-Thames where Bill and his pals (including Mike Read, the future Radio One disc-jockey and TV host) occupied a large house, for a singsong and/or jam. I still held out the vaguest of hopes of becoming a pop star and to be able to sing with a reasonably talented bunch of like-minded fellows kept this daft ambition tantalisingly and enjoyably alive. We even made a record (I am a prominent backing vocalist) which Bill and Mike had privately pressed and distributed, entitled 'Hello February's Child', under the band name Just Plain Smith. Needless to say it was not a hit but in 1999 individual copies were valued by oldie collectors at £150 each, considerably more than it cost to make in the first place. To this day I still sing with Bill's group and our repertoire at birthday parties and May Balls based around Beatles and Stones hits has hardly changed in thirty years. We are nowadays usually known as Wang and the Cheviots, with the question of which one of us is Wang unresolved for nearly three decades.

After a few months of independence, Norrie added a young composer named Nick Ingman to his team. Nick was a fine arranger and his principal job was to orchestrate songs for recordings that Norrie had either no time or no inclination to arrange himself. Norrie expressed the hope that Nick and I would write together, ignoring (perhaps deliberately) that I already had an established writing partner. I had in fact already dropped several hints that Andrew might have been a useful addition to the NP set-up, but for some reason Norrie had not responded. Nick and I did write a couple of half-hearted songs together, one of which, a fairly dire number featuring the manic American disc-jockey Emperor Rosko, a big name on UK radio at the time, actually secured a release as a pop single. But my writing partnership with Nick completely lacked the inspiration of mine with Andrew – it was a short-lived liaison. Besides, I was genuinely very concerned not to jeopardise my relationship with Andrew, despite Norrie's reservations about his prospects. This was a rare error of judgement on Norrie's part, not entirely made on musical grounds, and led before long to my leaving the Paramor Organisation.

But this momentous break was still some months away. The immediate excitement was the recording of *Joseph*. Norrie booked us into Decca's studio in Hampstead (coincidentally where I had recorded my demo of 'That's My Story' three years before) and generously left me, Andrew and Alan to get on with it, under the experienced eye of one of the top recording engineers of the time, Bill Price. It had been obvious that a mere twenty minutes was not enough to fill two sides of an LP, so Andrew and I had added a few numbers and extra verses to existing songs to fill the wax. One of these new songs was 'Potiphar', the portrait of Joseph's first Egyptian employer, who catches the star in a compromising position with his nymphomaniac wife. Andrew's choice of a witty vaudeville parody for the melody and arrangement was with hindsight a crucial move in the work's future development. After 'Potiphar' nearly everything we added was a send-up or steal of a well-known form of popular music. Calypso, French *chanson* and Country and Western pastiches were all in the pipeline, though not on the original NP Organisation recording.

Taking into account the almost total lack of studio experience of any of the principals, the sessions went very well, with Bill Price's contribution really that of a producer as well as that of engineer. His was a hugely encouraging presence, bearing in mind that he could not often have worked with such greenhorns. Indeed, there was one fine-tuning session at the very end of the week when we were briefly in the hands of another engineer, who made it perfectly clear that he thought both work and writers were way beneath his status. This charmer was Roy Thomas Baker who later became a phenomenally successful record producer with Queen and others, by which time I am sure he had grown sensitive to the needs of lesser mortals.

Joseph was still primarily an oratorio, with most of the numbers sung in narrative form, whether by Alan's choir, Malcolm and Terry, or David. I did quite a bit of the narration myself, in addition to the Elvis sequence. Alan conducted as 'undraggily' as he had done in concert and on the evening of the final session when we listened to the playback of the entire thing, Andrew and I had a sense of achievement we had hitherto never come near to experiencing in our three years of writing together. However this triumphant mood evaporated overnight. We were due to play the tapes to Norrie the following morning and somehow nothing seemed any good when we listened again at Harrington Court before heading for the NP HQ.

Andrew led the crusade of woe, certain that Norrie would loathe the tapes which were badly mixed, performed and edited. *Joseph* was a rotten piece which should never be issued on record as it would finish our careers before they had begun. Such pessimism was catching and both Alan and I, as we pottered over to Norrie's in Alan's cosy Morris Minor, found ourselves agreeing, if not in such exaggerated terms. It is amazing how different the same piece of music can sound in different atmospheres. From the first bar Norrie was smiling and by the end of side one we were all agreeing that *Joseph* was superbly sung, played, conducted, recorded and produced. It really sounded terrific and the wild acclaim given to our efforts by Norrie and his family spirited our despondency into thin air. Andrew's depression at the eleventh hour foreshadowed a habit that was to become more marked and less effectual as the years rolled by. I doubt whether he has ever written a show which he has not attempted to withhold from the public gaze at the last minute. Fortunately for his collaborators (and for him) his threats have never (as far as I know) materialised.

Novello had by now published a slim volume of the score of *Joseph* for schools. Annoyingly, it was only the original twenty-minute version and we instantly regretted not holding back with the book until after the expanded version as per the album was complete. Even more annoying, for me, was the fact that only Andrew's name appeared on the outside cover as author. When

I complained to Novello through Desmond, they replied that it was the custom only to credit the composer. This may not have worried Da Ponte or Ghislanzoni when they teamed up with Mozart and Verdi respectively, but it certainly worried me and a change was promised for the reprint, which Novello were clearly pretty confident would never be needed.

On the album though it was equal shares of glory all round. In my capacity as NP executive, I took charge of the post-production, pre-release, life of the album. We attempted to persuade Hugh Mendl, the veteran head of Decca's A & R, that our record should have a double 'gatefold' sleeve, with all the lyrics printed thereon and lots of glossy pictures of all concerned. The era of the domination of pop music by the album, as opposed to the single, was just taking hold and with every so-called progressive rock band wasting acres of cardboard with artwork and lyrics generally immodest and pretentious, we requested, immodestly and pretentiously, similar treatment. In the end we settled for a lively cover designed by Decca's in-house sleeve division, three black and white snaps of Andrew and me, of the Bag and of David Daltrey, and a lyric sheet included within the regular-type sleeve. However Derek Jewell, our distinguished supporter, readily agreed to write a sleeve note, and his kind comments gave the package a touch of class it otherwise lacked. Actually, to describe the photos as 'snaps' is very unfair to the late David Wedgbury, the photographer, whose portrait of me and Andrew in naff late Sixties clobber (I clutched a *Wisden* which we hoped would be taken for a Bible) was good enough to feature in a fascinating retrospective of his work published in 1992. It just turned out like a snap on the *Joseph* back cover.

The release of the album was scheduled for January 1969 and in the comparatively quiet time between the end of recording and its release I had plenty of other diversions, both personal and musical, to occupy the last months of 1968. Sara and I were still an item, but on occasions a tempestuous and/or rocky one. Following a delightful holiday in Malta together, where I became a reasonable water-skier, she announced she was going to New York for three months. Despite the gradual rise of *Joseph*, there had been no dramatic improvement in my economic situation and her stated motive for temporary emigration was to give me a chance to concentrate one hundred per cent on turning my promise into serious loot. She left in grand style on the final voyage of the old *Queen Elizabeth*. I had by now made good friends of her parents, Valerie and Richard, and as their invitations to me to spend any weekend I fancied at their beautiful mansion in Churt, Surrey, remained in place even without their daughter, I did not feel totally abandoned. In fact weekends *chez* Bennett-Levy were often more relaxed without emotional trauma thrown in, though physically the demands of my testosterone suffered.

Back at the NP ranch, I was entrusted with new artistic responsibility on Scaffold recordings. Their shot at the 1968 Christmas market was their adaptation of the old warhorse 'Lily The Pink'. I actually stood in for Norrie in the producer's role for one or two of the 'Lily' sessions, although Mike McGear did all the producing when Norrie wasn't around, and most of it when he was. I was roped in to sing along with the choruses, and in turn roped in Martin Wilcox, whom I had tried to involve in our work as much as possible, in gratitude for his bringing the Tales and the Bag to our attention. (Martin had played harpsichord, maraccas and acoustic guitar on the *Joseph* LP, for which he received a sleeve credit.) Martin and I actually had a bar to ourselves in the Jennifer Eccles verse of 'Lily The Pink', which verse was sung by Graham Nash, co-writer of the original 'Jennifer Eccles' hit for the Hollies, his group. I was at last mixing, on something approaching equal terms, with some important pop names, always hoping that Paul McCartney would drop in to a Scaffold session to check out how his brother was doing.

I dropped in on a Paul McCartney session before he dropped in on one of mine. The Scaffold, like the Beatles, worked at Abbey Road, and one evening I confidently strode into Studio Two, to find myself face to face with Paul. Wow! He had not only come to witness Mike in action, but he had turned up early and I was sitting in for Norrie! Overcome with inarticulateness, I found myself burbling 'Where's Martin?', meaning Wilcox, whom I had invited to attend the Scaffold session. It was only when I heard a very familiar voice emerge from behind the recording console replying, 'George isn't here yet', that I realised I was not in my appointed place. The voice was that of John Lennon and he assumed I was enquiring, in very disrespectful terms, about George Martin. Before either John or Paul could say 'Who the hell are you?' I was out of there, racing down the corridor to Studio Three. My embarrassment was acutely visible all evening, but I did not explain.

'Lily The Pink' went on to be a gigantic hit. It was Number One for a month over Christmas and the New Year, selling a million and giving the NP Organisation a terrific credibility boost. Unfortunately, as a novelty record, albeit a brilliant one, it did not herald a string of Scaffold best-sellers. I was promoted to co-producer with Norrie for the follow-up, 'Stop Blowing Those Charity Bubbles', but it failed even to creep into the Top Fifty. I was absolutely certain that anything following a massive Number One had to totter at least into the bottom of the charts, but despite Paul McCartney's guitar solo, 'Charity Bubbles' sunk. I was still hitless, in chart terms, in any capacity.

I never succeeded in finding a truly useful niche for Martin Wilcox, who had an unemployable streak. He adopted the hippie culture with an enthusiasm he seemed unable to give to the discipline of office life, even the shaky discipline of the music business. Many with limited patience misinterpreted his wish to be involved with whatever was going on as mere hanging-on, but he was a gifted, if totally unfocused, musician. He eventually moved to Brighton and dabbled in various artistic enterprises that kept the financial wolf from his door. Sad to say, diagnosed as epileptic in his early thirties, he could not keep the health wolf away and he died in 1993. The last time I saw him I fixed tickets for him and his girl friend to see Jason Donovan in the mega-glitz production of *Joseph* at the London Palladium in 1992, and he seemed a cheerful soul, enjoying his return to the show he had done much to help in its birth pangs. After his death, his brother gave me a tape of some of his wistful instrumental compositions, which deserved a wider audience.

In November we performed *Joseph* yet again, this time at the request of the Dean of St Paul's. A strange festival entitled 'Pop Into St Paul's' had been launched by the Dean, the Very Reverend Martin Sullivan, which included such items as the Very Rev himself parachuting from Wren's dome. The old team reassembled and though we felt that the third incarnation did not have quite the freshness of the previous shows, it was well received by packed pews and earned us a glowing review from Ray Connolly in the *Evening Standard*. Not every review to date had been as complimentary – a bloke named Meirion Bowen in the *Times Educational Supplement* ('Who is this rude woman?' I had angrily responded, never having come across a Meirion before or since) had not only ludicrously unfairly trashed Andrew's father's last-minute gratis contribution to our Central Hall show, but had harsh words for *Joseph* itself: 'no real dramatic structure . . . none of the tunes is exceptional'. But all in all the word was spreading, and by and large the word was good.

New Year – and the album was released. I designed and wrote the ad for the music papers and came up with the self-effacing slogan, '1969's most astounding album is here already'. Two singles were released – one taken straight from the LP of David Daltrey singing 'Close Every Door' and the other a re-recording by the Mixed Bag of 'Potiphar', an extended version as the album cut was barely two minutes long. Both flopped ignominiously and although the album sold 3000 copies in fairly quick time, nothing came near to penetrating the all-important charts. I cannot remember why we never considered the record's best and most commercial song 'Any Dream Will Do' as a single. Maybe we did not trust the lyric to make sense out of context to a public who knew nothing of the show. Novello's score was meanwhile selling tolerably well to schools but at best it looked as if we might only have written that hit Latin text book.

Chapter Thirteen

We staged a reprise Central Hall concert of *Joseph* in a desperate final bid to promote the album which had not excited much national or even musical press comment. This performance of the work was the least effective of the four we had organised to date and had it not been for the generosity of Bertie Holloway, my family's cosmetic king friend, who picked up the tab, it would have been a financial disaster. We allowed David Daltrey and his group to let rip as the support act and it is fair to say that their ear-splitting rendition of David's lengthy 'Planet Suite' did not go down as well as the more sedate classical selections various Lloyd Webbers and friends had delivered first time around.

However the album was to strike a powerful and crucial chord in an unexpected quarter. We had got to know a young singer/guitarist named David Ballantyne, a friend of a lady named Pamela Harrison who lived in the flat below the Lloyd Webbers, and he had been backed in his recent bid for pop stardom by a property tycoon called Sefton Myers. David had made a couple of heavily-promoted pop singles, and although neither had been a hit, it was clear that lack of publicity was not the reason.* We got the impression that Mr Myers was a man with a limitless source of funds which he could not wait to unload on to youthful

---

* I have seen a good deal of David over the past thirty years as he is lead guitarist with Wang and the Cheviots (see Chapter Twelve).

musical enterprises. Consequently Andrew wrote to him (without telling me) offering Myers not *Joseph* or a new songwriting team of stunning potential, but a slightly crackpot idea we had at times discussed about a museum of pop memorabilia. Presumably Andrew would have assembled Hank Marvin's first guitar, Cliff's underpants and the wreckage of Eddie Cochran's car in an emporium purchased by Sefton. Not surprisingly, this idea received the shortest of shrifts, but as Andrew had enclosed a *Joseph* album with his suggestion, Sefton Myers came back pretty pronto with a request to meet both Andrew and me.

Sefton had invested in many other hopefuls besides David Ballantyne and had to date only succeeded in being taken for several rides and in reducing his property profits. He thus formed a partnership, New Ventures, with a Wardour Street based agent named David Land whom he appointed his show business advisor, or at least con-man detector. David Land was not at that time a well-known name outside the entertainment world, but through his own agency and representation of such acts as the Dagenham Girl Pipers and the Harlem Globetrotters (when they were in England) had established a highly lucrative if low-profile operation. David Land too had made a good deal of his money in property, initially in Dagenham, where he had turned the local female bagpipe troupe into a worldwide attraction. The Dagenham Girl Pipers had even played Las Vegas.

Myers handed over Andrew's LP to Land, and at last received his colleague's rave review for something that had landed on his desk. David had been immediately taken with the album and always said that it was the line about Potiphar 'buying shares in pyramids' that clinched his conviction that New Ventures should move in. This they did by summoning the two of us to Sefton's office in Charles Street, Mayfair; Friday, 7 February 1969 thus being the date that I first met one of the most important people in my life – David Land. To our surprise we were offered a deal almost before we had sat down; what was more, a deal that promised us money. It seemed too good to be true and my initial reaction was to look for catches and to point out snags, such as Norrie Paramor and Desmond Elliott.

Sefton and David offered us £25 a week each for three years, roughly my Norrie Paramor wage of £1250 per annum. In return anything we earned from anything we wrote during that period would first go towards paying this money back. If we paid it back then Sefton and David would retain twenty-five per cent of any further income we generated. The twenty-five per cent management commission was a high one, but on the other hand they were putting money where their mouths were and furthermore by giving us the benefit of David's show-business expertise were offering quite a bit in return for their hefty cut. They also said we could have the use of an office in Sefton's building. I had noticed a very attractive receptionist called Joan. Although worried that they'd change their minds as soon as we left, we said we'd let them know.

What was, on the face of it, a pretty good offer to two unproven songwriters was the cause of the first major row between Andrew and me. Andrew, totally reasonably, was all for signing up on the spot. He was not yet twenty-one, had no job, but a burning conviction that he was a theatrical genius. I, almost as reasonably, hesitated. I had a very good job with a distinguished pop music personality, felt that at the ripe old age of twenty-four I was too old to take outlandish risks, and no strong belief that I had anything other than a lightweight ability to amuse. In a spirit of compromise we decided to try to get better terms before coming to a final decision. The New Ventures offer was sent to us in document form which meant we had to get a lawyer, absolutely essential but something we could barely afford.

Although we were both worried that daring to look this gift-horse in the mouth would instantly scupper the deal, we found legal representation – Mr Ian Rossdale of Burton and Ramsden, Piccadilly – my first return to a solicitor's office since my igno-minious exit from Pettit and Westlake, and my first ever visit to one on the client's side of the desk, a position I had innocently never expected to occupy. I was still blissfully unaware that a full-time career in the music business means a full-time relationship with armies of lawyers. Mr Rossdale ominously warned us that his help in guiding us towards a decision would be expensive, which statement paradoxically all but guaranteed that we could not afford to turn Sefton and David down. One of the first deal adjustments we requested was £500 each up front, primarily to pay for Mr Rossdale.

This and other demands were all met. It was mainly my half-hoping the deal would fall through that inspired our apparent greed. Eventually we had increased our weekly cheque to £30 a week for year one, £35 for year two, and £40 for the final year. We also managed to ensure that our wages for each year only counted against earnings for that year, i.e., if we made nothing in year one, but hit the jackpot in year two, we would not be liable to pay back the first year's pay from the second's windfall. We agreed that the deal could run for a further two years if Sefton and David wished, and for a further five after that if both sides agreed. Even I, Mr Caution, found it hard to contemplate anything that might or might not happen in 1979. New Ventures also undertook to establish at their expense that any surviving legal link (which we genuinely felt did not exist) we had with Desmond was severed. In retrospect, these were all tiny alterations as far as our prospective backers were concerned. They thought we were a good bet and would doubtless have been happy paying nearly twice as much for our signatures.

Thus, quicker than I had expected or hoped, we were now faced with putting our names to a very fair contract – and also with a 200-guinea bill from Mr Rossdale. Andrew therefore went little short of ballistic when I told him that I was still not convinced that I should sign. As if suspecting something murky was in the air, Norrie offered me a rise to £1500 p.a., plus the promise of increased production responsibilities, as a team with Nick Ingman, on recordings of artists both great and small. He hoped that Nick and I might even be able to write some songs for Cliff Richard. I hinted for the last time that maybe Andrew could be brought into the equation, but there was definitely no interest there whatsoever.

While Andrew seethed, I discussed my crisis with my parents, and with Sara Bennett-Levy's father, Richard, who had heard of Sefton Myers the celebrated property developer – and had heard nothing untoward. Richard undertook to find out what he could about David Land. He found nothing ominous whatsoever, indeed nothing whatsoever. No one I knew seemed to have any inside information on David, though most had heard of the Dagenham Girl Pipers. With great respect to an outstanding bunch of ladies, the news that I was considering signing up with their agent rather than remaining with Cliff Richard's recording manager, did not receive a hearty endorsement from my friends and family. Nonetheless my parents, not for the first time, were considerably less cautious about my prospects than I was.

My brother Jo, having read Oriental Languages at Cambridge, was now poised to go to Japan, to work for a trading company that had many personal and business connections with my father. Rice Minimus, Andy, having also completed five years at Lancing, was half way through his Cambridge career, reading Economics. The eldest son was definitely the one on the dodgy career path, apparently set on an even riskier route. But both mother and father, not to mention my ever-lively grandmother, disguised any reservations they must have had.

We weighed up the pros and cons. What had I accomplished so far, writing-wise? Of course *Joseph* was the prime achievement, but as yet a feeble money-spinner that did not seem to have much of a future. The fact it had been recorded at all owed much to Norrie. Apart from *Joseph* my writing with Andrew had resulted in one failed stage musical, two flop singles (four songs) with Ross Hannaman, one track on a staggeringly unsuccessful Sacha Distel album and the Danièle Noël EP which had shown that public indifference to our work had crossed the Channel.

Without Andrew, since the inauspicious start with 'That's My Story', I had written lyrics for a couple of B-sides for EMI losers, lyrics for an Emperor Rosko embarrassment, and words for some songs so grim that they hadn't even made it on to Sacha's album. The only solo creation of interest had been a tune (yes, a tune) I had composed for a Norrie Paramor/Nick Ingman instrumental unit called the Power Pack. But this little item, which I had romantically but uncommercially entitled 'Juliet Simpkins', merely indicated that I had even less potential as a tunesmith than as a lyricist. All in all, there was virtually no evidence to suggest a glittering songwriting future – unless I stayed with Norrie as a fully-fledged NP Organisation record producer with access to his stable of stars. And yet . . .

And yet – I handed in my notice to Norrie. I hated doing it, for he and his family had been a very kind and crucial part of my life. But something besides Andrew's pestering told me to go for it, however much it worried me that I was proving incapable of sticking in any situation for more than a year or two, and however likely it was that by 1972 we would be dropped by New Ventures. I tried not to think of unemployment at the lethally decrepit age of twenty-seven. On 17 April 1969, Andrew and I signed the deal with New Ventures (Theatrical Management) Ltd, pocketed £500 each and were taken to a celebration lunch at the White Elephant by Sefton and David. I was richer than I had ever been, even after handing over one hundred guineas the next week to Ian Rossdale.

What was that something which told me to go for it? (With hindsight it seems incredible, although Norrie's blandishments were strong, that I hesitated for even a moment.) I reminded myself just how impressed I had been with Andrew's talent the first day I had met him – a talent I had perhaps begun to take for granted after four years of modest progress together. That talent was still there and surely it just needed the right encouragement and support to thrive, items clearly not available to Andrew *chez* Paramor. It sounds grossly unfair to Nick Ingman to say this, but in writing with a less gifted composer, I could see that my own work would be unlikely to succeed. Nick's forte was (and is) as an arranger and orchestrator, in which fields he has long since prospered. Furthermore, Andrew and I had become very close friends; we spent a lot of time doing non-musical things together, from football matches to eating out – even in 1969 Andrew was regularly sending in reports to *The Good Food Guide*. We had similar senses of humour and by now a number of mutual chums. Not only that, I lived with him – the roof over my head was at stake.

I remembered a newspaper interview I'd read not long before in which Brian Jones of the Rolling Stones said that the principal reason he decided to give everything else up in favour of his unproven band was that he did not want to spend the rest of his life wondering if he could have succeeded in music – he had to know. I felt the same. Poor old Brian of course did not have a very long life ahead of him once he had made it, but when we signed our New Ventures deal his sad demise was still two months away and I never dreamed that fame and fortune could be a quick trip to the bottom of a swimming pool.

On the personal front, I was still obsessed with the sultry Sara, who was showing no sign whatsoever of returning from New York, where she had now long extended her three-month sabbatical and list of male admirers. I do not recall leading a monastic existence in her absence but it was certainly not an extravagant one. Throughout April 1969, in a desperate bid to analyse where my money was all going, I kept a record of every financial transaction, down to the last cheese roll. In the entire month I spent £93 16s 9d (£93.84) on day-to-day expenses plus a further £113 11s 4d (£113.57) on major items (Rossdale's bill plus the 1969 *Wisden* making up nearly all of this). A typical day (18 April) broke down as 8d on a cheese roll, 5d on a morning paper (presumably the *Daily Telegraph*), 2/6d on tube fares, 12/6d on lunch (which must have been quite a large one), 1/3d on magazines, 4/11d on a train fare (I don't seem to have come back) and 6d on a phone call. The entire action-packed day set me back £1 2s 9d (£1.14) and there were many more like it that month. I did splash out nearly £7 one evening for supper with Juliet. I called her in 1997 to enquire whether my reckless spending that evening had resulted in a night of passion, and if not, could I have it now? I received a dusty answer on both counts. I also note that I paid for supper with the Scaffold costing £5 13s (£5.65) on 16 April which must have been in drunken anticipation of the New Ventures cheque the next day.

Within days of signing our management deal all my doubts had disappeared. The freedom was fantastic. From dawn to dusk, and beyond, Andrew and I were able to do and write what we liked. We still would have been paid our weekly cheque even if we had absconded to the South of France, but such a dishonourable course of action never crossed our young, enthusiastic minds. David Land, already taking a day-to-day interest in everything we did, fixed us up with an office in Sefton's building in Charles Street, Mayfair, and in due course even signed a young PR man to help publicise our activities. The chap who drew the short straw in this regard was none other than Bill Heath's pal Mike Read, still a decade away from his own broadcasting fame and fortune. Mike (or Mick as I have always known him) was saddled with the task of trumpeting our talents to the world when he was quite reasonably more interested in trumpeting his own pop star ambitions. After four months and one story in the *Sunderland Echo* his services were dispensed with but my close friendship with him never has been.

The principal question facing me and Andrew was what should we do? Our first instinct was to continue in the one direction in which we had had a glimmer of success – school music. We still had a residue of a deal with Decca, who were not totally dissatisfied with *Joseph* sales and we persuaded the company to let us record a few songs with Alan Doggett's boy choir, dubbing them the Wonderschool. An interesting version of 'Bike', a number by Syd Barrett of the Pink Floyd, emerged from these sessions, together with a squeaky treatment of the Everly Brothers' 'Problems', but no one at Decca actually went as far as to suggest a release of any of the Wonderschool canon. We tried a song or two with the Mixed Bag and David Daltrey (mainly theirs not ours, or covers of old hits) but nothing worked.

Later in the year we managed to pester RCA into releasing a single we had made with a solo Doggett choirboy. One side was a new version, in a misguided bid to make the song more commercial, of 'Any Dream Will Do'. I changed the lyrics so that all references to coats and things philosophical were cut, thus destroying most of the appeal of the song. Barmy. The other side was much better, a re-working of an old Czech lullaby 'We Will Rock You'. I wrote new, rather melancholy, words of advice to the newly-born, to the well known melody,* but this too was firmly rejected by radio stations and public alike.

Alan had by now moved on to teach at the City of London School, so he suggested that we attempt a new work along *Joseph* lines for his new charges. It was obviously right that we should concentrate on our own writing rather than that of people even less

---

* My 'We Will Rock You' remains one of my favourite lyrics, sung at my son Donald's christening in 1977, and recorded again by Elaine Paige in 1982. 'Be a child while you still can/All too soon you'll be a man'.

established than we were, and we set about this fresh commission with gusto. Gusto was not enough.

The new idea (mine, I'm afraid) was the story of King Richard the Lionheart, king of England from 1189 to 1199. Although we tackled this tale with the humour and musical fizz we had given *Joseph*, and although it was another subject that would have natural appeal to teachers, combining music with English history, the story was simply not theatrically strong enough. It was too episodical and the central character not sympathetic. Richard spent most of his reign abroad on Crusades to the Holy Land, interested far more in slaughtering non-Christian foreigners than in attending to the needs of his subjects at home. The only feature of the story which had a good human slant was the devoted minstrel Blondel's European search for his imprisoned king. Love interest was limited to Richard's marriage to Berengaria, but as this was purely a political liaison, the king's inclinations in bedroom matters rarely involving females, there was little suitable romance that could be included in the story.

Come Back Richard Your Country Needs You (we went for another long-winded title) did nonetheless include some jolly tunes up to *Joseph* standard and the occasional inspired lyric, notably in a song entitled 'Saladin Days'. This was the tune that eventually became that of 'King Herod's Song' in *Jesus Christ Superstar*. In that famous incarnation of the song the most-quoted couplet is 'Prove to me that you're no fool/Walk across my swimming pool'. In 'Saladin Days' it was 'Hand me down my scimitar/Show me where the Christians are'. Even this was not the first version of this song as Andrew wrote the tune in the first place as an entry for the 1969 Eurovision Song Contest, in which Lulu triumphed in a four-way tie with 'Boom Bang-a-Bang'. The song was then called 'Try It And See'. I gave it a suitably inane Eurovision lyric, but not inane enough to make even the final fifty that year.

We performed *Come Back Richard* at the City of London School, and though both audience and participators appeared to enjoy it, once proved to be enough. We recorded only one song from the show – the title song, via a deal that David had done on our behalf with the newly independent RCA company. I was the singer. The song and its flip, a plea to Sara entitled 'Roll On

Over The Atlantic', totally unconnected with the *Richard* project, were both credited to Tim Rice and the Webber Group. The single died a death and whatever steam there had been in the whole enterprise slowly ran out. My daft obsession with this particular medieval tale did not similarly evaporate, as I was to return to the topic some thirteen years later when I re-approached the story with Blondel as the central character. Second time around the idea, now called simply *Blondel*, did make it to the West End but I was still getting something wrong as it turned out to be my first important stage flop.

Fortunately, Richard the Lionheart was not the only thought we had during our first year under the patronage of David and Sefton. We had considered the story of King David as a possible Joseph follow-up, but after writing half an introductory song, abandoned this in favour of the twelfth century. The tune Andrew produced for this briefest of ventures is now one of the best-known he has ever composed. When King David was in the frame the lyric began 'Sam-u-el, Sam-u-el, this is the first book of Sam-u-el'. Just a few months later I wrote 'Jesus Christ, Jesus Christ, who are you? What have you sacrificed?' to the same strident and unforgettable notes. Twenty-five years later I returned to King David.

We also wrote a few pop songs, but failed to get any of them recorded commercially. Norrie still had the publishing rights to some of our new material and through him the great Hank B. Marvin played guitar on one of our demo recordings. Another, a ballad entitled 'Like Any Other Day', was sung for us with great feeling by David Ballantyne, but neither of these talents helped to convince any third party to record a Webber/Rice number. In 1992, I was amazed to hear the opening bars of 'Like Any Other Day' on the radio – had David's demo at last been heard by a major star? Sad to say, no. Andrew had recycled the tune for Sarah Brightman and José Carreras. It was now called 'Amigos Para Siempre' with a lyric by Don Black and touted as the official song for the Barcelona Olympics.

Amazingly, Desmond Elliott was still hawking *The Likes Of Us* around and during 1969 we had a couple of meetings with him about this moribund show. One meeting also involved the leading impresario Harold Fielding and although nothing happened yet again, we were initially encouraged that Fielding should even spare us half an hour. We were contractually long since free of Desmond but felt that if he were mad enough to keep faith in a work that even we now considered to be seriously dated, we had nothing to lose by keeping that door open. I am ashamed to say we kept quiet about our continuing contact with Desmond, lest we fell foul of our new patrons, for they were as unproven to us as we were to them. But legally we were in the clear.

It was not King Richard, nor King David, nor pop songs, nor a resurrection of *The Likes Of Us* that finally justified our backers' faith. Nor was it any sensational improvement in the fortunes of *Joseph*. The chain of events that turned it all around began when I went to visit my old pal Mike Leander. The pop choir that he and Geoff Stephens had roped me into back in 1965 had been one of his few unsuccessful schemes. Four years later he was firmly established as one of the UK pop world's leading figures, having written, arranged or produced work with the Beatles, Paul Jones, Cliff Richard, Engelbert Humperdinck, Peter and Gordon, Marianne Faithfull, Vanity Fare, Billy Fury, his own orchestra and many more. His greatest successes of all, with Gary Glitter, were still three years away. In the summer of '69 he was head honcho of A and R at MCA Records, for whom he had recorded a version of 'Any Dream Will Do' with Joe Brown. He invited me to come up to MCA to listen and after I had expressed the obligatory enthusiasm (it was actually a good record, though in my then desperate state I would have raved about a Pinky and Perky recording of one of my songs) asked me what ever had happened to my idea to do a contemporary musical about Jesus Christ.

What idea? That was my first reaction. I hadn't discussed Jesus with Andrew. But of course, this indeed was something I had on occasion thought about over the years. Clearly I had once mentioned it to Mike and it had stuck. Ever since my stretches at both St Mary's in Tokyo and Lancing, where religious instruction, chapel and divinity had had top billing, my interest in the story of Jesus from an historical rather than from a believer's point of view had remained strong. From a very young age I had wondered what I might have done in the situations in which Pontius Pilate and Judas Iscariot found themselves. How were they to know

Jesus would be accorded divine status by millions and that they would as a result be condemned down the ages? Surely Judas was acting quite reasonably in seeing his contemporary and leader as nothing more than a man? Surely certain political considerations should be balanced against speculative spiritual ones? Not wildly original thoughts, but they had not to my knowledge been put over in any recent popular art form, with or without music. I had kidded myself for years that one day I would write a book, or a play, about the death of Jesus from Judas' point of view. Once involved in musical theatre, I actually had a plausible outlet for this idea.

Mike and I chatted more about Jesus Christ than about Joe Brown, as, with great respect to one of Britain's most entertaining musicians, has been the case on many occasions for nearly two millennia when two or three have been gathered together. Dennis Potter's television play, *Son Of Man*, had recently caused great controversy because it portrayed Jesus as part-hysteric, part-fanatic. I had not seen the play (it was the pre-video age and I still haven't seen it) but Mike had, and said that Potter's human representation of Jesus was the fascination – maybe it was the time for a musical about Jesus the man. Maybe it was. I left Mike's office inspired by an idea I had almost forgotten I had had. For some strange reason the Joe Brown record was never issued.

Chapter Fourteen

Andrew was immediately intrigued by the Jesus idea. I explained that it would be the story of Christ's last week on earth as seen through the eyes of Judas Iscariot. As the apostle who betrayed Jesus is given extraordinarily scant attention in the Gospels, bearing in mind his crucial role in the founding of Christianity, we would be able to put words into Judas' mouth without fear of being scripturally inaccurate. In other respects I was determined to be as faithful as possible to the story as per Matthew, Mark, Luke and John. We had no wish to offend or to be controversial, although we were well aware that we were entering sensitive territory. John Lennon's assertion that the Beatles were more popular than Jesus, made three years earlier, though taken out of context, had led, primarily in America, to death threats and to public burning of Beatles records. In the unlikely event of our work reaching America, or indeed anywhere beyond South Kensington, we had no wish to incur the wrath of fanatics.

We discussed possible adverse reaction with the Dean of St Paul's, who had been so enthusiastic about *Joseph*, and he assured us that our plans and approach to the subject as described by us to him were totally acceptable to any Christian who welcomed an honest challenge to, or enquiry of, the faith. His imprimatur gave us confidence, although he was certain that some feathers would be ruffled.

David Land was fairly horrified at our new wheeze ('I'm a good Jewish boy – anything but that!') but to his eternal credit told us that it was not his job to make the artistic decisions, even though ours with *Come Back Richard* had not to date been brilliant. Perhaps he thought the Jesus idea would all blow over in a few weeks and we would write something more commercial, but after he heard Judas' first song he was totally won over.

We wanted of course to write a musical, not a pop single. The first song of what we imagined was nothing more than one scene of a theatrical production was to be a tirade for Judas. As bashed out by Andrew on the piano in his salon, the number began with a deceptively simple three-chord rock verse that was suddenly taken over by a striking fanfare of a chorus whose tune was the one that Andrew had written for our extremely short-lived King David project. Memorable though this was, until we actually got into the recording studio, it was the lyric, and especially the title, that grabbed most of the attention. I found it very easy to write. I knew exactly the sort of questions I wanted Judas to ask, and by setting it in the twentieth century rather than in the first, the questions struck a strong contemporary chord. We had no idea at this stage how the song would fit into the completed show, but it was obvious it would be sung by a Judas who had somehow come back from the dead with two thousand years of hindsight.

The title was the last part of the lyric to fall into place. My first run at the chorus made no mention of 'Superstar', being simply:

> Jesus Christ, Jesus Christ
> Who are you? What have you sacrificed?

repeated twice each chorus. I had more or less settled on the rather dreary 'Judas' Song' as the title, until I saw a full page advertisement in *Melody Maker* proclaiming Tom Jones as 'The World's Number One Superstar'. I loved the word 'superstar' which seemed only recently to have been coined (though the Oxford English Dictionary lists an instance of 'super-star', with hyphen, being used as far back as 1925) and as it fitted the scansion of the hook of the chorus so perfectly, I wrote a new second couplet:

> Jesus Christ, Superstar
> Do you think you're what they say you are?

– probably the most important lines I have ever written, as far as our careers were concerned. They were at once shocking yet respectful and unforgettable. Thus the final lyric (mainly written at my parents' house one Sunday morning) read:

Every time I look at you I don't understand
Why you let the things you did get so out of hand
You'd have managed better if you'd had it planned
Why'd you choose such a backward time and such a strange land?
If you'd come today you would have reached a whole nation
Israel in 4 BC had no mass communication
Don't you get me wrong
I only want to know
Jesus Christ, Jesus Christ
Who are you? What have you sacrificed?
Jesus Christ, Superstar
Do you think you're what they say you are?

Tell me what you think about your friends at the top
Who do you think besides yourself's the pick of the crop?
Buddha was he where you're at, was he where you are?
Could Mahomet move a mountain or was that just PR?
Did you mean to die like that, was that a mistake or
Did you know your messy death would be a record-breaker?
Don't you get me wrong
I only want to know
Jesus Christ, Jesus Christ
Who are you? What have you sacrificed?
Jesus Christ, Superstar
Do you think you're what they say you are?

The title of the song was speedily changed to 'Superstar'. The word was soon to become one of the most over-used in popular culture with, very annoyingly, two other hit songs using the same title within a year of our album's release – one by the Carpenters and one by the Temptations.

So far we had just one song and a vague outline for the rest of the show, at that point called 'Jesus Christ'. Reaction from friends to the song was so positive that we thought it would be a good idea to see if we could get it recorded straight away – a hit single would make David Land's hideous task of flogging the show to a theatrical producer a little easier. Furthermore, if reaction to this one extract turned out to be overwhelmingly negative then it would be good to know early on, before we spent a year working on a doomed enterprise.

Naturally Mike Leander at MCA Records was our first port of call and he and the company's chief, Brian Brolly, a quietly-spoken, erudite (if occasionally long-winded) Irishman, were very enthusiastic. David negotiated a deal for the single, which entailed giving MCA rights to participation in every subsequent aspect of the project – album if the single hit, show if the album hit, film if the show hit. Ludicrous, we thought, but we were happy to agree as long as we could record 'Superstar'. MCA also got their hands on the publishing side of the action, i.e. control over the copyright of the actual work, as opposed to just our particular recording of it. Thus if, on some far-off date, the incredibly unlikely scenario of someone else recording all or some of our barely even started musical came about, MCA's music publishing outfit, Leeds Music, would benefit. So would we, but not as profitably as we would via any deal we could strike today. But we had little clout and 'Fifty per cent of something is better than a hundred per cent of fuck-all', as David so eloquently put it. We did however specifically exclude the grand rights, in effect the theatrical presentation rights to the score as a show. This was at Andrew's insistence and a good job for us both that MCA, a record company, did not seem to want a proportion of these.

The first thing we had to do was to find someone to sing on our single. We had no chance of persuading any established artist to do so and MCA-UK, being a very new company, had no tame in-house star who might have been suitable. I suddenly realised that the perfect singer, both in terms of availability and sheer talent, would be easy to sign – Murray Head, whose recording career had still not got off the ground since his departure from EMI in 1967. On the other hand his acting career looked like doing so as John Schlesinger was considering him for a leading role with Glenda Jackson and Peter Finch in *Sunday Bloody Sunday*. He had also just joined the cast of *Hair*, generally described in the popular press as the 'nudie' or 'drugs' musical. I had often been in contact with Murray since the 'Happy Together' fiasco that had been such a grisly end to his EMI relationship and he came to listen to Andrew and me sing 'Superstar'.

Murray did not seem to believe we were serious, but whether he did or not, he agreed to give it a go – more evidence that we had created something that was hard to ignore, whether loved or loathed, appreciated or misunderstood. Andrew had no intention whatsoever of letting anyone else muscle in on the orchestration of the song this time and began a most ambitious scoring of 'Superstar' which must have caused Brian Brolly's accountants to shudder. But Brian was genuinely committed and gave us everything Andrew wanted. In addition to a fifty-six piece orchestra and rock rhythm section, Murray was to be supported by two choirs – pop session singers and a gospel group. Most of these were booked through MCA's usual channels, but for the black choral sound Andrew wanted, we signed a Notting Hill Gate outfit called the Trinidad Singers, under the leadership of a cheerful character named Horace James. Murray recommended the perfect rock section, Joe Cocker's Grease Band, and he managed to persuade these eminent stoned heavies (without Joe) to join him in this weird experiment. We decided to return to Olympic Studios in Barnes, now one of the hottest studios in the country, thanks to the almost permanent residence there of the Rolling Stones.

Andrew delivered a most brilliant arrangement. The record began with a dramatic full-blooded orchestral treatment of the principal theme and then kicked most unexpectedly into the Grease Band's pulsating rhythm. Murray sang beautifully, with great strength and passion, as orchestra and choirs piled in around him, the pop vocalists (Sue and Sunny and Lesley Duncan) echoing his anguished cries of 'Don't you get me wrong' and 'I only want to know', the classical orchestral line-up adding all kinds of colour and mystery as the song built up to the climax of the chorus, sung by the Trinidads. The power of the music now easily matched that of the lyric and all concerned knew we had created something out of the ordinary. At one point Noel Redding, bassist with Jimi Hendrix, dropped into our studio and on hearing a bunch of gospel singers chanting 'Jesus Christ Superstar' in front of his buddies the Grease Band, left after five minutes convinced he was on a bad trip. It is hard to realise today just how astonishing such a lyric sounded in 1969.

With no other song from 'Jesus Christ' written, Andrew had a great time recording an instrumental B side which I called 'John 19:41', not a reference to Pearl Harbor as some Americans later assumed, but the chapter and verse of the fourth Gospel describing the place of Jesus' burial. The beautiful tune that was the first half of the flip side eventually became part of the finished musical, both in its orchestral form at the very end of the show, and with lyrics, as 'Gethsemane'. On this first recording, however, a frantic pub piano-dominated instrumental in 7/8 time inexplicably followed it. This side of the record was credited to the Andrew Lloyd Webber Orchestra. The principal recordings took place on 5 and 6 October 1969 at Olympic, and a few days later we went to St Barnabas' Church in Addison Road, Holland Park, to add the sound of the church's organ. Then it was back to Olympic for mixing.

Brian Brolly and Mike Leander were ecstatically happy with the results. When we apprehensively took the finished tape of 'Superstar' to Brian on 20 October and listened to it in the cold light of his office it sounded extraordinarily good. Brian played it twice and said it was quite magnificent and one of the best things he had ever heard in his music business career. This did not sound like the usual flannel and we knew it wasn't when Brian immediately began discussing promotional plans for the single. He was confident of a great reaction from radio and press. David Land was confident he could now place the whole show, albeit not yet written, with a West End producer.

MCA-UK scheduled 'Superstar' for release on 21 November. This gave the company time to plan a promotional campaign and early responses from the media were quite encouraging. The most exciting reaction came from the David Frost TV show team (David, then as now, having a great nose for anything potentially controversial), who immediately agreed to feature the song as long as no other programme featured it before they did. This was readily agreed to and the incongruous line-up that had made the recording were booked for their first live recreation of the epic (other than the fifty-six-piece orchestra, beyond even Frost's budget). The Dean of St Paul's readily agreed to write a short note for the record sleeve which we hoped would head off a lot of irate religious criticism at the pass:

> There are people who may be shocked by this record. I ask them to listen to it and think again. It is a desperate cry. Who are you, Jesus Christ? is the urgent enquiry and a very proper one at that. The record probes some answers and makes some comparisons. The onus is on the listener to come up with his replies. If he is a Christian, let him answer for Christ. The singer says 'Don't get me wrong. I only want to know.' He is entitled to some response.

The Dean also promised to consider a staging of the entire work at St Paul's.

Apart from the Frost interest, other responses were muted. One or two music papers reviewed the single, generally favourably, but although Christianity was suddenly infiltrating the pop consciousness with hits like 'Oh Happy Day' and 'Jesus Is A Soul Man' ('Spirit In The Sky', 'Let It Be' and 'Bridge Over Troubled Water' were all just around the corner) no allegedly hip music journalist saw anything of particular significance in our effort. Nonetheless, the few paragraphs we were allotted were generally kind. The music industry trade paper, *Record Retailer*, did state that this was 'possibly the most controversial record ever released', saying that 'it is a direct attack on the teachings and beliefs of Jesus Christ' but *Record Mirror* awarded the single 'chart chance' status and *Melody Maker* simply opined, 'I like this. But I don't know who it is. It's a great record.'

Radio One, the only pop station in the entire country, and Radio Luxembourg were even less moved and, with the notable exception of Alan Freeman, who played the single four weeks running on the most important radio show of the week, *Pick Of The Pops*, disc-jockeys and radio producers seemed nervous and hid behind a directive from above that perhaps this sort of thing should be handled with care, i.e. ignored.

The Frost show went ahead and sparked a mini furore. The

Daily Mirror reported that 'ITV programme chiefs will study a report today on viewers' protests over a song about Jesus Christ . . . written by former public schoolboys'. There were a couple of angry letters in the *Daily Mail*, blaming David Frost rather than us. A little half-hearted controversy fluttered around the show-biz columns for a day or two. All was going ominously quiet until a blast came from a most unexpected quarter:

BEATLE JOHN ASKED TO PLAY CHRIST

Several papers reported on 4 December that John Lennon was considering an offer to play the role of Jesus in our musical, to be presented in St Paul's Cathedral. A spokesman for John had apparently said that he was interested in the idea. Another report stated that he wanted Yoko Ono to play Mary Magdalene. This was all a total surprise to us as well as to the Dean of St Paul's, who by now must have been wishing he had not endorsed our pop single. At that time John Lennon and Yoko Ono were almost universally dismissed by the media as complete nutters. Their peace campaigning from venues such as a double bed in the Amsterdam Hilton and/or in a large bag, their support for a variety of anti-establishment causes, their drug busts, their looks, John's scandalous songs that used words such as 'fuck' and 'Christ', Yoko's films of cocks and bums and almost every utterance they made which emphasised how far John had moved on from being a cuddly Beatle (particularly his 'we're more popular than Jesus' remark), had made them little short of figures of ridicule in some minds. The idea that they could portray Jesus and Mary in a rock musical was all their birthdays come at once for the downmarket British newspapers.

The problem of course was that there was no plan to stage our show in St Paul's Cathedral, with or without John Lennon. The show wasn't even written and its first brush with the public, the 'Superstar' single, wasn't proving to be very successful. The whole Lennon saga was stirred up by the *Daily Express*, who called Apple, the Beatles' HQ, asking if John would like to play Christ. Receiving a non-committal reply from some Apple minion was enough for the paper to rush into headlines with the tale that

John was considering the 'offer'. We were on the front page, but hardly in the way we had planned, or even wanted. Still virgins as far as dealing with the media was concerned, our reaction was one of terror that we might have offended (a) John Lennon (b) the Dean of St Paul's and (c) the entire population of Britain. We issued denials, which made the front pages the following day, fearing that our musical had been laughed out of court before it had barely been started.

Certainly nothing more was heard of the St Paul's idea. After the John and Yoko farce, we returned to obscurity and faced the fact that our single did not look like leaping up the charts. It did limp into one trade paper's Top Fifty at number 39 and had sold a few thousand copies after a month, but it was 'Sugar Sugar' by the Archies and Rolf Harris's 'Two Little Boys' that really grabbed the record-buying public in December 1969.

However, Brian Brolly and his team at MCA-UK had not remotely given up on it. That team included (besides Mike Leander), a charming and funny Essex man before they had been invented named Alan Crowder, a beautiful half-Dutch baroness, Prudence de Casembroot, and Roger Watson, a former Stowe schoolboy who had been as batty as I had been about pop music since the age of ten and whose career in the music business had been strikingly similar to mine so far. He had worked at Decca, under Tony Hall, made a couple of flop singles as a singer, lived night and day for pop and pretty girls, and had now arrived at MCA-UK as A and R deputy to Mike Leander. It was a fairly incestuous line-up as Mike, Prue and Roger and their families were all friends from way back; the Chislehurst set, I gathered.

As MCA-UK was such a small company, access to any level was delightfully easy, especially as there were so few artists on their books. A visit to their high-ceilinged offices at 145 Piccadilly was like a trip to a club and Andrew and I were always received warmly by the entire staff. Other artists at MCA-UK included Leapy 'Little Arrows' Lee, the former Manfred Mann man Mike d'Abo and Paul Raven, who was fated to make records under a variety of handles such as Paul Munday and Rubber Bucket before hitting the jackpot as Gary Glitter in 1972. It was a wonderful contrast to the monolith of EMI, where getting an interview with the doorman was only marginally easier to secure than an audience with the Pope. The UK branch of MCA naturally had release rights to the American company's product, notably that of Neil Diamond.

Brian had enthused about 'Superstar' to all of MCA's operations abroad and we were slightly mollified after the British failure to hear that virtually every territory abroad intended to release the single. The most exciting news was that the parent company in America loved the record and intended to issue it in the States. Furthermore, Brian told us that he wished to take up the company's option on the recording of the entire piece, despite the disappointing reaction to date. We decided we would go away to make serious inroads into writing the rest of the show. David Land still reported no interest from the theatrical establishment in 'Jesus Christ' (as the 'forthcoming show' had been billed on Murray's single), so we began to revise our style and format of creation to suit a record album rather than the stage. This proved to be a brilliant move and, like most brilliant moves, it had been forced upon its perpetrators rather than cunningly planned.

Andrew, showing more signs of becoming an expert foodie (which was to culminate in his weekly *Daily Telegraph* restaurant review column begun in 1996) suggested that we emigrate to the Stoke Edith Hotel in Herefordshire, a recipient of great praise in *The Good Food Guide*, in order to extend our musical beyond its current length of four and a half minutes. We only stayed down there for three or four days, and spent a good deal of that time eating or looking at architecture in Hereford; but we did begin to write one or two new scenes and I began to construct a plot structure for the show. As the basic premise was the last few days of Jesus' life seen from Judas' position, Judas would sometimes be presented as a narrator, always as the central figure, which eventually and inevitably earned me brickbats for portraying Jesus in a secondary role.

In the meantime, just before Christmas, things began happening overseas – above all, in the United States. MCA executives in New York, particularly their International Vice-President, Dick Broderick, who had been at RCA in the days when Elvis Presley changed the direction of popular music, agreed most strongly with Brian Brolly's instinct that 'Superstar' was something special. MCA was then considered something of a dinosaur in the American record world, having not participated to any great extent in the Beatles-led British Invasion. They had relied on their vast back catalogue, notably in the Country and Western field, for too long. The Who and Neil Diamond were about it in their contemporary field. Elton John was soon to be their brightest star of all, but the arrival of 'Superstar' in their Park Avenue HQ encouraged many of their executives to feel that the slumbering giant might be about to lumber into action. It was given priority release on their principal, though ancient, label, Decca.

Broderick and Co. gave the single a big push as they sent it out to US radio stations and music press. The fact that MCA were so rarely behind anything vaguely modern undoubtedly helped their cause. Potential broadcasters and reviewers were more intrigued by a song with an outrageous theme than they might otherwise have been because it came from such a conservative record company. American radio in 1969 was far less formatted, in a far looser straight-jacket than it is today, and many different types of station were happy to play the record. Many who liked it did far more than just add it to their playlist. WQAM in Miami organised an entire show around the record with religious leaders in the studio and listeners were encouraged to call in to discuss the moral and religious questions raised. A Catholic priest in New Jersey used the lyrics as a basis for a sermon, announcing that 'this is exactly what the youth are asking for today'. The important trade papers *Billboard* and *Record World* each gave the record their seal of approval and very quickly it looked as if 'Superstar' was going to achieve a great deal more in America than it had in its native land.

The New Jersey priest was way off the mark when he suggested that the words of 'Superstar' articulated the most pressing concerns of American youth. American youth was more worried about scoring dope and avoiding Vietnam. There was no doubt though that our song had appeared at just the right time, when the rock and pop scene was beginning to take itself seriously. Intellectual appreciations of rock were now *de rigueur*, as exemplified by the rise of magazines such as *Rolling Stone*, and the generation who had first loved the Beatles were now six years older, still fond of the music but anxious for something a little more cerebral (plus more dope of course). Above all, the eclipse of the single by the album as the most important outlet for rock was all but complete and this was to be of huge significance for us just twelve months later.

MCA took out full-page ads in the US trade papers to plug 'Superstar'. In the Christmas issues their page read: 'On December 25th, MCA's offices will be closed in honour of Superstar's birthday'. On the last *Billboard* chart to be published in the Sixties, for the week ending 3 January 1970, 'Superstar' was listed for the first time at position 109. In *Record World* it was already at the dizzy heights of eighty-nine. The American charts! The Holy Grail! David and Sefton treated us to a celebration lunch. We felt we had made it in the Sixties by the skin of our teeth.

Chapter Fifteen

I suppose as 1970 dawned I was reasonably confident that we were on the right road but I do not recall any conviction that fame and fortune were around the corner. I still worried about what I would be forced to do in 1972 when David and Sefton had the right to drop our contract with them, but in the meantime there was no question that we were going to be very busy in the forthcoming year. Whether we would make any money was another matter and indeed it was to be another twelve months before we earned anything beyond our weekly guarantee. But when we did, it was a lot.

I was still living at Harrington Court with the Lloyd Webbers, paying Jean just £5 a week for my room, still with Andrew's granny, Molly, and John Lill as my flatmates. This cramped my style occasionally but not much for the unbelievably casual and shambolic friendliness from all generations continued to be the prevailing mood. John's star was rising fast and he was taking part in concerts and giving recitals all over the country. He would often arrive back from some far-off venue at about three in the morning whereupon he would put on Beethoven at full blast and challenge me to a game of chess (he always won). Sometimes when I returned at a slightly less wee small hour a comely companion would be waiting for his even later return (once to my surprise and delight in the bath) in which case my companionship was not required. John was also a short-wave radio ham and was liable to burst into my room at inconvenient hours with news of surfing prospects in

Brisbane or a stock market collapse in São Paulo. Molly was less likely to interrupt my nocturnal activities although in the middle of one night she roused me violently from a deep slumber to inform me that burglars were trying to break in. There was indeed a loud thumping at the door towards which I stumbled to investigate, forgetting that I was clad in only a brief T-shirt. Apparently I had told my chum Martin Wilcox that he could doss down on the bunk in the hall that night, an offer he only decided to take up at 4.30 a.m. Martin, though a fully paid-up hippie, confessed the next morning that even he was surprised to be greeted by an old lady in her nightie and me naked from the waist down.

Despite the relaxed atmosphere and ludicrously low rent I was beginning to feel it was time to move on – I could almost afford to. However Andrew beat me to it and left Harrington Court first, buying a basement flat in nearby Gledhow Gardens. Even when we were both comparatively poor, he seemed to be wealthy – I could not have contemplated purchasing any kind of property, and had been looking for somewhere to rent at around £8 a week. No. 10 Gledhow Gardens' principal features were a huge main room, perfect for Andrew's grand piano and music systems, and the close proximity of a chap named David Crewe-Read. Andrew furnished and decorated his new home with taste and not inconsiderable expense and it soon became a most congenial base for our musical and social activities.

David Crewe-Read and his wife lived on the floor above and he and Andrew soon became the closest of friends. David ran a shop called the Pine Mine and in addition to selling tables, chairs, chests and all things pine, dabbled in the art world, in which Andrew's interest was formidable. Crewe-Read was a very funny, likeable fellow, long and slim, who soon became a kind of court jester to Andrew's entourage, as well as his art advisor well into the years when Andrew had become one of the country's most important collectors. He affected a wonderfully disreputable and degenerate attitude to life (he enjoyed being referred to as Crude-Read) and Andrew, then very innocent in the ways of the world, greatly enjoyed the thought of living dangerously through David, acting the archetypal cad. But it was only a thought back then. In the early Nineties, Andrew and David had a falling-out about as

chen sink drama at the Lloyd Webbers, late Sixties, Harrington Court; *left to right*: Jean, Billy, vid Harington (no relation), Julian, John Lill, Andrew, Burmese cat.

e Dolly Dolly author – Adam Diment as Books pin-up in 1966.

Adam before the make-over, swinging from a rail with me (*centre*) and his brother Nick (*left*), as we often did in 1964.

The Shell, who had the misfortune in 1966 to be discovered by EMI's least influential and experienced record producer.

My first music business boss – the legendary Norrie Paramor. My early tasks included work with both Psyche and Petra (also pictured) and Cliff Richard. I took the first two for walks and booked recording studios for the third.

e first ever recording of a Lloyd Webber/Rice song, Olympic Studios, Barnes, 1967;
ss Hannaman (foreground) sings 'Down Thru' Summer' for EMI with Mike Leander (arranger)
d Bob Barratt (producer) in the background.

ooked daft even then – with Andrew and the 1967 *Evening Standard* Girls of the Year,
ny and Ross, at Royal Ascot. (*Evening Standard*)

The Mixed Bag – in rented leather for the *Joseph* album cover. *Left to right*: Bryan Watson, John Cook, Malcolm Parry and Terry Saunders. (*David Wedgbury*)

David Daltrey, precocious talent as singer/guitarist and composer at the age of fifteen in 1967; Andrew and I were unable to make him a star but he helped us up the ladder as the world's first ever Joseph in concert and on record. (*David Wedgbury*)

Martin Wilcox, EMI postboy, 1967, who brought both the Tales of Justin and the Mixed Bag to the original *Joseph* line-up.

th Andrew near Putney Bridge, 1968; a few days after the world première of *Joseph*, not far ay at Colet Court School, Hammersmith.

featured on the back cover of the original *seph* album, 1968; no Bible was to hand but I ely travelled without the current *Wisden icketers' Almanack*. (*David Wedgbury*)

The Scaffold, Roger McGough, Mike McGear and John Gorman – they let me sing on 'Lily the Pink', their first Number One (and thus mine too). (*The Scaffold*)

Sara Bennett-Levy, leaving me (again) – this time for New York on the *Queen Elizabeth*.

Prudence de Casembroot outside our leafy leaseho in 1970. Prudence became Mrs David Hemmings. wish I knew what happened to the Hacker Radio.

The Big Four of the first *Jesus Christ Superstar* album; *left to right*: Yvonne Elliman (Mary), Barry Dennen (Pilate), Ian Gillan (Jesus) and Murray Head (Judas).

Recording *Jesus Christ Superstar* at Olympic Studios in 1970:

Top left Alan O'Duffy the engineer;

Top right Henry McCulloch of the Grease Band;

Middle left Neil Hubbard (*left*) and the late Alan Spenner of the Grease Band;

Above (*left to right*) The Grease Band's Bruce Rowland, Alan Doggett and Andrew;

Left Mike d'Abo (*left*) and TR listening to a playback of his 'King Herod's Song'.

Working at Andrew's flat in Gledhow Gardens on *Jesus Christ Superstar*, 1970.

unpleasant as they come and David became a non-person. I take no sides.

My relationship with Sara Bennett-Levy was really struggling thanks to her ever-increasing absence from Great Britain and her involvement with an American boy friend. When she did come back home, he followed soon afterwards and it became clear, particularly after one Brian Rix-type episode in her aunt's Roehampton flat when I turned up uninvited for a showdown with Sara, unaware that my rival was there too, that I was at best in silver medal position. Sara's poor aunt spent a torrid hour hiding me in cupboards and the garage while attempting to persuade her niece to talk to me. We did eventually communicate for two minutes once my American counterpart had been, with great difficulty, persuaded to take the dog round the block but I merely learned my hopes of return to favour were slim. Sara soon went back to New York.

But I soon got over it. I had a mini-dalliance with a lovely and dotty lady called Nicola Kingdon, a promising artist whom I met in a Sussex pub. Three years later, to my absolute horror, I read of her death in a fire on a sailing boat. Her parents invited me to say a few words about her at her memorial service (I copied Mick Jagger's tribute to Brian Jones in reading an extract from Shelley's elegy to Keats, *Adonais*), which I found surprisingly cathartic on a perfect summer afternoon in the Sussex countryside. This tricky task has fallen to me more and more often as time rushes by and I always recall the ridiculously early end to Nicola's life and beauty when I am trying to speak about others who have gone. And I barely knew her.

My grandmother had moved down to St Leonards-on-Sea to live with her sister Gertie, after Uncle Arthur had died in 1957. Once, around the time when 'Superstar' first escaped, I was on a train to the coast to see her, and caught the eye of a truly beautiful young woman at the other end of the carriage. If she gets off where I get off, I'll ask her out, I thought. She did, and I did. She came from Jordan, her name was Lina. I saw her once or twice in London, with her friends who seemed equally exotic and powerful. Dark, fascinating and mysterious, she then mysteriously disappeared. Or maybe I lost her number. Like Bernstein in *Citizen Kane*, for whom not one month went by without him thinking about a girl he saw for one second on the Jersey ferry many years before, I often find myself, mainly on trains, thinking about Lina whom I hardly knew.

Much more seriously, I fell for the beautiful Prudence at MCA-UK. I have described her as a Dutch baroness, which was strictly true, but there were no windmills and tulip-clad estates to accompany her father's title, in Holland or anywhere else. Her parents were in fact both based in England, separated and as English as they come. I saw Prudence every time we went into MCA's offices to discuss the latest plans for our album and soon began going to the office whether or not we had any plans to discuss. I also became very good friends with Roger Watson. Soon I was seeing more of my new MCA colleagues outside the office than in and *Superstar* became a project that mattered nearly as much to Roger and Prue as it did to me.

Prudence and I decided to take the major decision of looking for a flat together. This upped the going rate for the maximum rent I could afford and by April we had taken up residence in a mews near Queensgate, in a quaint cellar named Jasmine Cottage. Another basement, but nothing on top of it and from the outside it did manage a passable impression of a country cottage, though once through the front door the only way was down. It was damp and basic, and no television ever worked in its murky depths, but we brightened its atmosphere to just the right side of gloomy and had a very enjoyable few months there during the hot summer of 1970. We even had a cat.

My parents' lives were also undergoing considerable upheaval. After nearly twenty years, they left Popefield Farm. We were all very sad to see the end of Popefield as the family home, but the sons had left and my father, at the age of fifty-two, felt it was about time he owned his own house. My father also changed jobs, leaving Hawker Siddeley to join Wheelock Marden, a company based in Hong Kong. They were a major engineering and trading corporation whose projects at the time included finance and construction of the Hong Kong Harbour Tunnel. My father was to head the London office but would obviously have to make regular trips out to the Far East. The change meant a welcome boost in income which in turn enabled my parents to buy (with mortgage) a house close to a golf course just outside Harpenden, on East Common, where my mother still lives today. We all knew Harpenden pretty well, thanks to Aldwickbury prep-school days. Jo was continuing to prosper in Japan, and had announced his engagement to my school friend Henry Speer's sister, Jan. She had shown great enterprise in following him out there, having taken a crash course in London in teaching English to Japanese, after successful completion of which she was flown out to put her new expertise into practice. The wedding was scheduled for later in the year in Japan, and I was hoping that someone's budget would stretch to getting me out there. Andy, who was just about peaking at six foot seven, towering over his mere six-foot-four brothers, was coming near to the end of his time at Cambridge.

These dramatic domestic matters however took second place to *Superstar*. Andrew and I had not really made a great deal of progress during our gastronomic-cum-creative jaunt to Herefordshire and we only really began to get into the writing of the final ninety-five per cent of the album by January 1970. In the meantime there was unexpected good news from abroad; not only was the single continuing to potter up the US charts, it was also breaking big all over Europe and even in more remote territories. All around the world sales of the single were booming – only in our homeland did Murray's record appear dead and buried. Brian Brolly's faith in our project was being amply justified, albeit a long way from 145 Piccadilly.

In the States, MCA were forced into an even more aggressive marketing and promotion campaign, thanks to the issue of a rival version of the song by a band named Silver Metre. This was an outfit fronted (or rather behinded, as he was the drummer) by celebrated British session veteran Mick Waller, who had cut their first, and as far as I can tell only, album in London during late 1969. The engineer was none other than the bloke who had given us a hard time recording *Joseph*, Roy Baker, who presumably was not the chap who suggested that Silver Metre cover *Superstar*. Their treatment was a pretty sparse one compared to Andrew's mega-arrangement, but their American record company decided to rush it out as a single once Murray's version began to make a little noise there. This galvanised MCA into serious action, a memo of 26 January from their promotions chief to the entire Decca label sales force reading:

> Whatever you've done in the past to obtain airplay exposure for our 'Superstar', I want you to triple your efforts now. That means each and every salesman and promotion man . . . I want this record carried in your car and played on every call that you make. I won't tolerate any account calling me and saying they haven't 'Superstar' in stock.
>
> GENTLEMEN I HAVE NO INTENTION OF LOSING THIS RECORD TO ANY COMPANY. YOU MUST RUN AND RUN HARD. I WANT THIS RECORD BROUGHT HOME!

Silver Metre's label's memo to its sales force was even less delicately phrased:

> Have your stations play them back to back – and *we* will get the airplay!! There *will* be CASH offered on Silver Metre.

Fortunately this blatant bribe failed to deliver the goods for Silver Metre's label, ironically, in view of the song's subject matter, a division of the Buddah record company. But though the threat of some other mob stealing our thunder had subsided, Murray's single still struggled to make really significant headway. Many stations, fearing the wrath of listeners and advertisers, were unwilling to play it and though we stayed on the Hot 100 for three months, we never got beyond seventy-fourth place.

Elsewhere we did a lot better. In Holland, apparently first becoming a major item in the gay bars and discos, the single rocketed up the charts to the very top, leaving even the current Led Zeppelin and Elvis singles in its wake, and Belgium dutifully followed suit. (I was not thrilled to note that on the initial pressings of the Dutch 'Superstar' single my name was printed as 'Tim Arce'.) In both Australia and New Zealand, 'Superstar' made the Top Ten, and in the even less likely Brazilian market we enjoyed another Number One. Had all these sales been in Britain, they would have been ample to give us a very big hit indeed. None of this brought us in any instant cash – songwriting royalties from foreign territories are notoriously slow to materialise. We had signed our copyright over to MCA's music publishing arm, Leeds Music, and requests for an advance were pointless as any we might have obtained would simply have gone (quite rightly) straight to Sefton Myers and David Land.

So we got on with the show. Two tunes we had already used in flop ventures were resurrected (how I wish lyrics were as easy to recycle), that of our Eurovision reject 'Try It And See', which had then briefly become 'Saladin Days', now wound up as 'King Herod's Song', and 'Kansas Morning' which was utterly transformed when it was turned into 'I Don't Know How To Love Him'. 'Kansas Morning' had been a pop song we had written back in 1966 under our deal with Southern Music, who were unable to persuade anybody to record it. From the period when Andrew was paying more than indirect homage to classical composers in general, and to Mendelssohn in particular, the beautiful melody kicked off with a striking resemblance to the opening phrase of the second movement of Mendelssohn's Violin Concerto in E minor before moving off into true ALW originality. In its first incarnation (Andrew's that is, not Felix's) I lumbered the melody with truly awful lyrics. Noting that plenty of hits of the time featured American place names ('Massachusetts', 'Lights Of Cincinnati', etc.) I concocted a complex storyline about a bloke in prison in Maine, dreaming of his home in Kansas. Maine was chosen because it rhymed with 'brain'.

> I love the Kansas morning
> Kansas dawn comes to greet me
> Kansas winds
> Shift and sigh
> I can see you now, we're flying high
> Kansas love of mine
> I long for Kansas morning
> Kansas mist at my window
> And the birds

> Those lazy birds
> Sing their wordless songs of love again
> Kansas on my brain
> I'm trapped in Maine

And there was more, but's that's quite enough. I occasionally sing this original version of 'I Don't Know How To Love Him' during talks or after-dinner speeches and it always goes down superbly – as a very funny example of abysmal songwriting. There is usually some wise guy at these functions who points out that there are plenty more examples from the Rice canon that have actually been inflicted upon the public as finished masterpieces. David Land had to buy the rights of 'Kansas Morning' back from Southern Music which he did for £100. Southern must have been delighted to have made so much from one of the most dire songs in their catalogue, but of course it was only the words that were dire. Version two of the song has gone on to earn literally hundreds of thousands of pounds, maybe more, to the great benefit of Leeds Music as well as of us. This episode shows how even a first-class melody can be dragged down by bad words. None of us (except possibly Andrew) really appreciated the potential of the tune. I didn't realise just how great it was until I managed to demonstrate it with decent lyrics.

We were unable to purchase 'Try It And See' back from Norrie Paramor's publishing company. MCA reluctantly accepted that one song in the show would not be their copyright and NP Music in due course did very well indeed from hanging on to their Eurovision tune. As Norrie's company also retained a copyright interest in *Joseph*, my brief time in his employment ultimately proved very profitable for my ex-boss. Confusingly, on American versions of *Superstar*, 'King Herod's Song' was often listed with its original title alongside and on several occasions US interviewers asked me about the artistic significance of this intriguing subtitle, only to receive a boring answer about music publishing.

The bulk of what we were now calling *Jesus Christ Superstar*, which was clearly a terrific title, was written in the first three months of 1970. It was more or less written in the right order, i.e., first songs first, with tune preceding lyric throughout. Before the tune for each scene was written or selected, Andrew had a fairly clear idea of what I wanted to say in that scene, maybe a title but no final lyrics. This was the way we had constructed *Joseph* and the way we would write *Evita* – plot, music, lyrics – Andrew's music the meat of the sandwich between my story and my words.

Although we knew we were writing something for a record album, we still felt that our ultimate aim was the theatre. Consequently we originally entertained the idea that the show would have a considerable amount of spoken dialogue between each number. This however would be absolute death on a record, unlistenable to after one hearing, however good the songs might turn out to be. We decided that for the album only, we would write the piece in operatic form, i.e., tell the entire story through song and music, and even after we had completed the recording, still thought it possible that we would have to alter huge chunks of it in order to accommodate spoken scenes for a stage version. Ditching the book turned out to be a masterstroke (just as issuing the score on record before the show existed proved to be), though impelled upon us by circumstances and never a conscious artistic decision.

Because we had to cram everything into just under ninety minutes (Brian Brolly had sanctioned a double album which gave us a maximum of twenty-two to twenty-three minutes a side of vinyl) we were far more concise than we would have been writing directly for the stage. I am certain that if we had written *Jesus Christ Superstar* for the theatre in the first instance, it would never have been a hit. It would have been long-winded, with dialogue continually interrupting the flow of the music, and would never have had the dynamic bang-up-to-date arrangements that we knew were vital for record success. Every musical is ten minutes too long (indeed everything in life is ten minutes too long) but the ten superfluous minutes in *Jesus Christ Superstar*, whichever ones they are, are not boring. The show started with a bang – no conventional overture hacking out the main tunes, but an exciting rock instrumental that eventually reappeared with words as the trial before Pilate. *Superstar* got on with it from bar one and never let up. It had to be different from the run-of-the-mill musical because of the constraints of the gramophone record, and those limitations constituted one of the main reasons for its sensational success.

The basic storyline was not one of my major problems – I had no intention of taking any liberties with the plot. After all, Jesus could hardly be let off by Pilate for a happy ending. I used no books other than the four Gospels (guided principally by John's Gospel), apart from *The Life Of Christ* by Fulton J. Sheen. This important work by a celebrated American Catholic bishop was written from a committed Christian viewpoint and was invaluable in making much of the political and historical background of the story clear to me. Where I was on my own was in the words and motivations of Judas Iscariot. What did he think about Jesus as God? How could he go along with such a staggering concept when he knew Jesus so well as a man, an extraordinary man, a good man, a great man, but surely no more than that? What did God think about Judas? As Bob Dylan had put it so brilliantly:

> Now I can't think for you, you'll have to decide
> Whether Judas Iscariot had God on his side

Seeing the magnificent Paul Jones sing 'With God Our Side' on a TV pop show with Manfred Mann in 1965 had made a great impact upon me, refuelling my schoolboy interest in this follower of Jesus who is eternally damned, perhaps simply because he had the bad luck to be around at the time. But without his betrayal, where would Christianity be? Judas' point of view had to be that the man he admired as a Jewish leader was in danger of bringing the wrath and murderous power of the Roman occupiers down upon the Jewish people because he was allowing his followers to get out of control, encouraging them to believe the unbelievable. So Christ in *Superstar* is seen only as a man, because Judas saw him only as a man. But even Judas has his doubts; before his suicide, flailing desperately, accusing Jesus of bringing about his death – perhaps Jesus was God! Perhaps he was, but in *Superstar* the question is left open.

My view of Judas was not original, although I had drawn my own conclusions. After *Jesus Christ Superstar* had become a hit album, I was both congratulated and cricticised for basing my work so closely on Nikos Kazantzakis's *The Last Temptation Of*

Christ, which I have still not read (though I have owned a copy since 1972). *Jesus Christ Superstar* was always intended to be a much more serious piece than *Joseph*, although we wanted it to be very contemporary. It had to be as we were going down the record route. I attempted to write words that could have stood on their own without the music, deliberately conversational rather than poetic for the most part. I still came up with several false rhymes, which annoy me now, but attempts to eliminate most of these, when Andrew staged a West End revival of the show in 1996, didn't actually make much difference. Indeed one or two *JCS* fans complained to me about the changes; for example I altered a priest's line from 'One thing I'll say for him Jesus is cool' to 'Infantile sermons – the multitude drools' in order to rhyme with 'Miracle wonderman, hero of fools', and received a letter from a young friend of my son suggesting that the entire flavour of that scene, if not the first act, had been lost. Sometimes technique is less important than a visceral approach.

Although *Joseph* type jokes and pastiche were by and large out of the picture, I wanted the words to have moments of light, if not daft, relief. Most of the characters in the action were not, after all, sophisticated dilettantes but rough or conniving peasants (including Jesus himself), soldiers or murky figures of crude authority. There would be little room for 'Baubles, Bangles and Beads' or 'You're The Top'. The leavening of the basically heavy and tragic (to put it mildly) story with humour and colloquialisms was an essential ingredient.

Only with the words of 'I Don't Know How To Love Him' did I venture into conventional Broadway territory, and the same was true for Andrew's music, although this was more a matter of presentation in his case. Many of his superb tunes in *Superstar* could, and subsequently have, worked just as strongly with a more conventional stage musical treatment. However, had they first been presented to the world in that way they would not have made the impact they did. I believe that Andrew barely put a foot, or note, wrong when he wrote the music of *Superstar* and, as had been the case with Murray's first single, his orchestrations were flawless and ensured that the work was never boring, no matter what the singers were ranting on about.

Consider the following melodies: 'I Don't Know How To Love Him', 'Heaven On Their Minds', 'Hosanna', 'Pilate's Dream', 'King Herod's Song', 'Gethsemane', 'Everything's Alright' and 'Superstar' itself. A stunning line-up, with another fifteen supporting them, which would have graced any show written in Britain or America since the war. This is more obvious to me nearly thirty years later than it was at the time, and is even getting through to the odd critic these days. Yet, immodestly, I am pretty sure that they needed an attention-grabbing setting and words that hit home quickly and directly for the unknown composer's talent to become recognised. The title alone of the show they were part of was enough to grab that attention in 1970, and the straightforwardness of the words was the final guarantee of their longevity.

Nothing of this analysis crossed our minds as we wrote. We were simply trying to tell an old story in a new way, and to write what we would have enjoyed if someone else had written it. We also wanted to get on with it, as we were worried that MCA would change their minds and pull the plug on the whole thing, despite the number of Brazilian record-buyers on our side.

Chapter Sixteen

A further pressure on our time (MCA wanted the double album for autumn release at the latest) was the fact that we had to find a cast to record it. This would inevitably entail considerable financial outlay and a lot of business hassle, which would necessarily be the province of David Land. We did not have a budget as such for the album, nor any money up front. MCA-UK merely agreed to meet all the bills as they came in. Whatever the final cost of the recording was, it would be considered our 'advance' payment, which would be deducted from our eventual royalties from sales, if any. We were already around £1500 in the hole for the single and anticipated something over £10,000 would be needed for the album, tiny sums in today's recording climate but hefty indeed for us to contemplate back then. Bearing in mind we were also in debt to David and Sefton, dreams of a dramatic improvement in my economic status, even if *Superstar* were to be a hit, were fading. I preferred not to work it out to the last cent, but we were only receiving a paltry five per cent royalty between us for producing the record, out of which percentage we had to cover all costs, including fees and royalties to other artists. Worse, this royalty would be halved overseas, where so far the only interest in our project had materialised. It seemed that the album would have to sell in Beatle-type proportions for Andrew and me to lurch into the black.

We already had Murray and the Grease Band in tow which solved the crucial problems of Judas and the rock rhythm section.

Murray opted for a royalty which would hit our five per cent take sometime in the future, but at least added nothing to the immediate costs. The Grease Band wanted session fees, noting that a double album on which they appeared on virtually every track would keep the readies coming in for weeks, very handy as they had no Joe Cocker work at the time. The performers we subsequently signed were keener to take a fee rather than a royalty, reckoning that a bird in the hand was vital, seeing that this was a wacky project in the hands of two unknowns, highly unlikely to sell. We tried to persuade most artists to take a royalty, as this would cost us nothing at all at this stage. Several who settled for a couple of hundred quid at the time were more than a little miffed seven million double albums later.

The Grease Band consisted of Bruce Rowland (drums and percussion), Alan Spenner (bass), and Henry McCulloch and Neil Hubbard (guitars), augmented by two non-Greasers, Peter Robinson (piano) and a former member of Murray Head's old band, the Blue Monks, Chris Mercer (tenor sax). Their performance was consistently scintillating, intense and exciting. Operating in a permanent haze of marijuana from dawn to dusk, their attitude to the project changed from friendly tolerance to genuine enthusiasm, with Bruce in particular taking a great interest in the overall master plan and making many invaluable arrangement suggestions. They had probably never worked with two such determinedly straight producers before and although we politely rejected all their offers to partake of their inexhaustible supply of dope, I was certainly fascinated by their tales of life on the road (they had played at Woodstock) and of the rock'n'roll lifestyle that we had never sampled at first hand. The Grease Band could never really understand how we could be making such a hip record without any of the correct cultural (i.e. drug) qualifications. Maybe if we had turned on, the record would have sold fourteen million.

MCA helped us in our search for a Jesus and our quest eventually came to the attention of Tony Edwards, a music entrepreneur who was just about to relaunch Deep Purple with their new line-up, including former Episode Six singer Ian Gillan. Tony came to see Andrew and me with tapes of one of his clients, whose voice was closer to that of Andy Williams than to the kind of wild vocal gymnastics we were after. Once Tony realised that this was a rock score rather than a Broadway one he returned smartly with a tape of Deep Purple's forthcoming 'Child In Time'. We had not heard Ian Gillan's voice before, but it only took a few seconds for us to realise that he was right up our alley, just as Tony Edwards had very quickly realised, probably more than we did, that *Superstar* was a project with enormous potential. Ian thus got the part of Jesus – and a royalty.

For Pontius Pilate we wanted a more conventional, older voice. Don Norman, a jazz world fixer and booker, friend and agent of the sublimely gifted but doomed sax player Tubby Hayes (heroin), had been recently employed by David Land to act as a kind of day-to-day manager for us as our work load increased. Don suggested the famous American jazz vocalist, Jon Hendricks, at that time in London, might be the answer. We had of course heard of Hendricks (or more precisely the distinguished vocal trio Lambert, Hendricks and Ross of which he was 33.33 per cent) and Andrew went down to the Pheasantry Club in Chelsea one night to hear Jon Hendricks in action. I can't remember why I didn't go but at around one in the morning I was roused by an excited Andrew on the phone, urging me to come down to the club at once because he had 'found Mary Magdalene'. He certainly had. As warm-up act to Hendricks, a young Japanese-American singer named Yvonne Elliman, still in her teens, was performing in her first London engagement, and she was magical. We had already recorded trial versions of 'I Don't Know How To Love Him' with other ladies without any success but we didn't even have to get Yvonne into a studio to know she was perfect for the part. Her manager, a rather aggressive lady, absolutely refused to consider the possibility of a royalty and insisted on a straight fee of £100, way above the going session rate. We agreed to this outrageous demand because Yvonne was so good, which saved us many thousand of pounds in the years ahead. Or rather it would have done, had we not been really decent about it. Her contribution was so significant, especially as both her tracks became hit singles, we decided a year or two later unilaterally to pay Yvonne a royalty. By this time her manager was doubtless earning some other innocent newcomer £100 somewhere.

Yvonne's career was helped by *Superstar* in ways other than financial, for she went on to play Mary Magdalene on Broadway and in the film. Through us she met Robert Stigwood, and through him the Bee Gees, leading in turn to a very strong run of hit records in the Seventies. The only other performer to progress from original LP to stage to film was Barry Dennen, whom we signed as Pilate after Hendricks showed no interest in the concept of Jesus and rock. Barry was an American singer/actor based in London, introduced to us by Murray Head. Barry was absolutely right as the cynical, weak, bewildered Pilate, a mature contrast to the rockers. Mike d'Abo, still on MCA-UK's books in his quest to carve out a solo post-Manfred Mann career, was roped in to sing King Herod. Of all the original *Superstar* team, Mike is the one I am closest to today, in part because of our mutual love of cricket. He is now very successful as a broadcaster, and as a performer with both the revived Manfreds and his own Mighty Quintet, although I feel his great talent as singer, pianist and songwriter has never quite received the acclaim he deserves.

Johnny Gustafson, an original member of Liverpool's legendary Big Three beat group, and subsequently a player with a variety of heavy outfits ranging from Atomic Rooster to Roxy Music, came to us via Grease Band connections and sang the Simon Zealotes song. Among those rounded up by MCA to fill in some of the minor roles was Paul Raven, still not quite Gary Glitter. Ex-Mixed Bag leader Terry Saunders even got a line and I also had my moments at the microphone, interpreting the part of a decrepit passer-by in 'Peter's Denial' with suitable croakiness, and as the odd leper.

Alan Doggett conducted; the vast orchestra Andrew continued to require featured the strings of Malcolm Henderson's City of London Ensemble, and the Olympic studios engineer entrusted with our creation was Alan O'Duffy, a tall, young, bearded, softly-spoken Irishman, whose contribution was massive. We were working with what then seemed state-of-the-art technology (we proudly asserted on the sleeve that we had used 'sixteen-track tape', although we actually used a sixteen-track recording machine – tape does not have a pre-assigned tracking facility) and Alan's mastery of every knob, plug and fader was crucial. He also had considerable musical know-how and a fascination with the angle my version of the story was taking. We discussed words and music with Alan as much as we talked about the nitty-gritty of recording technicalities.

After Andrew's quirky, arresting Overture, half wildly orchestral, half pure driving Grease Band, Judas' opening manifesto, 'Heaven On Their Minds', emerges ominously. An introductory verse ('my mind is clearer now') builds in intensity until the tune proper kicks in. A middle section in 7/8 time is a wonderfully ear-catching jolt and the piano by the end is truly flying.

> I remember when this whole thing began
> No talk of God then – we called you a man
> And believe me, my admiration for you hasn't died
> But every word you say today
> Gets twisted round some other way
> And they'll hurt you if they think you've lied

This track worked out so well, with Murray in majestic form, that we thought it might be worth mixing ahead of the rest in order to get a second single released immediately, particularly in the United States, where the first one had only just dropped off the Hot 100. Having had US airplay of 'Superstar' restricted because of the lyrical content, I very stupidly decided to rewrite parts of 'Heaven On Their Minds' purely for the proposed single version and Murray recorded the song all over again with lines such as:

> Crazy people in control, laughing weeping dancing souls
> You would think that rock'n'roll's all that we do
> Never time to catch a breath – fighting, lying, dying, death
> Death . . . death . . . nothing is true

Even if these and other lines had been (a) good and (b) not deeply depressing, it was really foolish of me to forget that the airplay that we had achieved with 'Superstar' was precisely because of the lyrical content, not despite it. MCA did release 'Heaven On Their Minds' in the States, but very half-heartedly and it sunk without trace.

After Judas' initial statement, the Apostles, portrayed throughout the work as John Lennon had described them in his notorious Jesus interview, as 'thick and ordinary', launch into 'What's The Buzz', a phrase I don't think I invented, but if I did I wish I hadn't. While I maintain that most of the words in *Superstar* have not dated a great deal, it's hard to deny that 'What's the buzz' is hardly common linguistic currency these days, if it ever was. But the mercifully short song is a suitably simplistic chant for the blinkered disciples and is soon interrupted by a blazing argument between Judas and Jesus, ostensibly about Mary Magdalene.

JUDAS
It seems to me a strange thing, mystifying
That a man like you can waste his time on women of her kind
Yes I can understand that she amuses
But to let her stroke you, kiss your hair, is hardly in your line . . .

JESUS
Who are you to criticise her? Who are you to despise her? . . .
I'm amazed that men like you can be so shallow thick and slow
There is not a man among you who knows or cares if I come or go!

This brief but explosive clash is then stifled by Mary Magdalene's first major scene, 'Everything's All Right'. In irresistible 5/4 time, this very straightforward song is a highlight of the album, and of my entire work with Andrew. The lyrics sung by Mary are pretty simple – pretty and simple – but very effective:

> Try not to get worried, try not to turn on to
> Problems that upset you – oh
> Everything's all right, yes, everything's fine
> And we want you to sleep well tonight
> Let the world turn without you tonight
> If we try, we'll get by so forget all about us tonight

I find it difficult to be so uncomplicated today. Some director would have got hold of me and gone on about motivation and dramatic arcs. Yet all I wanted Mary to say was 'relax, don't worry' and that's all the song says. Or Mary's part of it anyway. In between her sweet major-key verses the argument continues between Judas and Jesus in minor-key tension. More weighty themes are briefly tackled: Judas' distress that his leader is dissipating their funds, which could have been given to the poor, on ointment; Jesus' resignation that the poor will always be around – but he will not be. The entire five minutes holds together as a most catchy and seductive song, of which the last two minutes are nothing more than a long, long fade repeating the final phrases of Mary's verse. We just didn't want it to end, though in subsequent stage versions Andrew had to give the number a big ending rather than let it drift away. I have always loved pop records that faded as I feel I could hang on to the song just that little bit longer than even the creators intended and let it go when I wanted it to end.

Throughout *Superstar* Jesus gets little chance to demonstrate any of the power or charisma that earned him such devotion and the belief that he could be the Son of God, but then I had the luxury of assuming that most of my potential listeners would know what had happened before his last week of mortal existence. Some have said that the work fails because the Jesus of *Superstar* is never seen to be capable of the inspiration that led him to be considered divine, but even if they can't take that as read, it is Jesus as a man facing death who is the protagonist in *Superstar*. He is greater because, whether God or not, he had human failings and fears, and these must have dominated his final days on earth. Were he simply God, his suffering would have been non-existent.

After establishing (I hoped) the three main good guys of the piece (or at least sympathetic guy in Judas' case) we switched to introducing the bad guys. In the first instance this meant Caiaphas and the High Priests, terrified lest Jesus' popularity should lead to an uprising against the occupying Romans, in turn bringing about an end to the tolerance that Rome showed to the Jewish religion and customs. Caiaphas, a bass man, portrayed with rumbling malevolence by Victor Brox on our record, leads his motley crew of holy leaders (including me as Priest Two and the future Gary Glitter as Priest Three) in an almost comic number which yet manages to convey an aura of sinister panic as the crowd sing 'Jesus Christ Superstar' outside. On stage most directors have played this one for black laughs.

> ANNAS
> Listen to that howling mob of blockheads in the street
> A trick or two with lepers and the whole town's on its feet . . .

And:

> PRIEST 3
> What then to do about this Jesusmania?
> ANNAS
> How do deal with the carpenter king?
> PRIEST 3
> Where do we start with a man who is bigger
> Than John was when John did his baptism thing?

There were also references to Jesus being 'cool', a 'miracle wonderman' and being 'top of the poll'. I even managed to squeeze in a nod to one of my favourite pop hits of the year before, Creedence Clearwater Revival's 'Bad Moon Rising' with Caiaphas' line 'I see bad things arising' but no one noticed that.

Next came an upbeat choral number 'Hosanna', the crowds praising Jesus as he rode into Jerusalem on Palm Sunday. Its nonsense chorus of 'Hosanna, Hey-Sanna, Sanna Sanna Ho . . .' was a straight pinch (lyrically) of the style of 'Good Morning Starshine', one of the magnificent songs from *Hair*, which chorus contained the immortal words 'giddy glup glooby, nibby nabby nooby, la la la lo lo'. Caiaphas attempts to break up the party:

> Tell the rabble to be quiet, we anticipate a riot
> This common crowd is much too loud
> Tell the mob who sing your song that they are fools and they
>   are wrong
> They are a curse, they should disperse

A pity that I had already used the crowd/loud rhyme in 'Heaven On Their Minds'. Jesus points out to Caiaphas that his quest for silence is a lost cause:

> If every tongue were still the noise would still continue
> The rocks and stones themselves would start to sing

before leading an ebullient reprise of the chorus himself, the only moment in the entire work where Jesus appears relaxed and in total control of the situation. For the stage version a year later, we added a second verse and chorus for Jesus to make a little more of his moment of triumph, and to prolong the choreographic possibilities of the scene.

'Hosanna' leads into Simon Zealotes' rabble-rousing call to Jesus and his followers to turn their spiritual crusade into a political one. John Gustafson made the most of his one solo spot, investing Simon's driving rock aria with real frantic tension, alternating with the self-seeking yells of the mob who miss the Zealot's point entirely:

> Christ you know I love you
> Did you see I waved?
> I believe in you and God
> So tell me that I'm saved

Simon's plea that they should use their numbers to overthrow Roman occupation elicits only a resigned reaction from Jesus who sings a gentle lament for Jerusalem, prophesying the city's downfall and linking it to his own:

> If you knew all that I knew my poor Jerusalem
> You'd see the truth but you close your eyes
> While you live your troubles are many, my poor Jerusalem
> To conquer death you only have to die, you only have to die

I remember being particularly pleased with the last line of the above verse, despite the false rhyme of 'eyes' and 'die', but although my brother Jo ventured the opinion that it was the best line in the show, it has signally failed to make any impression on dictionaries of quotations ever since. The *Superstar* couplet that has hit the quote books was a throwaway gag about a swimming pool. In 1996, I changed 'but you close your eyes' to 'but you live a lie', which at least corrected the rhyme.

Continuing with the 'Poor Jerusalem' melody, we next introduced Pontius Pilate relating a disturbing dream, which in the Bible is credited to his wife. However introducing another character for just one brief scene was impractical, mainly for economic reasons, so we had no At Home With The Pilates number. Pilate is simply seen and heard in no particular time or place, struggling to understand his vision of a meeting with a 'a Galilean, a most amazing man' whose ultimate fate seems to be sad, and Pilate's fault. Pilate's one troubled appearance in the first half of the show makes his second-half dialogue with Jesus infinitely more powerful, and his Dream is one of the best tracks on the album, understated and sensitively delivered by Barry Dennen.

Around this point in the proceedings, we wrote a comic song sung by Jesus, to the tune that King Herod was to use later, in which Our Lord viciously condemns a fig-tree to permanent barrenness. This incident is recounted in Mark, chapter 11, and seemed to us to be an opportunity to show something of Jesus, the frustrated human being, capable of being annoyed by trifling earthly inconveniences such as being unable to find fresh figs. However the words of the song we wrote seemed hopelessly out of character with the rest of Jesus' pronouncements, and the tune unsuited to his character (but not to Herod's), so I decided to use the scene with the lepers, the lame and the poor to illustrate Jesus, the man, flying off the handle. I recall the fig-tree song being rather funny but I've lost the lyric.

The choral sequences in the Temple, when Jesus flings out the money-changers, and immediately following, when he is beset by beggars and paupers, the ill and the deformed, are not the strongest words and music in the piece, but had a dramatic pace that always worked well on stage. In fact some of the lyrics were little short of ridiculous, notably 'see my tongue I can hardly talk', which in every theatrical presentation for the following twenty-six years was inevitably sung by an actor with beautiful diction and projection that hit the back of the upper circle with spine-tingling clarity. For the 1996 revival I changed this howling error to 'see his tongue, he can hardly talk' – not that anyone had ever complained or even noticed the impossibility of the original statement.

After Jesus finally shakes off the multitudes clamouring for a miracle, he is comforted by Mary Magdalene, with a short reprise of 'Everything's All Right' and then, as he sleeps, she sings 'I Don't Know How To Love Him'. Andrew's arrangement for this first recording of what was to become a standard was brilliantly subtle. He wheeled in an instrument known as a Positive Organ, which the *Oxford Companion to Music* describes as an organ of fixed position, not easily moved. Although not a massive instrument, it was indeed quite a job to get this contraption into Olympic Studios, but the breathy pipe sound coaxed from it by Peter Robinson justified the removal costs. The Grease Band in gentle mood played quite superbly, notably Henry McCulloch on acoustic guitar. Although the full sweep of a string section dominated the brief instrumental reprise of the bridge, the feeling throughout the track was one of quiet passion – less was more. Yvonne was wonderful and it sounded like a standard, if not a pop hit, from the first few bars. 'Kansas Morning' had made a remarkable recovery.*

I wrote the lyric to 'I Don't Know How To Love Him' in maybe just two or three hours at my parents' dining room table in Harpenden. Normally, love songs are the hardest to write, taking weeks, primarily because everything has been said so many times before, but also because the choice of vocabulary is much more limited than it would be in a novelty, humorous or unromantic number. Slang, puns and smart-arse gags are usually unsuitable too. By and large, the number of syllables a lyricist is given to express his passion is fewer when he is working with a potential ballad than with an uptempo melody, so every word has to get straight to the point. The lyricist has to be extremely concise – no room to ramble down entertaining sidetracks. All these

---

* The morning after I wrote the above paragraph about Yvonne I received a letter from her in Encino, California. Happily married with children, she has not performed professionally for many years, and is now 'dying to sing again'.

restrictions are increased when the tune comes first, which was the case with virtually every line of *Jesus Christ Superstar*, indeed with almost everything Andrew and I ever wrote together. Yet these very problems can sometimes bring out the best in a lyric writer, and I believe this to have been the case with 'I Don't Know How To Love Him'.

It is always easier to write a lyric that is part of a larger story, as the situation of the singer is immediately apparent. Given the tune in isolation, I came up with 'Kansas Morning', a sensationally grim love lyric, but knowing Mary's situation was that she did not know how to express her love for a remarkable man, there was little danger of such a disaster second time around. The title, just a prosaic statement any woman in that position might use, was strong and direct, leading me quickly to a natural succession of thoughts. It was not necessary to use a great deal of rhyme, usually the sign of a truly strong melody. I have often been guilty of excessive rhyme, which can sometimes distract from the message of the lyric, particularly if the rhyme can be seen coming a mile off. One of the greatest lyrics of all time, 'Some Enchanted Evening' has no rhyme at all in its verses, and 'I Don't Know How To Love Him' has very few.

The words were however contemporary with lines such as 'I've had so many men before' and 'so calm, so cool', identifying the song as a creation of the Seventies and ensuring that it did not seem out of place in the context of the rest of the work. I was somewhat disappointed when singers of later versions of the song sometimes changed 'I've had so many men' to 'I've loved so many men' – an alteration that makes the entire song rather bland, as if sung by a Mills and Boon reader rather than a woman of experience who has been around but never really fallen in love before.

I have always enjoyed writing songs from the feminine point of view, and many of my most successful lyrics have been for women, obviously written from observation rather than direct personal experience. I have never been (yet) a prostitute touched for the first time by true feeling for a man ('I Don't Know How To Love Him'), a wronged wife or distressed mistress ('I Know Him So Well'), a manipulative vamp ('I'd Be Surprisingly Good For You') or an older woman in love with a young gay man ('Ziggy' from

Starmania) but these and other female-centred songs have been among those I am most proud of. Neither have I ever addressed a crowd of 100,000 from a balcony in Buenos Aires wearing an expensive dress and decked out in extravagant jewellery.

The first half of *Jesus Christ Superstar* closed with Judas' deal with the High Priests, 'Damned For All Time'. In a way, this frenetic, riff-based rocker, featuring some masterful tenor sax from Chris Mercer, is the essence of Judas' crisis, the main expression of his dilemma, following on from his 'Heaven On Their Minds' tirade:

> I came because I had to, I'm the one who saw
> Jesus can't control it like he did before
> And furthermore I know that Jesus thinks so too
> Jesus wouldn't mind that I was here with you
> I have no thought at all about my own reward
> I really didn't come here of my own accord
> Just don't say I'm
> Damned for all time

Judas makes excuses, attempts to justify his actions, grovels and fears for history's verdict. He knows what he is doing is of monumental importance, believes it has to be done, yet is terrified by potential consequences. The Priests despise their informer and joke about the thirty pieces of silver they hand to him ('cash on the nail'):

> Think of the things you can do with that money
> Choose any charity – give to the poor
> We've noted your motives, we've noted your feelings
> This isn't blood money – it's a fee, nothing more

Judas tells them where they can arrest Jesus in safety and a heavenly choir intone the deliberately unheavenly phrases:

> Well done Judas, good old Judas

Andrew and I always felt that the first act ended at this point, but in the majority of the stage productions around the world, the break seems to have worked better after the Last Supper and Gethsemane scenes.

'The Last Supper' is a lengthy sequence in which the final showdown between Jesus and Judas is played out against the background of the Apostles getting more and more drunk and sleepy, blissfully unaware of the dramatic clash going on around them. Their singalong chorus, 'Look at all my trials and tribulations', is enjoyably daft and gets dafter as the wine kicks in. Words are slurred and confused by the third time around and I also included a pot reference ('What's that in the bread? It's gone to my head') as a tribute to the dominating atmosphere in Olympic Studio Two at the time.

But the core of the scene is the Jesus/Judas argument. Jesus in *Superstar* does not actually consecrate the bread and wine on the table, declaring them to be his body and blood. He tells his drowsy followers that their food and drink might as well be his body and blood for all they care. After his death I envisaged the Disciples half-remembering these words and interpreting them, through guilt and confusion, as an instruction to commemorate Jesus through bread and wine – the misguided creation of Holy Communion and the doctrine of transubstantiation. This is not the concern of Jesus in this scene. He knows his destruction is imminent and he lashes out at his friends and at Judas:

> Look at your blank faces! My name will mean nothing
> Ten minutes after I'm dead!
> One of you denies me, one of you betrays me—

Judas, the only Apostle following his master's train of thought, shouts at Jesus to 'cut out the dramatics' and Jesus simply tells him to get on with his betrayal. As the diners get more and more out to lunch, so to speak, the argument becomes more and more frenzied and after a foretaste of Judas' 'Superstar' song, the betrayer runs off to do the deed. Andrew's musical illustration of the altercation was superbly constructed – heavy rock music, almost heavy metal, being ideal for the clash and switching wonderfully at unexpected moments to the inebriated corn of the Apostles' chorus. At the conclusion of the supper, all are asleep and a deserted Jesus makes his final plea to his God through 'Gethsemane'.

'Gethsemane' is Jesus' big moment in *Superstar* and in Ian Gillan the song was blessed with an outstanding first interpreter. Influences of 'MacArthur Park' and Del Shannon's 'Runaway' (in the chord progression of the middle section – a progression suggested by yours truly) abound, but the beautiful opening and closing melody remains one of Andrew's most inspired to this day. Jesus' doubts, his eleventh-hour hope that perhaps he might be excused his horrific destiny, are there in St Luke and I hope in our 'Gethsemane' too:

> I only want to say
> If there is a way
> Take this cup away from me, for I don't want to taste its poison
> Feel it burn me, I have changed, I'm not as sure
> As when we started
>
> But if I die
> See the saga through and do the things you ask of me
> Let them hate me, hit me, hurt me, nail me to their tree
> I'd want to know, I'd want to know my God
> I'd want to see, I'd want to see, my God
> Why I should die . . .

Later in the song, he accepts his fate:

> God, thy will is hard
> But you hold every card
> I will drink your cup of poison
> Nail me to your cross and break me
> Bleed me, beat me, kill me, take me
> Now, before I change my mind

The use of 'thy', instead of 'your', the only use of the ancient possessive in *Superstar*, was deliberate – a reference to the Lord's Prayer which, despite unpleasant modernising moves in recent times, still packs most power today in its original form.

Barely has the final note of 'Gethsemane' died away, than Judas returns with the Priests and soldiers. Too late, the Apostles awake to the situation and there is a brief reprise of 'What's The Buzz' in which Peter attempts to confront the arrest party. The fatal kiss of betrayal is planted and Jesus hustled away. To the tune of 'Strange Thing Mystifying', Peter then denies any link with Jesus when challenged by a trio of accusers, notably me in the roles of Soldier and Old Man.*

Jesus is brought before Pilate and quickly passed on to Herod by a sarcastic, barely interested Pilate, in confident contrast to the man earlier troubled by his dream. The fickle mob reprise a mocking version of the 'Hosanna' chorus as Jesus is brought before the debauched Jewish monarch. 'King Herod's Song', the Eurovision reject, turned out to be a show-stopper, with its nasty lyric a sinister counterpoint to the jaunty, *Cabaret*-influenced melody. Mike d'Abo sang with great gusto, ad-libbing 'Get out of my life' at the very end. This ad-lib was later singled out as the best line of the entire work by an American Christian reviewer, the very essence of the entire show – I was highly praised for pointing out that we are all determined to push Christ out of our lives. Only I hadn't – Mike d'Abo had.

The couplet that always got the big laugh was of course

> Prove to me that you're no fool
> Walk across my swimming pool

and, as mentioned before, has found its way into several books of twentieth-century quotations. I always regret not being able to come up with an equally good couplet for the final verse, 'Feed my household with this bread/you can do it on your head' being rather an anti-climax, not to mention a weak re-use of the bread/head rhyme, already heard in the Last Supper singalong. Despite this, the number has always been ecstatically received over the years.

Perhaps Murray's finest hour on the album, 'Judas' Death',

---

* The part of Peter was played by Paul 'Sandy' Davis, the lead singer of Gracious, one of the bands that Norrie Paramor had briefly signed during my time at the NP Organisation. Gracious eventually made a couple of intelligent progressive rock albums but neither Sandy nor the band ever achieved substantial commercial acceptance.

begins with a reprise of the melody of 'Damned For All Time' and after a final bitter exchange with the Priests, Judas gradually slips into madness and suicide via twisted versions of 'I Don't Know How To Love Him' and 'Heaven On Their Minds'. We are then back in Pilate's court and this time Pilate is forced to take an interest, egged on by the Priests. The music reprises the ominous excitement of the Overture. Pilate inflicts thirty-nine lashes upon Jesus in the hope that this will satisfy the blood-lust of the mob ('to keep you vultures happy I shall flog him') but in vain. Jesus will not defend himself. Pilate is baffled. He finally loses patience and screams out his wish to be rid of the problem, handing him over to the execution party:

> Don't let me stop your great self-destruction
> Die if you want to, you misguided martyr!
> I wash my hands of your demolition
> Die if you want to, you innocent puppet!

The trial scenes contain some of the most sophisticated musical passages in the opera – rock meets Prokofiev with melody, discord, unexpected time signatures and intriguing orchestral touches, combining to demonstrate Andrew's musical eclecticism at its most appealing. The words do not always match the panache of the music. Rhymes (not always true ones) often took precedence over content, but there is a good dramatic flow to the Pilate/Jesus/mob correlation. Some of the lines, and the concept of thirty-nine lashes, came from an *Eagle* comic re-telling of the story back in the Fifties, some lines from the more conventional source of the New Testament. The trial was expanded for the stage a year later, and for once expansion improved the original. I made a few mini-improvements to the words for the 1996 London revival.

Pilate's hand-washing outburst led straight into 'Superstar' – the one track we already had in the can. Jesus doesn't get a resurrection, but Judas does. It was a great relief to find that the number recorded a year earlier fitted seamlessly into the rest of the score. It was followed in turn by the Ligeti and Penderecki-influenced Crucifixion during which Jesus' final desperate words were spoken by Ian Gillan – more or less as per the Gospels. Satanic laughter, hammer sounds and electronic effects segued into a freaky jazz drum and piano pattern underneath wails and moans. All came to an abrupt finish with the words 'Father, into your hands I commend my spirit'. All that remained was the beautiful orchestral rendition of the principal 'Gethsemane' theme, John 19:41. The freaky piano coda to John 19:41 that had been part of the B side to Murray's original *Superstar* single was ditched.

By the middle of July, five months of recording had been completed. The vast majority had taken place at Olympic Studios in Barnes, with the odd excursion to other venues when more distinguished artists such as the Rolling Stones were occupying every spare Olympic slot. Andrew, Alan O'Duffy and I had been present for virtually every minute of every session and our nervousness as Alan stitched the entire epic together was understandably huge. Had we missed something out now that all the performers and musicians had gone home?*

What had we done? Was the whole concept completely mad? Would we go through the experience we had had with our *Joseph* album, feeling that, after all our efforts, the final result was mediocre in the extreme? Would others then reassure us that it was really quite good? Had we been blasphemous, pretentious and/or just plain incompetent? How much did we now owe MCA and how many millions would we have to sell to be able to get out of their debt? (Towards the end of the sessions, MCA refused to pay around £10 for a Chinese takeaway that we claimed was an essential contribution to one all-night session, which we took as a lack of confidence in the whole project.) Would our managers decide to pull out of our agreement if the recording failed? Paranoia struck deep.

---

* No, but we found to our horror that we had mistakenly erased half of one of Barry Dennen's lines and Barry was now out of the country. Fortunately, Murray came in to do a very good Dennen impersonation for the words 'this unfortunate'.

Chapter Seventeen

*J*esus Christ Superstar sounded terrific when Alan O'Duffy, Andrew and I listened by ourselves to the complete eighty-seven minutes and sixteen seconds of tape. We had just squeezed under the wire as far as the restrictions of a vinyl LP were concerned – twenty-two minutes a side was roughly the upper limit before sound quality began to deteriorate, thanks to grooves being forced too close together (I am aware that technically there is only one groove per disc side). Side three of our two-disc set actually clocked in at over twenty-three minutes but Alan was confident he could cut the master of even that side to a satisfactory standard. Cassettes were not yet a major force in the market, indeed they were still slugging it out with eight-track cartridges as the principal alternative to vinyl. CDs, still over a decade away, were not even a twinkle in a record company manager's eye.

It still sounded wonderful when we played it to David and Sefton and to Brian Brolly and other MCA personnel. It sounded just fine when we played copies of the tapes at home. Even Andrew still liked it. When those who had played and sung on the recording heard it, they too were extremely enthusiastic. Among others, Murray Head, Chris Mercer, Ian Gillan and Bruce Rowland all called to say they had had a few doubts but on hearing the finished master were now convinced this was something special. To receive the endorsement of heavy rockers was a great artistic boost for us; to receive that of our management and record company was an economic relief, for we were promised one hundred per cent promotional support for our 'concept album', formally dubbed a 'rock opera', these two terms not yet being unfashionable albatrosses.

Brian Brolly swung into immediate action, promising worldwide co-operation from all the MCA offices, especially from those in America. He started chasing designers for the cover and plotting a promotional campaign. David Land began to do the rounds of theatrical producers yet again, now that he had something more than one single and John Lennon to talk about.

I took the opportunity at the end of July to go to Japan for my brother Jo's wedding to Janet Speer. I could not possibly afford such a jaunt but my parents were keen that there should be at least one family representative there. My father fixed me up on the cheapest of cheap flights via a charter airline vaguely linked to Wheelock Marden. I stayed with my brother and did best man duty in stifling heat and a heavy suit at the British Consul's house in Kobe.

After the happy couple had gone to Guam for their honeymoon, I visited Tokyo to see what I could remember from 1955 and to meet up with one of my former masters at Lancing, Harry Guest, and his wife Lyn, then writing and teaching in Japan. Harry had struggled with me and Virginia Woolf in 1962. The Tokyo I knew when I was ten, including our home in Shibuya, had been razed to the ground, and the district in which we had spent that summer totally unrecognisable. The Emperor's Palace was almost the only landmark I recognised from fifteen years back, although the sounds and smells of the city, not to mention the humidity and the taste of Brierly's Orange Juice, took me straight back to 1955. I returned home via a glorious week in Hong Kong, staying in luxury with my father's boss's family, and on a succession of unorthodox flights, cargo planes and company aircraft that eventually deposited me and a crew of air hostesses (I and 3000 shirts being their only charges from Calcutta onwards) at Luton after, among other highlights, one night in Istanbul and a terrifying storm over the Himalayas.

Japan was not the first major trip abroad I had made in 1970. Half way through the *Superstar* sessions, out of the blue, Andrew and I had received a telegram from Father Christopher Huntington of the College of the Immaculate Conception in Douglaston, Long Island, New York. The College was staging *Joseph* and Father Huntington offered us an all-expenses paid trip to see the show. We didn't take more than a minute or two to fire back a telegram of acceptance and happily postponed for a few days the Olympic sessions we had planned from 7 May, trusting that MCA would not blow their tops at our desertion of the cause – or be charged cancellation fees.

Everything about that trip was more than just exciting for a young man who had grown up with American popular culture the dominant interest of his childhood. I felt I already knew New York like a native, and determined to walk the length of every one of its avenues and streets. I longed for the record stores, radio stations, swathes of TV channels, skyscrapers, Greenwich Village, burgers and fries, and even Broadway theatre. We could pester MCA in their headquarters about their plans for our album, and I might even risk calling Sara, although she was by now firmly ensconced with her American lover, the rotter. The flight out on a Pan Am Jumbo was the first thrill – the 747 had only been in service for a year and it was still a form of transport sampled only by the privileged minority. We were in economy but didn't mind. There were head-sets with eight music channels and a movie, and though drinks weren't free at the back of the plane then, they were cheap. The thing I remember about the flight best of all was that I read my first P.G.Wodehouse novel, *The Code Of The Woosters*. A late but soon devoted convert.

We were met at JFK by Father Huntington who was delighted that we had responded to his call but gloomy because of the shooting of Kent State University students by President Nixon's National Guard a couple of days before. He told us that it was a sad time for his country and during the drive into Manhattan we saw plenty of evidence of the impact this event in Ohio had made – petitions being signed on street corners, protesters marching. Of course the shooting had been a big story in England, but had already faded from the headlines. I was reminded that the United States had a life beyond entertainment and sensed even before reaching our mid-town destination that young people seemed to be far more involved in politics and anti-government activity than they were in England. Or maybe just more than I had ever been. Complacency is easier when there is no danger of the Vietnam draft.

Our mid-town destination was none other than the Harvard Club on West 44th Street, a very conservative introduction to New York living. Apart from two trips out to Douglaston to see the students there perform *Joseph*, which they did with great zest, we were free to do as we pleased and we indeed trawled the record stores and covered many blocks of Manhattan on foot. We discovered the delights of New York cabs, thinking that we were very unlucky in that the first one we tried was a filthy, smelly, cramped wreck with no suspension and a driver who neither knew the English language nor his home town. We soon discovered they were all like that.

We went to MCA on Park Avenue, were received cordially, and renewed our acquaintance with some of the executives we had met on their UK visits, notably Dick Broderick. Dick managed to produce a gold record for us, allegedly for sales of the single in Brazil, but it might not have been totally authentic for when we removed it from its frame and played it back in England, it turned out to be a Brenda Lee song. We optimistically discussed plans for the half-finished album, but nothing could be set up as no one in New York had heard very much of it (and had probably been discouraged by the weak 'Heaven On Their Minds' release). We reckoned the US team were still hedging their bets, and in fact subsequently discovered that only Brian Brolly's refusal to comply prevented the American record chiefs from aborting our expensive, crazy venture before we had barely begun the album sessions.

We did manage to persuade MCA to give a US release to a single we had recorded during the *Superstar* sessions with Paul Raven, the future Gary Glitter, our then current Priest Three. Still demonstrating my obsession with American places I knew nothing about, I wrote a lyric entitled 'Goodbye Seattle' about a loser from Boston failing to make it in Washington State. The Grease Band gave Andrew's simple rock melody a boisterous treatment and Paul/Gary hollered appropriately, but the result was rather a shambles and although actually receiving one reasonable review in a US music trade paper, sunk without trace, as had 'Heaven On Their Minds'.*

We went to see our first Broadway musical, Stephen Sondheim's *Company*, which had opened at the Alvin Theatre two weeks before our arrival. It was directed by Hal Prince, in seven years' time to be contracted to direct *Evita* for us in London. I was lamentably ignorant about both these giants of the musical in 1970. I quite enjoyed *Company* but did not get a great deal of its Manhattanese. It seemed a whole world away from *Superstar*. After five days, when the Father Huntington tab ran out, Andrew decided to go back to England, but I hung around for a few extra days, even going up to Boston for the weekend to see Sara and her boyfriend, rather a nice chap, flying back from Logan airport overnight on 16 May. As my love life was now in full swing with Prudence, I was quite happy to be a spare part in Massachusetts.

Throughout August, we worked closely with MCA-UK to prepare for the album's release. The artwork and packaging were our main concern and we were delighted that we were to be allowed to have a booklet with all the lyrics, photographs and detailed credits included. A company named Graphreaks were contracted to design the package and a weird and shoeless individual from that organisation quickly convinced us that their concept was perfect. In all honesty, it turned out a bit of a mess with erratic semi-biblical lettering over a huge yellow, red and purple photo of the sun. The inside featured twelve portraits of Jesus by artists ranging from Leonardo da Vinci to children at a South London school which worked well, but the major problem was the construction of the package itself. Instead of a normal double-album gatefold cover, the two discs and booklet were squeezed into a ludicrously tight slot behind a complex four-pronged sleeve, whose interlocking bits could be opened or closed only with a book of instructions. It was rather like opening a milk carton – one reviewer complained that it took longer to get the discs out of the sleeve than it did to play

---

* Somehow, during the *Superstar* sessions we found time to record yet another flop single, 'Bridge Over Troubled Water' by 'Harold and Ted'. This was a spoken word version of the recent Simon and Garfunkel hit by actors impersonating Harold Wilson and Edward Heath, released to coincide with the 1970 General Election. It seemed funny at the time.

the album. However, once the record began selling in prodigious quantities, MCA reverted to a conventional double-album sleeve. In America they never even used it in the first place.

Brian Brolly was confident of good media coverage and hopeful that Radio One, the only station that counted and indeed almost the only one that existed, would play the record. Reaction from the sales force was good and 16 October settled as release date. A strong advertising campaign was put in place. Many MCA companies around the world, most of which had had a hit with Murray's single earlier in the year, were committed to an equally high-profile release in their respective territories. Brian had sent a memo to the MCA New York heavies saying, 'This is a truly monumental work . . . I have no doubts at all of its outstanding aesthetic values and absolutely no doubt that creative and agressive [sic] selling and promotion will make this set one of the biggest selling albums in our history.'

How right he was, about the sales anyway. Andrew and I owe an enormous debt to Brian for his total belief in the record, without which it might never have been completed, let alone issued. Sad to say, Brian is a non-person in the ALW world these days, but I am sure Andrew would gratefully acknowledge Brian's contribution to our first significant success together, which in turn led to one of the most remarkable show-business success stories of the century. And to my career too.

All the same, at the time I was not one hundred per cent sure that the American office was completely on board and I fired off a lengthy seven-point letter to Dick Broderick on 3 September, outlining my view of how the record should be promoted in the States. I was probably hoping to wangle another trip to the States as much as anything, but I did agitate about a variety of topics such as radio, TV, press (both establishment and underground), how cast members and of course ourselves would happily fly anywhere at the drop of a hat, the idea of film clips (this was in pre-video days), Canada (I wanted to go there too) and whether we could listen to the US test pressings of the record before they committed to running off half a million albums. I never got a reply.

Looking back at my files today, I am surprised how much of this sort of thing I did, rather than Andrew, whose interest in every single little detail of the promotion and production of his work is now legendary, taking up more of his time than composing. But then composing doesn't take much time anyway. Hard to believe today, but in many respects I was the leader of the duo as far as PR and business aspects were concerned, though fortunately much of the latter was left to David Land.

Having told MCA how to run their US campaign, confident that anything that could be done around the globe was being done, I took a short break in Scotland with Prudence and the family of Alan Crowder of MCA-UK. This was my first visit to what I consider the most beautiful country in the world. We wound up on the remote island of Tiree where even today I doubt if any of Andrew's or my shows has ever played.

Meanwhile David Land was still trying to interest theatrical producers in London. He still failed to make any headway, was told time and time again that rock never worked in the theatre (despite *Hair*) and that anything religious was either too boring or too controversial to be touched by any sane impresario. We did not see how one work could be simultaneously boring and controversial, but not even David's highly individual selling techniques convinced anyone to invest time or money in *Jesus Christ Superstar*. We would just have to put all our energies into the record.

By this time we had known David for over a year and I had already formed a deep affection for him. He was beyond any doubt a one-off, and became one of the most important influences in my life. Andrew and I had originally been given office facilities in Sefton's HQ in Charles Street, but we soon outgrew the space there and David installed us in a second-floor office opposite his in Wardour Street, whence we could carry on all the non-creative aspects of our work. David's own office, at number 118/120, was so small and untypical of a show-biz tycoon that we not unnaturally assumed the poor bloke must be struggling to make ends meet, doubtless financed heftily by Sefton. He liked to say that the décor was 'early hideous'. He shared his tiny domain with the distinguished orchestra leader and film composer Stanley Black, plus two secretaries crammed into a pigeon hole and a murky back room stuffed full of Stanley's scores going back to the war. Stanley did have a piano and a little breathing space in his room, but

David, who hoarded for England, had great difficulty in pulling up a chair for visitors without knocking over piles of ephemera, old records and tapes, toys, tins of sardines, airline bags and freebies, strange clothes and ancient photographs, snooker cues and footballs, collected since his days of flogging reject crockery in Dagenham as 'Dave's Stores'. His office was a forerunner of the car boot sale, and as the awards, posters and gold discs mounted during our long association, he was lucky not to have his office declared a health or fire hazard.

He was most reluctant to venture out of his eyrie, thus, unlike every other manager or agent I have ever heard of, being extremely easy to get hold of. He was always there. He boasted that if anybody was prepared to come and see him in his office, they must genuinely want to see him and would therefore be unlikely to waste his time. The only complaint I ever had about his premises was his refusal to switch from old-fashioned sandpaper-type lavatory paper to the soft but strong tissue kind. I assumed he must have bought a consignment of 10,000 pre-war toilet rolls around 1946.

I had no idea that he was a truly wealthy man until one evening in the late summer of 1970. I had been working late in our office at Number 145 and found at around seven o'clock that I was locked in, presumably by the last of the other occupants of the building to leave. I had no master key and exit via the second-floor window was not a practical option. I rang David at his Crawford Street flat and fortunately he was there. He said he would be around in fifteen minutes and I sat at the window watching out for him. Maybe he would be on foot, having caught a bus down Oxford Street, or in his wife's Mini. After a quarter of an hour a huge Rolls-Royce purred gracefully down Wardour Street and stopped outside my front door. David got out and released me. Once it was clear that this was David's car I never worried about him starving again. Further proof of his extremely comfortable financial status cropped up regularly thereafter, with his vast Webber-Rice earnings becoming the ultimate icing on his cake.

David was above all a very funny man and totally unpretentious. He would joke that he was only interested in 'the ackers', but while this was clearly one of his motivations, he had genuine appreciation of what was worthwhile and what was not; like me, he found that a lot of things he genuinely loved were highly commercial and popular. David pursued talents and ideas because he liked them rather than because he thought they would make money. They usually did, though.

He was short, rotund and I cannot think of him today without a smile on his face and a smile coming to mine. He was fifty-one when I met him, just a year or so younger than I am as I write these words. The son of Polish Jewish immigrants, he won a scholarship to the Davenant Foundation Grammar School in London. At the beginning of the Second World War he joined the Royal Army Service Corps as a volunteer. His career in entertainment began in 1945 when he produced concerts featuring such wartime favourites as Vera Lynn, Anne Shelton and his lifelong friend, Stanley Black. That year he married Zara Levinson, a graceful and beautifully-spoken lady who was the perfect foil for his irrepressibility. Soon the Harlem Globetrotters and the Dagenham Girl Pipers became his two most reliable sources of income. He presented innumerable British and international cabaret acts for the Variety Club, including an early London performance by the Beatles.

David was just as happy chasing two 'impossible to get' tickets for a pal for an opening night (he always got them) or doing a deal with the fruit stall in Berwick Street market, as he was dealing with the moguls of Hollywood or Broadway. His humour and down-to-earth attitude dominated his approach to all matters, great or small. He formed a company called Hope and Glory Limited, just so he could answer one of his many telephone lines with the words 'Land of Hope and Glory'. Another company of his, called Dee Land, was continually being phoned in error by fishermen applying for rights to catch salmon on the River Dee. For a year or two he attempted to refer the sportsmen to the correct authority, but eventually found it more fun to give permission which he imagined leading to scores of angry anglers squabbling over prime areas of the Dee's banks. He was in many ways an Arthur Daley of real life, but unlike the brilliant creation of *Minder*, trustworthy and supremely successful.

He was fiercely patriotic (a great expert on the life and times of Winston Churchill), and felt almost as strongly about Arsenal football club. Beyond doubt, his luckiest break was meeting me and Andrew, but ours was meeting him. As a manager, he was fully supportive of everything we tried to do, even when he had initial doubts about the project, as he did for about three hours with *Superstar* and for about six with *Evita*. We soon became close to his family as well as to him, his daughter Lorraine and son Brook as enthusiastic about their old man's newest protégés as David and Zara were.

Sefton Myers did not play anything like such a major day-to-day role in looking after our activities – financial support was his vital contribution, but he understandably maintained a great interest in our progress. In the early days we were often most generously entertained by Sefton and his young wife (we were invited to their wedding not long after we signed the management deal) and we would play him our latest material, keeping him fully informed with the artistic side of things. His daughter by his first marriage, Judie Tzuke, barely a teenager when we first met her, became a very successful singer/songwriter in the late Seventies. Sad to say, he was diagnosed as having cancer just as things were beginning to happen with *Superstar*, living only long enough to know that his last show business venture had been the kind of success he had always hoped would match his property triumphs. It was a tragedy that we were not able to know him better and that he never knew just how magnificently his final entertainment investment was to be rewarded.

At the beginning of 1970 Andrew met Sarah Hugill, a sixteen-year-old schoolgirl, and it seemed to be only a matter of weeks before he announced he was going to marry her. As he had hitherto never shown much evidence of being a ladies' man, though he had several good and amusing female chums, this dramatic announcement took those who knew him well by surprise. It would not be stretching a point to say that few believed he would ever go through with it, but those doubters were proved wrong when they married in the following July. Andrew and Sarah were clearly devoted to each other and Sarah's combination of adolescent innocence and innate good sense, not to mention her charm and virtuous good looks, made Andrew's obsession totally comprehensible and Sarah a pleasure to have around. Every time Andrew has fallen seriously for a lady, he moves, if possible, extremely quickly into marriage, in marked contrast to my indecision in these matters.

My own personal life was still based around Prudence but towards the end of 1970, just as *Superstar* preparations were beginning to take off, she announced she was going abroad for a while, to work on a cruise liner's discotheque in the West Indies, my lack of long-term commitment to our relationship undoubtedly a factor. Was I incapable of any long-term commitment? This question briefly crossed my mind, and the answer that came back was not one which reflected well on me. On the other hand, nearly all my important relationships so far had ended against my wishes – and I was still only twenty-five. I loved Prudence but selfishly looked forward to being more of a free man when I made my next visit to America, for the release of *Superstar* over there at the end of October.

Before this trip, we had the release of the album in England. As promised, MCA-UK swung a powerful promotional campaign into action and although we got a good deal of press, the all-important factor of radio and television support was not so positive. From *The Gramophone*, a magazine devoted almost exclusively to serious music, to *Melody Maker* and *Disc* in the pure pop corner, we received extensive and wildly conflicting coverage. Most of the pop papers gave us raves, as did William S. Mann in *The Gramophone*. David Wigg, still going strong nearly thirty years later as the *Daily Express* showbiz man, stated that it failed to sustain interest and that some of the lyrics were 'nauseating', although strangely he simultaneously professed 'nothing but admiration' for us. Derek Jewell, in the *Sunday Times*, loyally and genuinely loved it as much as he had *Joseph* – 'as an artistic exercise in musical drama is every bit as valid (and to my mind often more moving than) Handel's *Messiah*'; whereas his opposite number in the *Observer*, Tony Palmer, stated that in just one short song, 'Father Of Night', on his new album, Bob Dylan 'says it all with greater power and precision'. Geoffrey Cannon in the *Guardian* headed his piece 'Making God Tedious To Generations'; *Music Business Weekly*'s headline was '*Jesus Christ Superstar* A Superb Masterpiece' (as opposed to an appalling masterpiece, I suppose). These opposing poles of critical reaction were soon to be repeated even more extremely in America.

David 'Kid' Jensen, then a heavy underground disc-jockey on Radio Luxembourg, was one of our few fans on any radio wavelength, but none of our songs was played very much on the less esoteric record shows, either on Lux or by the BBC. And there wasn't much else on the UK radio dial in those days. Any flicker of interest from television usually faded when the cost of reassembling the forces on the record for live performance was calculated. Miming was not allowed in Britain and most of the cast weren't available anyway, Ian Gillan for one back on the road full-time with Deep Purple and the Grease Band reunited with Joe Cocker.

Sales were reasonable, but not dramatic. Things looked more hopeful on the Continent, but our greatest concern was America. We had heard very little from MCA over there, although they had asked us to return for the launch in New York. We set off on our second US trip with the feeling that our grand project was coming unstuck and that we would have to come up with something new pretty quickly. At least we would have another trip to New York and there was the prospect of the odd European jaunt when we got back. I stoically reckoned that if eighteen months' work had only got me a few freebies around the world that was, in one of David Land's immortal phrases, 'better than a dead policeman'.

Chapter Eighteen

The few days that we spent in America on our second trip there from 23 October 1970 irrevocably changed our lives. We left England (for some forgotten reason, on an Air India flight) convinced that we had still not quite got it right; we returned home after just two weeks with the realisation that we had created not merely a common or garden hit record but a work of massive cultural impact. I am of course not claiming that *Jesus Christ Superstar* is a sophisticated composition of genius but, stone me, it was popular. It was praised to the skies and derided to the basements, but in less than a year it was to be described by *Variety*, king of entertainment publications, as the 'biggest all-media parlay in show business history'.

In America *Superstar* was primarily a recording album phenomenon. For all its subsequent life in concert, theatre and film, it was as an album that its impact was revolutionary. Nearly thirty years later, I continue to be amazed and flattered by the number of Americans around ten years younger than me who tell me that *Superstar* was *the* record they recall with most affection and enthusiasm from their school and college days. In England the album was never anything like such a big hit and the entire *JCS* bandwagon only really began rolling on our home turf when the West End stage production opened in mid-1972. By then, and in that setting, it was already rather a conventional piece, totally acceptable to all save the hip end of the market, original and exciting though the London production was. But it was

just another show, albeit a very good and staggeringly successful one.

We got our first surprise when we were met at JFK, not by
an MCA office junior, but by three or four of their fairly senior
executives (notably Ellis Nassour who became our personal New
York City tour guide), plus a frenetic publicist named Barry
Kittleson. As we were limousined into Manhattan, we were regaled
with information about the number of press and radio interviews
that had been lined up. We were deposited in large adjoining
suites, stocked to the gills with champagne, in the Drake Hotel
on Park Avenue. As the MCA team got stuck into the drink, their
promotional campaign was outlined to us, and it was impressive.

Then they showed us the US version of our album. The British
artwork had been completely dumped and replaced with a solemn
brown box with a striking gold double angel design the only
external intrusion, a design that was to become a Rolls-Royce
of a logo over the years. A stylish matching booklet and the two
discs, with a designer label, rested within. Not even the heaviest
of rock acts had the privilege of their own label design in those
days of vinyl uniformity. The whole thing looked more like a
classical album than a pop one, which we briefly worried might be
commercial suicide, but we were told this was precisely the point,
and MCA were right. By treating the whole project as a serious,
up-market venture, the media and record-buyers were encouraged
to do the same, and feel intelligent and sophisticated as a result.

The album's release was still a few days away, but already some
radio stations were playing it in its entirety. Presentations of the
record were scheduled for churches in New York, Los Angeles
and Toronto (so they were releasing it in Canada). Bill Levy,
the company's art director, had supervised the assembly of an
intricate slide show to go with the playing of the principal tracks
to the large media contingent invited to attend the presentations.
Andrew and I were to introduce the show in the three cities and
submit to questions afterwards. I was amazed to see that at the
run-through of the sound and vision show one or two of the MCA
team were moved to tears. One such was the legendary veteran
record producer, Milt Gabler, who had supervised the recording
of Bill Haley's 'Rock Around the Clock' in 1954. I wish I could

claim that one of my works has made me cry, but this has never happened, not even in the theatre. I am unusual in this regard in a business where weeping even at auditions has been known. Affected yes, moved even, but by performances rather than my own contribution, and to date no tears.

Nothing seemed too much trouble for MCA. We felt strangely wanted – quite a turnaround from our trip in May when few in the record company took great interest in our unfinished work. Dick Broderick became our father figure within the empire and others moved sharply to our slightest bidding, often to the point of obsequiousness. I could not get over the luxury of the first decent hotel I had ever stayed in and was amazed that they would even do your laundry. We were both very reticent about outwearing our welcome and worried whether we dared phone home or order a club sandwich. We must have been the best hit clients MCA had ever known, polite and grateful, undemanding and trying desperately to keep costs down. A change from acts who insisted on the most expensive suites with all the trimmings, mainly so that trashing them would be more fun.

We also did well at interviews. On radio shows we had plenty of female callers ringing in just to say how much they liked our accents but the majority made it clear to us that *Superstar* was an album that they profoundly liked and longed to discuss. The presentations were wildly successful, even with the odd technical glitch, and ridiculously good reviews began rolling in. Chris van Ness in the L.A. *Free Press* called it 'the greatest pop recording produced since the first African ever pounded a drum'. As this put 'Heartbreak Hotel', 'You've Lost That Loving Feeling' and the entire Beatles catalogue into our wake, we were quite pleased. Other comments were almost as favourable and even *Rolling Stone* was kind. *Time* magazine, which had only discovered rock music about a year before, picked it as an album of the year and *Playboy*, another publication which had considered rock beneath it for over a decade, bizarrely voted it the best big band album of the year.

Wandering down Park Avenue, David Land, who had flown out to join us once we reported what was going on, noticed on a board outside a church on Fifth Avenue that that Sunday's sermon was entitled 'Jesus Christ Superstar'. We sneaked into the back row and were staggered to witness a christening of a baby 'in the name of Jesus Christ – Superstar'. I recall feeling that things were getting out of hand, worrying that we had bitten off more than we could chew. I really hadn't wanted to change the liturgy of the Christian Church and dreaded giving offence to conservative believers, and even more important, to armed nutters. We became more and more respectful of the New Testament as the record's fame increased, more conservative, more cowardly.

But America was determined to take *Superstar* seriously and the churches rushed to embrace it. A cartoon in the *New Yorker* showed two priests, one saying 'Jesus Christ Superstar has grossed $30 million – where did we go wrong?' Mail from all over the country flooded in as the record began to sprint up the charts within days of its release. We were only able to read a tiny selection, but nearly all thanked us for making the Gospel story clearer and relevant. There were a few noises of protest from the Bible belt but, by and large, we felt that God was on our side. As I said in one interview, He either didn't exist or liked it.

Los Angeles was a great excitement. Driving down Sunset Boulevard for the first time in the back of a huge stretch limo, all expenses paid, our own songs blasting out on the radio, was all my teenage dreams come true. I was not actually a pop star, but this was a minor detail as we lapped up the glamorous treatment. We felt brave enough to spend a few bob recklessly, but only on shirts, records and the odd present for Mum. We had tea with Linda Ronstadt, hoping she would record 'I Don't Know How To Love Him' (she didn't). The presentation went down as well in California as it had in New York and scored just as well for a third time in Toronto. We barely had time to see much of the cities, but more than enough to become hooked on America. By the time we staggered home, the album was selling at a rate that required MCA to ditch the box sets in favour of a simpler and quicker-to-manufacture regular gatefold sleeve.

After a day back home, we heard the great news that we had crashed into the *Billboard* Top 200 LP chart at Number 40 – a very high entry in the only chart that really mattered. Within two weeks it was in the Top Ten and we were back out there on another round of promotion and glory-basking. I made my US

TV début on a game show called *Tell The Truth* in which the panel of celebrities, none of whom I had heard of, had to guess which was the real one of three Tim Rices. Both the fakes signed up by the station were Australian which I felt made the quest rather easy, but no celebrity noticed the difference in accents. We began to spot *Superstar* merchandise in shops, none of it authorised. I bought some psychedelic *JCS* posters and a *Superstar* rubber stamp. Merchandising, which these days is often more lucrative than the music or show that inspired it, was not even past the embryo stage in 1970 and no one, other than the bootleggers, spotted the enormous potential of our work in this department.

MCA's kindness this time round even extended to the provision of a delightful nocturnal companion. I was pretty slow on the uptake when asked if I was at all lonely in New York. This was the last thing I had been. Everybody wanted to know us and we had been out every night, sometimes with famous people. We had met Neil Diamond, Paul Newman and either Paul or Peter from Peter, Paul and Mary, I forget which, if I ever knew. We had been introduced to MCA's other big hit act of the day, a newcomer who, like us, had been almost totally ignored in his native England, Elton John. Elton had become an overnight sensation in America and we were taken by MCA to the famous Fillmore East to witness this new star in action. He was brilliant, but we went back to our hotel that night worried lest MCA put all their energies into promoting Elton rather than us. These unworthy thoughts caused us to be a little cool about Elton's first hit album. How wrong can you be?

Paul Newman introduced himself to us on an aeroplane when we were flying from LA to New York. He had a cassette of *Superstar* in his pocket and, as he was of almost Elvis-level stature, we were awestruck. We became pals for a while, the three-hour chat on the flight being followed by dinner in New York and eventually an invitation to spend the weekend at his house in Connecticut, which Andrew bewilderingly declined. I had a marvellous time *chez* Newman, playing pool with him on the table that had starred in *The Hustler*, and becoming entranced with his wife, Joanne Woodward, and one of his daughters, Nell, then only around twelve, who owned and trained a falcon. I was too shy to ask Paul or Joanne if I could have a photo taken with them and, instead, my lasting souvenir of the stay are some pictures of a young girl with a mean-looking bird on her arm. Career-wise, Newman was as hot as he ever was at that time, *Butch Cassidy and the Sundance Kid* having been his most recent triumph. He was the most dominating of personalities, but not in an arrogant way, an icy armour of detachment slipping into place when on public display, replaced by a slightly intimidating warmth when with family and friends. I shall never forget Joanne Woodward bringing me a cup of tea in the morning.

Anyway, when I had finally cottoned on to the fact that MCA had a phone number for me that could mean a night of fun, I agreed that I was lonely and spoke to a lascivious-sounding young woman who invited me round to her place. It was a huge and well-appointed apartment, not only as far as the fixtures and fittings were concerned. My new friend, Robin, answered the door in her nightie and I left three hours later, exhausted and relaxed, wondering if the cost would be deducted from our royalties. I didn't dare tell Andrew (who as far as I know hadn't been offered a phone number) and when the truth slipped out a few months later he was deeply offended. Travelling with Andrew at that time was a little like travelling with a maiden aunt in that I didn't think it was good for his constitution to know about this sort of thing. Not that there was that much of this sort of thing, not enough really, but when meeting beautiful young women who were performing in one's own show in those early *Superstar* days around the world, I did form one or two extremely brief but extremely tempestuous relationships, and it seemed best to hide the sordid truth from Andrew.

The danger of loneliness on those early trips to New York was diminished still further by the fact that Sara seemed to have rekindled her former enthusiasm for me. In fact at one point the story got out that we were engaged, probably a confusion with Andrew's status, and I received several letters of congratulation before an official denial could be issued. I am glad to say that Sara and I remain good friends and that she sensibly eventually married another American. I had probably never been less likely to have considered marriage at this particular stage of my life, though I missed Prudence, still gallivanting around the Caribbean.

The next crucial development in the *Superstar* story was the arrival of Robert Stigwood. Andrew and I had approached the highly successful Australian-born entertainment entrepreneur when we were casting the *JCS* album, hoping that one or more of his stars (the Bee Gees, Eric Clapton, etc.) could be persuaded to play a part on the album. Robert couldn't or didn't want to deliver any of his big names, but when the record began to skyrocket in the States, he moved quickly to re-establish contact. Simultaneously, David and the ailing Sefton knew that *Superstar* was becoming too big for their modest enterprise to handle, and that a collaboration with a larger showbiz entity was inevitable. All at once, impresarios who had rejected our work out of hand were pestering David to be allowed a second chance to develop the property. David began a policy of sending back all offers with every figure doubled, as he freely admitted that he had no idea what the norm was, and how much *Superstar* could be worth. These less favourable deals were still happily accepted, so David redoubled. The three of us agreed that this couldn't go on indefinitely, but even if the numbers zoomed into the stratosphere, we were afraid that we would still get it wrong and go with the wrong people in the wrong direction. While David dithered, the interest increased, the album reached Number One in the US charts, and Stigwood made his move.

David did deal with another problem with decisive speed. News of our great US success was beginning to trickle back home and several friends and acquaintances called or wrote to say well done. One of these was Desmond Elliott, from whom we had heard zilch for more than a year. He sent a congratulatory cable from 'Your agent, Desmond', which I took to be a sporting self-deprecating joke about his having lost our representation just before we hit the big time. David did not quite see it that way and I was firmly instructed not to respond in any style, jocular or not. The telegram was whisked off to a lawyer. To my absolute amazement, legal proceedings lurched briefly into action, to which I had no wish to become party. As far as I am aware, David emerged unscathed. I was staggered that Desmond tried it on, although when I next ran into him, at a book fair in the mid-Eighties, he seemed perfectly affable.

Robert, one of the most remarkable and likeable show business moguls of the past thirty years, had achieved enormous success in the years since he arrived in London from Adelaide in 1957, without a bean. His first success was as manager of John Leyton, who had a good run as a pop star in the early Sixties when Stigwood, some years ahead of his time, recognised the enormous potential of television as a medium for flogging pop records. Leyton was a straight (and rather good) actor playing a pop singer in a soap called *Harper's West One* and as the character Johnny St Cyr (sincere!) performed his latest release, 'Johnny Remember Me', on the show while simultaneously issuing the record in real life as John Leyton. The song became an overnight smash and shunted Leyton's career into a completely new direction as a pop idol, which he sustained until the arrival of Beatlemania two years later.

Robert also launched Mike Sarne via a string of witty novelty hits such as 'Come Outside' and, though he suffered a major setback when his fast-expanding entertainment empire collapsed in 1965 after the notorious P.J. Proby tour, when shocked theatre owners cancelled bookings en masse, alleging that Proby's trouser-splitting was immoral and liable to corrupt Britain's youth, he soon bounced back as part of Brian Epstein's NEMS management, with whom he discovered and launched fellow Aussies, the Bee Gees.

Robert never thought big – he thought massive. In both private and business lives he combined a sense of fun with a sense of the cannily outrageous. He was very good at anticipating public taste, mainly because his own tastes were solidly and genuinely commercial. Enough of his stunts and imaginative promotions paid off to place him in a key position in Epstein's empire by 1967, which was of course the year Epstein died. There was a brief moment when it looked as if he might inherit the Beatles, but unsurprisingly the group were not keen to replace Epstein with anybody at that stage, and NEMS fragmented, with Robert taking the Bee Gees and Cream (Eric Clapton, Ginger Baker and Jack Bruce), the first so-called supergroup, comprised of leading members of former hit acts – another concept in which Robert led the way. This time around his own organisation was in no danger of going under.

One of Robert's less successful early campaigns was for a pop singer named Simon Scott, whom Robert plugged by distributing a stone bust of the young warbler with every promotional copy of his first single. The single stiffed and the busts became extremely valuable collectors' items. It was with great joy that Andrew was eventually able to trace one of these tacky bonces for Robert's birthday in 1971.

By the time Andrew and I were beginning to make a noise with *Superstar*, Robert was as important as any manager or agent in the business and headed an organisation that embraced television, theatre, movies and music. Among many others, it represented Frankie Howerd, and Galton and Simpson (the most successful TV comedy writers of the time, with *Hancock's Half Hour* and *Steptoe and Son* their most famous creations). He operated from vast, plush offices in Brook Street, Mayfair, only half a mile but half a world away from David Land's cupboard in Soho. Robert was also planning to open offices in New York where he had appointed Brian Epstein's former Number Two, Peter Brown, to man the controls.

We were starting to get used to the high life in New York on about our third trip. By this time every agent and/or manager and/or theatre producer and/or conman in the book had been laying siege to our hotel with offers, which we dutifully referred back to David, who in those days generally preferred to mind the shop in England rather than zip around the globe with his young protégés. The need for some sort of deal with a serious player was now becoming urgent and David told us that Robert was looking like the best bet. Robert was English (well, sort of), a nice guy, a top dog and clearly genuinely enthusiastic about *Superstar*, beyond just the cash prospects. This impressive CV was supplemented by Robert's smart move of coming to New York and sending a fun-packed limousine to take us round to his rented house to be wined and dined. We met Peter Brown, an immaculately attired and well-spoken Brit (though he became a US citizen in 1997) and the four of us got on very well. We were primarily interested in hearing tales of the Beatles from Peter and of Eric Clapton and the Bee Gees from Robert. The Gibb brothers had spent the previous two or three years splitting and re-forming, but were about to make their first of many major comebacks; Eric and his band were somewhat out of it at this stage. But we must also have discussed our own careers, and Robert's huge ambitions for *Superstar* in every conceivable guise, as we tottered back into the limo convinced that this was a team we could trust, as long as David remained part of the equation.

So before long a deal was struck between Robert and David and Sefton's New Ventures company. Robert bought half the shares, for a price I have never known, and the name was changed to Superstar Ventures. Our basic deal with David and Sefton remained unchanged. This alliance was to forge a lifelong friendship and business partnership between Robert and David; for the moment we were delighted to have gained a new management limb without losing any of the old.

Thus David had made a mini-killing; and so did we. Part of the deal involved Andrew and I being paid £10,000 each – I cannot recall if it was an advance against future earnings or not, and if so, which future earnings, but I lost little sleep about this. Up to this point (December 1970) we had survived on our New Ventures wage plus apparently limitless petty cash from MCA. Not that we needed to spend very much on ourselves anyway, as virtually everything we did, from travel to nightclubs, was paid for by somebody else. The ten grand was the first positive sign of real earnings and I couldn't wait to pay the cheque into a bank. I raced down Brook Street after the signing ceremony and into the nearest Barclay's, but to my annoyance and chagrin the lady behind the counter didn't blink as I handed in my paying-in slip.

Christmas 1970 was therefore a fairly cheerful holiday in the Rice household. My parents were, to put it mildly, amazed and thrilled that I had at last brought home a little bacon. My grandmother expressed less surprise, devotedly declaring that she always knew this sort of thing would happen and she was the only member of the clan (including me) who never harboured the doubt that this might all be too good to last. I began to experience the unease of earning more than my father. Worse, he was now fighting to re-establish himself in business in the UK having fallen out with his Hong Kong colleagues. He resigned on a matter of principle (over which he was quite right). At this point my money was not yet rolling in hand over fist, but my Christmas presents to the family were very noticeably more extravagant than in previous years.

As my success to date had been almost exclusively achieved overseas, the true incredible potential of what might be round the corner was not really obvious to my England-based family and friends. One chum of my mother's asked me what my job was and when I informed her that I wrote songs, she replied, 'Wouldn't it be wonderful if you could earn a living doing that?' At the time my album was in the Top Ten in the US and about ten other countries and I knew I would probably earn at least £100,000 in the next year. And this was 1970! But I did not disillusion her.

Around the very end of 1970, Prudence's and my Jasmine Cottage lease having run out (as had Prudence), I temporarily and cheerfully returned to home life with my mother and father in Harpenden. Brother-wise, Jo was still in Japan, but I saw a lot of Andy, coming to the end of his stretch at Emmanuel, Cambridge. It seemed daft to continue renting in town when I was spending less and less time in England, let alone London. I took up gentle jogging around the Harpenden lanes as I had noticed a certain expansion in the lower shirt and upper trouser area.

There were many requests for Andrew and me to go around Europe to promote the album, which opportunities I relished. A three-day trip, all expenses paid, to Italy, Germany or Sweden was right up my alley. In Milan we attended a manic press conference in which half the assembled throng appeared to be violently anti us and half equally strongly pro. We stared in bewildered amazement as the rival factions screamed and slagged each other off, barely interested at our presence, nor asking us any questions – not that we would have understood them anyway. The Italian schizophrenia about the project was best illustrated by the fact that the Italian state radio banned *Superstar*, only to find Vatican radio endorsing it enthusiastically. No matter, it was a massive hit there.

In Brussels, I took my pal Roger Watson to join me on a TV show to mime to the voices of the singers on the album. Murray Head, Ian Gillan and Co. were never free to appear anywhere, but most European TV shows didn't seem to mind as long as someone from the project could lip-synch to the tracks. Roger did a moving interpretation of Pilate and I wiggled with delight as I mimed Judas' greatest hits. Not quite *Top Of The Pops* but fun enough. We spent two days in a church in a remote part of Holland (if anywhere in Holland can be remote) where an hour-long tribute to the LP was staged at no mean expense. We also went to Zurich, Stockholm and Luxembourg, to the latter just a few months after my trip there as the guest of the *Sun*, following my triumph in their Prophesy Next Month's Top Ten competition.

The best jaunt of all at this time was to Vienna. For once, a genuine performer on the album, Yvonne Elliman, agreed to take part in a European TV special. I decided I would like to drive to Austria. I had purchased my mother's ageing Mini for a knock-down £250. The only car I had ever owned before had been the ninth-hand Austin Cambridge which I had bought with a loan from my grandmother during my EMI days, which had lasted just three months before finally giving up the ghost near Baldock, where it may well still be rusting. Already becoming a bit of a nervous flyer, I persuaded Yvonne and Don Norman, the jazzer roadie employed by David Land to accompany us on trips David didn't fancy (most of them), to squash into the Mini for three days each way.

We set off at dawn's crack one chilly, damp, rainy February morning, ludicrously cramped, Yvonne, her baggage and a huge guitar in the back. I had bought an eight-track cartridge player and a huge supply of tapes in this format, which I was convinced would eventually see cassettes off. I was as wrong about this as I was to be later about Betamax videos versus VHS. With the Doors and Simon and Garfunkel, Elvis and *Superstar* itself blasting away, we made Strasbourg by night one, Rosenheim in Germany by night two, and rolled into Vienna after exactly 1000 miles on the road on the third afternoon. I spent several of the wee small hours of night two fruitlessly searching for disgusting things to do in less than swinging downtown Rosenheim, only to discover from Yvonne many years later that we could have had more fun in the hotel.

I cannot remember much about our media blitz in Vienna, other than noting that Austria was yet another country that had ignored the cool reception given to our album in its country of origin.

Everywhere I went in 1971 I was in the charts; albums and singles – local cover versions of many of the show's songs proliferated – except in the UK.

The journey home was made memorable by a party to celebrate some remote French village's football success. Having decided to drive through the night to Calais, we were fog-bound at midnight in a tiny hamlet somewhere near Lille. We attempted to kip in the car, difficult for three in a Mini, however friendly they might be. Yvonne did drop off in the luxury of the back seat, insulated by a number of towels she had borrowed from the Vienna hotel, but Don and I decided to leave her snoring and search for the million-to-one shot of an all-night bar.

We soon heard singing and stumbled into the village hall where a massive bash was in full cry. No one objected to our gate-crashing, as the local team's triumph had spread goodwill and munificence around the entire arrondissement. For two hours we ate and drank in style, sang along with the band and made several close friends. We eventually tottered out into the morning, now miraculously fog-free. Yvonne was still comatose and even a quarter of a century later does not believe she missed a great party. How we got to Calais I prefer not to recall, but I was violently ill in the ferry car-park. I do recall that we returned to Blighty on the first day of decimalisation – a depressing event that I complained about blimpishly for a good six months afterwards.

Yvonne Elliman was one of the best singers ever to grace our songs. She was also one of the nicest. Very much a child of the late Sixties, she was intemperately carefree and limitlessly trusting – hence some of her career problems over the years. If you told her it could be smoked, she'd smoke it.

She asked few questions – it was not until the rehearsals for the Broadway show of *Superstar* that she realised that Mary Magdalene was not Mary the mother of Jesus. 'I always wondered why his mother would have sung that song,' she said when it was explained that the character she had portrayed on seven million albums was another Mary. So much for dramatic motivation. Yet no one has ever sung that song better than Yvonne. She never looked beyond the next five minutes and appeared simultaneously bemused and amused by everything and everyone around her. She had a deep and filthy-sounding contagious chuckle.

With a Japanese mother and an American father (big in mayonnaise) her looks were both delicate and striking – not a classic beauty but a beautiful original. She had been brought up in Hawaii and had somehow found her way to England via the saxophonist Stan Getz. After Andrew spotted her in the Pheasantry Club her career began a steady climb that continued for well over a decade, and in the late Seventies she was one of the most popular contemporary singers in the world. She wound things down when she had children from her second marriage in the early Eighties, but I am sure that she could pick up the threads whenever she wants.

I remember how much I enjoyed those very first days of feeling successful. Based at my parents', I had no mad desire to spend, spend, spend but basked in the unfamiliar sensations of not having to worry about buying a hardback book rather than a paperback, or ten albums in one trip to the record shop. In many respects I still find the greatest pleasure of financial security is the ability to purchase comparatively small things without a qualm, whereas even now I worry about investment in anything more substantial, such as a car or a painting – an illogical concern but one I shall never quite shake off. Moreover, these were the days without too much money, no feelings of guilt, no obligation or indeed the resources to give huge chunks away, no pressure of responsibility to friends and family less fortunate. The downside of wealth was yet to come, but I would be hypocritical to pretend that the massive advantages do not vastly outweigh the problems.

When not gallivanting around Europe, I continued much as before; devouring books, magazines and records, playing gigs with Bill Heath and David Ballantyne as Just Plain Smith, jogging and playing a little squash, playing soccer some Saturdays with the Lancing College Old Boys Fourth XI, sitting for hours in pubs with Roger Watson and other pals, and still dreaming up a variety of musical or literary projects.

One of the first things I purchased with my £10,000 was an adding machine. Unbelievable as it may seem now, this was just before the age of the pocket calculator which was to sweep the globe in a matter of months. I bought the refrigerator-sized machine in order to work out the all-time Football League table, adding up every First Division team's records from the 1880s to the present time. I eventually got the results of my labour published in *The Times*, thanks to a most friendly reception to the idea from their distinguished Association Football correspondent, Geoffrey Green, one of the greatest writers and characters this country's sport has ever produced. I also began work on the definitive history of Tom and Jerry, then as now a regular fixture on BBC TV. I never completed this one, but spent many enjoyable hours in MGM's screening rooms in Soho, taking copious notes and laughing hysterically at the brilliance of Hanna and Barbera. (The later Tom and Jerry films, after the creators had left MGM in the mid-Fifties, were pretty ropey.)

Something I would never have suggested before my affluence was an offer I put to the lovely Flea Wallinger, secretary to Robert Stigwood's partner David Shaw. We were having dinner together at the White Elephant when we happened to discover that we both had our passports on our persons. Fortified by wine and doubtless inspired by lust, I proposed that we should drive immediately to Heathrow and get on the first plane to anywhere. The first part of this plan was easily accomplished, but the second abandoned when we discovered that the next flight out was the six a.m. to Birmingham. So, no manic adventure and/or romance, for which I am sure Flea was profoundly grateful in the cold light of day. I felt like James Bond on the way out to the airport, and like Tony Hancock on the way back.

Having been on TV in nearly every country in Western Europe, I was beginning to wonder if I could wangle some trips further afield – had our album not been Number One in both Brazil and Australia? – when we were summoned back to the United States. Now that we were part of the rampagingly ambitious Robert Stigwood Organisation, it was made clear by both David and Robert that we (me in particular) would soon have to stop flitting around Europe miming to Ian Gillan on obscure Dutch channels and chasing foreign pleasures in order to take a grip on the US situation, almost out of control in terms of our work's acceptance.

Superstar finally reached the top spot in America in February 1971. After a couple of weeks in pole position it dropped down a place or two, but returned to Number One in April. MCA's market research revealed that it was now selling in massive numbers to an adult market. Suddenly we found our work was now perceived to be a middle-of-the-road extravaganza, rather than the hip rock, cutting-edge phenomenon it had started out as. We began getting some really dire reviews from the kind of publication that would have raved about the album three months earlier, but success had stuffed us critic-wise. Having been overpraised, we were now over-slagged off, but the realisation that we were well on the way to the biggest-selling British album in history was some consolation. It was flying out of the stores all over the country as fast as MCA could get the platters in. An unknown Australian singer named Helen Reddy had covered 'I Don't Know How To Love Him' and both Reddy's version and Yvonne's were shooting up the singles charts. Murray's original *Superstar* single was also now a *bona fide* smash and dozens of other cover versions of songs from the show appeared, performed by a quite extraordinary range of artists from steel bands and military ensembles to José Feliciano and Peggy Lee. There were even a couple of male versions of the most popular song, retitled 'I Don't Know How To Love Her'.

The success of *Superstar* inspired the record releases of other, usually dire, 'rock operas', usually with a religious bent. None of these efforts, I am glad to say, were hits. Our own *Joseph*, having been ignored by every US record company for two years, was hurriedly repackaged and released by the somewhat unorthodox Scepter label, admittedly the home of the Shirelles and Dionne Warwick. Scepter had done a hasty deal with UK Decca and shoved the David Daltrey/Mixed Bag LP out in a new cover that looked extremely like the US *Superstar* album. Even this made the charts. Andrew and I made the front covers of most of the music trades, on *Cashbox* in tandem with MCA's other big new act, Elton John. As an anorakish pop chart follower from way back, it was doubly exciting to follow one's own progress on the lists that had gripped me since my early schooldays.

This was all very well, indeed better than all very well, but the question of a stage show had to be addressed urgently. Never before had there been a hit score from a show that didn't exist, and Robert was concerned that we mount a show as speedily as possible, preferably before the record dropped off the charts, and before someone else attempted a bootleg production. We succeeded in the first aim, mainly because the record stayed on the American charts for two years, but failed in the second.

Chapter Nineteen

Robert Stigwood moved fast to get *Superstar* on to Broadway, but not fast enough. Shortly after he had begun to put the production team together in preparation for an October opening at the Mark Hellinger Theater, the problem he feared surfaced: an unauthorised staging of the work. Worse, it was not just one illegal show, but literally dozens. If I find it hard to recall just how huge *Jesus Christ Superstar* was in the United States in 1971, looking back at the details of the Stigwood battle against armies of dubious or downright shady operators cashing in on the absence of a show to go with the smash score, is a staggering reminder.

The record was still selling prodigiously and had become far more than a merely musical phenomenon. In the US religious sphere everyone chipped in, from Billy Graham ('the music, in my opinion, is excellent, but the lyrics, while at times reverent, at other intervals border on the sacrilegious . . . to me, the work leaves a great deal to be desired') to the Rev. K.C. Ptomey, Jr, of the First Presbyterian Church, who preached a sermon entitled, 'What you always wanted to know about Jesus Christ Superstar, but were afraid to ask'. There were ominous rumblings in the wind of accusations of anti-Semitism in *Superstar*. Editorials were written about the work, business and women's groups held seminars about it, thousands of letters poured in from all over the nation, mainly telling us how we had opened their eyes to the real Jesus (some saying we had shown he was just a man, others that we had demonstrated his divinity), hundreds of church choirs sung all or some of the piece during their services, MCA's music publishing arm was forced to print versions of the score for every conceivable musical line-up from solo piano to marching bands, the cover recordings mounted. The original record grossed $35 million dollars by May, and then the full-blown illegal shows sprung up.

This was a serious crisis. Not only were these cowboys making money hand over fist without paying royalties to the owners of the copyright, we had no control over their artistic merit and ran the risk of tacky or simply abysmal productions irrevocably damaging the status of the work. The issue was over the grand rights. Without going into too much detail, these are the rights that enable writers to earn from theatrical presentations of their songs, normally by taking a percentage of the gate. This could mean big money, millions compared to the thousands that the songs would earn from record and radio play. To this day, the income I receive from innumerable theatrical presentations around the world of *Superstar* (and from most of my other shows) dwarfs the still substantial sums I earn from CD royalties and the like. Furthermore, it comes through very quickly compared with the sluggishness of recording and non-theatrical performance money.

The principle that Robert's army of lawyers (eventually more than fifty of them) had to establish when attempting to close down unauthorised shows was that *Superstar* was not simply a collection of songs which anyone could perform, provided they paid the modest licensing fees per song, but a theatrical piece, whether or not performed with sets and costumes, over which Robert's company, through his purchase of New Ventures, retained absolute control. Thanks almost entirely to Andrew's insistence back when we signed the original deal with MCA in London that the grand rights should not be part of the publishing side of the deal, we (and Robert) had a huge interest in making sure that these rights existed and that no one could mount a show without our approval.

Illegal productions crawled out of the woodwork. Companies such as the National Rock Opera Company (they also made their own LP of the show), the American Rock Opera Company (strangely, from Canada), Century Productions and a ragbag of other hastily-assembled companies swamped the country with their versions. Our Number One adversary was a formidable lady named Betty Sperber, who operated under a variety of different company names. Some of these stagings were quite good, judging from reviews, and some clearly dire. *Life* magazine featured one pirate show on its front cover. Andrew and I would have loved to have gone to see one, but were firmly restrained from doing so, in case our very presence implied approval. We protested that we were virtually totally unknown visually in the USA, but were told that there was always the faint chance of someone who knew us being there. Thus, extremely annoyingly, millions of Americans saw live performances of *Superstar* well before we did.

Robert's legal team, headed by the celebrated John Eastman (Paul McCartney's father-in-law), were pretty successful in closing down most of the pirates in due course. The opposition tried every trick in the book to prove they were not staging *Superstar*. They billed their show as 'extracts' (which meant they cut one song), or added in selections from *Godspell* or other religious tunes, some of which they wrote themselves, to prove that it was really just another concert. The actions, in over twenty different States, cost Robert over a million dollars, but he knew this was peanuts compared to what the potential income control of the grand rights could generate. But, in a way, the pirates did us an enormous favour by showing that there was massive potential in *Superstar* as a live show without the trappings of Broadway and legitimate theatre. On the 'if you can't beat 'em, join 'em' principle (even though he did beat 'em in the end) Robert's masterstroke was to set up his own touring concert version.

While still proceeding flat out with Broadway plans, Robert began to assemble a rock concert tour of *Superstar* at even more breakneck speed. Auditions were in full spate, and we were now looking out for singers to go out on the road as well as into the Mark Hellinger. These auditions took place in Los Angeles as well as in New York (more plane travel) and were enlivened for me by the occasional appearance of a faded rock star, such as Gary Puckett or, one of my special heroes, Ricky Nelson. A delightful audition pianist named Joanne also brightened up the West Coast auditions for me. Sad to say, none of the old rockers made the final cut, often because their agents still felt they were worth an astronomical wage.

I myself auditioned – in full drag – for Mary Magdalene. Most of the production team were in on the joke, but the audition pianist (it was not Joanne) became so offended at Robert and Andrew laughing out loud at my dire efforts that he walked off the stage in protest at such insensitivity to a struggling actress. On another occasion Robert was the victim of a dressing-up gag when we persuaded a real actress, posing as an Australian nun, to serve Robert with a writ. One of the most publicised features of Robert's lawyers' anti-bootlegging campaign had been his successful action against the Loretto nuns of Sydney, Australia (America was not the only country to generate unauthorised shows), who were mounting a substantial staging of the show, charging $12 a ticket. The nuns claimed that they had first rights to Jesus, but Stigwood prevailed and put their show, which was beyond doubt as commercial a venture as they come, out of business.

The only two survivors from our record to make it into the theatre were the two Americans, Yvonne Elliman and Barry Dennen. Had we wanted to cast Murray Head or Ian Gillan, and had they been free from pop commitments, it would have been highly unlikely that we would have got them past the less than enlightened mandarins of the actors' trade union, American Equity. Unknowns in the shape of Jeff Fenholt and Carl Anderson landed the parts of Jesus and Judas respectively, and together with Yvonne and a host of young, largely inexperienced and chaotically exuberant (but talented) actor-singers were rushed into concert rehearsals.

In great contrast to the extravagance planned for the Broadway show, the concert presentation was simple in the extreme. There was no set, no formal costumes (although Jesus wore a kaftan and most of the cast's everyday hippy-look matched the story satisfactorily), and precious little acting or direction. In short, it was just like an early Seventies rock concert, when staging and lighting effects were still fairly primitive. With no star names involved, the fate of the concert would obviously depend entirely upon the strength of the performances and *Superstar* itself.

On 12 July what was billed as the official World Première of *Superstar* opened in Pittsburgh, in front of 13,640 people who paid $66,262 for the privilege, beating the record at that venue set by Tom Jones the previous year. The top-price ticket was just six dollars. Not only did this tour prove the final nail in the coffin for Betty Sperber and Co., it gave the cast two months of extremely useful practice with the score. A rock band named Randall's Island were signed to be the Grease Band of the enterprise, and they too were booked for Broadway.

The concert tour was a mammoth success. As every bootleg tour had been wildly popular, this was not really that surprising. Before long Robert had two other tours criss-crossing the States, and all played to packed, enthusiastic houses wherever they went. When those chosen for Broadway were removed to start rehearsals in New York, replacements slotted in without a break in the run, which made no difference whatsoever to the reception. The show was the star. Even the reviews were pretty good, *Variety*'s rave including the prediction that *Superstar* should be very big on Broadway, and its comment, 'Outstanding from a trade point of view was the dominance of family groups in the audience. All ages were seen everywhere in the crowd', highlights a crucial reason for our work's commercial clout. Once more, by accident, we had stumbled upon a new way in which our work could be hugely successful. I gave thanks yet again that no one ever wanted to put *Superstar* on stage before the record.

As things turned out, *Variety*'s Broadway forecast was not really accurate, but as a rock concert *Superstar* could hardly have gone better. In fact I believe the work is seen at its best in a rock setting, preferably a stadium, with the full paraphernalia of a rock event, from noise to joints to bewildering lighting and over-the-top effects, much of which was still in its infancy in 1971. The version that became the biggest commercial success of all, in Australia in 1992, was a wondrous rock concert which made more money more quickly per show than any *Superstar* before or since. Most people prefer rock music to Broadway music, as I do.

I was not in Pittsburgh for the world première, unwittingly presaging my tendency to miss quite a few of my own opening nights over the following three decades. However I did not skip Pittsburgh voluntarily. Around three or four weeks earlier, I had collapsed in the Waldorf Astoria in the middle of a production meeting in Robert's suite – nothing remotely serious, really just a half-second faint. A doctor was summoned and put the fear of God into me by saying my blood pressure was up and that I should have tests for everything. I had frankly been burning the candle at both ends as well as in the middle and was simply knackered – besides all the gallivanting around New York I had nipped over to Tokyo via a stop-off in Hawaii (where I had dinner with Yvonne's parents), just to see Jo for four days – but immediately assumed that I was about to have a stroke, heart attack or had contracted some lethal virus. It was from this moment that my hypochondria burst into full bloom and I have never shaken it off since.

I decided to go straight back to England to face a less aggressive UK doctor and clocked in to see the very distinguished medicine man John Henderson, who attended many of the great and good from royalty downwards, though my hearing of him came through his friendship with one of Prudence's close chums. John assured me that 'common things are commonest' and put me through the ropes both at his own Knightsbridge HQ and with a succession of Harley Street specialists. Nothing sinister was revealed and I was merely diagnosed as being a bit clapped out. The cure was a holiday and, coupled with my decision at that time that I could not face getting on to another aeroplane, ever, ruled out my return to the States in time for Pittsburgh on 12 July.

I suspect that a small element of my hypochondria was caused by guilt at having suddenly made so much money, together with a need to have something to worry about when everything else had gone so perfectly. Certainly I never worried for a moment about my health until after my financial bonanza, and have always had it on my mind ever since – but I can usually convince myself that stress or jet lag is more likely than a terminal disease. Of course, one day that will not be true.

My nervousness about flying was ironic in that my father had spent most of his working life in the aviation business, but around this time it did become a bit of a problem. On my insane scoot over to Japan, I had undergone some fairly bumpy sectors plus a six-hour wait on the ground in a Jumbo while Pan-Am wrestled to get an engine to start. In the end I caused a fair amount of hassle by switching flights, convinced this one was doomed. I have to admit

I was half-hoping to read the next day that it had gone down, but I am now extremely glad to report that both it and the one I changed to got back to New York. I eschewed any kind of flight until the very end of 1971, when I plucked up the courage to go by air to Copenhagen with David Land to see the Danish version of *Superstar*.

Throughout all my candle-burning no one had held one (a candle, that is) to Prudence and she, having returned from her Caribbean foray, and I were soon together again whenever we could be. So for me to be ordered to take a holiday presented a pretty good opportunity for us to ease a little stability into our erratic partnership – as long as she came on the holiday too, of course. We decided to go to Biarritz and we had a terrific ten days in that wonderful Atlantic resort, wondering if Andrew, David and Robert were enjoying Pittsburgh. The only setback during this 'cure' came when I read that Jim Morrison, around my age, had died of heart failure in Paris. I did not know then that Jim's approach to the good life had been considerably more exotic than mine and passed a gloomy hour by the pool, worrying that the Grim Reaper might wish to claim a second exhausted mid-twenties victim having a break in France. But during the other hours, I began to feel less neurotic about dying and my relationship with Prudence was definitely on the most even keel it had enjoyed to date.

Feeling refreshed, with some rather nice relaxing pills prescribed by John Henderson as the only physical evidence of my feeble ailments, I had to re-address the problem of returning to the States. I wanted to see the concert and to take part in the Broadway plans, hotting up fast. I wound up making four Atlantic crossings by boat, two on the *QE2* and two on the long-since put-out-to-graze French liner, imaginatively called the *France*. Prudence joined me on one double voyage. The five-day trips were great fun, even though I was almost the only passenger under the age of fifty in First Class. I thus sneaked into the steerage discos and plebby clubs most nights and sang rock'n'roll with the *QE2* band after all the aged punters had gone to bed.

George Harrison was on one of my four trips and, armed with my new status as hit record producer, I felt bold enough to introduce Prudence and myself and share the odd beer with him. George's recent solo début, '*All Things Must Pass*'* had been almost the only British LP that year to have challenged the sales of *Superstar*. I found it strange to be talking to one of my idols from the position of having just had an even bigger hit than he had, but relative sales were not discussed and George could not have been more charming. He sang a few bars of 'Dear Prudence' on introduction to the lovely Miss de Casembroot, which went down pretty well. I also recall meeting Troy Shondell's mother. Shondell was an American pop singer who only ever had one hit, 'This Time' back in 1961, and to one fascinated by obscure pop stars this was a meeting made in heaven, as Troy's mum told me how young Gary Shelton (Troy's real name) won his moment of glory.

One of the many films I saw on board was Frank Loesser's *How To Succeed In Business Without Really Trying*, during which I was amazed to hear what sounded remarkably like the tune of the chorus of the song 'Superstar' but entitled 'Rosemary'. How dare they nick Andrew's melody, I thought, but then realised that the film predated *Superstar* by several years.

Back in the States, I drove down to Roanoke, Virginia, to see the concert tour, now a month into its stupendous run, and felt all my pop-star ambitions fulfilled when I went on stage at the end to be screamed and yelled at by over 8000 souls. The show was a triumph and I saw for myself that the audience covered all age groups – grandparents to kids. Many had the booklet from the album with them and followed the words therein avidly, pausing only to holler with fanatic lungpower between each scene. Yvonne was sensational as Mary Magdalene and the two unknown male leads, Fenholt and Anderson, seemed to me to be the equal of Ian Gillan and Murray Head. It was a weird (and slightly chilling) moment seeing the black man playing Judas kissing the white man playing Jesus in front of a huge crowd in one of the Southern States of the Union, knowing that my work had led to this happening, but no one in the huge audience raised a whimper of protest.

Returning to New York to put the Broadway show together, it was all systems go. One of the delights of that particular

---

* Like *Superstar*, George Harrison's album had a marked religious flavour, 'My Sweet Lord' being the most popular song of the collection.

pre-production period was that no one ever queried the actual quality of the work. Andrew and I were never told to 'improve' our work, as has happened so often since. It is strange but true to say that the longer I have been in this business, presumably quite competently if only because I have survived so long at it, the more others tell me how to do my job. Of course if a record has sold zillions of copies and taken a nation, if not most of the world, by storm, it is difficult for colleagues to suggest that wholesale changes are made, but in more recent times I know that everyone from the director downwards (or upwards, I sometimes feel) is going to have his or her view on how the writing, in particular the lyrics, can be improved. *Joseph* and *Superstar* were never tampered with by those who knew better, and *Evita* only a little – and that by someone who might have known better, Hal Prince.

I bitterly regret altering massive chunks of the original album of *Chess*, which had been hugely successful two years before we mounted the show in London – by which time suggestions from at least eighteen others had been incorporated, each one beyond doubt to the detriment of the original concept. Part of the problem arises from sheer success; once you become a major player then others are much keener to become involved as early as possible and too many cooks emerge. The three big hits I wrote with Andrew were virtually free from interference in this way, and much better for it. I don't tell directors how to direct, much as I would have liked to on occasion.

Anyway, for *Superstar* on stage the only change we made from the album version was a straightforward addition of one new song for Mary Magdalene, i.e. Yvonne. On the record, her character disappears completely after half-time and this would not have been satisfactory when we had such a marvellous singer in the part, and one who was becoming quite well known. The new number was in fact a duet between Mary and Peter, entitled 'Could We Start Again Please', in which two of those who loved Jesus the most wish hopelessly that the clock could be turned back. This number turned out rather well and we decided to double the length of the Trial sequence too. But nothing of the original score was actually altered.

Andrew did have to put up with a Broadway arranger being

dragged in to do what everyone assumed Andrew wouldn't know how to do, i.e., the orchestrations. As this had been one of the most outstanding features of the album, it seemed a strange decision and ALW was not best pleased. The arranging cove in question, Hershy Kay, was a man with a distinguished Broadway track record, precisely what this score did not need, but after several close encounters of the explosive kind, more or less reproduced Andrew's work note for note, with any alterations simply taking into account the fact that the orchestral resources available in the Mark Hellinger pit were smaller than those on the LP. I think in the end Andrew even got the credit on the posters for the orchestrations, as was only right and proper. My only other memory of Hershy is that he was so tiny that we more than once put our feet into it by talking about him without realising he was lurking behind a speaker. I am not trying to denigrate a much-respected Broadway veteran, but he was the wrong bloke in the wrong job.

The first director Robert signed for the show was Frank Corsaro. I had never heard of him, but then I had never heard of any directors. Frank was an affable chap who had had considerable success in both Broadway and operatic fields. He had made his name off-Broadway when off-Broadway barely existed, shortly after the war, with dynamic productions of Sartre, Strindberg and Shaw (I'd heard of at least two of these gents) and had staged important New York premières of works by Shostakovich and Prokofiev, incidentally two of Andrew's favourite composers. Corsaro had done great work too at the New York City Opera. All in all he seemed a perfect choice – innovative, respected, at home with all kinds of musical drama. He brought with him a multimedia design team, Gardner Compton and Emile Ardolino, and we were enthralled by their ideas which involved great emphasis on a mix between film and live action. Frank also said he wanted Jesus completely starkers on the cross. I had my doubts about that one.

We were pretty happy with the way the look and concept of the show was going, but Robert, unknown to us, was beginning to have doubts. He may well have begun to consider Frank to be too respectable, unintentionally destroying much of the flash and splash of the work, but in any event Robert had to dump him when poor Frank was badly injured in a car crash at the end of July. Corsaro received $40,000 severance pay (and later a lot more by suing the driver of the other car) and his cards.* Robert turned to Tom O'Horgan, the director who had turned *Hair* into a worldwide phenomenon and soon we found ourselves attending meetings with a weird bunch of largely gay, zonked hippies. One chap in O'Horgan's squad wore a rather fetching frock to most meetings which I found a little disconcerting; maybe that would not seem quite so outrageous now, but in 1971 it made me wonder whether my conservative middle-class upbringing had been the best training for this sort of working relationship.

O'Horgan squeezed a very generous deal out of Robert and set to work at a manic pace (he had to, as the opening was only about ten weeks away). I must admit he pulled off some great strokes. He was more or less stuck with principals from the cast that was now out on the road, although he insisted on one major change, Ben Vereen as Judas in place of Carl Anderson. As Carl had been so brilliant in the concerts nearly everyone not in the O'Horgan camp, so to speak, were very anti this move. However O'Horgan got his way and Vereen the part. Ben, Broadway to his boots, of course went on to become a big star for a while and certainly proved to be a very strong Judas, but I missed Carl's more contemporary vocals and more striking looks. In the end Carl came up trumps, performing the role both in the Los Angeles stage production and, more importantly, in the movie. He was still touring with a road version of *Superstar* as recently as 1996, so I trust he has paid off a few mortgages through his association with our work.

O'Horgan's work methods were somewhat unorthodox. In order to get the cast to 'bond with Jesus', he poured honey all over Jeff Fenholt and encouraged other cast members to lick it off. His designers' sets and costumes were outlandish. The actors loved this radical new approach to Broadway and confidence, not to mention the cast, was high. I actually took very little part in the production plans from here on, returning to England for most of

---

* David told me that Frank had been given the DCM. 'The DCM?' 'Don't Come Monday.'

August and September. I found it hard to raise colossal interest in rehearsals and had plenty of pressing reasons to return (by sea) to England, not the least of which was that I had recently bought a house.

Andrew spent much more time in New York than I did at this stage, but most of his efforts were concentrated on fighting musical battles. When I was on one side of the Atlantic, and he on the other, we spoke regularly and very amicably, when he would generally predict disaster (David and Robert bubbled with enormous confidence). I was becoming a little immune to Andrew's dire forecasts but what I had seen made me feel he could have a point this time. I genuinely wished I could nip over to offer more support, but still couldn't face an aeroplane. There again, Robert had made all the right moves so far – I would just have to wait and see and both inexperienced young writers felt at this stage of their careers that waiting and seeing was all we were entitled to do.

The money had not really started to roll in (my performance royalty cheque for July 1971 for plays of my songs on British radio was only £40) but I hadn't spent much of my £10,000 and it was a pretty safe bet that by the end of the year I would be sitting on quite a bit more than that. After a few weeks in a pretty ghastly flat in the Edgware Road, I found a modest four-storey terraced house in Northumberland Place, Bayswater, and shelled out £2100, being ten per cent of the asking price, taking out a mortgage for the remaining ninety per cent.

I then took out another mortgage in order to buy a flat for my grandmother, by then eighty, though still in the most sparkling form, in order that she and her older sister, Auntie Gertie, could be near my parents in Harpenden, instead of a hundred miles away in St Leonards-on-Sea. This set me back around another £1000 and lumbered me with a second set of monthly repayments, but even I, ever one to worry about going broke, felt relaxed about the commitments. The solicitor for both deals was my schoolfriend, Henry Speer (by now of course Jo's brother-in-law) in conjunction with a chap named Michael Campbell-Bowling, an insurance broker who amazed me at our first meeting by his uncanny visual and vocal impressions of Peter Cook. Michael remains part of my financial advisory set-up today, ever perplexed by my lack of interest in wheeling and dealing, trusts, pensions and insurance. But he seems to get most of it right, and if he helps keep the taxman at bay, I'll write the lyrics.

I have warm memories of 33 Northumberland Place, a quiet road quite near the Portobello markets, in W2, one of the best of London arrondissements. Few taxi drivers seemed to have heard of this leafy back street, and both I and several friends enjoyed erroneous trips to the more celebrated Northumberland Avenue, near Trafalgar Square, over the years. Very few cabbies haven't heard of Northumberland Place now, as it was made famous by Peter Mandelson in 1998. The government minister's purchase of a house exactly like mine led to his resignation after questions about his purchase methods. By this time houses in Northumberland Place were changing hands for around three quarters of a million pounds, and the street was well established as a trendy Notting Hill boulevard.

No. 33 had a tiny garden, and this provided me with the excuse to buy something I had yearned for ever since the passing of the one my parents had – a boxer dog. Bonzo, for such was the poor mutt's name, was a fine representative of his breed, bouncy, terminally friendly, thick as a post and barking mad. Prudence moved in, followed in quick succession by another dog, Stanley, a surly Lhasa Apso, which I bought for her in a very weak moment, and by my youngest brother Andy, now down from Cambridge and planning a drive across Africa.

I was accumulating advice quicker than cash and that of my accountant, Leonard Woolf, a colleague of Sefton's, plus that of Henry Speer and Michael Campbell-Bowling, was that I had to turn myself into a company. Personal tax rates were then, I think, at their highest of all time, with top slices of earnings being hit for eighty-three per cent, with unearned income suffering a fifteen per cent rate on top of that. Consequently there was little incentive for high earners to invest in the stock market or other straightforward wheezes, when they only kept two pence in the pound. You had to be a company and hit it for as many tax-deductible expenses as possible and thus I formed Heartaches Ltd. This was not an expression of how I felt about the UK tax laws, but a tribute to one of my favourite Elvis recordings, 'That's When Your Heartaches

Begin'. A stupid name, really, but Heartaches is still going strong, its profile today maintained primarily by my cricket team, named after the company – Heartaches CC. Several other company names I came up with over the years were even dafter.

Saving like mad for his African trek, Andy was employed by Heartaches and became a vitally useful personal assistant (and dog walker). I also found I needed a secretary, for my overseas fame was beginning to filter through back home, and I was embarking upon a crazy timetable which persists to this day, only worse. Flea Wallinger (the lady I had attempted to spirit away from Heathrow) had a close friend named Fiona Mackenzie and after a one-minute interview, Fiona was signed up. Heartaches opened its offices on the top floor of 33 Northumberland Place. Fiona was shortly to become engaged to a young property dealer named Anthony Deal, and thus two more quarter-century-plus (so far) friendships were formed. Heartaches bought me a car (a rather boring Triumph saloon) and I issued shares in the company to my parents and brothers. The cheques eventually began streaming in, minus of course Superstar Ventures' twenty-five per cent. I was getting used to becoming wealthier than in my wildest dreams, although I doubt whether I made more than £50,000 after tax by the end of 1971.

I bought a juke-box, an exotic hi-fi system, dozens of albums and books, cameras, bikes and ate out every night. I became, for the only time in my life, a theatre fanatic, and went to nearly every new musical or play. One around this time, and one of the best, *The Philanthropist*, was written by my former Lancing colleague, Christopher Hampton. Another OL, David Hare, was also making his dramatic mark, though at this point in his career I didn't care for his work as much as I did for Christopher's. I engaged a brilliant young architect to wreak havoc in my kitchen and drawing room, which he did with great gusto. Piers Gough CBE is now one of the most celebrated architects in the country.

I also found that I was becoming recognisable. I had always longed to try my hand at broadcasting and David wangled me on to several radio and TV programmes – all pretty trivial stuff, but I found I had a reasonably fluent media manner and began to crop up on more and more minor quiz and chat shows. I even judged a Miss England competition. An American writer based in London, Michael Braun, who had written a very good book on the Beatles' rise to fame, and knew all about our US success, latched on to me and Andrew. He seemed to be with one or other of us every night we were in England (David Land said he had 'A-levels in scrounging', which was perhaps a little unfair) but we were flattered by his attentions and by his declaration that he wanted to do a book on us. He seemed to know everyone, though, and I shall be permanently grateful to him for inviting me to a Neil Diamond concert and dinner in the company of Julie Christie.* We were still a bit of an unknown quantity to the British public at large, however, with the foreign Superstarmania resolutely refusing to duplicate itself at home.

I wanted to do everything – I wanted to be a pop star (still do), a disc-jockey, write articles for the papers, write my history of the record business, write a play, anything now I had the attention of those who could help this happen. Andrew and I set up a record production company with Polydor with *carte blanche* to record what we wanted, within a fairly generous budget. This company we called Qwertyuiop Ltd, from an obvious source, though we never actually registered what we thought should be its subsidiary, Asdfghjkl Ltd. (the second line on the typewriter keyboard). Polydor doubtless hoped we would write and produce another rock opera but they got lumbered with a succession of singles by me and/or Roger Watson, under names such as Huddersfield Transit Authority and Vocal Refrain. Covers of old Del Shannon and Tiny Tim hits failed to dent the charts, but we had a laugh making them. Slightly more intelligently, we recorded a version of *Peter and the Wolf* with Robert Stigwood client Frankie Howerd as narrator and signed Yvonne for future solo projects. But Qwertyuiop cheques have never set the taxman's heart beating.

Andrew somehow found the time to write the score for Stephen Frears' first feature film, an excellent private-eye spoof entitled *Gumshoe* starring Albert Finney. I wrote a lyric for one cod

---

* I met Julie Christie again in 1998 and she strongly, very strongly, denied ever having seen Neil Diamond, and thus presumably me, in her life. I still stick to my version.

rock'n'roll number in the picture entitled 'Baby You're Good For Me', sung by former Rebel Rouser Roy Young, whom I had last met at EMI when I attended Cliff Bennett's hit 'Got To Get You Into My Life' session. Andrew's main theme for the movie was a strong tune that he has resurrected time and time again over the years, eventually as the tune of the title song of *Sunset Boulevard*, where I guess it has now ground to a halt. My first set of lyrics for the melody were pretty grim, under the title 'Finally', which we recorded with a singer Andrew spotted on *Opportunity Knocks*, but the lady was no Yvonne, and the song no 'I Don't Know How To Love Him'.

Family and close friends were now becoming aware that I was actually coining it in, and this is not always easy to cope with. My attitude to cash has always been dominated by a feeling of panic that it won't last. I am happiest with large (positive) numbers on my bank statements. 'Who isn't?' I hear you cry, but my desire for such a situation derives from my quaint faith in cash as the only real evidence of wealth and security. I don't quite believe in anything else, and would probably be even happier with banknotes under the bed. My father's rocky career patch at this time didn't make things easier. He would never have dreamed of asking me for help, and I felt awkward about making the offer, incapable of coping with a reverse father/son support situation. Not that he was on his uppers by any means. Gradually over the years we both came to terms with the ludicrous imbalance of the rewards our respective careers had given us and by the time his working life ended with great distinction with four years in Jordan attached to the diplomatic service, we had both adjusted to my ridiculous earnings and I had helped him along the way. But never as much as he had helped me over my first twenty-five years.

Others were not so backward in coming forward for loans or help. Requests from charities materialised from all sides and I was happy to do what I could, though always felt it more worthwhile to give my time rather than merely hard cash. I participated in a primitive form of hospital radio at the Royal Marsden and gave the odd talk to churches and fundraising groups for a variety of causes. Best of all, I played in a charity cricket match for the Lord's Taverners, before long to become my number one charitable outlet. A glorious day's cricket at Blenheim Palace made me realise how much I had missed the game, having never struck a ball in anger since leaving school. I don't pretend that at this point I was doing much for worthy causes, but I discovered that there were thousands of them around and it was important for me to feel, as ninety-nine per cent of showbiz winners feel, that I was doing my bit, or a bit of my bit.

Old friends from way back with insoluable financial crises kept popping up. It was never close chums who needed the odd grand, but friends of friends or people I hadn't seen for a decade. One bloke, an American actor friend of Roger Watson's, stung me for £250 (multiply by at least ten for today's equivalent) which was only to be a sum that he would stick in his bank account and leave untouched for three months in order to convince the immigration authorities that he was solvent and thus worthy of a British work permit. Needless to say, he was on the plane home days after I gave him the cheque and probably had enough left over for a good holiday. He was not the only conman who took me for a ride.

But those who mattered to me, brothers, parents, Prudence and my long-term pals, delighted in my good fortune and made no demands. I was delighted to have them help me enjoy it. I was never shy about admitting that I was earning big money, and even went on to a current affairs TV show to confess that I was pulling in around £1000 a week. This was not simply an excuse to brag, but part of the programme's probe into the insane tax levels of the day. I was able to demonstrate how little of the money I would keep unless I went through absurdly complicated hoops with armies of experts, all earning a living by trying to deny the government its income. Even then one didn't really keep much more than half. I was told that I should become a tax exile, but in 1971 that entailed not setting a foot in the country for 365 consecutive days, and I didn't want the extra that badly. And what if a family crisis cropped up during the year out? As Ian Anderson of Jethro Tull said, 'If you leave the country to avoid tax, you can afford to stay.' I stayed.

Andrew was always much happier setting up schemes and (perfectly legal) dodges than I was and soon dispensed with Sefton's accountant contacts, in favour of a team recommended by his new wife's father. It seemed that at the start of every tax year in the Seventies, on 6 April, he would announce that he was leaving the country but he never held out much beyond the beginning of May. All the same, he displayed a superb grasp of personal economics even before he shot into the supertax bracket, and I have no doubt that he kept a lot more of his income than I ever did. He liked the money meetings and had a powerful business instinct. He tended to play down his earnings drastically in private and in public, his claim in one interview that he was not even a 'lire millionaire' rather hard to swallow.

How I had time to fire on so many cylinders in England when I still had to be in New York for *Superstar*, and going there and back by boat, I cannot now imagine. But come the end of September I was back in Manhattan, with Prudence, for the big opening.

Chapter Twenty

A host of family, friends and fans descended upon Manhattan for the Broadway début of *Jesus Christ Superstar*. David Land had chartered a plane for the bulk of the supporters' club and two days before the scheduled opening 200-plus of our nearest and dearest, investors, UK critics, gossip columnists and assorted hangers-on were wandering around New York, eagerly anticipating what Robert had promised would be the opening night of opening nights and the party of parties on 12 October 1971. Among the sightseers was my entire close family, parents, brothers and grandmother, the latter making her first trip to America at the age of nearly eighty-one. Prudence and I had arrived by boat a few days earlier and had seen a couple of previews. I wasn't sure that I liked what I had seen, but frankly I didn't really know what I thought; it seemed a bit of a mess in places.

In the frantic days before any first night, panics and disasters abound, and *Superstar* had more than its share. Three previews had to be cancelled at a loss of $36,000 to the box office because of problems with radio mikes on stage, then gadgets in their infancy. They kept picking up alien signals such as police radios and, deliberately or otherwise, the clearest sound always seemed to emanate from an actor wired for sound when he or she was off-stage, more often than not in the lavatory. In the end they were nearly all ditched and hand microphones installed in their place, their leads disguised rather feebly with leafy décor which at times gave the impression that the action was taking place in the

Garden of Eden rather than Jerusalem. The complexities of Tom O'Horgan's sets caused further problems. I have learned since that sets cause nearly all of any new show's teething troubles and have become convinced that costumes and lighting, neither a tenth of the trouble of scenery and furniture, are the visual aspects of a musical upon which one should lavish time, skill and attention.

We also had to cope with various professional protesters. These were almost exclusively complaining about the content of the show, i.e. the lyrics. I did not know whether to be flattered or frightened by this. First into the ring was Rabbi Marc H. Tanenbaum, representing the American Jewish Committee. They compiled a hefty document which concluded that the show 'unambiguously lays the primary responsibility for Jesus' suffering and crucifixion to the Jewish priesthood', and found evidence of anti-Semitism in almost every line. Rabbi Tanenbaum was remarkably available for radio and TV interviews and cropped up all over the shop in the days before the opening.

I agreed to go on to one television programme to defend the work, a strange semi-chat show compered by Leonard Nimoy, Dr Spock of *Star Trek* (in this mode, *sans* Spock's ears). Most of the programme consisted of Nimoy reading his less than moving poetry but during the brief exchanges Tanenbaum and myself were allowed, I made a fair fist of establishing my anti-anti-Semitic credentials, by quoting 'Close Every Door' from *Joseph* and pointing out that, as both victim and oppressors in our show were Jewish, it was illogical to argue that we were siding with the bad guys. I never got into the more complex point that our Jesus, just like the Bible's Jesus, had plenty of opportunity to avoid his earthly fate, but accepted what he felt to be his destiny, in other words he was largely responsible for his own mortal end. Neither did I get the chance to point out, cliché though it be, that many of my best friends, many involved with this production, were Jewish. I did manage to query why Tanenbaum had kept quiet during an entire year when the work reached millions of record buyers around the world, yet felt it necessary to beef when it was about to play to a fraction of that audience on Broadway. Could it be he relished the publicity that a Broadway opening guaranteed?

We also got it in the neck from black activists for the casting of the black Vereen as Judas. However, Robert decreed that the best policy was to ignore all complaints and, apart from my one encounter with Rabbi Tanenbaum, we kept our heads below the parapet, avoiding direct confrontation. On the opening night itself a motley collection of placard-carrying religious maniacs picketed the theatre, but as most of them loudly denied ever having soiled themselves by listening to the album or by attending a preview, their campaign lacked a certain amount of authority.

Many critics, both before and after the opening of *Superstar*, compared us (usually unfavourably) with *Godspell*, the other Jesus musical that appeared at the time, which endeared itself to the media by virtue of the fact that it was small and unpretentious, whereas we were a massive, overblown hype. When we first heard about this John-Michael Tebelak–Stephen Schwartz show, which had opened off-Broadway in May, we were extremely worried. It seemed that this was yet another outfit from nowhere ripping off our idea, only this lot would be impossible to deal with along the lines of other bootleggers because they had had the wit to write a completely new piece around a story that not even Robert's lawyers could claim was our copyright.

Andrew and I went to see the show and our worries were quickly laid to rest – the show bore no resemblance at all to ours. It was a modest show, just a dozen actors and a small rock band, which portrayed Jesus as the Son of God, albeit dressed as a circus clown. Furthermore, we enjoyed it very much. In the end the presence (and success) of two Jesus rock musicals was a huge help to both shows. Commentators and critics were able to ramble on about a 'trend', which meant that most people who went to see one then felt obliged to see the other, to get the full picture. In reality (as far as we knew) the simultaneous creation of both shows was nothing more than a coincidence. David's philosophical gem No. 7, which stated that 'where there's room for one hamburger bar, there's room for two', was once again proved right.

Other exciting pre-opening moments included sharing a Waldorf-Astoria lift for thirty floors with the Duke of Windsor and a huge black retainer, the latter carrying a set of golf clubs. My first conversation with a past, present or future monarch was Brechtian in its stark simplicity. 'Going down?' was my contribution; 'Up', the former Edward VIII's. Travelling from our humble floor to Robert's penthouse suite, I was, I am sorry to relate, wearing no shoes or socks, and little more than a vest and jeans, and found myself pathetically hoping that the tiny Duke had not detected my English accent. He certainly looked at me with the enthusiasm of a Ku Klux Klan member at a reggae festival but this might have only been because his elevator was normally efficiently protected from contamination by any alien passenger.

I also had a spot of bother with one of the backstage team making extraordinarily persistent advances after a long evening's production meeting, finding it a salutary experience to be in the position I had more than once placed a woman. I knew that however strong his blandishments and flattery, I would not give in. How many of the ladies I had chatted up over the years felt exactly the same? I learned a lesson, but soon forgot it again.

What of the show itself? Well, it wasn't perfect. O'Horgan's production was never seen again outside Broadway, unusual for a hit show, and although it never even ran for two years at the Mark Hellinger, *Superstar* was technically a hit in that the investors got their money back. Just. O'Horgan did restage the work himself in the summer of 1972 in Los Angeles, where his excesses found a more sympathetic setting in the new Universal Studios Amphitheatre, a near-4000 seater outdoor venue overlooking the San Fernando Valley. Mountains, the sunset and the Pacific Ocean were backdrops to match the director's profligacy and this second attempt earned considerably more critical praise than had his first.

The Broadway show contained some dazzling, often vulgar, special effects to which I will concede our material lent itself rather easily; it was, after all, basically a contemporary rock score which had a considerable built-in shock quotient. But too often the spectacle overwhelmed or distracted from the actors or the songs, so the emotional and dramatic power, which the virtually effect-free concert tour had surprisingly delivered, was almost absent. During the overture a silver chalice rose from the depths and eventually fell open like a flower to reveal Jesus high above the stage; when Judas sang 'Superstar' towards the climax, Jesus was raised again with a huge golden coat falling from his

n the road with Yvonne, 1971; a drive to
enna and back in my mother's old mini, to
me on Austrian TV.

David Land redecorates his office.

drew and I were the stars when the *Superstar* album shot to Number One in America, but
body knew what we looked like. So I was a perfect candidate for the game show *To Tell The
uth*, in which a panel of celebrities had to guess which was the real Tim Rice. They all guessed
, which was probably because the producers insanely booked two Aussies as the fake Tim Rices.

Above My first secretary, Fiona Mackenzie, now Mrs Anthony Deal, outside her place of work which doubled as her boss' home, 33 Northumberland Place, W2, 1972.

Above right Although my first trip to Oz in 1972 was blighted by the immigration authorities' refusal to let my sister-in-law enter the country, I was quickly won over by the locals.

The late, great Anita Morris (*below*), about to drive to Boston with me, Andrew and Bill Oakes (*right*), early 1972.

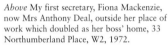

ve The front of the Palace Theatre looked like this
1972–1980; when *Superstar* closed it had become
longest-running musical in West End history, a record
beaten by almost everything. (*Doug McKenzie*)

t Felicity Balfour, captivating dancer in the first
End *Joseph*.

w The signing of the *Superstar* film deal at the offices
MCA, Universal City, Los Angeles; *left to right*: TR,
e Maitland (MCA Records boss), Andrew Lloyd
ber, Robert Stigwood, David Land and Ned Tanen
versal Pictures chief).

The Huddersfield Transit Authority, aka Tim Rice and Roger Watson, deliverers of several expensively unsuccessful singles to Polydor.

Boxer obsession continues as limp-wristed Bonzo (two) and master (twenty-eight) relax on the pavements of not yet trendy Notting Hill.

On the air at Capital Radio; being paid to play my own records as I had more oldies than they had.

With a frail Benjamin Britten at his home, the Red House, Aldeburgh, in 1974, during the recording of one of my *Musical Triangles* programmes.

Above Romeyns Court, at Milton, Oxon.

Left, main picture 19 August 1974; marriage on a sunny Monday morning.

Left, below 19 August 1974; evening celebrations at the Savoy – me with three Rices: the groom and family.

Right With Jane in the garden of Romeyns Court soon after taking possession. Why am I reminded of the Bob Dylan song 'I Threw It All Away'?

With Jane and Eva Jane Florence, the latter just an hour or two old.

Two great American chums: Tyler Gatchell (*left*) and Peter Brown, Long Island in 1974 (though the latter only became American in 1997).

shoulders to envelop a large part of the playing area. A massive green head disgorged King Herod relaxing in a pink shell; a vast plastic box of stars hovered above Jesus during 'Gethsemane', and Judas' death by hanging was a drawn-out, twitching trip to the skies that must have worried the show's insurers as well as Ben Vereen's loved ones. The first act ended with the stage rising up to become a wall, separating Judas, who had just betrayed Jesus to the High Priests, from the rest of humanity. The costumes for the authority figures of the piece were particularly unrestrained, with hideous platform shoes and towering helmets as much a lumber for the actors as were their hand microphones. The colours were rarely vivid; browns and mauves, faded greens and wash blue stick in my mind – a welcome shot of subtlety amid the brash mechanics.

The cast performed pretty well and, when the sound system wasn't playing up, most of the lyrics and textures of orchestration got through. 'I Don't Know How To Love Him' always hit home as Yvonne's lovely voice and poise were all the spectacle needed. But this was 1971 – still the stone age of amplification on Broadway. It was loud and the bulk of the audience had never been to a rock concert. The younger element, whose ears had been raised on rock, rarely ventured into a legit New York theatre. The oldies didn't get it, or couldn't take it, and the kids didn't go – so after 711 performances Robert threw in the towel.

Jeff Fenholt, the young man who played Jesus, had a simultaneously sweet and powerful voice, which had little difficulty echoing the vocal gymnastics of Ian Gillan. He never achieved any kind of subsequent commercial theatrical or musical success, but did make another mark on twentieth century culture via his liaison with Salvador Dali's wife, Gala, around fifty years Fenholt's senior. This affair and obsession (on Gala's part) caused Dali much unhappiness during his final years. Jeff later turned up as a born-again Christian on religious channels, singing and speaking the praises of the Lord on those unspeakably fascinating God-TV shows. Curiously, his first child (not by Gala) was born on Christmas Day. Ben Vereen was never anything less than supremely professional, Yvonne was Yvonne, which is more than enough, and Barry Dennen as Pilate proved that there was a place for acting in rock musicals.

Looking back, I feel that Tom O'Horgan's *Superstar* might have got rather a bad deal. Every time I recall an aspect of his extravaganza these days, it seems strange that I had reservations about it at the time – but I did. I guess I was almost as resistant to innovation as the Broadway regulars. Impossible to bring about, but I would love to see an exact replica of his production today, with all the technical advances in sound and sets available. It was beyond doubt ahead of its time, both in its conceit and its actual staging. Robin Wagner (sets) and Jules Fisher (lighting) barely put a truck or a bulb wrong, even if sometimes the mechanics hampered their contributions. Though O'Horgan never again directed a show that made any great impact, through *Hair* and *Jesus Christ Superstar* alone he is entitled to be considered an important figure of the twentieth-century musical. These two shows were nothing if not mould-breakers and began the process of dragging Broadway into a new area of music. It has still some way to be dragged.

So at the time I didn't really think the show had done our work justice – and neither did Andrew. He minded much more than I did – undoubtedly the more praiseworthy and understandable writer's reaction – but I found it easy to shrug off the disappointment with the thought that we had had an amazing year and had already achieved more than I ever dreamed we could have done. That sounds rather flippant, but I'm afraid it's the truth.

Most of our fans from England felt the show was not quite what they had hoped for, whatever that was, but for many, the whole razzamatazz of the week in New York more than compensated. The opening night party at the Tavern on the Green in the middle of Central Park was a hoot, even more exotic than the show itself. Transvestites and drag queens mixed with slightly bewildered black-tie traditional first-nighters; it was as if there had been a double booking mix-up featuring the Gay Liberation Front and a Wall Street seminar. There was a fair smattering of American celebrities, few of whom meant anything to the British delegation.*

---

* One of the strangest social feelings I know is to be in the presence of someone famous, but not to you. The reaction of fans to the celebrity whom you don't know from Adam seems beyond all comprehension and logic.

The cheerful atmosphere at the bash was slightly dented in certain quarters by the less than ecstatic review in the *New York Times*, which arrived shortly before midnight. Its theatre critic, an Englishman named Clive Barnes, laid into most aspects of the show, notably the lyrics:

> [Mr Rice] does not have a very happy ear for the English language. There is a certain air of dogged doggerel about his phrases that too often sound like a deflated priest.

Bloody rude. A few months earlier, we had been taken by MCA to Barnes's flat to meet this vitally important writer, in the hope that Barnes would be won over by the charm and youthful exuberance of his fellow countrymen. This wheeze obviously failed. I am very glad to say I have not met him since, though he is still plying his trade in a less prestigious New York paper. Nonetheless, his tepid review (he was at times quite nice about Andrew) was a rave compared with many we were to receive from his successors on the *New York Times* in subsequent years, both for shows we did together and separately. However, Douglas Watt in the *Daily News* gave *Superstar* a terrific write-up which provided plenty of quotes to stick up outside the theatre. He began:

> *Jesus Christ Superstar*, which as everybody knows opened last night at the Hellinger, is so stunningly effective a theatrical experience that I am still finding it difficult to compose my thoughts about it. It is, in short, a triumph.

What a perceptive fellow. All in all, we could truthfully claim the reviews were mixed, something I would have been absolutely thrilled to say about most of the recent receptions of my theatrical efforts in New York.

But I enjoyed the opening hoop-la. It was great fun to show my clan around the city, particularly my grandmother who was up for anything and charmed the socks off even the most degenerate assistant director. We all returned home half-convinced that we had triumphed and I for one was nothing but chirpy about the next twelve months. The road shows were going great guns, the

Broadway box office looked good if not great, the Los Angeles show was in preparation, there were the Danish, French and Australian versions coming up in the immediate future, the London show was scheduled for the late summer and, best of all, a deal had already been done for the movie. And the record was still selling by the truckload. Maybe we should even start thinking about a new project. Maybe not, Christmas was coming.

The investors in the New York *Superstar* eventually got their money back, plus a tiny profit. They would have done better leaving it in the bank, although their local branch would not have thrown in a huge party in Central Park. A determined investor can usually get a fair chunk of his money back via food and drink on the opening night. Much of the $800,000 (roughly £320,000 then – well under a twentieth of the cost of a big musical in the Nineties) that the show cost was funded by the Robert Stigwood Organisation, and by MCA and their associates but I undertook to raise a small portion ($50,000) by offering my friends and family the chance to buy a share in the production. Here was a foolproof way to enable others to benefit from my good fortune – I took no investment share myself. Around fifty first-time 'angels' (as those who finance shows are called) purchased a tiny piece of the action, generally at about $1000 dollars (then around £400). A thousand dollars gave a punter one-eighth of one per cent of the profits and as those profits came in, they were paid out around every three months to the anxious investors. Stigwood paid my group's income directly to me, and Fiona and I then divided it up pro rata among our lucky backers.

Unfortunately they did not turn out to be very lucky. The first payments were hefty and prompt, but as the show's box office wilted, the final instalments took longer and longer to materialise. Most of my investors were uncomplaining and reassured by my confidence that they would eventually see a positive return, but one or two (inevitably the friends of friends) got rather stroppy towards the end of the run and demanded to inspect the full accounts. Their disgruntlement was doubtless fuelled by the fact that the statements they received revealed that I was personally making around £1200 a week from the enterprise, my royalties (a straightforward percentage of the weekly take) unaffected by the overall status of the show's economy, being based on income not on profits. And I was easily making that again from the road shows. I was mightily relieved when I was able to send out cheques to my supporters that took their payback over the one hundred per cent mark, but they never got more than a few pounds beyond that. Towards the end of the saga I suggested that the modest cheques should be invested elsewhere and included racing tips in the payout letters. A couple of these recommendations stormed home, turning a final two per cent profit for my syndicate members into one of around five per cent, at least for those who backed the selections.

As the vast majority of musicals dispose of angels' shirts, trousers and most visible means of support, these *Superstar* virgins were in fact extremely lucky not to take a bath. I have generally followed the rule that one should never back one's own shows – if they are hits, the creators earn anyway, if they flop, at least you haven't lost anything other than your time, effort and sanity. The one time I broke this rule in a big way was still many years in the future, when I sunk (unwillingly, but that's another story) a small fortune into the Broadway production of *Chess*, an unmitigated financial disaster. I never had a penny of my own money in my biggest hit of all, *Evita*, nor in the recent hugely profitable revivals of *Joseph*. I have occasionally put a few grand into other people's shows, but have rarely backed a winner. I even shot myself in the foot over the one investment venture that did pay off handsomely – the film of *Monty Python and the Holy Grail*.

Through connections I cannot recall (it may have been through the impresario Michael White who had been involved as co-producer of the first West End version of *Joseph*), I was asked if I would like to invest in the first Monty Python feature film of original material. This was in late 1972 or early 1973. I agreed to put in £4000. Both David and Andrew were rather miffed that they had not been given the chance to invest in what sounded like a copper-bottomed smash, as I casually bragged about my show-biz acumen and movie connections. I was then invited to see a (very) rough cut of about half of the picture and thought it looked a complete mess. My four grand had surely gone down the drain. When David and Andrew next mentioned the film, I shamelessly and disgracefully intimated that I might just be able to involve them in my investment and relieved them each of £1000 in return for half of my stake. When the finished movie came out, it was brilliant and a huge hit. My £4000 is still paying out today, having made me well over £50,000 in the past twenty-five years. But of course I have had to hand over half of this to my two colleagues – poetic justice in view of my murky behaviour.

At the start of 1972, my income was soon to be boosted even further by the proliferation of *Superstar* productions around the globe. For some strange reason, the first European version to emerge was in Denmark and David Land persuaded me to get on to an aeroplane for the first time in eight months to attend the Copenhagen opening. The highlights of our trip were a visit to a live sex show (where David was nearly thrown out for barracking the performers and asking the management whether they were paying Robert Stigwood royalties for the use of the Bee Gees' *Greatest Hits* as background to the squelchy cabaret) and meeting John Fogerty, legendary leader of Creedence Clearwater Revival, on the plane out. I recognised him immediately, but could not understand what he would be doing on a flight from London to Copenhagen. (It turned out, inevitably, that there was a woman involved.) Once I found the nerve to introduce myself, and confirmed that it was him, we had several turbulence-calming glasses together during which I asked him, rather rudely really, whether he ever resented criticism that Creedence were a three-chord group. 'Three chord group?' replied John. 'We're a *two*-chord group.' Indeed, many of his greatest songs such as 'Green River' and 'Bad Moon Rising' were simplicity itself, but therein lay their greatness. Oh, the Danish *Superstar* was quite good, and a big hit.

In the first half of 1972 I went to openings of *Superstar* in Paris, Munster in Germany, Stockholm and Sydney, Australia. Because of the general lack of confidence in the O'Horgan version, all of these were brand new productions, and none bore any resemblance to the Broadway show. Robert had decided that he would not entrust the London show to O'Horgan, and it was extremely useful for us all to see other ways it could be done before we set up in the West End. Robert, however, was still moving at high speed, determined to open at the Palace Theatre (these days owned by Andrew's Really Useful Group) in August. There was never a great likelihood of a Swede or Dane being called in for London, but the Paris production, in the hands of the English actor/director Victor Spinetti, and the Sydney show, under the control of the young Jim Sharman, provided directorial possibilities for the UK.

As ever, the European trips provided me with more opportunities to behave like a pop star, at least off stage, and I have more recollections of being up all night in bars or actresses' flats than of the actual shows. The Swedish show was more or less a transplant of the earlier Copenhagen one. I became entranced with Stockholm on my second visit there and became friends with Stig Anderson, the country's leading music mogul, whose publishing companies represented our copyrights in Scandinavia. This contact proved to be extremely useful eleven years later when I wanted to meet Bjorn Ulvaeus and Benny Andersson of a group Stig managed (ABBA) with a view to writing a show with them. The German show we attended was staged in a huge ice-rink in Munster, and was really more of a concert version which was to tour Germany at similar venues for over a year in its first incarnation. The Thirty-Nine lashes scene went down so well in Deutschland that Pilate nearly made it Seventy-Eight.

I loved the Paris version, but not many Parisians did. The French are not known for their support of musical theatre – even *Les Miserables*, written by their own countrymen, flopped there – and the huge hype that surrounded Victor's production made the local critics even less disposed to like it. It ran for a few months in the Palais de Chaillot, a (then) modern hall near the Eiffel Tower, but despite all the efforts of the wickedly energetic French producer, Annie Fargue, one of Robert's closest chums, it never caught on. Salvador Dali stole much of the opening night glory, preening his exotic garb and demeanour with Wildean satisfaction from the most visible box in the house. A brief encounter between Dali and Frankie Howerd was alone worth the price of admission. It was Mr and Mrs Dali's enormous enthusiasm for *Superstar* that led to the fateful Gala Dali/Jeff Fenholt situation when they came to see the show again in New York. In Paris the cast had beautiful voices and Victor's staging was simple, fluid and sympathetic to the work, but this was not enough. Some of the songs were, however, big hits in the French charts, including both Petula Clark and Anne-Marie

David (Mary in the show) scoring with the French version of 'I Don't Know How To Love Him'.

The dynamic mighty atom that was Annie Fargue was determined to give *Superstar* another shot in her home town and once she knew the Chaillot version was doomed, set up a smaller concert version in the most famous music hall in the land, the Olympia. This was the Palladium of Paris, the venue in which Edith Piaf most famously carved out her legend. To my astonishment, Annie asked me if I would direct this new pared-down version. No one knew the show better than me, she argued, the casting was already in place, I spoke tolerable French and I would have the chance to spend a few weeks in a city I loved and knew pretty well.

In the event I only needed to be there for around three weeks. I did my best and although I doubt whether Harold Prince and Peter Brook combined could have broken through the Parisian determination to stay away from *Superstar* in droves, my first and last attempt at directing was fairly enjoyable. Perhaps not as enjoyable as a renewed acquaintance with my Sorbonne sweetheart, Solange, but there were no major crises or cock-ups with the show – other than the indifference of the locals. Speaking French nearly all the day did wonders for my Parisian social life, but the Mark Two French *Superstar* was no more successful than Mark One. Even Annie lost heart after the second failure, but I am very grateful that she tried so hard.

It was the Australian show, as Robert had suspected, that provided us with the new inspiration for the West End. The young man (he was, like me and Andrew, then in his mid to late twenties) Robert invited to direct the Sydney *Superstar*, to première there in May 1972, was on a roll Down Under. Jim Sharman was a descendant of a very famous family of Australian touring boxing booth shows, who began his career as a director in the non-musical theatre. He first showed his skill for handling the musical side of things when he staged a notable production of *Don Giovanni* for the Australian Opera, and then, moving to the contemporary, the Oz version of *Hair*, which was enormously well received. He was the obvious choice for Sydney, and Robert was very optimistic that his fellow Aussie would immediately demonstrate he could also be the man for London.

I was red-hot keen to go to Sydney for the opening, not just to check out Sharman, but because my long love affair with cricket had made me a confirmed Aussiephile. Ironically, my first ever trip to a country I have returned to at least a dozen times since 1972, coincided with the arrival of the Australian cricket team in England. It was the start of the Australian football season and the one thing I had no chance of doing there was to see any cricket. However, I was not the slightest bit disappointed by Sydney – it is of course almost impossible to imagine anyone failing to be enchanted by this beautiful city. The Opera House was still under construction and the cosmopolitan buzz that is such a characteristic of Sydney these days had barely begun to sound, but its matchless harbour and beaches, its relaxed and open people, its sun, its space, its architecture mixing so many traditional nineteenth- and twentieth-century English styles, in both city and suburbs, with a twist or mantle of indigenous modernity and/or provision for a warmer climate, were more than was needed to ensure my first taste of Australia would not be my last. I loved hearing old Aussie pop hits from the Fifties and Sixties which I had never come across before on the radio and brought back happy memories of a time I had never known – Col Joye, Johnny O'Keeffe and Slim Dusty. How is it possible to feel nostalgic for times or places one never experienced in the first place? Movies set between the wars have that effect on me, too.

In a spirit of staggering generosity, I invited my brother Jo and his wife Jan to join me in Australia (from Japan) for the opening. Although I quickly found I had several new Aussie best friends, and two old Lancing friends called my hotel within hours of my arrival, Andrew had decided not to make the trip, and I needed some close allies in tow. (Incidentally, one of the advantages of celebrity, even at my then Third Division South level, is someone from your past, wherever you go, will read about you in the local press and get in touch. High-flyers from lower-profile industries must miss dozens of reunions as they zip in and out of foreign parts; many would be more than happy about this, but I am a sucker for the good old days and really enjoy catching up, even with people I barely exchanged five words with during five years at school.)

Japan seemed like a short latitudinal hop from Tokyo to Sydney. In fact, while obviously a whole lot less than the slog from London, it was still a ten-hour flight. I drove out to the airport to meet Jo and Jan a few days before the big night, only to spend three hours witnessing several Jumbos disgorging passengers from the Far East, but none of them my brother and his wife. Eventually a seething Jo emerged with the news that the Aussie authorities would not let Jan into the country as she had not had the required smallpox jab. This despite Qantas in Tokyo assuring them that a certificate stating that Jan could not be given the inoculation because of her asthma would get her past the border guards. We spent a couple more hours fruitlessly protesting to anyone we could find behind a desk or in a uniform, but all in vain. In order to avoid further contamination of New South Wales, Jan was carted off to a quarantine centre on a remote Sydney cliff-top to spend twenty-four hours with illegal immigrants and consignments of bananas affected by fruit-fly, to await a plane back to Tokyo the following morning.

Jo and I spent most of the day pulling every string we could find to get this cruel decision rescinded, but to no avail. I slagged off the Australian immigration squad on radio, tried to call the Governor-General and spoke pompously to several newspapers. We enlisted the help of the extremely well-connected local producer of *Superstar*, the larger-than-life, near-legendary Harry M. Miller, but even his contacts, threats and wheels within wheels were unable to spring my sister-in-law. When it became clear that Jo and Jan were in Australia on a day trip, I took my brother on one of the all-time quickest sightseeing tours of Sydney and its environs. His day, which had not by any standards been a successful one, ended in further disaster when he was arrested as he attempted to join his beloved late at night in the quarantine compound. They got away the following morning without further humiliation, having featured on the front page of a couple of Sydney papers, 'Superstar man's brother turned back at airport' being one headline. At least I eventually got a full ticket refund from Qantas who admitted their cock-up.

So I went to the opening without family support. An exciting feature of the night was an attempt at sabotage at half time, when an unknown hand (allegedly that of an affronted Christian), cut the main cable linking the conductor to his orchestra via closed-circuit television. The Twelve Apostles and Jesus came out to begin the second act unaware of this communications breakdown and patiently sat at table waiting for the opening notes. After a few minutes it was clear that something was wrong, unless Jim Sharman had decided at the last moment to include a biting attack on slow restaurant service. Our Lord and his disciples shuffled off and the audience sat for another three-quarters of an hour before the main course was finally served. No one seemed to mind too much about the hold-up, except for a few critics meeting deadlines (ha ha), although the Capitol Theatre did get swelteringly hot. The principal result was extra column inches in the press the next morning. The saboteur was never caught.

Sharman replaced the tricksy, complex, tacky elements of O'Horgan's staging by an almost spartan space-age set. Much of the scenery, dominated by a huge dodecahedron, was clear plastic and the costumes of no identifiable time or place. Sharman treated *Superstar* with considerable respect, in contrast with O'Horgan's apparent wish to emphasise brashness, vulgarity and shock value – not that these are not elements of the piece, but I never felt they were the most important ones. Nonetheless, Sharman's version was highly innovative and very much of its time, very un-Broadway. The cast were strong, led by major Oz rocker Jon English as Judas and Trevor White as Jesus. I took a great liking to Jim and although I had a few reservations about some of his ideas, I was more than happy when Robert offered, and Jim accepted, the London job. Jim stated before the Sydney show even opened that he would not simply repeat himself in the West End.

The Sydney show was a big hit and after nine months moved to Melbourne where it did equally well, despite the appearance of a rival show called *Jesus Christ Revolution*, aims unclear, which I never saw. I left Sydney after a quick nip down to Melbourne (where I stayed with our childhood nanny-cum-lodger, now Edna McKaige) and Adelaide (where I renewed another ancient friendship – with a former Hertfordshire teenage chum Lesley Loch, by then the wife of an Australian dentist, David Wright). I had really enjoyed my visit, professionally and socially, had loved the country, and in Jim Sharman and the very high-profile Sydney actress Kate Fitzpatrick, made (I hope) good friends. I vowed my next trip would be during their cricket season.

In the very early part of 1972 I spent a few weeks in New York, working on a new album with Yvonne and continuing to enjoy my new status as a B-list celebrity there. I became involved with Anita Morris, one of the actresses in *Jesus Christ Superstar*, probably the most talented of the entire cast. Anita was a vivacious redhead from South Carolina, with an accent and body to die for. She was a superb dancer who had little chance to shine as a humble chorus member of the New York company, but her talent certainly got through to me. She did eventually become pretty well known, graduating to leading Broadway roles (in such hit musicals as *Nine*), and substantial movie parts, such as when she co-starred with Bette Midler and Danny de Vito in the marvellous *Ruthless People*. She also made a memorable and torrid appearance in the Rolling Stones video 'She Was Hot'. We had a lot of fun together in New York, often in the company of Yvonne and her new husband Bill Oakes, a young Englishman who worked in the Stigwood empire, and who became a close chum. Bill is now a film producer in Los Angeles (and no longer married to Yvonne) and around every two years we discuss the major picture we are going to make together. One day.

I lost touch with Anita for nearly twenty years after it became clear that this was yet another affair going nowhere, but when I found myself spending a great deal of time in Los Angeles working for Disney in the early Nineties, I saw Anita cropping up regularly on TV there and made contact. We had a few nostalgic lunches together. She still looked a million dollars, but to my horror she was in reality not well at all. She died of cancer aged barely fifty, tragic and ironic in view of her dedication to keeping in the best possible dietary and physical shape. I sometimes wonder if this health kick isn't bad for the middle-aged human frame, but more often wonder why exceptional people like Anita are denied the long and happy life which they deserve.

From these accounts of my re-dalliance with Solange in Paris and of my time with Anita in New York, it's finger-pointingly obvious that I was not committing myself to Prudence. So often

I so nearly did, but an indefinable reluctance, or cowardice, or selfishness, held me back. So, before too long, Prudence moved out of my life again, at least taking Stanley the grumpy Lhasa Apso with her. She had been working for a while for David Hemmings and he gradually became more important in her life than I was.

In addition to producing Yvonne's album which, rather insanely from Andrew's and my point of view, contained no new material by us but a dozen reasonable-to-indifferent rock-tinged ballads by everyone from Stephen Stills to the blokes in Yvonne's backing band, I also somehow found time to renew my links with the Scaffold. They had long since left Norrie and now seemed happy to work with me, with my one mega-hit behind me, at the controls. I rowed in Roger Watson as co-producer. We booked into a new studio in the grounds of a manor house in Oxfordshire, owned by a very young and very shambolic entrepreneur named Richard Branson. I liked Richard very much but felt certain that this guy would never make it in any business venture as he seemed to be flying by the seat of his pants in all of his many enterprises. We spent two chaotic weeks there, bedrooms and food being thrown in (often literally) as part of the deal and came up with rather a good album entitled *Fresh Liver*. This was a combination of Roger McGough's poetry, Mike McGear's rock songs and John Gorman's less subtle but very funny novelty numbers. One of these, 'I'm In Love With W.P.C. Hodges', was the single released to highlight the album, but this sad tale of unrequited love on the beat failed to emulate 'Lily The Pink' and the LP barely got out of the starting gate sales-wise. Neither did Yvonne's over in the States.

There were plenty of other projects Andrew and I were pursuing together and separately at this time. I was enjoying myself appearing on more and more radio panel games, and even graduated a few times on to *Any Questions*, where I fear I was less than brilliant, on one occasion inspiring a lot of hate mail for daring to suggest that teachers should regard their profession as a calling rather than another job, and look elsewhere for employment if money was their *raison d'être*. On less taxing shows such as *Many A Slip** and *Pop*

---

* I was particularly pleased to get to know Steve Race well on *Many A Slip*; Steve was a mainstay of Children's TV when I was a broth of a boy and I had always followed his musical and broadcasting careers with enjoyment ever since.

Score I was pretty good. I even graduated to TV and *Call My Bluff*, appearing with the great Frank Muir which delighted my father more than Broadway had. Ned Sherrin asked us to work on a new movie of *Peter Pan* (we gave that about ten days' attention) and the ubiquitous Michael Braun, whose paperback about *Superstar* had finally staggered out after endless arguments and perhaps justified attempts by Andrew to stifle it, took us away to the country for a few days to work on a new film version of *Alice In Wonderland*, financed by Roman Polanski.

I think there is no doubt we were distracted from moving ahead as speedily as we should have done on new projects by the sheer size of the *Superstar* phenomenon. The album had broken through to parts of the world most records did not easily reach. It had become a major underground hit in the Soviet Union. The recording had been banned by the authorities and we read that both original and bootleg copies were changing hands there for over £100 – a fortune in the early Seventies. From Estonia, then behind the Iron Curtain, came a request from a fan named Uno Viigand, whose only copy of *Superstar* was a very low-fi cassette recording a friend had taped from Finnish radio – could I possibly send him an album? I could and did – but it took about five attempts as (Uno told me) each LP sent was intercepted and stolen by customs officers. In the end he suggested I put *Superstar* into a Prokofiev sleeve as no-one at customs would nick Prokofiev. He was right. Uno became a regular pen-pal. We finally met in London in 1997 (by which time he had shelves of my stuff on LP, tape and CD) when he interviewed me for his Estonian TV programme.

We spent most of the week we should have been working on *Alice in Wonderland* playing snooker. We began to realise that whatever we did next should be something that we ourselves instigated. Besides, we had to pay some attention to both the film version and the London opening of *Superstar*.

Chapter Twenty-one

Robert's amazing energy continued in full flow as he set to work in the summer of 1972 to bring our hit show home. The American and indeed near-global success of *Superstar* had at last penetrated British indifference to their two young countrymen's theatrical achievements and we were not short of advance publicity or bookings. The album even lurched into the UK charts, selling consistently rather than sensationally. Jim Sharman took quiet and measured control and casting proceeded speedily. The part of Jesus went to Paul Nicholas, a young singer/actor who had made an impact in Robert's London production of *Hair*. The less established Stephen Tate won the part of Judas and the role of Mary eventually settled upon Dana Gillespie, after the original lady selected proved unsuitable – not untalented, but not right – and Dana was promoted from the chorus at the eleventh hour during previews. A crazy American based in London named Paul Jabara was signed as Herod and John Parker played Pilate. Among total unknowns in the chorus was a young actress named Elaine Paige.

The entire cast (after the brief glitch with Mary) proved highly satisfactory and morale was high. I recall a panic over costumes which were changed radically from first-century Oxfam to timeless desert chic with about one preview to spare, but otherwise the only hiccup was a last-minute wobbly from Andrew when he told Robert with three days to go that the whole enterprise was doomed and that he was removing his score. Once again,

I found Andrew's pessimism catching and as we drove out to Robert's Stanmore mansion one night to plead the case for total abandonment, even I was briefly convinced that we were heading for irretrievable disaster if we didn't send Jim and his cast packing the next morning. Robert dealt with our ludicrous quest with tact, calm and a lot of champagne.

One of the pluses of the London show was that the cast were all such nice people. Or stoned, at least. Paul Nicholas is one of the most unpretentious and amusing characters in British entertainment and I have never been surprised by his subsequent substantial success, doing well in almost every field of entertainment, as a pop singer, musical actor, TV star and more recently theatrical producer. He sang Jesus like a bell, fortunately keeping his wonderfully filthy laugh for off-stage activities, sometimes difficult when one heard of the tricks played on stage during the show. Paul shuddered every time he opened a chalice during the Last Supper, knowing that some foul memento of backstage life would inevitably have been placed therein. Dana Gillespie, who had achieved a certain notoriety via her appearance in Bob Dylan's documentary of his 1965 tour of Britain and, it must be said at the risk of being sexist, via her quite magnificent breasts which inspired admiration and gave consolation to her fellow workers, was beautifully earthy as Mary and gave the song an edge that even approached Yvonne's interpretation. Stephen Tate was strong on anguish and of voice, in good tormented contrast to Paul's ethereal Jesus. Paul Jabara delivered Herod with extraordinary camp panache, white suit and tails, glitz and degeneracy. There were no weak links even down to the humblest member of the supporting cast. I wish I could state that Elaine stood out but she was merely one of many great movers and singers. No one watching the original *Superstar* cast would have named her then as the one to become the biggest star of all, but only because they all seemed capable of almost anything.

Jim's show was very different from his Australian production. He ditched many of the space-age trappings of his first effort, including the huge plastic dodecahedron that had slightly cramped his room to manoeuvre in Sydney. The set (by the Sydney *Superstar* designer Brian Thomson) was stark and bare; the central playing area a large box with a slightly raked, lit floor surrounded by three walls, wide and high, over which members of the chorus clambered throughout the evening. A Piccadilly Circus display of lights flashed up occasional words of information such as 'Jerusalem, Sunday'. The simplicity of the basic staging generously allowed the words and music to become the main driving force of the story, but there were many moments of great visual impact, primarily through the movements of the swirling chorus, with lights, dry ice, colourful banners and artful choreography (by Rufus Collins).

There was also a good deal of humour, which always helps. The priests and Herod were both jokey and sinister. The crucifixion was spectacular but restrained, as Jesus' cross rose from the depths. (Extremely restrained on the opening night when a safety catch clicked into action for over a minute, trapping Paul on the cross in the basement. This delay seemed like an hour to conductor, orchestra and cast, desperately holding on to one note of anguish which they did not have to act to convey, and to two panic-stricken authors standing at the back of the stalls. Eventually the contraption lurched into action just before we felt we should rush on to stage to apologise, or rush out of the Palace altogether, by which time most of the theatre had been filled with smoke that had been pumped out for much longer than intended. If anything, the delay added to the dramatic tension of the climax of the show.) Anthony Bowles, who had been the conductor in Paris, marshalled the musicians and singers with crisp authority and was hugely helped by a sound system that suffered few of the Broadway embarrassments. We were getting better at rock theatre technology.

By the time *Superstar* opened in London on 9 August 1972, it was established in Britain as a cultural phenomenon, albeit a more middle-of-the-road one than it had been in the countries that had gone for it in a big way from record one. Robert's opening night party at his home in Stanmore was a tremendous bash (even though for some reason I eschewed booze for the occasion), complete with a couple of fights and mass skinny-dipping. It was clear that the show was going to be a massive hit and by and large the reviews were not too bad at all. Shortly before we opened

Peter Hall wrote a big article in the *Observer* which analysed 'the phenomenal Broadway success and significant failure' of the work, which damned us with faint praise and trashed most of Tom O'Horgan's work. I thus found it hard to sympathise when his own attempt at a rock opera a few months later, a sci-fi shambles entitled *Via Galactica*, lasted just three days on Broadway.

Superstar never won any significant awards during its initial spell of glory in the early Seventies. It missed out on Grammys, Tonys and British theatrical prizes such as the *Evening Standard* Awards. We were briefly miffed by this but after David Land told us he could probably get the shows that had defeated us (*Applause* won the *Evening Standard*, *Two Gentlemen of Verona* the Tony*) to give us their trophies if we gave them our box-office take, it didn't seem to matter so much. I'd be even less keen to hand over my *Superstar* royalties in 1999 for a Tony than I would have been in 1972. My attitude to awards ever since may well have been fuelled by those early rejections. I am unable to take any of them very seriously, although by and large I would rather win than lose. Those I have won over the years seem more often than not to have been for the wrong things, or for just turning up. The only one that really means anything outside the self-obsessed showbusiness world is the Oscar, and in 1972 I was still a long way from breaking into that circle.

Thanks to *Superstar* in London, I met one of my heroes, the great Australian cricketer, Richie Benaud. I spotted him in the interval at the Palace Theatre during a preview and boldly introduced myself. I sensed poor Richie's inward shudder as yet another fan pestered him but as soon as he realised that I was actually a co-perpetrator of his evening's entertainment he and his wife Daphne were sweetness and light. They are musical buffs and wanted to talk about the shows; I wanted to talk about Greg Chappell and Dennis Lillee, but we got on just fine.

From the release of Murray's single of 'Superstar' to the London first night, we had enjoyed almost three years of roller-coaster thrills with the show. We had succeeded beyond our most opti-

---

* *Superstar* did not even pick up a nomination as best musical in the 1972 Tonys, let alone win.

mistic hopes, almost beyond our comprehension, having made the biggest impact with a British musical since *Oliver* or possibly even way before that. The London show was to run for over eight years, establishing a new record for a West End musical of 3358 performances. Over the next few years there were dozens of new productions all over the world, but even I became less desperate to attend every single one. But we still put ourselves around a bit, with trips to Reykjavik and Tokyo in 1973 being standout recollections. In fact there has hardly been a time in the past quarter of a century when some major new version hasn't started up somewhere. The Budapest open-air production on an island in the middle of the Danube in the late Eighties; the gigantic Australian stadium tour in 1992; the Prague show that has run for more than three years as I write; the big London revival in 1996; an interminable tour of the States from the early Nineties starring Carl Anderson and Ted Neely – it just goes on and on. I'm still not quite sure where we went right.

Carl Anderson and Ted Neely played Judas and Jesus in the movie. They had both eventually sung the roles on Broadway, taking over from Ben Vereen and Jeff Fenholt, and I was particularly pleased that Carl, unlucky to be passed over as the first (legal) Judas on stage anywhere in the world, was signed by Norman Jewison for the film. It is quite staggering that both he and Ted should still have been on the road with *Superstar* in their fifties, but old rockers never die.

Our contribution to the *Superstar* movie was minimal. In stark contrast to the ultimate fate of *Evita* (the Alan Parker/Madonna epic appeared nearly twenty years after the stage show), the film was set up at breakneck speed by Robert and MCA, via MCA's Universal Pictures. The director was to be Norman Jewison. This was good news: (a) I had heard of him, (b) he had directed one of my favourite films of all time, *In The Heat Of The Night*, with Sidney Poitier and Rod Steiger, and (c) had just completed an excellent musical film, *Fiddler On The Roof*. Indeed it was while he was shooting that picture, in Yugoslavia I believe, that our Pontius Pilate, Barry Dennen, who had a part in *Fiddler*, introduced Norman to the *Superstar* album, firing the distinguished Canadian's enthusiasm for our work.

We met and liked Norman and his team, who were to be based

in England, at Pinewood Studios, for the duration of the *Superstar* film. I was asked to write the first draft screenplay. I set about this with great enthusiasm and minimum concern for budget, certain that a massive *Ben-Hur* kind of treatment was essential. Tens of thousands of extras would soon be thanking me for a boost to their incomes. After all, *Superstar* had not got where it had by excess subtlety or by its creators thinking small. Obviously all the words were already in place (though Andrew and I did expand one of the High Priests' scenes in a futile bid to quash further anti-Semitism charges at the pass) so it was merely a question of pointing out which massive visual effect accompanied which song. Should the procession of camels enter from the left or right of the frame? What was the best marching formation for the Roman legions? These were the only kinds of problem I faced, so that within two weeks of being asked, I had submitted my script. Certain that I would not be required to do anything more, I sat back to await the invitation to Israel to see my extravagantly brilliant ideas transferred to celluloid.

I was right in that I was not required to do anything more. Norman and Robert rejected my screenplay outright and signed Melvyn Bragg to write another with a cast of dozens rather than thousands. I was fast learning how feebly writers vibrated on the film world's Richter scale. I was not even asked to have a re-think; Melvyn was signed without my knowledge or consent and he, too, unencumbered by actually having to think up any plot or lyrics, delivered his screenplay in next to no time.

I suppose I was fairly narked about this at the time, but not half as annoyed as Andrew was by the refusal, yet again, of anyone to trust him with the orchestrations. The insane decision, a repeat of the Hershy Kay episode on Broadway, was taken to hand over the baton to André Previn. As had been the case with Norman Jewison, we had at least heard of him, and I had quite liked one or two of his Sixties jazz albums, but as he made no effort to hide his basic loathing of the score (he went into print some years later describing *Superstar* as 'shit', making one wonder how he could have so debased himself as to accept the job) we were unable to register much enthusiasm for his appointment. Previn had even less to do than Melvyn, as he merely rehashed Andrew's original arrangements, for which he was ludicrously nominated for an Oscar. Mercifully, he didn't win.

Consequently, Andrew and I took a total back seat. The production however roared ahead without us. The cast were a hundred per cent American (why?) and were soon out in Israel filming. Robert and Universal Pictures naturally ran into a bit of opposition re their choice of location but the eventual approval of the Israeli government was a big plus for the film's credibility – and PR. David Land, Andrew and I went out for just three days to have a look at things, and we continued to exert no influence on proceedings, spending most of our time sightseeing in Jerusalem, Jericho and the Dead Sea. We teamed up with the hip writer, Nik Cohn, who was on an assignment on behalf of *Playboy* magazine to write an article on *JCS* in Israel. I was a great fan of Nik, who had written one of the first intelligent histories of pop music, a wildly witty tome entitled *A Wop Bop A Lu Bop A Lop Bam Boo*. He duly delivered a highly sarcastic and fairly abusive piece about *Superstar* to the famous socially desperate magazine. He incidentally hit the jackpot a few years later when Robert Stigwood turned a slender article of his about New York kids' Saturday nights out into the basis of *Saturday Night Fever*.

My principal memories of our visit to the filming were hilarious van trips around Israel with David Land in top form, regaling us with his wartime experiences ('first man away at Dunkirk') and less than politically correct views about the Arab-Israeli situation, often delivered astride a camel. Yvonne and her husband Bill Oakes were almost the only people involved with the picture whom we actually spoke to and they joined us for my twenty-eighth birthday celebrations at a Jericho tavern with an unusual menu. We remember the joint to this day as the Angus Snake House.

The film was eventually released with reasonable fanfare in the summer of 1973, barely a year after the début of the West End stage show (still going more than strong). It was neither a huge success, nor a complete flop. The basic concept that (presumably) had been Norman's and/or Melvyn's idea was that a bunch of wandering hippy actors, arriving in the actual places where Christ had lived and died, decided to do the show right then and there. So the action was really set in the 1970s, with Israeli war-planes and tanks occasionally intruding; the net result was a little confused and dated almost before the prints had come back from the chemist. The choreography was by Pan's People out of *Hair*, the costumes were mid-period Who, and despite some beautifully photographed sequences and one or two fine performances, for the first time in its meteoric streak across the showbiz heavens, *Superstar* seemed out of touch and out of fashion. In some ways it was; it had completed its supernova burst into prominence and would henceforth be an establishment musical, rarely dipping in overall popularity, but never again a work with the power to shock or provoke. Maybe a more literal *Ben-Hur*-type screenplay would have given the movie a longer lease of life, although it still earns a crust or two on television every so often. Maybe we would have done better to have waited twenty years before making the film.

Another reason why the closing months of 1972 did not find us over-occupied with the motion picture business was a totally unexpected new surge of interest in *Joseph*, this time from the professional theatre. We had received a request earlier in the year from Frank Dunlop, then Director of the Young Vic, for permission to present the show at the Edinburgh Festival, as part of a Dunlop concept called *Bible One*. This was a two-part entertainment, billed as 'Two Looks At The Book Of Genesis', the first part being Medieval Mystery Plays and the second *Joseph*. Alan Doggett had been roped in as musical director and he asked me if I minded some of the lyrics being switched from the third person to the first, in order that the words could be shared around a bit – otherwise the choir, or Narrator would be telling the entire tale. I happily agreed and forgot about it.

The next thing I remember about the Young Vic production was purchasing a *Daily Telegraph* at Nice airport en route back from a holiday in Corsica in September. There on the arts page was a rave review of *Bible One* with particular attention being paid to *Joseph*. There was a prominent photograph of Gary Bond in the title role. Another first night missed. I shot up to Edinburgh the next day and witnessed a remarkable show at the Haymarket Ice Rink. Frank had transformed the piece into musical comedy of the highest order for all ages, without destroying any of its innocence or appeal to children and unwittingly set the pattern for thirty years (so far) of commercial productions. The brothers in particular emerged as wonderfully comic villains, eleven for the price of one, getting much bigger laughs out of the text than a solo narrator could hope to do, though the part of the Narrator was still a crucial one.

The cast was splendid: supporting the effortlessly charming and tuneful Gary were Peter Reeves as the Narrator and Gordon Waller as Pharaoh. This was the first I had seen of Gordon since my Norrie Paramor days. He seemed to have found a springboard for a new career in musical theatre, if his electric performance as Elvis/Pharaoh was anything to go by. The long-established musical star (*Grab Me A Gondola*, etc.) Joan Heal was somewhat under-used as Wife to both Jacob and Potiphar, but I was thrilled to discover that she was now in a show I had written. One of the brothers who went on to greater things was Ian Charleson, who came to international prominence a dozen years later in *Chariots Of Fire*. It is terrible to report that both Gary and Ian died of AIDS in recent times. In 1972, of course, no one had heard of the disease.

The Medieval Mystery Plays, some five hundred years senior to *Joseph*, were also presented by Frank in a marvellously light-hearted manner, and both sides of the evening were rapturously received by audiences and critics alike. There was virtually no set, and the show was performed in the round. A choir of schoolboys and a seven-piece rock band maintained close ties with the original Alan Doggett production, Alan himself proudly conducting with panache. It was obvious to all (Robert Stigwood and David Land soon raced up to Scotland) that our first published piece had a future beyond educational establishments, although I am glad to report that the brilliant Dunlop reincarnation has never affected the continuing popularity of the work in schools.

Every production of *Joseph* since the Haymarket Ice Rink owes a huge debt to Frank's original vision in late 1972. I have long since lost count of them all. The immediate post-Edinburgh move was to the Round House in North London and thence (February 1973) to the Albery Theatre in the West End. It was felt that the medieval part had to be ditched for the Albery (too intellectual!)

and Andrew and I were urged to come up with an entire new first half, double-quick.

We almost achieved the impossible. We decided the most logical story to tell in Act One would be the events in Genesis that led up to the Joseph story, i.e. the story of Joseph's father, Jacob. There was quite a bit of good material to work with, notably Jacob and Esau and the mess of pottage, Jacob working for Laban for fourteen years in order to marry two of his wives, his becoming Israel and being chosen by God to continue the Abrahamic covenant. Reckoning we didn't have time to write a full new sung-through act, our first attempt consisted of a script (by me) with four or five new songs inserted at various points.

My début as a comic script writer was not a huge success, although having to master this new skill in less than a fortnight might have put even Alan Ayckbourn under pressure at a similar stage in his career. After a couple of readings, it was mutually agreed that the songs were okay but the bits in between were definitely not. Consequently, Robert commissioned the genii behind *Hancock's Half Hour* and *Steptoe And Son*, Ray Galton and Alan Simpson, who were conveniently represented by the Stigwood Organisation, to do the dialogue to what was now called *Jacob's Journey*.

Ray and Alan did their stuff and managed to accommodate our new songs into their story reasonably successfully. The finished result was satisfactory, but no more than that. There were some very good laughs in the script, and one or two competent songs such as 'Seven Years' as Jacob slaves away for his uncle Laban, and 'And Did He Notice Me'. The latter was a pretty love ballad sung by Rachel, the tune of which was the tune of 'Song For Solange', first warbled by Sacha Distel five years before. For all this, *Jacob's Journey* lacked the freshness and guilelessness of *Joseph* itself and the two halves sat uneasily together. The box office was not snowed under with punters, even though reviews were reasonable. After a few weeks of middling business, it was decided to phase out *Jacob's Journey* completely and stretch *Joseph* still further to be the entire show.

Amazingly, *Joseph* proved to be stretchable yet again. We wrote three new songs for the brothers, a country-and-western spoof,

'One More Angel In Heaven', as they broke the news to Jacob of Joseph's apparent death, a cod version of 'Island In The Sun' entitled 'Benjamin Calypso' and the French chanson parody, 'Those Canaan Days'; and elongated several of the other songs to their absolute limit with new verses, instrumental passages or blatant repetition of existing lines. We also salvaged a song the youthful Jacob had sung in the original Act One entitled, 'I Don't Think I'm Wanted Back At Home', and gave it to the youthful Joseph just before his brothers get rid of him. For some reason Andrew never liked this number and it was the only item of the 1973 expansion not to survive beyond the Albery run. Finally, we encored about a third of the show at the end; a feature loved by *Joseph* fans now, but back then, when the piece had not yet become ingrained in the popular culture of Britain, it looked rather like what it was – a desperate attempt to fill time.

Even this could not save the show, which carried on losing money for Robert and his backers with modest consistency. Eventually, Robert pulled the plug in September, after 243 performances. Not a total embarrassment, but a feeble run compared with *Superstar*, which was continuing to pack 'em in at the Palace. However, the work we did on the show during its first London run proved invaluable and helped ensure its longevity; we had created a piece that was now long enough to stand on its own as a venture for professional companies to tackle, and as soon as the Albery show closed, David Land was inundated with requests from commercial theatres around the country (and soon the world) for the right to produce it. And of course interest from schools and amateur companies was increasing all the time. Often when professionals are putting on a show, amateurs are denied access to the rights in the daft belief that they might detract from the earning power of the bigger versions. David wisely insisted that schools and colleges and the like should always be allowed to produce *Joseph*, no matter what was happening elsewhere. The Really Useful Group came in for some flak in 1991 (including from me) when they foolishly tried to ban amateur productions in advance of their massive London Palladium extravaganza.

Everyone who wants to put on a version of *Joseph* has to pay, even the humblest kindergarten or most stricken repertory theatre.

This may seem cruel and heartless, but is of course the situation with any work still in copyright. Our main aim is to protect the copyright and to make sure that no pirate versions, over which we would have no control, start roaming the world. To allow even one tiny operation to do it without official permission and for no fee would set a dangerous precedent. Naturally, schools were only charged a nominal fee, unless they were clearly an Eton-type set-up. David usually asked for barely enough to cover the cost of postage and phone calls in dealing with each request, eventually a virtually full-time job for one of the girls in his ever-more cramped office, by now overflowing with *Superstar* and *Joseph* files, souvenirs, merchandising and gold discs. Eton did in fact do *Joseph*, under the direction of the irrepressible Rev. Roger Royle, now a media star and wonderfully risqué after-dinner speaker. They paid a few hundred quid for the privilege and it was a jolly good show.

I was beginning to realise, during all these rewriting and expansion sessions of 1973, that maybe I was lumbered with the short end of the song-writing stick. The writer of the tune can easily re-use a melody that hasn't worked in one situation in a completely different setting; this is generally impossible for the lyricist. Had *Evita* flopped, I would have had a far harder task getting the words of 'Don't Cry For Me Argentina' into another show than Andrew would have had with the tune. Words also take a lot longer to write than music; if you can do the latter at all, a basic melody will usually crop up within minutes, and once verse one of a tune is written, so are verses two, three, four and five. In the case of all these *Joseph* extensions, most of the 'new' tunes had done service elsewhere in abandoned projects: 'One More Angel In Heaven' was originally part of the aborted 'Come Back Richard' score and 'I Don't Think I'm Wanted Back At Home' was a tune from way back, from *The Likes Of Us* when it was called 'You Won't Care About Her Anymore'. 'And Did He Notice Me' was Sacha Distel's flop 'Song For Solange' with new words. And so on. This is not a criticism of composers in general or of Andrew in particular (honest) – I know if I wrote tunes I would recycle with the best of them – but occasionally composers are inclined to forget that the words are a longer slog and unfair (sometimes) charges of laziness have been known to surface.

Despite the undistinguished first West End run, *Joseph* became an instant sell-out all around the country, with most leading provincial theatres mounting their own version in the following few years. The most successful of all producers to take up the *Joseph* cudgels was Bill Kenwright, whose version (which he himself directed) has been selling out all over the UK for the past twenty years. It has starred a variety of Josephs but more often than not Jess Conrad, apart from a three-year hiatus when Jason Donovan and then Phillip Schofield reigned supreme for the Really Useful Group in London. Bill's version was perhaps not the most subtle (nor was the Really Useful version, come to that), but was irresistibly charming, funny, and never let up for a moment. The goodwill and energy that flowed both ways, from cast to audience and back again, was always incredible to behold, as were the box-office takings. Bill has worked wonders for the show over two decades and I would be happy to let him tour it until he drops. I expect he will and I am delighted that he has said that his success with *Joseph* has often enabled him to take a chance with less infallible musicals and plays. One member of his cast, Peter Lawrence, who played Jacob from the very start of Bill's regime, made it into the *Guinness Book of Records* when he played over 5000 performances in the same part.

Over the years Andrew and I have made a fortune out of *Joseph* – far more in the Nineties than in the Eighties, and in turn the Eighties earned more for us than did the Seventies. In 1988 Andrew, through his Really Useful empire, purchased the balance of the copyright from Filmtrax, the company which had in turn bought out Novello & Co. some years before (a deal which caused huge acrimony between me and Andrew) so it is probable that his income from the show now vastly exceeds even mine; but against that, as producer of the show in some of the more obscure North American venues, he and/or the RUG may well have taken the odd bath, which I, as mere writer, avoided. More of that murky piece of business anon – but not in this volume. *Joseph* returned to London for a limited season in each of the years from 1979 to 1982 (twice with Paul Jones, twice with Jess Conrad) and finally became a *bona fide* long-running West End smash with the massive Palladium treatment of 1991–4. Without becoming quite so much a part of the national consciousness, the piece has grown enormously popular in the United States, notably on the road starring Donny Osmond, and in South Africa, where a production mounted by the Performing Arts Corporation of Transvaal in 1975 became one of the biggest musicals ever staged there. Even the Aussies quite like *Joseph* and in most other English-speaking countries it has been pretty popular, school productions in all corners of the globe being the key to its longevity. Unlike most big British musicals, *Joseph* has never done quite so well in other languages. I suspect this is because the style and humour of the words are so very English, very dependent on outlandish rhymes and puns, and the music, while absolutely perfect for the piece, is not particularly spectacular in its own right. I like to think that its comparative failure in foreign parts is a kind of compliment to the lyricist.

I actually starred as Pharaoh in two professional shows, one for three weeks in Oxford at the Apollo, where I played opposite Leonard Whiting's Joseph, and once for a few days in Johannesburg, in the South African smash, filling in for the local Elvis when he was on holiday.

Superstar had been banned in South Africa (although I was presented with a gold disc there for presumably one hundred per cent illegal sales) and I think I was briefly on some black list for daring to venture into the evil regime, but I was keen to see South Africa for myself, and also my brother Andy, who had by then settled there. He had spent most of 1972 driving from London to Johannesburg by Land Rover, crashing only once, just before boarding the Dover ferry. He decided to stay in South Africa where, apart from one stretch in the mid-Eighties, he has been ever since, primarily working in advertising and PR. Back in 1975 I was both encouraged and depressed by different aspects of the country, but on balance did not feel an overwhelming urge to hurry back.

The only significant further lengthening to *Joseph* came in 1981, when a production under the bright management of two young women from Baltimore, Gail Berman and Susan Rose, finally got the show to Broadway. Before that, its principal American production had been under the aegis of good old Frank Dunlop at the Brooklyn Academy of Music in 1977 – just a mini-season of twenty-four shows, starring Cleavon Little, a Broadway name whom I knew of through his hilarious role in Mel Brooks's *Blazing Saddles*, and David Carroll, many years later to star in one of my shows on Broadway, *Chess*. The English actor/director Tony Tanner (whom we had first met way back in the mid-Sixties when Desmond Elliott approached him to play the lead in *The Likes Of Us*) directed the Berman/Rose show, and his and our main stroke of genius was to give the part of the Narrator to a woman. At last the appalling imbalance between male and female roles in *Joseph* was put right and since Laurie Beechman's quite magnificent narration at the Royale Theatre on Broadway, ladies have more often than not been given the second most important part in the show – actually a bad Narrator can often be of greater damage to the show than a below-par Joseph.

But I am running a little ahead of myself; it's the end of 1972 and Andrew and I are beginning to be regarded as something more than one-hit wonders who struck lucky with a God show. The pressure to come up with a new show was mounting – pressure from ourselves mainly. We wanted to break away from the Bible (though we were tempted to stick with a winning formula and discussed various ideas from King Saul to Saint Paul) and after considering a rather wacky (but maybe brilliant – I shall probably never know) idea to write a musical about the Cuban Missile Crisis, settled on a complete contrast to our two forays into Holy Scripture – P.G.Wodehouse and Jeeves.

Chapter Twenty-two

I was truly keen to get on with a brand new project by early 1973 but there were a few distractions. Running my home and office at 33 Northumberland Place seemed like two full-time jobs. I had lost the assistance of brother Andy to Africa and even with Fiona working long hours on my pay-roll I was beginning to find plenty of excuses, some genuine and some spurious, not to devote myself to writing. There were so many other things I wanted to do. ALW too had many new extra-curricular interests.

One common to both of us was art. Andrew had long been purchasing pictures and objects but it was a brand new experience for me to be able to think of spending money on something purely to hang on the wall or to look at and I loved it. An old school chum of mine, Ian Bennett, was linked to Sotheby's as a consultant of sorts (his special subject being carpets) and he took me round galleries and salerooms. Through him I made my first serious purchase, a large painting by the late Victorian artist, J.W.Waterhouse, entitled 'Nymphs Finding the Head of Orpheus', painted at the turn of the century. I forked out £5200 for this beautiful work, at a time when Waterhouse never even made it into the catalogues of Victorian painters. He was of the Pre-Raphaelite school, albeit a late entrant, and Pre-Raphaelites were about to go through the roof.

Andrew had always been a fanatic admirer of these sentimental, colourful, realistic pictures and we were both smart (Andrew) and lucky (me) to move into this market before it took off. My first

Waterhouse would now fetch rather more than £5200. Andrew has virtually cornered the market these days having built up the most stupendous pre-Raphaelite collection, but back in the early Seventies I matched him purchase for purchase for a while. I broke the record for a Strudwick, by paying £12,000 for a picture of a knight in armour kipping in a leafy grove, which I foolishly sold a couple of years later for about twice what I paid for it. One art critic described this investment as insanity, but I am glad to say there are just as many ill-informed art critics as there are theatrical ones. I wish I still owned the two Strudwicks I bought then. I have not sold any of my Waterhouses.

Gradually my knowledge and appreciation of art increased, without too many disastrous purchases over the years. With the assistance of Ian and another independent art advisor, James Dugdale (now Lord Crathorne), I moved quickly into different areas of painting, within three or four years owning, among others, a Degas, a brace of Pissaros, a terrific Hockney still life, Peter Blake prints, Rembrandt etchings, and three magnificent Old Master drawings by Annibale and Lodovico Carraci. Plus a small smattering of works by contemporary, unknown artists and a few intriguing pots and vases by Christopher Dresser and the like. This sounds a pretty impressive list, and I appreciate my good fortune in being able to dip into this sometimes selfish pastime, but in reality I did not spend a fortune on art in the early Seventies. I was lucky to be well-advised. By the end of the decade I slowed down quite a bit on the purchases, with other expensive and more essential commitments, e.g. children, demanding attention. Then in the mid-Eighties, with the money not rolling in quite so prolifically, I ground to a virtual halt in this area, only resuming my enthusiasm to buy art in the Nineties, when Walt Disney enabled me to afford it again.

I spent quite a bit of cash on 33 Northumberland Place itself, and the office facilities were constantly being improved. The fabulous basement kitchen which Piers Gough had designed now incorporated a Carillon jukebox and Gottlieb pin-table. The latter proved highly addictive and not just as far as I was concerned. Friends would stay up all night flipping away in pinball wizard mode, as did the builders, who eventually had to be rationed to one game an hour in order that their work might be finished by 1980. The pin-ball machine enabled me to have the honour and thrill of entertaining Peter Cook for several hours one night after we had met at some reception or other. Both slightly tired and emotional, mention of my personal amusement arcade resulted in my hero returning to Northumberland Place to demonstrate his considerable skills thereon, and to perform his celebrated Elvis impersonation over and over again to the strains of 'Suspicious Minds' and 'Burning Love' (selections A3 and A5 on the jukebox).

One of my great regrets is that I never got to know Peter Cook better. I did meet him on rare occasions after his night of the long jives at Northumberland Place, but failed, largely because of being rather in awe of him, to turn this into any sort of friendship. The popularity of the *Beyond The Fringe* LP when I was at Lancing was quite phenomenal, and though I never saw the actual show, I must have seen virtually every item in the flesh over the succeeding thirty years, or at least on television. Many of the funniest sketches were included in Peter and Dudley's early Seventies show, *Behind The Fridge* which metamorphosed into *Good Evening* on Broadway. I saw that show four or five times and after one performance of *Good Evening* managed to persuade an extremely convivial Peter to record a brief insert for my Capital Radio oldies show. His great taste in popular music was well illustrated by his choice of record, 'Let The Little Girl Dance' by Billy Bland.

I felt, perhaps rather presumptuously, that Peter and I had much in common. We came from similar middle-class backgrounds, attended public schools of around equal standing (Peter was at Radley) and had fathers who spent much time abroad. Our enthusiasms were generally unsophisticated, popular culture and sport, and we were both newspaperholics. I sensed too that we shared a low boredom threshold, finding our own work and careers pointless at times, even when going well. So far I have not succumbed to some of the excesses that bedevilled Peter in his later years, but at times I have felt that I have the potential to give him a run for his money. Both our long-standing partners went on to staggering success after the split. Dudley and Andrew were both small, Peter and I both six feet four. While never claiming to have been as devastatingly handsome as the young Cook, I noted a common decline in our physical attributes over the years. We were both born under the sign of Scorpio, but of course Scorpios don't believe in astrology. I am sure I am flattering myself with these comparisons, but my sadness at his early death was compounded by the ability I had to identify with the great entertainer, beyond doubt the funniest man of my generation and rightly acknowledged thus by so many of his colleagues and admirers.

Andrew and I continued to spend a great deal of time together in non-working hours and I remember many wonderful evenings around his piano in his new home at Brompton Square, usually after a noisy supper in one of the many restaurants that Andrew knew extraordinarily well. He was still firing off reports to *The Good Food Guide* and really knew his onions re where to eat. One of our favourite haunts was a now defunct Covent Garden restaurant called the Grange, where one night we introduced ourselves to a man I recognised from my prep school days, a fellow old Aldwickburian, David Fingleton, now magistrate and opera critic. Unaware of our childhood link, he had not long before written a few kind words about *Superstar* in the *Tatler*. David has been an extremely useful ally on many occasions since in his capacity both as a music and food critic – generous reviews or mentions in his columns and a free dinner now and then.*

At some point around this time, we were approached by Frank Dunlop to make a contribution to a revue he was directing at the Criterion Theatre, entitled *Hullabaloo*. This grisly concoction was an extremely camp and extremely ropey entertainment featuring drag queens named Rogers and Starr and the great Jimmy Edwards (who was not known, by me anyway, at that time to be anything other than majestically heterosexual). The entire production was set in a gents' lavatory, and that was one of the more tasteful aspects of the show. In feeble company, our songs failed to stand out. We never got any royalties at all from the producer Harold Fielding, which was probably more than we deserved.

Having to this day an irresistible fascination with pop stars, it

---

* His younger brother, John, considerably larger than life, joined my cricket team in 1976. Detailed discussion of the celebrated 'Fingers' must await a future volume.

was very satisfying that so many of them seemed to be cropping up in my work and in my life and when Andrew and Sarah organised a dinner for Neil Sedaka at Brompton Square my cup runnethed over. Neil is one of those artists who will do his act at the drop of a hat and I recall scoring many points by knowing the words to every one of his greatest hits (e.g. 'dum doobe-doo down down') – despite my interpretation of some of the high bits. At this time Andrew and I were as close as we had ever been; we had had a few minor tiffs over the years, but nothing by 1973 had ever indicated to me that our partnership would not be one for life. Threats to our relationship generally grew out of Andrew's feeling that there were things I would rather be doing than working with him on the next smash show. There were times when I wished to pursue extra-ALW professional activities, but from my point of view our partnership was still the most important aspect of my show-business ambitions.

I expect Andrew was more than a little peeved by my continuing desire to make pop records. Some of these involved Andrew as well, notably an album we recorded with one of the original brothers from Frank Dunlop's *Joseph* production, Maynard Williams, good-looking and a powerful warbler, the son of the actor/comedian Bill Maynard. This LP was drearily entitled *Ten Songs* and contained several new Webber-Rice compositions (at least the lyrics were all new), plus a selection of covers, including one written by our new best friend Neil Sedaka. MCA, still catering to our every whim as various *Superstar* albums continued to sell healthily around the globe (even the film album sold around two million globally), issued Maynard's album, but it died the death.

One interesting track was entitled 'Down On The Farm', with a good but extremely uncommercial lyric about the industrialisation of agriculture; the memorable tune eventually made it into *Evita* as 'High Flying Adored'. Another song, 'The Red Room', again with a lyric I was proud of, this time about a bloke being unable to resist returning to a brothel, was to become the melodic basis of 'Buenos Aires' in the same show. Then there was yet another re-working of what was one day to become 'Sunset Boulevard', in this guise entitled 'Turning', and re-hashes of two of Andrew's oldest melodies, of 'Down Thru' Summer', our first flop with

Ross Hannaman back in 1967, and of 'Make Believe Love', a song Andrew had written before we even met, which now became 'Marisa', in tribute to Marisa Berenson, a beautiful actress I had met at a David Hemmings' dinner party. None of these gems helped save the album, which doesn't sound too bad today. The problem was it didn't sound too good then.

We also recorded a pretty dire single with Gary Bond, called 'Disillusion Me', the tune being that of 'Seven Years' from the ill-fated *Jacob's Journey*. This was inspired by my latest love affair, with Felicity Balfour, an actress/dancer in the less than triumphant West End *Joseph* production, and is a good example of how passion does not necessarily bring the best out of a writer. On my own, I released a version of the old Buddy Holly hit 'Not Fade Away', a job I was presented with by my pal Roger Watson, now a Chrysalis Records producer, when the original chap scheduled to do the vocal had to be wiped off the track when it was revealed he was under contract to another label. This vocalist was George Fenton, now an Oscar-winning composer.

All these flopped, as did a project I hoped would be a Christmas Number One, 'How Much Is That Doggie In The Window', sung backwards. This was a daft idea originally performed on the children's TV programme *Whirlygig* by Humphrey Lestocq and Mr Turnip. For some reason this insane interpretation of what was never the most cerebrally challenging of songs had stuck in my mind since around 1954. At the fag-end of a *Joseph* recording session (we had also around this time decided to make a definitive studio album of what we then assumed would be the final complete version of the work) I persuaded the rhythm section to lay down the basic track of the 1953 Patti Page hit, over which the quartet of me, brother Jo, *Superstar* engineer Alan O'Duffy and Bee Gees musical director Geoff Westley sang every line of the entire number backwards, obviously beginning 'Window The In Doggie That Is Much How'. Under the name Rover, this catastrophic concept was actually issued by Robert Stigwood's label and, despite a promotional campaign that involved the distribution of dozens of dog bowls to radio stations, was rejected forcibly by the nation. I can still sing the entire song in reverse, occasionally a useful skill at struggling parties.

Other diversions to delay getting down to our Jeeves idea included my ever increasing involvement with Good Causes, notably the Stars Organisation for Spastics and the Lord's Taverners. The combination of an inability to say No, a strong sense of guilt, the generally highly enjoyable functions that raised the cash, a chance to meet stars and/or cricketers, and the fact that here were two charities that actually delivered, rather than acting as a front for self-congratulatory gong-chasing balls (in both senses), led me to give quite a bit of time to both the SOS and the Taverners. The SOS looked after victims of cerebral palsy, the Taverners provided sporting facilities and buses for under-privileged children. For the latter, playing cricket was one of the less onerous tasks and to turn out on the same ground as the likes of Bill Edrich, Denis Compton and Jim Laker was even more exciting than singing 'Breaking Up Is Hard To Do' with Neil Sedaka.

I devoted much time to other sporting matters. In 1973 Sunderland justified my unflagging support for the first time since I began to follow them twenty years before and won the cup as complete outsiders. Through David Land, able to get tickets for anything, I went to nearly every round of their triumphant run and found myself virtually in the royal box for the final. As a new recruit to the MCC, I spent a lot of time at Lord's. But the most significant sports-loving move that I made that year was the creation of my own cricket team, Heartaches Cricket Club. More than twenty-five years later this has become one of my most satisfying creations, a huge social success and a source of many friendships, business arrangements and happy summer days.

Heartaches CC was never conceived as anything other than a private pastime, deliberately non-show-business, non-charity, and low-profile. It has proved to be a wonderful way for me to keep in close touch with two dozen or more friends, their wives, lovers and families, and the same is true for every one of them. The line-up of players has changed gradually over the years, but not significantly – many of the players who turned out in the first few years are still frighteningly keen to strut their stuff a quarter of a century on. Only now, many of their sons also put on the Heartaches colours (red, pink and green). The Hearts, as we affectionately refer to ourselves, have now played around 400 matches, winning almost as many as we have lost, and have played as far afield as South Africa and North Carolina. It costs me a bit now and then, and maybe some of our opponents could not function in the sometimes affluent style which I am able to bestow, but in essence it is proud to be just another regular wandering side, taking on villages and fellow nomads in quiet English surroundings without crowds, fanfare, publicity or opulence.

Every year since 1975 I have produced a privately printed *Heartaches Cricketers' Almanack*, modelled on *Wisden*, which contains a ludicrously detailed literary and statistical account of the season just past. This usually takes up more of my time than lyric writing and, among other therapeutic benefits, enables me to return to my childhood delight of playing with numbers without too much embarrassment. Designed by the cartoonist Robert Duncan even in the years before he cornered the greetings card market, it costs a packet to produce, but the briefest and most pathetic innings by the most transient of signings is recorded therein with mind-numbing accuracy for all time.

Perhaps the most reckless example of extravagance in connection with a Heartaches game was when I chartered a helicopter in order to dash one hundred miles across the country immediately after the last ball was bowled in East Anglia in order to fulfill a speaking engagement an hour later at a school in Kent. Unfortunately the helicopter landed in the wrong school and took off again without me before I realised this fact. Furthermore, being a Sunday, I was locked in. It took me longer to clamber over the walls and stagger on foot, carrying my cricket gear and with the faithful Bonzo on a lead, from one Sevenoaks school to another than it had for me to fly from Suffolk.

My brother Jo was an early star of many a Heartaches match, having returned from Japan after several years there working for Cornes and Co., a trading company in Tokyo. Never the most dedicated of businessmen, he decided to come home in order to pursue his own writing ambitions. Shortly after his return, Jan gave birth to their first child, Alex, now just about the best bowler in Heartaches' ranks, but then merely a large mound of sound. Jo signed on to the Heartaches payroll and I rented a moderately shady office in Paddington from which he, I and Fiona masterminded several new ventures, notably a satirical football magazine called *Foul*. This publication, a cross between *Private Eye* and *Football Monthly*, was years ahead of its time, anticipating the slew of anarchic soccer fanzines by at least a decade. Sad to say, despite being the first journalistic home of several distinguished football writers of the future, such as Steve Tongue, *Foul* never paid its way and collapsed after two years, during which time we were never sued by anyone important enough to give us credibility. A final, desperate attempt to stay afloat involved the printing of 10,000 copies of *The Best Of Foul*, of which 9500 were still in my garage at the end of the decade.

Luckily Jo had several other literary assignments to keep him occupied and the wolf from the door and he seemed to spend a good deal of his first months back in England shooting around the globe for various colour supplements, including, ironically, a return to Japan. But the most important creative venture we began to put together was the idea which eventually became the staggeringly successful *Guinness Book of British Hit Singles*. Andrew and I had recently met a bright young UK-based American journalist and broadcaster named Paul Gambaccini, who had been asked to interview us for the British edition of *Rolling Stone* magazine. This took place at my house in Northumberland Place, though Paul arrived an hour late, having been taxied, as so many others had been, to a Ministry of Defence building in Northumberland Avenue. After the interview, Paul and I found we had a mutual fascination with the history of pop, and that we both owned a then extremely obscure US chart reference work by a gent named Joel Whitburn. This volume simply listed all the hits that had ever reached the American Top 100 and, together with Jo, we were certain that an English equivalent would be a winner. It took us some time to get it all together, but eventually we assembled all the raw material for the research (every pop chart from 1952) and a fourth author, my old chum Mike Read, by now beginning to move rapidly up the radio ladder. We formed a new company, GRRR books (Gambaccini, Rice, Rice, Read), with a growling boxer logo, and spent more than two years collating the huge amount of information.

It was not until late 1975 that we felt able to approach a major publishing company with our idea, and we went first to Guinness Superlatives, the undisputed leaders in the field of reference books. I called them out of the blue and asked to speak to either Norris or Ross McWhirter, founders of the hugely successful imprint. To my surprise, I was put straight through to Norris, who may well have recalled that *Jesus Christ Superstar* had featured in the *Guinness Book of Records* for a while as the biggest-selling British LP of all time (it probably really was the biggest by the end of 1971, though long since surpassed by many others). A few days later Norris met me and Jo and expressed great interest in our book. Our delight was dashed the very next day with the terrible news of Ross McWhirter's murder by the IRA. The McWhirter we never met had bravely but tragically offered a reward for information about IRA activities and paid the ultimate price. It was at least three months before we felt able to re-contact Guinness Superlatives, who fortunately told us it was business as usual and that our book was definitely still wanted. I am running ahead of myself a little, but the first edition finally emerged in mid-1977 and proved to be the forerunner of more than thirty best-selling books we authored during the following twenty years. In 1996, having sold around one and a half million books, all but about fifteen in the UK, we felt we had lost our grip and interest in the charts and flogged the concept back to Guinness.

I greatly value the close friendship that Paul ('Gambo') and I have formed over the years. We have different backgrounds and different political and social sensibilities, but I have never had anything other than great admiration for this highly civilised man who has more than once enabled me to see events and people from a new perspective, though we parted metaphorical company as far as his admiration (at various times) for Kajagoogoo, New Labour and Bill Clinton was concerned. His knowledge of all types of artistic endeavour is prodigious and each subject he broadcasts or writes about is always immaculately and entertainingly conveyed. He knows as much about baseball as I do about cricket and never uses autocue.

Mike Read is an enigmatic figure of enormous warmth and wit, who at times drove Paul and Jo in particular to distraction when his radio and television fame was at its early Eighties peak, preventing him from pulling his full weight with our Guinness books. In fact in the end he got eased out of the GRRR empire but fortunately not out of my life. On the one hand he seems to have achieved every middle-aged man's dream of never growing up, on the other he is a sophisticated poet and authority on poetry, having most recently written a biography of Rupert Brooke and also musicals about Brooke, Betjeman and Wilde (Oscar, not Marty). In any hectic life, one often only has time to make friends with those with whom one works – I am lucky that these two guys were the fellow pop maniacs on the Guinness books.

So there was a lot going on to delay a new show, and a lot of cash still rolling in to lessen the incentive. I was still doing my best to help dodgy businessmen and scroungers with ill-placed loans and investments, but with *JCS* going so well in so many countries in both stage and movie form, 1973 was proving to be an even better year financially than the previous two. I guess I must have slipped into at least half-millionaire status around this time (when half a million was a lot of money) but taxes were ludicrously steep and the overall state of the nation's economy dire, with inflation galloping and Edward Heath's three-day week doing little to make even the highest earners feel super-secure. One particularly daft venture I allowed myself to be sucked into involved the manufacture of a truly hideous kind of plastic ornament and/or lampstand entitled Shattaline. I sunk £5000 into Shattaline after meeting one of the titled directors who was wheeled out by the managing director of this struggling concern to show how reliable and kosher the whole enterprise was. The nobleman in question was a bloke named Lord Lucan. Could the collapse of Shattaline have contributed to his decision to 'lie doggo' when he had a little domestic difficulty in late 1974?

But Jeeves could be delayed no longer. I think the original suggestion that we should musicalise the immortal P.G. Wodehouse stories of the supremely intelligent manservant, Jeeves, and his intellectually challenged Hooray Henry master, Bertie Wooster, was mine, but Andrew and I were both unshiftable fans of the books and equally convinced that this would be the perfect, unexpected, type of follow-up to our two biblical shows. Of course we were not the first to come up with the idea. Wodehouse himself had had a go. Indeed one of the problems that affected the lengthy negotiations that David Land and Peter Brown (still Stigwood's main man in New York) had with Wodehouse's agents to obtain the relevant rights was that Wodehouse and his long-time collaborator Guy Bolton (the veteran dramatic author) had written their own musical, *Leave It To Jeeves* (music by Robert Wright and George Forrest). Wodehouse had written the lyrics, and Bolton the book. I am not quite sure when this show was actually written, but I suspect it had been lying around for some time by the time we came on to the Jeeves scene.

Consequently we found ourselves dealing with Guy Bolton as well as with Wodehouse's advisers and we were bombarded with advice and suggestions from the great dramatist as David and Peter were simultaneously bombarded with legal work. Guy Bolton was then nearly ninety and P.G. Wodehouse a couple of years older but both were one hundred per cent on the ball. They had written a number of hugely successful musicals in the early decades of the century, working with many of the greatest composers of all time, such as Jerome Kern, Cole Porter, George Gershwin and even Franz Lehar. We were extremely small fry in comparison and I was acutely aware of the fact that even if Wodehouse had never written a single novel, he would still have been remembered as one of the foremost theatrical lyricists of his era. Both Wodehouse and Bolton, British born, were American citizens.

We began work on our new show in Italy. Andrew's aunt, Vi Johnstone, a former actress (as Vi Crosby) had retired with her husband George, a doctor, to a villa in Ventimiglia, on the Mediterranean coast close to the French border. Vi, Andrew's mother Jean's sister, was a vivacious and highly amusing lady, larger than life and a great fount of rude and scandalous tales. Andrew was very close to his jovial aunt who had encouraged his childhood love for the theatre and she received us with great hospitality. We drove down to Ventimiglia in my spanking-new BMW, a hideously orange motor that creamed down the autoroutes. So thrilled was I with my exotic automobile that instead of going to bed one night I decided to take an all-night spin, driving to Pisa and back between one and eight in the morning. The sight of the Leaning Tower in a deserted Pisa at four in the morning more than compensated for the loss of a day's creative juices as I slept my drive off the following day. I am not sure whether Andrew or Vi ever believed my explanation for a day in bed, doubtless assuming I had crept out to some place of ill-repute in Ventimiglia or San Remo.

Even without my nocturnal tourist excursions, we did not make dramatic progress with Jeeves. Our original plan was to write a conventional book musical, i.e. with spoken dialogue scenes interspersed among the songs, and my first job was to draft a plot. Basing my outline primarily on the story of *The Code Of The Woosters*, with one or two scenes purloined from other Jeeves classics, I constructed a twenty-two-scene synopsis, telling the tale of Bertie's antics with the Drones, terrifying aunts, disastrous engagements, stolen cow-creamers and the vile neo-Nazi Roderick Spode. Then we started at Scene One to flesh it out with songs and dialogue. I found myself trying to keep the spoken bits to a minimum, instinctively preferring to tell as much of the story as possible through song. This inevitably slowed things down a bit and after a fortnight or so we had only completed a scene and a half. The first number featured Bertie Wooster on the banjo, singing about his mastery of the instrument and recalling an embarrassing incident when he was arrested for stealing a policeman's helmet on Boat Race Night. The song does not appear to have had a title and the lyrics were, at best, mundane:

> It's only been lately
> My life has changed greatly
> It's all come about since I bought my banjo
> I was a Philistine
> But now I've checked my sad decline
> They'll all line up to hear me soon
> For I've nearly learned Jingle Bells,
> Carousel's
> Highlights and half of Blue Moon

Actually, even mundane seems over-kind twenty-five years on. It probably sounded better with the music, but not much.

Back in England, we repaired to Andrew and Sarah's new

country retreat, a delightful farmhouse named Summerleaze, near East Knoyle in Wiltshire, in order to stagger at least past Scene Two. Progress was again fitful, and I decided to go away somewhere on my own in an attempt to speed up the faltering process; I went to stay in Exeter with Harry and Lyn Guest – Harry being the former Lancing teacher whom I had last seen when he and his wife were teaching in Tokyo, and who was now writing (several well-received slim volumes of poetry*) and teaching in Devon. It was great to see the Guests again but, left to my own devices during the day, I continued to struggle with the as yet entitled musical. I more or less completed two more lyrics – one to the tune of 'Down On The Farm', the song we had recorded with Maynard Williams and still three years away from its final resting-place as 'High Flying Adored'. This time around it was called 'If I Were Keats' and proved that I was definitely not:

> Oh if I were Keats,
> Or Tennyson or Rod McEwan
> Then I could begin to describe my thoughts to you – an
> Easy thing for Keats
> Who knew his words and rhymes . . .

Verse two was no better:

> Oh if I had the time,
> I'd paint for you around the clock – well
> That's if I were Waterhouse, Michaelangelo or Norman Rockwell

I also just about finished a lyric entitled 'Suddenly There's A Valet', which managed to mention the great between-the-wars cricketing partnership of Hobbs and Sutcliffe and had a couple of reasonable gags about breakfast trays and 'worldly pleasures at full throttle/let's not beat about the bottle' but it was becoming increasingly clear to me that all I was doing was making the master, P.G. Wodehouse, unfunny – quite an achievement.

I drove back from Devon knowing that I wanted to pull out of

---

* Much of Harry's poetry was published by the Anvil Press, owned by Peter Jay, himself a poet and a contemporary of mine at Lancing.

Jeeves. This was not only because I knew I was writing badly – I was convinced I had a much more exciting idea for a new show. A few weeks earlier, I happened to hear the tail end of a half-hour radio documentary about Eva Peron, as part of a series called *Legends Of Our Time*, or something like that. I was on my way to a dinner party in London and only because I was horrendously late did my few minutes in the car coincide with the last few minutes of the programme. I did not know anything about Eva Peron other than the fact she was Argentinian, glamorous and dead, and that she was known as Evita. Even this was probably more than ninety-nine per cent of the British population knew about her in 1973. I remembered her from my childhood stamp collecting days; her image on Argentina's stamps had always been one of my favourites, and I vaguely remembered reading, and feeling sorry about her death way back in 1952 – this is true for, as I have earlier recalled, I was well into newspapers by the time I was seven. What also intrigued me about this programme was that it was announced at the end that the following week's legend would be James Dean. Now I did know a lot about the eternally fascinating James Dean and immediately thought that if Eva Peron was in his league then I wanted to know more about her too. I managed to get a copy of the full Evita programme from the BBC and I was hooked.

Before I could begin to think about how to tackle a musical about a deceased Argentinian dictator's wife, I had to get out of Jeeves. This was a nightmare prospect – there were so many people to tell and presumably let down. In fact, everybody – Andrew, Guy Bolton, David Land and P.G. Wodehouse himself – took the news extremely well. I thought perhaps that Andrew would also wish to abandon ship, and I mentioned my Evita idea, but this cut no ice and he said he would proceed with another lyricist.

I broke the news to both Bolton and Wodehouse by letter. I had met Guy Bolton several times in London, and P.G. just once, at his home in Remsenburg, Long Island. Peter Brown took Andrew and me out to meet him one day shortly after we had decided to tackle Jeeves, and we spent a delightful afternoon in the company of the master and his wife. This was undoubtedly the best moment of my entire involvement with the Jeeves saga and made up for all the subsequent agonies. Wodehouse happily posed for photographs with us but of all the hundreds of rolls of film I was zapping off around the world at this time, this was the one that I wrecked by opening my camera at the wrong moment. I never got another chance for a picture with the man I consider not only to have been one of the greatest comic writers ever, but one of the greatest writers of any type, ever.

I wrote to P.G. telling him:

I have come to the conclusion that almost any attempt on my part to transfer Jeeves from book to song would do Jeeves and Bertie no good at all. Naturally they would survive (they are immortal) but I would hate any failure on my part to be responsible for linking your magnificent characters with adverse criticism.

I received a most gracious reply:

September 27, 1973
Remsenburg
Long Island
New York 11960

Dear Mr Rice:
I appreciated all the nice things you said about me in your letter, and I am of course sad at the thought that your Jeeves show has fallen through, but, as the fellow said, that's show business, and you were certainly wise to issue a *nolle prosequi*, as Jeeves would say, if you didn't feel comfortable about going on with a job which was certainly about as tough a one they come.

I had a feeling that it was a bit dangerous doing Jeeves after your stupendous success with *JCS*. I don't know how the critics would have reacted, but there is nothing they like better than to jump on somebody, especially if young, who has started off with a big winner. 'We'll show him', they say to themselves.

Great pity of course, but I'm sure you have been wise.

I am halfway through a new Jeeves novel. It looks pretty good to me, but there is a block comedy scene coming along, and if that doesn't come out all right, I'm sunk. So I am not cheering just yet.

All the best
Yours

P.G. Wodehouse

Guy Bolton also responded most generously to my letter. Writing from Buck's Club in Clifford Street, he was kind enough to close by saying, 'I greatly admire you both as craftsmen and I feel it is sufficient reward for what time I have given to the enterprise to be counted among your friends'.

Phew. I was still dogged by a nagging panic that I had just walked out of the biggest hit musical since – well, *Superstar* – and was almost tempted back in when Andrew recruited Alan Ayckbourn, no less, to write the book. I was asked to think again about writing just the lyrics, but after another look at my efforts to date, decided to stick to my guns. As Andrew and his new team continued with their *Jeeves* (for such was now its official title), bringing in a highly distinguished set of contributors, including David Hemmings, Prudence's man, as Bertie, I often felt like the man who had turned down the Beatles, but more often (just) felt my instincts were right.

So they proved to be. The story of *Jeeves* after my desertion is fortunately not one I am able to tell, but it turned out to be a major disaster. It ran rather shakily in Bristol before coming to London, but closed after a few weeks at Her Majesty's Theatre (where Andrew was to triumph over a decade later, and is still triumphing, with *Phantom Of The Opera*). By the time Stigwood called a halt to *Jeeves* it was May 1975, and I had made considerable progress on my own with what was now *Evita*.

I don't really know why *Jeeves* failed so ignominiously. There were endless clashes between various members of the team, but these were probably a consequence rather than a cause of the disaster. It was certainly far too long when it first hit the stage, but there have been plenty of long-winded hits before and since. The music was certainly not to blame, for the LP of the show contains a very pretty, if inevitably, because of the subject matter, lightweight selection of tunes, including some old favourites from Andrew's past and some that were to be recycled later.

Many years later, in 1996, Andrew and Alan reworked the show at Alan's Scarborough theatre and this time around it worked much better, eventually enjoying a short run in the West End. But the basic concept made it an unlikely bet for a mega-run; sad to say small musicals hardly ever work any more and I believe this is as true at the end of the century as it was in the Seventies. The main difference now is that a lot of big musicals aren't working either. It all comes down to the old cliché: the three most important things in a show are the book, the book and the book. In other words, a good idea is the essential initial peg on which every other element must be hung. A musical adaptation of P.G. Wodehouse, however professionally executed, is never going to appeal to non-Wodehouse fans and will probably alienate Wodehouse lovers by being unable to improve on the brilliant novels. Why add music when the humour is all? Of course many of the finest musicals of all time have been adapations of works by the greatest writers – Shakespeare, Shaw, Hugo – but the originals were stories that have universal appeal and did not depend solely on linguistic brilliance to strike a chord. With Wodehouse, the style of the writing was ninety per cent of the genius, the plots almost irrelevant. Andrew and Alan were only retaining the other ten per cent.

The parting of our professional ways did not at this point threaten to drive any kind of permanent wedge between Andrew and me. I was still red-hot keen to work with him again, and felt that my Eva Peron idea could be the vehicle. I suppose we were both accumulating permanent distractions and commitments in diverse areas that meant we could never be as close as we were when we lived under the same roof with little else to do but write and play together, but we never had any serious arguments and while the *Jeeves* musical was still lurching towards fruition, continued to write the odd song together.

Andrew was commissioned by the film director Ronald Neame to write the score for his movie of Frederick Forsyth's *The Odessa*

File, starring Jon Voight and Maximilian Schell. There was a need for one song to be heard on a car radio on the day of President Kennedy's assassination, and I was more than pleased to provide the words. As the movie was set in Germany, and the time November 1963, we wrote a Christmas song which owed more than a little to Elvis Presley's 'Wooden Heart', even down to a German verse (not written by me) in the middle. The song was recorded for the movie by Perry Como, which was an honour, and even lurched on to the bottom of the US Hot 100 in December 1974, our first brush with the American charts for quite a while. We also included it on Maynard Williams's album, but it really wasn't an outstanding song and Maynard's single release increased our list of pop flops by one. The opening couplet, a rather cringe-making 'Watch me now here I go/All I need's a little snow' was misinterpreted as a reference to cocaine in certain insalubrious American circles but even this unintentional bid for underground acceptance failed to boost sales. One of the principal themes used by Andrew in the score was yet again the melody that was one day to wind up as 'Sunset Boulevard'.

While devoting a fair amount of time to researching the life of Eva Peron – a tricky task, as back then there was almost nothing available about her life in print in English – and waiting for *Jeeves* to resolve itself one way or the other, I managed to secure myself a slot playing oldies on the brand new commercial radio station, Capital Radio. I happened to be sitting next to one of the station's directors, Richard Attenborough, at a charity lunch a few weeks before Capital's launch and told him of my dreams to be a disc-jockey and, more important, of the size of my record collection. The next day I was called by Capital's managing director, Michael Bukht, and was invited to see him. I probably got the job because the fledgling station had no oldies of their own. I called the show *You Don't Know What You've Got*, after a rather obscure 1961 hit by an Elvis sound-alike, Ral Donner, and was signed (and paid) to play my own discs every Saturday morning for an hour, which I would have done anyway at home for nothing. But the most significant result of my thirty minutes at Capital (then based in Piccadilly) on 4 July 1973, was the sight of a beautiful lady working there as a temp, Jane McIntosh.

Chapter Twenty-three

S ince my first brush with celebrity, my love life had been fairly hectic, if not in the Division One rock star league, time-consuming and erratic, with the combination of youth, money, travel and success pushing a few more opportunities my way than might have been the case had I remained a trainee solicitor, or even had I qualified as one. Though some liaisons were brief in the extreme (not always my fault), I was still at heart a romantic, and whenever I fell hard for somebody I tended to feel that this was definitely it. I'd been this way since 1956, as Jerry Leiber memorably said in 'Love Potion Number Nine'. My affair with Felicity, the delicate and fragile inspiration for my Gary Bond lyric, 'Disillusion Me', had moved from it to exit around the time I first met Jane McIntosh. Felicity and I had had a good six months or so together, including one holiday to Jamaica and Florida, but I am afraid that as a consequence of my inability to commit to anything and Felicity coming to her senses, she and her cat had moved out of Northumberland Place by the end of 1973.

The second time I met Jane was at Capital Radio's new HQ in the Euston Road soon after the station had got under way and I had two or three oldies shows under my belt. Apart from confidently announcing that Bobby Darin was alive and well on the day that superb pop singer died of heart failure, my programme was relatively glitch-free and seemed to be going down well with Capital's bosses, mainly ex-BBC men (there was nowhere else any radio man could have come from in those days), such as Aidan Day and Peter James. I really enjoyed my Saturday spot and relished working alongside some true radio greats such as Kenny Everett and Roger Scott. There was a great team spirit at Capital in those early days and the station quickly caught on with the London public. I set some competitions not usually associated with a pop oldies show, e.g. involving Etruscan pottery or retired cricketers and often brought in chums such as my art advisor Ian Bennett or brother Jo to liven up the chat. I also allowed a young hospital radio disc-jockey, Chris Reed, the odd five-minute slot. Few of these diversions would have been possible then within the BBC's bureaucracy but at Capital most broadcasters had much greater freedom to run their shows the way they wanted and it paid off in the listening figures.

The greatest perk my stint as an oldies disc-jockey gave me was an opportunity to meet battalions of ancient pop stars, both British and American, heroes of my youth, in the flesh, the more obscure the better. There has always been a loyal audience in Britain for former US hitmakers, particularly in clubs 'up North', a mysterious but obviously lucrative circuit. Usually the blast from the past included the odd London gig in a venue that did not require too much filling and most weeks I was able to pin down a rocker from my childhood who, not overburdened with the press attention of his glory years, was normally delighted to give an interview, either live in the studio or pre-recorded at his hotel. In this way I met the likes of Frankie Valli, Fabian, Tommy Roe, Johnny Tillotson and, best of all, Del Shannon, creator of the immortal 'Runaway' back in 1961. I had even recorded 'Runaway' myself, under the pseudonym Huddersfield Transit Authority, a couple of years before and, of all the self-indulgent pop singles Qwertyuiop Productions had made in the afterglow of the success of *Superstar*, my Del Shannon cover had been the one that came closest to hitting the charts, selling around 3000 copies. Del had not heard of the Huddersfield Transit Authority, nor of me, but he had heard of *Jesus Christ Superstar* and when I managed subtly to slip into our interview the fact that I had written it, he was suitably amazed that one of its creators should be slumming it with golden oldies on a local radio station. I also dug up several less-than-household former British pop names for exclusive chats, including Gary 'Top Teen Baby' Mills and Michael 'Angela Jones' Cox.* Heaven!

Jane McIntosh was only working at Capital between theatrical ventures; she had spent most of her time since coming down to London from Scotland some seven years before as a freelance theatrical production assistant. When we met two of her most recent shows had been musicals, *Grease* and *I And Albert*. She had also worked at the National Theatre during Laurence Olivier's regime. *I And Albert* was an American musical about Queen Victoria with music by Charles Strouse and lyrics by Lee Adams; they were both well-known Broadway veterans although I was more familiar with their one big pop smash, 'Born Too Late', by one-hit wonders the Poni-Tails in 1957. Charles's biggest hit, *Annie*, was still in the future. *Grease* was not yet the phenomenon it has since become and the first UK production was a failure, despite the fact that it starred Richard Gere. But Gere was then also some way from becoming a household name and I took a particular interest in him solely because he was going out with Jane when I first met her. For some reason, I am not often believed today when I say that Jane moved from Richard Gere to me.

The second time I saw Jane at Capital she was clad from top to bottom in motor-cycle gear, helmet, boots and leathers. Consequently I did not immediately recognise her as the irresistible lady I had noticed during my interview a few weeks before, and made a mental note that there were at least two wonderful women at Capital I should investigate. It soon transpired that these two visions of pulchritude were one and the same but I was not disappointed. Far from it; I felt she was the most beautiful woman I had ever met. I still do.

Jane was nearly twenty-seven when I first met her, a little less than two years younger than me. She was Scots through and through, the second daughter and third child of Colonel Alexander 'Sandy' McIntosh, OBE, and his wife of Scottish and sometime Maori descent, Artereta. They lived way up in the Highlands, on

---

* I played in a Lord's Taverners cricket match with Michael Cox a year or so later and he held one of the most stunning close catches I have ever witnessed at any level of cricket. Michael also surfaced later as a striking Pharaoh in one of the many *Joseph* national tours.

the Black Isle, just north of Inverness. I came to love the trips we made to see her parents in this beautiful and remote part of Scotland. Sandy and Artereta were Scots to the core and both Jane and her elder sister Fiona became much more Scots in accent and manner once north of the border. Their brother Colin seemed to be a true McIntosh wherever he was, which was usually France. Sandy had spent many years with the family furniture firm after his army service but was now a semi-retired estate manager for vast tracts of land around the Black Isle, which, needless to say, was neither black nor an isle. He was a champion, but fortunately a very interesting, talker. Both parents were around seventy when I first met them but their attitudes belied their years.

Artereta's Maori ancestry enabled me to come up with a laboured pun on our first meeting, when Artereta revealed that one of her grandfathers was half Maori. I suggested that he founded the Half a Maori School of Dancing, which was received with polite bewilderment. Eerily coincidentally, the real Arthur Murray of Dancing School fame died within two days of good old Artereta. I had no idea the old boy was still alive when I read his obituary just after attending Artereta's funeral on the Black Isle in March 1991. Well he wasn't alive by then of course, but you know what I mean. Arthur had made it to nearly ninety-six, and Artereta was not far off ninety when she died, fit and alert to the very end. And one of Artereta's brothers was called Arthur . . . but you can find coincidences everywhere if you look hard enough.

Jane had been, for reasons still unclear today, sent to a now defunct boarding school in North Wales, winding up her education loosely attached to Winchester for a year, where an uncle of hers taught. Secretarial training was followed by her move to London and the theatre. She was actually married when I met her, though she had been separated for some time from her husband, the theatrical agent Michael Whitehall. I fell for her in a big way and it was not long after we started walking out together (as she put it) that I felt, for the first time in my life, that here was someone I could not contemplate losing. I was old enough, and financially secure enough, to consider marriage and it was on my mind from the first time we had dinner together. Whether I was mature enough is another question, but that did not occur to me.

By the end of 1973 we were a serious item and I have terrific memories of a most enjoyable pre-Christmas weekend at her sister Fiona's home in Sussex, at which I first outlined my serious intentions. Fiona is a true one-off whose hospitality and verbal exuberance are legendary in her wide circle; her husband John Armstrong, a big wheel in shipping insurance, copes with this via imperturbable aplomb, i.e. agrees with every word and does his own thing. I loved all of Jane's relatives and fervently hoped I would be admitted permanently into their line-up.

Despite the happy turmoil in my heart, or perhaps inspired by it, I was moving on well with my research into the life of Eva Peron. The only problem was that there was precious little published material in print in English. Since the worldwide success of *Evita* the show, there have been literally dozens of books about Eva Peron, none of which give our work any credit whatsoever for reintroducing awareness of this fascinating character to the non-Latin world. I do not think I am being arrogant when I state that none of these books would ever have seen the light of day had the musical not been so popular, so to be ignored or attacked by a succession of scribblers doing little more than jumping on the bandwagon has sometimes been a little hard to take. Most post-*Evita* authors or journalists have accused us (me in particular) of wild inaccuracies, total misunderstanding of her personality and motivation, trivialisation and/or glamorisation of her story and, most outrageously, of choosing the subject purely for commercial reasons.

However, many who were actually around in Eva's time and place and who knew something about the lady all along, have given us more credit. Apart from the device of using fellow Argentine Che Guevara as a narrator, there is nothing in the text of *Evita* that does not stand up to historical scrutiny, and although I am well aware that Guevara never met Eva, it is more than likely that his subsequent career was at least in part influenced by his early life under, and a distaste for, the Peron regime. Indeed, in our original recording of the work, we never even stated that the narrator was Guevara. He was referred to simply as 'Che', a nickname in Argentina roughly equivalent to the English 'mate'.

I genuinely feel that the kind of character Eva Peron was,

obsessed with personal aggrandisement, power, image, fashion and self-importance (often justified), but yet smart, driven, stylish, self-confident and attractive, makes a musical by far the best way of portraying her brief but blazing existence with any accuracy. The above qualities are all too often to be found within the milieu of show business and it takes one to know one. The snobbery of the majority of self-appointed Evita scholars trailing in our wake, who attempt to analyse her appeal and influence with words alone, probing her intellectually rather than emotionally, usually has the effect of making her boring, the one thing Eva never was.

Looking desperately for written info about Eva, all I could find back then were two sources – first, a 1957 book by Frank Owen, a former Labour MP, journalist and editor, *Peron: His Rise And Fall* (Cresset Press), which I borrowed from a Kensington public library and I am ashamed to say I have still not returned. There was also an excellent paperback by Richard Bourne entitled, *Political Leaders of Latin America* (Pelican, 1969), which consisted of six articles on six leading figures of the region, including one on Eva herself and one on Che Guevara. It was Mr Bourne's book which made me aware of the fact that Guevara was Argentine; I had always assumed he was Cuban. My initial synopsis for *Evita* made use of a fictional narrator, Eva's hairdresser, whom I imaginatively named Mario. Once I realised that Guevara was in Argentina for the years of Eva's ascendency, Mario was consigned to the hair-cutting room floor; the opportunity to include two Argentine icons in one story was too good to miss. I was also keen to point out that in his own way Guevara was just as ambitious, self-obsessed, fanatical and intolerant as Evita. All the same, my initial outline for the show's structure, completed by mid-1974, and featuring Mario, was not changed greatly by the substitution of Che as narrator/critic.

I contacted Richard Bourne and we had a fascinating (for me anyway) lunch at which I learned a little more about my new leading character, the illegitimate daughter of a middle-class Argentine landowner, born Eva Duarte in 1919, who rose by means fair and foul to become wife of President Juan Peron of Argentina when she was still in her mid-twenties. Eva, however, was never content to be a mere cipher at Peron's side, and in a male-dominated, class-ridden society became an icon, a near-saint for millions of *descamisados*, the 'shirtless ones', the workers, who worshipped her with untrammeled and unquestioning devotion. She was despised with equal vigour by many of the establishment figures she challenged. Her death in 1952 from ovarian cancer at thirty-three, produced an outbreak of genuine public mourning in Argentina matched in Britain since then only by that for the death of Diana, Princess of Wales.* Bourne, in contrast to almost everyone else who heard about my idea at this time, probably did not think I was barking mad to choose Eva Peron as an all-singing all-dancing heroine, but he was one of the few who knew something about her back in the early Seventies.

Perhaps my most important source of Evita knowledge, however, turned out to be a television documentary entitled *Queen Of Hearts*, filmed a quarter of a century before Princess Diana gave the title global renown, and for that matter eight years before Dave Edmunds's chirpy hit record of that name. *Queen Of Hearts* was directed by Argentine film-maker Carlos Pasini, then working in London. He was not a complete exile from his home country, but the chaotic and dangerous political situation which existed in Argentina at that time made many in artistic or allegedly subversive pursuits wary of too high a profile there. Eva died in 1952, Peron (who had been President since 1945) was overthrown by the military in 1955, and from then until 1972 there were eight Argentine administrations, none of which halted the sad slide towards bedlam and lawlessness. Consequently, as those seventeen years went by, more and more people in Argentina came to feel that Peron's years in charge were not so bad after all. His decade seemed almost calm and efficient by comparison with the subsequent chaos. Furthermore, it had been blessed with the magic of Evita.

In November 1972, Juan Peron, with his third wife Isabel, returned to Argentina after seventeen years in exile. In September the following year he was re-elected President, with Isabel ironically and unsuitably achieving the position that Eva had desired but had ultimately been denied, the Vice-Presidency. His

---

* Sir Winston Churchill's death in 1965 was of course an event that inspired great national mourning, but he was ninety and grief was respectful not hysterical. The Rice family were among the huge number who filed past his coffin as he lay in state.

return did little to arrest Argentina's disastrous decline into violent anarchy and he died of heart failure in the middle of 1974. He was succeeded as President by Isabel, whose desire to be known as Isabelita was never as keenly adopted by the populace as she had hoped.

Carlos Pasini's documentary told the story of Eva's life and after-life, the film beginning with the removal of her body by Peronists from an unmarked grave in Milan in 1971, whence it was delivered to the President-in-exile in Madrid. Narrated by Diana Rigg, it had been shown on English television (by Thames TV) a few months before I became interested in Evita. I was able to obtain a copy of the film from Thames, and to meet the director, who became a great help to my early research. In addition to the information I had already gleaned from his film, Carlos provided me with many other photographs and posters which I was able to use when we came to launch and promote the first recording of our musical version of Evita's story. *Queen of Hearts* was a clear and gripping hour of Argentine history which conveyed with great clarity the charisma and power of this remarkable woman, and the extraordinary reactions of both love and hate that she inspired.

But the most enjoyable piece of research I undertook was a trip to Argentina. I invited Jane to come with me and I have to say that an offer of a trip to South America is a pretty good chat-up line, although I believe that our relationship was going well enough by early 1974 to have survived without the wonderful two weeks we spent down Argentine way. I told virtually nobody where we were going and certainly intended to keep a low profile once we got out there, as both the planned stage and film versions of *Jesus Christ Superstar* in Buenos Aires had met with fairly strong critical reaction. The theatre where the stage show was scheduled to open had been burned to the ground and the cinema due to show Norman Jewison's film bombed. I was not confident that introducing myself to the Argentine media as the bloke who had written the words for *Superstar* and who was now embarking upon a show about their most hated and/or loved female would have been a wise move. I am not sure exactly who was responsible for the pre-*Superstar* violence but the Argentine reaction to our work has enabled me to remain a little more relaxed about even the most unpleasant of home critics who can only wound with words.

An executive of the international movie distribution company, CIC, Fred Sill, whom I had met during the promotion of the *Superstar* film, had extensive contacts and experience of South America in general and of Argentina in particular, and he supplied me with a number of Buenos Aires contacts. Fred, who sends me Evita postcards and memorabilia from South America to this day, emphasised however that I should not advertise my reason for the trip or tell anyone about whom I was meeting to discuss the project. The country was certainly in a shambolic state and plagued by evils committed by various factions, often with official approval, so it was not a trip to be embarked upon without a little care.

All this, plus the fact I was travelling with a beautiful new loved one, made me feel rather more daring than I was entitled to be, as nothing remotely along John Le Carré lines happened during our idyllic week in Buenos Aires. But I did meet some Argentine film-makers and journalists out there and every one added to my fast-increasing knowledge and fascination with Eva Peron. Seeing many of the places where Eva had lived and operated was also a great help to me in preparing my outline for the musical, atmospherically at least. I did not have the contacts, nor of course the guts, to attempt to meet Peron himself, who was nearing the end of his short come-back as President when we were out there, partly because I was having such a romantic time sight-seeing and partly because I didn't want to be taken to a deserted railway siding, shot and dumped in the River Plate. I probably flattered myself imagining that I was of sufficient interest to any pro- or anti-Peronist to warrant such a fate but as I was never quite sure whose side my musical was on, I thought it best to avoid all possible chance of interrogation and torture.

Jane and I spent a week in the Plaza Hotel in Buenos Aires, a magnificent joint whose parade of shops included a jeweller once patronised by Evita. From there it was a short stroll to many of the places where Eva had operated, notably the Casa Rosada, the pink presidential palace in the Plaza de Mayo. It was from the balcony of this stocky edifice, impressive but a little drab and architecturally unadventurous, and not actually that pink, that Eva made many of her melodramatic speeches, and where we were to represent her singing 'Don't Cry For Me Argentina' after her husband's inauguration as President in 1945. I would have been surprised, to put it mildly, to have been told in 1974 that twenty-two years later a full-blown re-staging of Evita's greatest moment would have been filmed on that very balcony, with full Argentine government approval, using our words and music and someone called Madonna Louise Veronica Ciccone, then an unknown seventeen-year-old just starting out on a singing and dancing career.

We loved Buenos Aires and although I spent a fair amount of time in our hotel room hammering away at my outline for the show we occupied ourselves with equal dedication sight-seeing and just drifting around. We went to several good restaurants, but one thing we never did in a nation famous for beef was to eat it. The incompetence of successive administrations had led to beef rationing – a ban on its public purchase or consumption for half of every month and we happened to be there in a beefless half. We shopped at Harrod's in Calle Florida, went to the cinema on Avenida Corrientes, crossed the widest (425 feet) street in the world, the Avenida 9 de Julio, and drove a few miles out of town to the riverside suburb of Olivos; all places with Evita connections and most of which I managed to incorporate into the lyrics of *Evita*. After a terrific week we flew up to the beautiful and gargantuan butterfly-thronged waterfalls at Iguazu, where the borders of Argentina, Paraguay and Brazil conjoin, and then to Rio de Janeiro, where we lazed around on the beach for three days before returning to the murky three-day weeks of England and the first of two General Elections that year.

Around this time, having been outed as a natural Conservative through my somewhat confused orations on *Any Questions*, I was approached to lend my political avoirdupois to the Tory cause by youthful, fast-rising MP John Selwyn Gummer, then dating even faster-rising political socialite and writer Arianna Stassinopoulos. I attended one or two not very star-studded meetings in not very smoky Westminster drawing rooms and was entrusted with a couple of afternoons on a soapbox in what was then John's constituency, Lewisham West. Fortunately I was not recognised by many of the electorate there who were determined to be unmoved by my speeches and leaflets. John lost his seat and the Conservatives sort of lost the election. The people's verdict was more or less a plague on both your houses, though eventually the Labour party proved the less incapable of forming a new government and Harold Wilson was returned to Number 10. Neither Wilson nor Edward Heath inspired much fervour and the country was lumbered with another election in October, when the result was almost as inconclusive. Around this time an astrologer in (I think) the *Daily Mirror* tipped me as a future Prime Minister. Wrong. So far.

Although I was now genuinely devoting a lot of time to *Evita*, I still fired off like a loose cannon in various other directions and with various other schemes. Andrew was, after all, still busy with *Jeeves*. I wrote a set of lyrics for a children's album *Barbapapa*, a spin-off from a phenomenally successful Smurfs-type Dutch TV series, which unfortunately never caught on in this country, despite the signing of Ed Stewart for the English version (I also brought in Alan Doggett's London Boy Singers for the sessions). I wrote some allegedly topical lyrics for a couple of Esther Rantzen's *That's Life* programmes and vaguely remember contributing a pro-monarchist song about Charles the First to the Chichester Festival. I turned up on more and more media panel games, thrilled to be asked back several times to *Call My Bluff*, with both Frank Muir and Patrick Campbell unfailingly convivial, amusing – and tall. I was even offered my own television series, *Musical Triangles*.

Musical Triangles was the brainchild of a young producer at Thames TV, Simon Buxton. The most important result of our pairing was that Simon became a regular member of the Heart-aches cricket team, for whom he still makes an occasional guest appearance, and with whom I usually opened the batting during the side's markedly untriumphant early years. The musical triangle of Simon's series was that of (classical) composer, instrument and performer and I was presenter and interviewer. Composers covered included many obvious ones such as Mozart, Purcell and Vivaldi and one or two I had barely heard of, such as Villa-Lobos and Rameau. The musicians involved were fairly stellar, including Julian Bream (the lute and Dowland), Paul Tortelier (the cello and Beethoven), James Galway (the flute and Vivaldi) and for me the most interesting of all, Peter Pears (the voice and Benjamin Britten). The programmes were filmed on location rather than in a studio at spectacular venues such as St Bride's Church in Fleet Street, the Duke of Wellington's HQ at Stratfield Saye, my old stamping-ground of Hatfield House (where an exact contemporary of mine at Lancing, Robin Harcourt-Williams, was in charge of the library and other treasures) and Benjamin Britten's home at Aldeburgh.

The highlight of *Musical Triangles* for me was the recording with Peter Pears. The world-renowned tenor had also been educated at Lancing, though considerably before my time.* I was intrigued to discover that Peter had been a more than useful schoolboy cricketer. Benjamin Britten and he were of course an artistic (and personal) collaboration of rare distinction and our little programme turned out to be the last to feature Britten himself on camera, although the composer felt too frail to participate in the recording. I was very moved to see the two lifelong companions walking slowly around their garden, Pears supporting Britten each step of the way. Britten had written his St Nicolas cantata for Lancing's centenary in 1948 and my first introduction to his music had been as a hand-bell ringer in *Noye's Fludde* during my first year at the school. Despite my lamentable ignorance about most of these two colossi's work, we thus had much in common and my off-camera conversation with Britten was relaxed and enjoyable. I have heard quite a bit of Britten's *oeuvre* since 1974, and wish I enjoyed it more.

Musical Triangles went well and the initial series of six programmes led to a second, of seven more. My diffidence as a result of my lack of expertise in the world of classical music turned out to be an asset, making my enquiries and desire to learn seem genuine, which they were. The shows were usually broadcast at whatever the opposite of prime time is, but even twenty years later I received the odd repeat fee (usually less than a tenner) for a transmission in some remote latitude at an even remoter hour. I

* A highly regarded classical composer who taught music during my time at Lancing, Christopher Headington, a friend of mine until his death in 1996, wrote biographies of both Britten and Pears.

was doubtless seen by many more viewers when I became a team captain on a pretty inane pop quiz series called *Disco*, which was compèred by Terry Wogan, and travelled to a succession of grotty dives and clubs where Freddie (of the Dreamers) and former Miss Worlds replaced Bream and Tortelier as my co-stars. At least I was covering both up and down markets in my rather lacklustre bid for a television career.

I continued with Capital Radio, though by now having run out of oldies to play (it was only 1974), I switched to the current American charts, in particular the Country and Western arena, of which music I had become a great fan. I was now persuading US country stars such as George Hamilton IV, Tanya Tucker, Bill Anderson and the hilarious Jimmy Buffet to come in to talk to me at Capital. But the greatest thrills of all were the great divas Tammy Wynette, already long established in America and shortly to top the best-sellers in the UK with her masterpiece 'Stand By Your Man', and Dolly Parton. I think I was the first person to play Dolly's first English hit, 'Jolene' in England but I dare say she would have made it without me. I met her for the second time in 1991, when I was asked by Disney to act as 'music consultant' on her movie *Straight Talk*. She was just as modest and funny (and outrageously beautifully proportioned) as she had been at Capital Radio all those years before. Inexplicably she did not recall our first get-together.

I went to see Tammy Wynette at the Hammersmith Odeon with Michael Campbell-Bowling, my insurance pal. We had trouble getting into our extremely good seats because the bloke positioned right next to them was bandaged and plastered from head to toe. Even tapping his foot would have been out of the question and we idly wondered just how keen a Tammy fan he was to be lowered into a theatre seat in his painfully rigid condition rather than into an intensive care unit, or even a tomb. Half way through the show the immortal Tammy launched into a moving speech. She said she wanted to introduce the audience to one of the bravest and most inspiring men of our time, at which a spotlight leapt into life and illuminated Michael. Admittedly I had only known Michael for a few years, but I was nonetheless surprised to hear that he was so highly rated by one of the all-time Country greats. Just as

Michael was warming to his applause, the man on the light got it right and shifted the beam to the wrecked individual beside us, whom Tammy now revealed to be Evel Knievel, the motor-cycle daredevil. At that time he was a household name for his manic biker stunts, such as leaping through space (on a motor-bike) over the Grand Canyon or a row of London buses. Evel had recently missed the bus as far as a recent exploit had been concerned, or rather hadn't, as machine and man had failed to clear the final double-decker, resulting in a lot of extra business for English surgeons. Evel did his best to smile in response to his acclaim, but showed more noticeable emotion when Michael tactlessly asked him for an autograph.

But the one thing that often took my mind off *Evita* during 1974 was Jane. Not long after our return from South America I asked her to marry me, and not long after that she discovered she was pregnant. We were both thrilled by this turn of events and only the fact she was still technically married clouded the skies. However, she had no problems finalising the divorce (no settlement was necessary, no children were involved) and we planned the wedding for a Monday morning, 19 August 1974, at the registry office in Marloes Road, Kensington. Neither of us wanted a big bash, so we told virtually no one about our decision until fairly late in the day, eventually roping in the two families and two or three close chums (Roger Watson acted as best man) for the ceremony itself and a slap-up dinner at the Savoy in the evening. Half an hour after the marriage, I took Bonzo for a walk in the park and ran into Malcolm McDowell, the actor who was then in the middle of a hot streak of hit movies, such as *O Lucky Man* and *Clockwork Orange*. I didn't know the poor bloke but was so keen to tell someone, anyone, about my new state, that I buttonholed him and did so. He offered genuinely profuse congratulations and as I seem to run into him by chance around every eight years since then, we always recall our first meeting with amusement.

Shortly before Jane and I got married, we bought a house. Romeyns Court was a quite beautiful house in the village of Great Milton, some six miles south-east of Oxford, near Thame. I bought it at auction in June and paid a lot more than I, or the sellers, had bargained for. The expected price for the six-bedroomed mansion, with around nine acres of field and garden, had been around £75,000 and I actually made a pre-auction offer of £90,000, so taken were Jane and I with the property after a weekend of looking at several houses from fifty to a hundred miles west of London. Once we saw Romeyns Court we knew it was the place for us and we cancelled all future house-hunting plans in order to concentrate our strategy on landing it. The owners (after a lot of thought) rejected our sneaky offer and, wisely as it turned out, decided to go ahead with the auction at the Randolph Hotel in Oxford.

The auctioneer gave Romeyns Court such a build-up before starting the show that he almost put me off it. There must be a catch, it sounds so ideal. I was put off even more when immediately the bidding started a loud voice from the back called out, 'One hundred thousand pounds'. There followed a collective gulp as most of the prospective purchasers realised they might as well go home, and then a longish silence. The hammer was about to fall when I felt I should at least make a token gesture of bidding, so I nervously volunteered one hundred and two thousand. Quick as a flash the chap at the back came back with one hundred and ten. Another pause, then I heard myself offering one hundred and twelve. Yet again, an instant riposte, this time of one hundred and twenty. My nerve almost gone, I raised him a feeble grand – one hundred and twenty-one thousand. At last, a pause against me, except I was now petrified that I was at least thirty thousand beyond my budget and almost longed for him to crush me completely with a hundred and thirty. But he faltered and eventually came back with a mere hundred and twenty-two. Somehow I knew I had him and it was now my turn to go for broke, as it were. I shot back with a confident 'One hundred and twenty-five thousand pounds' and that was it. My unseen opponent retired hurt and the gavel descended. The vendors were ecstatic, as well they might have been. My own ecstasy was delayed while I got over a minor panic attack, but after those few minutes Jane and I never again felt for a moment that we had made a mistake. We called in on the way back from the sale. The house was perfect, it was ours and it needed a lot of work. So did *Evita*.

Chapter Twenty-four

Jane and I went to America for our honeymoon. Fiona Mackenzie had married Anthony Deal and left the Heartaches empire, and after one or two short-lived signings to help me and Jo in our cheerless Paddington office, a great friend of Jane's from Capital Radio, Linda Brooker, became my new secretary. Of her many qualities, the most intriguing was that she was closer than close to Elvis Presley's music publisher, Freddie Bienstock, a giant in that business, his Carlin Music and related companies having published countless hits all around the world for decades, most notably the songs of Jerry Leiber and Mike Stoller, two of my greatest song-writing heroes. Leiber's lyrics were the wittiest in rock music, ranging from the out and out comedy of 'Yakety Yak' and 'Love Potion Number Nine' and the wry humour of 'Jailhouse Rock', via the romance of 'Stand By Me' and 'Loving You', to the social comment of 'Is That All There Is' and 'Spanish Harlem'. And dozens more; Elvis alone had recorded over twenty Leiber-Stoller songs, starting with 'Hound Dog'. Freddie told me and Andrew that he might be able to get Elvis to record something of ours if we made a suitable demo recording – and of course if he got the publishing rights. Fair enough, he could have had my house and car in return for an Elvis recording.

Linda was going out to join Freddie in Las Vegas to see Elvis in concert shortly after our wedding and suggested that we drop in while she was there to see the King ourselves. I had by this time probably been to America thirty or forty times, enjoying every trip enormously, but had never really been there solely on pleasure bent, for a long holiday. Neither had I shown Jane any of my American haunts and longed to go there as an expert and to discover some new places as well. So we planned an extensive trip: Los Angeles, Las Vegas, Denver, Jackson Hole and the Rocky Mountains, Yellowstone National Park, winding up with a few days in New York.

I had actually seen Elvis live in Vegas a couple of years before, in the company of Andrew, David Land and Robert Stigwood, after one of our trips to Los Angeles in connection with the *Superstar* movie. MCA-Universal had fixed that excursion, and we were also accompanied by one of their up-and-coming record stars, Olivia Newton-John, which added much-needed glamour to our party. I recall wandering around the still buzzing hotel casinos and nightclubs at around four in the morning (we spent an hour watching a brilliant female hypnotist act) with Olivia, who was totally unrecognised. She was about to enjoy a truly staggering run of record success in America and, speaking as one who has met her many times over the years since, she has been unchanged and unfazed by it. We saw Elvis two nights running at the Las Vegas Hilton and it was a surreal experience for me to see the most famous star in the world in the flesh – he had existed so powerfully in my mind as a remote and inaccessible icon, as an image that had become so familiar and commercial that his human form appeared artificial; he seemed like an Elvis impersonator. But I loved his shows, although most of my companions expressed severe disappointment. He had appeared to lose concentration at times, carelessly sauntering through many of his greatest hits while he threw scarves and fluffy hound dogs to the matrons in the front row, but when he put a bit of effort into it, as he usually did with the big ballads, it was clear his voice was still up to it. Loving it or hating it, no one could take their eyes off him. Two years on, I could not wait to see him again, especially as Linda said we would be invited to his after-show party.

The Elvis shows Jane and I saw on that trip were more varied than the 1972 performances I had caught. Elvis seemed totally distracted one night, insisting that his competent but bland backing vocalists, a trio called Voice, sang four or five songs on their own while he skulked in the wings, which was not what the punters had come to see. He followed Voice's unwanted set with 'It's Now Or Never' at breakneck speed, somewhat reducing the intensity and passion of the song. He then noticed the singer Vikki Carr, who had been warbling elsewhere in town, come into the auditorium and asked her publicly whether she had missed 'It's Now Or Never'. Ms Carr had, so Elvis did the song again, even faster, and then repeated other chunks of his act for her benefit. He introduced the audience to one or two other stars and then to his ex-wife, Priscilla, his current girl friend (I forget who), his karate teacher, his dad, the policeman who had given him a drug squad badge and several others linked to him in ever-remoter ways. At one point, almost out of control, he threatened all those who accused him of being strung out on drugs with violent retribution. This was actually gripping, as it was Elvis, but very disturbing. But yet again, when he tried, his singing was magical, and his versions of 'Fever' and the normally excruciating 'American Trilogy' were spine-tingling. He didn't really need the huge, brash Vegas lounge band. He didn't need anything, except a good manager.* A phenomenal talent. A phenomenal tragedy.

The second show we saw on our honeymoon trip was the final show of Elvis's stint at the Hilton, and afterwards Freddie took us up to the penthouse floor of the hotel to the end-of-engagement party for the Elvis band and crew, and presumably for Elvis as well. Once past the armed guards, we took up position near the snacks and cased the joint. Elvis had of course not yet turned up and the atmosphere was subdued, if not funereal. Rather than being part of the wild rock'n'roll extravaganza we had been expecting, with me and Elvis trading vocals on 'Don't Be Cruel' as exotic ladies danced, as food, drink and substances flowed, we felt more as if we had crashed a Home Counties Senior Citizens get-together.

Eventually things livened up to dreary, and a little more eventually, to something approaching entertaining, as we swigged Elvis's beer and munched his peanuts. At last the King materialised – we missed his entrance, it was as if he had been teleported into the

---

* Freddie Bienstock introduced us to Colonel Tom Parker, Elvis's manager, who was a permanent fixture at the tables, which was why Elvis got trapped in the Vegas circus at least 500 shows too long.

suite by thought processes – and was immediately surrounded by his rhythm section who hung on his every word, annoyingly just out of earshot. He looked good close-up. He was not going through one of his fat periods, was dressed fairly soberly in shirt and slacks, and seemed very cheerful. It was strange looking around a room of people at a fairly staid gathering, one of whom was Elvis Presley. He needed no stage or lights to draw all eyes towards him. He looked so like himself that it couldn't be – as if he were the only man at the party who'd thought it was fancy dress and had come as Elvis. Then he dematerialised again and after another hour of small talk with the third trumpeter and (mainly) among ourselves, we decided to scarper. The sun had come up and after a few minutes' gawp at Vegas and the desert, the lights of the casinos and hotels still flashing pointlessly in the dawn, we headed for the door.

Just as we were on the threshold, a side door right next to the suite's main door opened and from what I had thought must have been a cupboard (maybe it was) out stepped Elvis. We were all too obviously facing the wrong way to pretend that we had just arrived, and too nervous to change our minds about leaving in front of our host. But we did shake his hand and thanked him for a great party. 'Thank you for coming,' drawled the King and we were back out with the armed guard. Descending to our humble floor, I assured Jane that next time he'll have recorded one of our songs and we can meet him properly. We were quite happy with that briefest of introductions, until of course the night of 16 August 1977, when we heard that the King had left the building forever.

Elvis did eventually record a Lloyd Webber-Rice song. We broke away from *Jeeves*, *Evita* and sundry other distractions for a couple of days and came up with two numbers we thought right up his boulevard. One was a country-ish ballad entitled 'It's Easy For You', which dealt with a marriage break-up and the subsequent desertion of a mistress, and the other, a Chuck Berry pastiche entitled, 'Please Don't Let Lorraine Come Down', about a lady of ill-repute living on the floor above. Freddie got our demos to Elvis, who finally got around to recording 'It's Easy For You' in his studio at Gracelands in 1976, and although the arrangement and production sounded as if they had been phoned in, Elvis's vocal wasn't at all bad. The thought that Elvis must have spent at least fifteen minutes studying our words and music is a humbling one. Freddie thought Elvis might also have had a shot at 'Lorraine' but it has not yet surfaced and as virtually everything Elvis ever sung, spoke or grunted near a tape machine has been issued in the twenty years since his death, I fear that he never got around to our second effort.

'It's Easy For You' was eventually issued as the final track on his last album, *Moody Blue*. Almost as soon as we were celebrating its release, we were mourning his death. His transfer to heavenly status did of course mean that the album sold in millions, rather more than it deserved to artistically, although our royalties for the song have remained mysteriously modest over the years, indeed non-existent for over a decade. There was a rather gruesome coincidence for me in that a song I wrote with Marvin Hamlisch entitled 'The Only Way To Go' turned out to be the last track on the last album Bing Crosby issued before *he* died. When Whitney Houston recorded 'I Know Him So Well', which I wrote with ABBA's Bjorn and Benny for our musical *Chess*, and placed that as the last track on her new album in 1986, I was mightily relieved when she survived the curse of a Tim Rice album-closer. I'm afraid I didn't warn her beforehand in case she took the title off her album.

One final Elvis anecdote: for about five minutes I was convinced that I was the only person in England who knew that he had died. I was watching the ITV *News At Ten* at Romeyns Court one evening in August 1977, when I received a phone call from my old EMI pal, Alan Warner, in Los Angeles. Alan and I have been exchanging calls and faxes, almost on a daily basis sometimes, since he moved out there in the early Seventies, swapping news and views of the music and film business. Alan knows more about these two worlds than anyone else I know and has been a highly sought-after music historian and researcher to many major film and record companies in America for twenty years. This time his call was not for merely another show-biz gossip. He had just heard on the radio out there that Elvis was dead. I could not believe this – I was watching Reginald Bosanquet live and there had been no mention of this appalling news, which surely would have rated reasonable billing. We were already into the Scottish football results. But Alan was the most reliable of informers and assured me it was not a hoax. I instantly rang the *Daily Telegraph* and this was news to them too. I don't think they believed me – how could I tell the world? Then, just as Reggie was shuffling his papers and wishing us all goodnight, he stopped in his tracks and announced that there were unconfirmed reports that Elvis Presley had died in Memphis. Then straight into the weather. Bearing in mind Reggie's reputation for something less than rock-solid reliability, I might well have been the only person watching to have believed him. Within about a quarter of an hour, the whole country believed and talked about little else for days.

Our honeymoon continued with a flight from Vegas to Denver, Colorado. We loved the Rockies (John Denver country) and Yellowstone. We saw 'Old Faithful', the king of geysers, and drove around Colorado and Wyoming and through places such as Cheyenne and Jackson Hole. We called in at the famous Caribou Ranch recording studio, where nobody the slightest bit famous happened to be recording. We nipped into Montana and drove through Idaho. We had trouble keeping to the ludicrous fifty-five m.p.h. speed limit, listened to country music stations, bought cowboy boots and hats and stayed the night wherever we happened to fetch up, finally driving to Salt Lake City for a plane to New York. Here we caught up with a few shows and spent a long, wonderful weekend out in the Hamptons on Long Island, on the beach and in the ocean, with Robert Stigwood, Peter Brown and Tyler Gatchell and numerous of their cronies, mainly male.

Tyler Gatchell was one of the greats. He was a New York City theatrical producer and his company had been signed by Robert to handle the day-to-day running of his shows; *Superstar* had of course been the first of these. Tyler soon became the first person Andrew or I would call when we hit Manhattan, as he knew everyone, every new club and restaurant, every scandal and rumour. Furthermore, he would drop nearly everything to entertain us. In those days he drank, smoked and behaved badly with the best of them, but even when he gave up all vices towards the end of the Eighties, he remained as lively and sociable as ever. Tyler at least had the excuse of a heart attack to justify his change of lifestyle. The vast majority of the grim puritan health maniacs who are sweeping California in particular, and the United States in general, into the dreariest of social fabrics have no such excuse. Tyler lived for the theatre but was not over-theatrical. He never seemed like a luvvie, nor even gay. He barely seemed American, for that matter, apart from his accent, having an English feel for the ridiculous and using the wit of understatement as the basis of his great sense of humour. Not that being overtly luvvie, gay or American would have mattered a jot, but he defied labels or categorisation. He could have been a bank manager and been exactly the same delightful companion. His life was ended by another heart attack in 1992, when he was still in his fifties.

Jane and I returned to England after three glorious weeks in the US, then still reeling from the Watergate saga. I had had great fun, particularly in New York, annoying my American pals by defending Nixon (what really annoyed the liberal élite was that President Ford had just pardoned him), maintaining that he was a highly efficient operator as President, no worse a human being than many who had occupied the White House, and whose petty crimes and dishonesties were less likely to harm the US in the eyes of the world than the premature removal of the leader of the Western world. I certainly preferred Nixon to Clinton.

I had even made a pop record intended to highlight the dangers of letting the Watergate fiasco do permanent harm to the American presidency. This was a song for which I wrote both words and music, though the latter was basic in the extreme and owed a good deal to Phil Spector's composition for the Crystals, 'Then He Kissed Me'. My song, 'The President Song', was simply a list of every President from Washington to Nixon with a chorus that went:

> They all made you what you are today
> Please don't throw it all away
> It's easy to destroy the whole thing now
> I wouldn't tell you how

Subtle, huh? The first verse began:

> George Washington, John Adams, Thomas Jefferson,
> James Madison, James Munroe . . .

and so on, the verses featuring every single Chief in the correct order; rhymes had to go out the window. After the names of the four Presidents who had been assassinated, I inserted an echo-laden pause. The final verse was very short:

Lyndon Johnson, Richard Nixon—

and then another echo-laden jolt, and the record was over.

I had recorded this epic, with me as vocalist, some weeks before Nixon got the chop and sent it off to MCA in America, our *Superstar* patrons, still coining it in from the various incarnations of our smash. To my amazement, they loved 'The President Song' and released it with the fanfare of a full page ad in *Billboard*, the record industry's leading publication. The singer was not billed as Tim Rice, but as Victor Trumper, the name of one of Australia's greatest cricketers. There would have been little chance of anyone in America thinking I was the original Victor Trumper, even if he hadn't died in 1915. Several radio stations began playing the disc, and I started to plan my promotional tour of the States as Victor. But everything was brutally nipped in the bud when a station in Boston interpreted the platter as an incitement to assassinate Nixon. The exact opposite had been my aim, but the damage was done and the record was pulled off every airwave. It has only ever been played since as a curiosity on English oldies programmes by my close friend Mike Read.

I had another go around this time at writing a tune, and came up with a rather more sophisticated melody by my standards, in that it had seven chords, entitled 'Hey Love (What A Way To Spend The Night)'. Barbara Dickson recorded the demo, beautifully, and I hawked it around publishers and record companies. In the end the only artist who wanted to sing it was me, and I managed to persuade Elton John's old label, DJM, to finance and issue my version. I rather liked the finished result, and so did Stephen James of DJM, but we were about the only two. It was a sad tale of a chap spending the night at Heathrow's Terminal three, waiting in vain for his lover to return. Despite being released twice, it never took off.

Then Robert Stigwood asked me to provide a lyric for a TV

movie he was making of John Osborne's *The Entertainer*, starring Jack Lemmon, with a score by Marvin Hamlisch. There had already been one film made of Osborne's great play about a music-hall star at the end of his professional and personal tether, starring Laurence Olivier, and I could never quite see the commercial potential of a re-make so soon after a magnificent original, but the prospect of working with Hamlisch was exciting, and Lemmon had always been one of my favourite film actors. Marvin was on a sensational roll in 1974, having won three Oscars at once that year for his work on *The Sting* and *The Way We Were*. He was also just about to enjoy huge Broadway success with *A Chorus Line*, a show whose music and lyrics have been grossly underestimated over the years in deference to the admittedly excellent staging and choreography by Michael Bennett.

I first encountered Marvin in his pyjamas when I called in at his Park Lane apartment to hear his ideas for *The Entertainer* and, not bothering to introduce himself, or to get out of his nightwear, he dived straight to the piano and hammered out a catchy melody. I was back out in the street with a cassette before he had cleaned his teeth. The melody eventually became a song called 'The Only Way To Go' which to date has been recorded by just three people, Jack Lemmon (in the movie), Bing Crosby and George Burns. Not an undistinguished line-up, and though I have never earned more than a pittance from the song, to have those names on my CV made the enterprise extremely worthwhile. It also enabled me to become good friends with Marvin, and we have often talked of writing a show together. So far it's still just talk.

1974 was beyond doubt one of the best years of my life. I was happily married, was eagerly anticipating fatherhood for the first time, owned a beautiful house in the country (even if builders were taking their time enabling us to move into it), a stream of income that showed no sign of drying up, for which I had to do very little work, and last but not least was convinced that I had a great new musical in the works. Hardly a scenario to evoke sympathy from the average reader. 1975 was probably even better.

The most important event of that year for me and Jane, indeed of almost any year, was the birth of our first child, Eva. Although I nobly attended one expectant fathers' class run by the legendary

Betty Parsons, Jane absolutely refused to let me be present at the actual birth of our daughter. I was perfectly happy with this decision, in fact extremely relieved, and when the time came, early on the Sunday morning of 9 February, I was more than content to pace the corridors of the Middlesex Hospital in time-honoured fashion. A father today (assuming he hadn't already left the mother and assuming she knew who he was) would be very lucky indeed to get away with such half-hearted involvement in the actual moment of delivery,* but political correctness and the cult of the New (i.e. Wet) Man had not then quite taken root. All went well inside the delivery room without me, and mother and daughter were both pretty perky soon afterwards.

It is extremely boring to hear any new parent go on about how wonderful their offspring is, and I certainly struggle to show interest or shower praise upon anything under about fifteen years old not produced by me. Suffice it to say that Eva was a most beautiful, intelligent, well-behaved child and the surviving pictures of her in her early months that show her as a bald, porky and bored infant are a distortion of the truth and the fault of the photographer. We gave our daughter three Christian names – Eva, sort of after Eva Peron, but also because it was a good old English name, notably popular at the end of the nineteenth century, Jane (after mum) and Florence (after my grandmother). Eva Jane Florence and her mother came home just a few days later, but to 33 Northumberland Place, as Romeyns Court still resembled a bomb-site.

Jeeves meanwhile had expired. I saw the show twice, once in Bristol during its out-of-town try-out and on the West End opening night at Her Majesty's Theatre in London. It was pretty ghastly in Bristol, partly because it was more than three hours long, and although desperately pruned and reworked for the West End the London première was still a night to remember with a shudder. Mercifully P.G. Wodehouse (promoted to Sir Pelham just in time) had died a few months before *Jeeves* did. Andrew had been showing more and more interest in *Evita* as *Jeeves* headed down the tubes and the morning after a set of almost universally

---

* Though I was in 1998.

dire reviews were published he called to say that we should waste no more time tackling Argentine history. I was delighted, and more than happy to abandon my minor songwriting sidelines, none of which had advanced my career an iota.

Andrew had obviously taken a bit of a knock, but as he was to say so often over the years, the nightmare of *Jeeves* taught him a great deal, primarily that he wanted to have total control over his works in the future, i.e. produce them as well as write them. But he was not in a position to do that right away, certainly not with *Evita*. We had recently confirmed our continuing management relationship with Robert Stigwood and David Land, in effect signing on for a further five years, which would mean they would represent us at least until the middle of 1979. Even the ever-optimistic Robert must have had slight misgivings about our ability to repeat the *Superstar* magic, bearing in mind the weirdness of our new topic and the total failure of *Jeeves*, which had cost him a packet as co-producer (with Michael White).

Andrew did express some doubts about whether we should continue with Robert and David, but this may have just been posturing, as there was really no credible alternative. Apart from anything else, both men were so nice, and so funny, to work with. A cash sweetener or two helped the deal along, as did much typically generous and extravagant Robert hospitality. One Sunday lunch at Robert's Stanmore manor around this time ended with my depositing one of his go-karts at the bottom of his swimming pool, doing severe damage to both machine and pool, but not to our relationship. Robert thought the incident hilarious and left the kart at the bottom of the pool for days as a tourist attraction, rather like a forerunner of a Damien Hirst sheep-in-formaldehyde creation.

Andrew and I slipped comfortably back into partnership. We were a shade more independent of each other than before, with wives, serious homes, and ever-increasing lists of extra-curricular activities making demands on our minds and time that had never been present in the days of creating 'The Likes Of Us', *Joseph* or *Superstar*. But we approached our fourth joint creation with the same zest and method with which we had the first three. The difference now was that for the first time we knew that if our work was any good at all, and probably even if it wasn't, it would make its way on to record or stage. For the first time we had a production plan for the life of the musical – very early on we decided that we would make an album, so that all our energies could be focused on getting the words and music right. A director and staging, a producer for the theatre (which would almost certainly be Robert) could come later. We had been forced to record *Superstar* to launch the work; but we did the same thing with *Evita* from choice.

I was a little worried that because we now knew what we were doing, we would cock the whole thing up, but the writing of *Evita* went extremely smoothly indeed. We made very few diversions from my outline and more or less wrote the songs and scenes in the order they appeared. The first tune Andrew came up with was quite magnificent, and if some in the West End thought, after *Jeeves*, that ALW was just a flash in the pan, I was immediately reassured that his great gift for melody was not on the skids. The tune was eventually to become best-known as 'Don't Cry For Me Argentina' but the first lyric I wrote for it was entitled 'Oh What A Circus', Che's opening diatribe against Eva Peron at her funeral.

After a week or two we decided to go away, as we had done with *Superstar*, to a remote hotel in an attempt to crack the first few scenes. Now we were both richer, we were able to go somewhere more exotic than Herefordshire, and we decided to go to Biarritz, to the Palace Hotel where I had spent a few days recovering from hypochondria in 1971. A piano was wheeled into our suite and although we were often lured away from work by the usual temptations, such as restaurants and the casino, we had a very productive few days, writing four or five important scenes, including the Perez Prado/Dean Martin pastiche 'On This Night Of A Thousand Stars', 'Eva Beware Of The City', 'Buenos Aires', 'I'd Be Surprisingly Good For You' and 'Another Suitcase In Another Hall'. This was a pretty good workrate by any standards, let alone our own, though I was reminded yet again how much longer lyrics take than music. Our writing procedure was as before: plot (already done), music, then lyrics.

Jane and Sarah joined us for the last few days of our French jaunt, but it was clear that not all was well with Sarah, who looked like death warmed up for a good part of their stay. Shortly after she got home, her condition was diagnosed as diabetes, and back in England she spent two difficult and at times even dangerous weeks in hospital and was warned that it could be very risky to have children. But Sarah has much of Andrew's determination and refusal to accept life's apparent restrictions, and before long she was pregnant. Her illness obviously checked *Evita*'s progress for a short while, but before long we resumed our task at Andrew's stately pile, Sydmonton Court, a massive house near Newbury which Andrew had bought a year or so back; a sixteenth-century edifice with many Victorian adapatations within twenty acres. The effort and love he has poured into the property in the past twenty-five years matches that which he gives to his writing; he now owns thousands of acres around the house (including Watership Down).

In the summer of 1975, Jane and I were still waiting to move into Romeyns Court, about an hour's drive from our house in London, which we were anxious to flog as soon as we could get the builders out of our new home. Jane's redoubtable sister Fiona, a distinguished interior decorator, was in charge of operations at Romeyns Court, but even her explosive methods of negotiating with builders seemed to have little effect on their speed. But we were, it seemed, virtually starting again from scratch, so dilapidated was so much of the house once we stripped away the outer layers. I wasn't too concerned – I reckoned we would be there for a lifetime at least, which would in due course make the eighteen months between purchase and move seem a mere stitch on the tapestry of time. I briefly attempted to lay down a cricket pitch but there wasn't quite enough room and we settled for renovating the shabby tennis court instead. Better yet, the house had a squash court, disused for years, but soon put back into immaculate shape. We held back on a swimming pool – the builder's bills were huge and I did not think the *Superstar* money would keep rolling in for ever (and I was terrified of children drowning).

So in the last half of 1975 I found myself regularly hammering down the M4 to Sydmonton, sometimes via Romeyns Court to check on progress there (usually less spectacular than the progress around Andrew's piano). We continued in fine form and although we were aware that many of our friends and all of our enemies (i.e.

the millions who felt we were mighty lucky to have got away with *Superstar*) thought Eva Peron was a ludicrous idea for a show and bound to fail, I was sure it wouldn't. Or at least it wouldn't be the fault of the idea or the score if it did.

Most said that it couldn't work because nobody knew anything about Eva Peron, an exact reverse of the forecast of our previous show's prospects, which was that it would fail because the story of Jesus was too well-known. In 1996, when the release of the *Evita* movie gave a whole new slew of reviewers a chance to attack us, I was not best pleased to see more than one sage accuse us of choosing the subject of Evita back in the Seventies because it was so obviously commercial.*

I really felt that what we were doing was our best work yet. Andrew's tunes were just outstanding; since Biarritz he had added 'High Flying Adored' (a.k.a. 'Down On The Farm'), 'Rainbow High', 'The Money Kept Rolling In' (that one admittedly with rather a lot of help from a Peronist marching song), 'Waltz for Eva and Che' and 'The Lament' to name but five powerful new goodies. And I felt my lyrics matched them, although I still did not have a complete lyric or a title for the most important scene, which would be the principal airing of the tune that had already featured as both 'Oh What A Circus' and (sung by the dead Evita) as 'Don't Cry For Me Argentina', but the latter title would clearly not make sense for her big balcony scene.

Time to worry about that later – the overall shape of the score seemed right; there was a fine variety of rhythm, emotion and mood. I managed to get quite a bit of humour into what was essentially a serious story about some fairly murky characters. The ending, or rather the fifteen minutes before the death-bed scene at the very end, was not panning out quite as satisfactorily as the rest, but all in all we were brimming with confidence. I enjoyed the regular spins down to Sydmonton, and above all returning home in the evening with yet another rough (very) cassette recording of me and Andrew singing the newest *Evita* number blaring away in

---

* Tom Shone, a film critic on the *Sunday Times*, informed the world in 1996 that our only interest in Evita was to put bums on seats. As he was only seven when we wrote the piece, his comment revealed a remarkable ability to bark up the wrong tree at an early age.

the car. Jane could never wait to hear the latest fruits of our labours and seemed to like what we had done even more than I did.

I don't think Andrew (while we were writing anyway) was quite as certain as I was that *Evita* could be as big as *Superstar*. Nor did he really feel in those early days that *Evita* was his show. But paradoxically, that is why I think his *Evita* work was so outstanding. He was not thinking about promotion, publicity, commercial gimmicks or business, simply about doing the very best he could as a composer, determined to prove that he could bounce back from the humiliation of *Jeeves*. He was subconsciously relaxed in that I would cop most of the flak if it flopped – not that he would have wanted to have blamed me if it had. The outline for the show had been handed to him on a plate and all he wanted to do was to compose the very best music he could to bring my story to life.

He proved to be surprisingly uninterested in many of the promotional activities that inevitably had to be faced in due course. As with *Superstar*, I handled the vast majority of the ancillary promotional duties that led up to the release of the album – the album design, the sleeve notes, the audio-visual show that accompanied the first public playing of the album and so on. Undistracted by that end of things, he gave his all to his music – and it showed. I feel sure that on occasion, for all his incredible success, some of his later works have suffered a little because he has been doing too much in other areas. *Evita* was also the last show he wrote of which great things were not automatically expected, the last time either of us were able to write without an army of wannabe directors, producers and promoters scrambling to be involved before a single song has been written. Too many cooks at the start is usually a recipe for trouble.

On 23 December 1975, Jane, Eva and I finally moved into Romeyns Court where we had a terrific family Christmas (both families). Even my great-aunt Gertie made it. We had sold 33 Northumberland Place for £39,000, not a killing bearing in mind the rampant inflation of the time and the thousands I had spent on it. I had demo tapes of a virtually finished new show to play to my nearest and dearest who received it with polite interest (they were eating my turkey) but, save Jane, not with unalloyed raves. Who was this Eva Peron anyway?

Chapter Twenty-five

Sometime in the early days of 1976 Andrew and I played what we had of *Evita* (which was most of it) to David and Zara Land at Andrew's Eaton Place flat. I think they were impressed, but not totally convinced that we had created anything with a tenth of the commercial potential of *Superstar*. The one song that really got to them was 'Another Suitcase In Another Hall' but all in all I felt their reaction was subdued admiration at best. *Evita* was of course a hard piece for two dodgy male singers and one piano to sell. A good deal of the score was written for a seriously gifted female voice and there was not as much rock content, easier for us to sing with gusto, than there had been in *Superstar*. Nonetheless, Andrew and I were bubbling with confidence and David was never going to advise us to abandon ship; he had originally had his doubts about *Superstar* but to his great credit had backed our conviction all the way that time around. He suggested we made a few presentable demos with a good singer or two and he would attempt to fix a record deal.

Our problem was who on earth could we persuade to sing for us? The only indisputably brilliant lady vocalist we had worked closely with to date had been Yvonne Elliman and she was now resident in the States. Furthermore, we felt we needed someone who was an experienced musical actress. Fate stepped in about ten minutes after we began worrying when we caught an episode of a TV series entitled *Rock Follies*, the seamy (for Seventies television) tale of a trio of aspiring rock chicks, played by Julie Covington, Charlotte

Cornwell and Rula Lenska. Written by Howard Schuman with music by Roxy Music maestro Andy Mackay, the hit music-biz soap made a big impact in 1976/7. We remembered Ms Covington from the London version of *Godspell* as a fiesty gamine and *Rock Follies* reminded us that she could certainly hold a contemporary tune with power and conviction. She could act. We got in touch.

Julie Covington is a one-off, a singular artist. Many now, in the late Nineties, will have consigned her to the 'Where Are They Now?' category, but if she has faded somewhat from the public eye, I am sure this is because she wished it so rather than from any decline in her great talent or in lucrative offers. She seemed to have an aversion to success, almost as if she felt it was unfair that not every singer or actress could enjoy the rewards that came her way, or that anything too popular must be discouraged. She attempted to play down her feminine charms, in dress and in attitude, but they always overcame any attempt she made to appear even less sexy than a Greenham Common protestor or a lesbian co-operative chairperson. Within her slender form a feminist activist and a sensual diva fought for recognition. Whichever prevailed at any one time, her sense of humour and sparky intelligence ensured she was consistently beguiling.

When Julie first heard our story of Evita and some of the songs the character would sing, she was immediately intrigued. Eva's struggle was something she could readily identify with, and she thought the songs were great. She probably thought that it was a highly uncommercial idea for a show and therefore became even more interested. Her voice suited the principal songs perfectly and we moved double-quick from Andrew's living room to a studio to make the first ever recordings of 'Don't Cry For Me Argentina', 'I'd Be Surprisingly Good For You' and 'Buenos Aires', simple demos with Andrew on piano as the only backing. They sounded breathtaking and David was instructed to sign her up a.s.a.p. to the company we had formed especially for the projected *Evita* album.

Of course, before we could sign anybody to our fledgling recording company, we ourselves had to have a deal with a slightly more established outfit. Once again, the chiefs of the music world did not fall over themselves to obtain the rights to a

Webber-Rice project and it was no great surprise to us when David revealed that we were once again going with MCA, who probably took us on mainly because in the unlikely event of *Evita* being another *Superstar* they would look daft if they'd missed out.

The MCA team that had been behind *Superstar* on both sides of the Atlantic had undergone a virtual one hundred per cent turnover in staff since our first escapade with the company's record division. Furthermore, the centre of the company's US and thus worldwide operations had shifted from New York to Los Angeles. The US boss at the time of our signing a global deal for *Evita*, the album, was Mike Maitland who, along with most of his sidekicks, had had no involvement with our previous effort and presumably felt that as we hadn't had a hit album release since October 1970 we were dead in the water. I dare say the British executives who did the *Evita* deal with us did not win employee of the month awards. But we had such enthusiasm from the UK end of the empire indifference 5000 miles away barely mattered, at least when we were recording the work.

I can't recall exactly what the original record deal was, but we certainly got no money up front for ourselves. Basically, it was more or less the same as the *Superstar* deal, but with a slightly better royalty rate. MCA would advance us the cost of the recording, which we would have to pay back out of our royalty, which I remember being something in the region of ten per cent, rather than the paltry five per cent we were given first time around. Once again payment for all the featured artists was our responsibility; once again we tried to persuade most of them to accept a one-off fee. This time around none of them bought that idea and most of them (quite rightly) received a royalty (and a fee, in some cases). Even with the return of Andrew's huge orchestras and choirs, a lengthy recording schedule and the rapidly increasing costs of studios in those days of great inflation, the overall initial cost to MCA was not huge in comparison with the amount of loot major record companies would have expected to pay in advances alone to a leading five-piece rock band in the mid-Seventies. *Evita* came in for £74,827.83, so that was in effect our advance, every penny of which we spent on making the recording. (*Superstar* had cost less than £15,000.) But no one expected *Evita* to be a hit – to many over at head office in Universal City, California, it was the price the company had to pay for the fluke success of those two weird English guys five years back.

Luckily, one MCA office had faith in *Evita* – the still modest London branch, now headed by Roy Featherstone. I had first met Roy way back in my management trainee days at EMI. He had been the executive co-ordinator of the A and R department, responsible as much as anyone there for telling me and Andrew that our pop singles were not going to be issued. He was now head of the entire MCA set-up in Great Britain, supported by a small and enthusiastic staff, notably his number two Stuart Watson and a former music journalist Peter Robinson, who years before had written one of the first positive pieces about *Superstar*, as head of MCA's press and marketing. We never had anything less than total support from Roy and his colleagues and this was an absolutely vital factor in the record's ultimate massive British success.

Having secured the talents of Julie Covington, we proceeded to chase up other voices for the supporting roles in our epic. One lady we both admired greatly was Barbara Dickson who, after making her name in the Willy Russell musical *John, Paul, George, Ringo and Bert* (and making the demo recording of my flop 'Hey Love'), had recently broken through to the pop charts with a revival of 'Answer Me'. Barbara would have been a fine Eva Peron, but all that was left to offer her after we had signed Julie was our song for Peron's mistress, 'Another Suitcase In Another Hall'. Fortunately Barbara and her manager, Bernard Theobald, loved the song and were happy to participate for just one track on the album. No doubt they reckoned 'Suitcase' could be a hit single for Barbara. They were right.

We were also lucky with our first-choice for Peron, as Paul Jones, by 1976 an established West End actor, but still in as fine voice as he had been when fronting Manfred Mann, accepted the part of the project's Denis Thatcher (sort of) with alacrity. The other principal role, that of our narrator/commentator Che (not billed as Guevara anywhere in the score), proved harder to cast. We had a meeting with Steve Marriott of the Small Faces (and Humble Pie) but friendly though he was, he seemed a little lacking in the concentration department. I even called my hero (and Copenhagen flight colleague) John Fogerty, but he politely declined, probably without having a clue who I was.

A few tentative trial sessions with Murray Head didn't really reproduce the magic that his portrayal of Judas had and we eventually turned to an unknown Irishman named Colm Wilkinson, whom Anthony Bowles, the *Superstar* stage show musical director, strongly recommended. Colm had recently played Judas in the West End *Superstar*, still going strong at the Palace. When he came in to wrap his tonsils around one or two *Evita* numbers, it only took a couple of verses to know he was our man. Other vocal roles were assigned to ex-King Herod Mike d'Abo, to his then musical partner Mike Smith (the former Dave Clark Five front man), to Tony Christie, MCA-UK's answer to Tom Jones, who had had a couple of substantial British pop hits, and to Chris Neil, another *Superstar* stage alumnus – Jesus himself this time.

We decided to repeat the *Superstar* formula as far as venue and engineer were concerned and had no trouble rebooking our favourite Olympic Studio, but had to make a switch engineer-wise, in that Alan O'Duffy now felt he deserved a royalty for any future work with us, a view we would not have warmed to even if we had had any room left for royalties after carving several chunks off our slice for all the singers. So we worked with one of Olympic's in-house men, David Hamilton-Smith, who could not have been more efficient, more inspired and, above all, more funny. We would have liked to have returned to the Grease Band, but they were no longer a unit, and although former Greasers Henry McCullogh (who had joined Paul McCartney's Wings) and Neil Hubbard put in an appearance or two, we formed a new rhythm unit of Simon Phillips (drums), Mo Foster or Brian Odgers (bass), Joe Moretti and Ray Russell (guitars) and Ann O'Dell (keyboards). David Snell had an important role on harp at various moments. Hank B. Marvin contributed to 'Buenos Aires' when we needed a bloke to play just like Hank B. Marvin, and Chris Mercer repeated the elegant sax work that had graced *Superstar* with a fine solo on 'I'd Be Surprisingly Good For You'. Anthony Bowles was appointed to conduct the London Philharmonic Orchestra, no less, and Alan Doggett, who was principal conductor for the

Superstar album, was gently relegated to directing the London Boy Singers, the choir he had formed since leaving regular school employment. This was a pretty solid musical line-up.

Even I cut back a bit on side projects as we began to settle into our second summer, six years after the first, of travelling to Barnes to record a project that no one outside our closest circle thought worth a prayer. 1976 proved to be an even hotter summer than 1970 had been, which was a great start to our summers at Romeyns Court but not so appealing when experienced from the inside of a windowless, albeit air-conditioned, recording studio. Almost the only day on which it rained between May and October was the Saturday of the Lord's Test Match.

I note, however, that in 1976 I fulfilled one of nearly everyone's great ambitions, to appear on *Desert Island Discs*,* the week after an opera singer I had never heard of called Pavarotti. I doubt whether Luciano matched my choices of Elvis, Del Shannon and the Everly Brothers, but in order not to appear a complete Philistine I flung in Mendelssohn and Puccini (and *My Fair Lady*). Jane and I also flogged up to Gordonstoun where I spoke to the pupils about my life and times, taking tea beforehand with the teenage Prince Andrew. There were a few other visits to schools, often to see *Joseph*, Heartaches cricket matches, occasional forays into *Call My Bluff* and minor chat shows, several Lord's Taverners and other charity bashes at which I was beginning to hammer out a reasonable turn as an after-dinner speaker, but by and large *Evita* held sway throughout the heatwave. Romeyns Court had very quickly become the most beautiful and happy of homes and, prevented from making the most of it because of our recording commitments, I was not as keen as I had been on too many sideshows denying me even more of my time there.

The three or four months we spent huddled in the bowels of Olympic during the heatwave, ran smoothly. We were confident that our new piece was as good as *Superstar* and those who were present as it took shape shared much of our enthusiasm. We were that much more experienced in the studio and as we

---

* Having worked with Roy Plomley, the creator of *Desert Island Discs*, for several series of *Many A Slip*, of which he was chairman, it was hard for him to avoid inviting me on to the island.

put together massive and disparate forces for the second time to create a musical without paying attention to anything but the score, we almost got to feel that we really knew what we were doing, boosted no end by Roy's MCA team expressing ecstatic reactions to virtually every crotchet and word. David Hamilton-Smith, as Alan O'Duffy had before him, became virtually a third producer. Like nearly everyone behind the scenes in the music business he was a frustrated performer and, like me, he made sure he had the odd solo line on the album.

Evita begins with a brief scene in a Buenos Aires cinema on the day that Eva's death was announced. During our 1974 trip to Buenos Aires, I had asked one of the few Argentinians Jane and I actually spoke to then, a pal (anti-Evita) of Fred Sill's, where he was when Evita died on 26 July 1952. He had told us he was in a cinema and that the film suddenly ground to a halt, annoying him intensely even (and especially) when he heard the reason – that the First Lady of Argentina had passed away. This struck me as a great opening scene and Andrew had a lot of fun writing a section of deliberately dire early Fifties film music over which Carlos Pasini and a girl friend emoted, in Spanish, an equally grim script. In the eventual stage version, an actual clip from an early Eva Peron movie was used, one of the few surviving extracts from the then Miss Duarte's cinema career.

After the ponderous actual announcement of death, we crashed straight into Eva's funeral. This was Andrew at his best, combining melody, dissonance, and straightforward and complex time signatures with the full forces of orchestra, choir and screaming guitar, primarily laying down the tune that was to close the show as Eva's dying lament. Few words were needed – just 'requiem' and 'Evita'. From this powerful mélange emerged the first proper song in the show, Che's 'Oh What A Circus'. Andrew never allowed the fact that he was dealing with a Latin story to drag his music into a parody of Latin styles; some complained later that the score was not close enough to the feel of the time and place it portrayed, but they might as well have criticised *Superstar* for not featuring enough first-century Jewish music. *Evita*, like *Superstar*, was a re-telling of a foreign tale in modern English musical terms. In any event, there were throughout *Evita* many references to Latin forms, but never were they too dominant.

'Oh What A Circus', the first words I wrote to the 'Don't Cry For Me Argentina' tune, was an upbeat and almost cheery contrast to the doom and gloom of the funeral, tango-rock, if you like. Colm captured its mixture of anger and mocking envy from the first take. Che, as narrator /commentator/critic, ridicules the national grief for a woman he perceives as little more than a jumped-up whore who fooled millions:

> Oh what a circus! Oh what a show
> Argentina has gone to town
> Over the death of an actress called Eva Peron
> We've all gone crazy
> Mourning all day and mourning all night
> Falling over ourselves to get all of the misery right

> Oh what an exit! That's how to go
> When they're ringing your curtain down
> Demand to be buried like Eva Peron
> It's quite a sunset
> And good for the country in a roundabout way
> We've made the front pages in all the world's papers today

I had fun with the idea that a country could go to town and that 'mourning all day' might be misconstrued as 'morning all day', also by rhyming lines across the verses ('show/go', 'town/down') though some less perceptive observers missed this and complained that 'town' did not rhyme with 'Peron'. Che continues by asking 'Who is this Santa Evita?' and 'What kind of goddess/has lived among us?' He mocks: 'You let down your people Evita/You were supposed to have been immortal' before the crowd's wailing takes over again. Thence he explodes into a violent outburst, a new hard rock melody:

> Sing you fools! But you got it wrong
> Enjoy your prayers because you haven't got long
> Your queen is dead, your king is through
> She's not coming back to you

Once we heard Colm's finished vocal on 'Oh What A Circus' we knew we had a male voice to match Julie's.

The people are unaware of any dissenting voice and an echo-swamped choir sing yet further lamentation, climaxed with a heavy, emotional orchestral reading of the verse of 'Circus' 'Argentina', before the voice of Eva is heard for the first time – the dead Eva, singing from the grave.

> Don't cry for me Argentina
> For I am ordinary, unimportant . . .

Here the famous line was heard for the first time; when it was recorded we had no intention of using it at any other point in the show. I was still wrestling with a selection of terrible first lines for Eva's big balcony scene.

The story now flashes back nearly twenty years to Eva Duarte's liaison with a popular tango singer of the day, Agustin Magaldi, who came to play the fifteen-year-old Eva's home town of Junin in 1934. I have an actual Agustin Magaldi LP in my collection and it's not exactly catchy. The tune with which we lumbered our Magaldi in *Evita*, 'On This Night Of A Thousand Stars', bears no resemblance whatsoever to the real man's rather delicate high-pitched offerings; rather more to Perez Prado's 'Cherry Pink and Apple Blossom White' as sung by Engelbert Humperdinck. It was meant to be pretty cheesy in all departments, and we felt it succeeded in that aim, though it still picked up some serious cover versions in due course.

Tony Christie, our Magaldi, is best remembered perhaps for 'I Did What I Did For Maria',* a beat ballad about a man who is to be executed for doing away with a love rival, which he sang with the cheery exuberance that graced all his recordings. This, and others, had hit the charts in the early Seventies but by 1976 he was not always to be found in Britain's entertainment heartland. Andrew and I had been up to Cleethorpes to offer him the role of Magaldi and he accepted after we had seen him in action on the

---

* Though he did return to the charts in 1999 with 'Walk Like A Panther', singing with the group All Seeing I.

pier there. Tony, conveniently under contract to MCA Records, gave 'On This Night Of A Thousand Stars' and his other scenes the perfect reading and we were so impressed we also wrote another song for him, nothing to do with *Evita*, entitled 'Magdalena'. This did escape as a single, but to no noticeable effect.

The scenes in *Evita* that were set in Junin feature an argument between Magaldi and the young Eva. He sees her as a one-night stand and she sees him as her passport to better things; she insists that he takes her to Buenos Aires and her family back her up, threatening to make public Magaldi's seduction of a minor. Julie's rendition of Eva's diatribe against the middle class, which she sees as the enemy who denies her access to her own father's funeral, was formidable. Che, the observer, has a few one-liners. The clash comes to a climax with 'Eva, Beware Of The City', during which I paid tribute to 'Over The Rainbow' with a couplet, 'Birds fly out of here so why/oh why the hell can't I?'. Besides the city, Magaldi also warns her to

> . . . beware your ambition
> it's hungry and cold – can't be controlled, will run wild
> This in a man is a danger enough
> But you are a woman, not even a woman
> Not very much more than a child
> And whatever you say
> I'll not steal you away!

But Magaldi has barely finished this verse, when we cut to 'Buenos Aires' and we know that Eva has got her way. The pretty, pleading tune that was 'Eva Beware Of The City' is reprised orchestrally and segues into one of Andrew's best creations, a funky samba praising the delights of Argentina's capital:

> What's new? Buenos Aires?
> I'm new – I wanna say I'm just a little stuck on you
> You'll be on me too!
> I get out here Buenos Aires
> Stand back – you oughta know what'cha gonna get in me
> Just a little touch of star quality!

This number worked a treat. The melody was strong, as it had been when used as the basis of a song called 'The Red Room' on our album with Maynard Williams, and the arrangement driving and wonderfully varied. The middle section used the tune of the verse of 'Down Thru' Summer', one of our Ross Hannaman flops. Hank B. Marvin played his solo, I managed to get a reference to nearly all the places in Buenos Aires I had actually visited – the River Plate, Florida, Corrientes, Neuve de Julio – and by the end of a dynamic three minutes and forty-three seconds I reckoned we had painted a pretty good picture of the city of the teenage Eva's dreams.

It took Evita quite a few years to make her mark in the big city, but we rushed through this in three and a half minutes with 'Goodnight And Thank You', a cynical lullaby with some great ALW brass parts, in which Eva worked her way through a line of lovers, each more prominent than the last. This was a very theatrical number, which Hal Prince was eventually to stage with terrific aplomb and revolving bedroom doors. By the end of the sequence, Eva is an established radio star and aiming to hitch her wagon to even higher things – the military political leadership. 'Goodnight And Thank You' contained a somewhat misanthropic chorus, with which I confess I have some (not total, and not always) sympathy:

> There is no one, no one at all
> Never has been and never will be
> A lover, male or female
> Who hasn't an eye on
> In fact they rely on
> The tricks they can try on
> Their partner
> They're hoping their lover will help them or keep them
> Support them, promote them
> Don't blame them
> You're the same

Next, we felt we had to clue in those listeners who were still with us with a little of the historical and political background to the Buenos Aires of 1944, in particular some information about

Juan Peron, now one of several army heavies sniffing around the presidency. We did this via our narrator Che, and a straightforward rock number called 'The Lady's Got Potential'. This number was dropped for the stage show, but reinstated (with new lyrics, natch) for the movie twenty years later. Hal Prince felt that neither the tune nor the lyrics were suitable for the theatre – the former simply too loud and repetitive, the latter too complex to be absorbed at one sitting and too concerned with a subplot about Che's own capitalist ambitions.

In my research into Che Guevara's life, a subject on which I was almost as ignorant as the millions of students who had pinned his picture on to their walls during the previous ten years, I discovered that in his own student days he had attempted to market an insecticide. Delighted to find that he had briefly espoused capitalist leanings, I decided (still without actually saying our Che was Che Guevara) to incorporate this strange ambition into the show, enabling us to suggest that Che and Eva were really cut from the same grasping cloth, implying that Che had only become a revolutionary after failing to make a million. This mischievous viewpoint was referred to at odd points during the original album of *Evita*, but disappeared at the request of just about everyone in subsequent versions. The first time it crops up is in 'The Lady's Got Potential', this number thus dealing simultaneously with Peron's career to date, the state of Argentina's politics in the early 1940s, Che's fly-killing plans and Eva's moves in Peron's direction. I have not written many other lyrics with quite so broad a remit.

Much of these messages would pass a listener by on one hearing, but if followed with the lyric sheet, they are not too incomprehensible. There were also one or two good lines that I was sorry to lose when it came to the staging, such as the description of Eva as 'the greatest social climber since Cinderella' and of Peron's early army days as a frustrated ski-instructor. 'Sure Peron could ski but who needs a snowman?' Che's promotion of his fly-killer would have delighted any advertising agency's jingle department:

> Now my insecticide contains no dangerous drugs
> It can't harm humans but it's curtains for bugs
> If you've got six legs I ain't doing you no favour

and the political faction that Peron joined, the GOU (Government, Order, Unity) was highlighted in the couplet:

> They thought that Hitler had the war as good as won
> They were slightly to the right of Attila the Hun

But all these gems were doomed to remain etched in vinyl alone.

Colm sang the rock number with heavy-metal-meets-Chuck-Berry panache and the song also featured the first appearance of Paul Jones's Peron, loudly announcing the GOU's murky fascist programme.

The seventh track on the album brings Eva and Peron together for the first time, after both Magaldi (as cabaret, reprising 'On This Night Of A Thousand Stars') and Peron (as rabble-rouser) perform at a rally in aid of victims of an earthquake that struck the Argentine town of San Juan in early 1944. After a short scene depicting the rally, Eva and Peron seduce each other with 'I'd Be Surprisingly Good For You'. This minor-key, shuffling, almost night-club, ballad is both tender and ominous in Andrew's subtle arrangement and Julie's sexy delivery. Peron's response as per the confident Paul reeks insincerity. Chris Mercer delivered a snaky sax solo and once the two principals have hooked each other they reprise, but not to each other, the brutal chorus of 'Goodnight And Thank You' – 'They're hoping their lover will help them or keep them . . .'

Almost until the last minute before recording, the lyric of 'I'd Be Surprisingly Good For You' contained a howler with the line 'I'm sure there's more than this for you and I'. It probably would have been laid down as such for posterity but for Jane's father pointing out that it should be 'for you and me', which scuppered a rhyming scheme. The line became, 'That's not the reason that I caught your eye', which is clumsy but at least grammatical. Rod Stewart used my line 'creeping home before it got too light' in his hit 'I Was Only Joking' two years later, which I like to think was a subsconscious tribute to 'I'd Be Surprisingly Good For You'.

But after this song which, in establishing their relationship, ought to create a sense of well-being, Andrew inserted a harp passage foretelling disaster. This short, brilliantly uneasy, section is shaken off as Eva summarily ejects Peron's under-age mistress from his apartment:

> Hello and goodbye!
> I've just unemployed you
> You can go back to school
> You had a good run
> I'm sure he enjoyed you

Which in turn leads to the one song that we felt had a good shot of being a hit single – 'Another Suitcase In Another Hall'. It did indeed become a hit for Barbara Dickson, but was of course overshadowed by the song we never thought could be a success out of the context of the whole show, 'Don't Cry For Me Argentina'.

'Another Suitcase' is one of my very favourite songs, especially in the original Barbara version. In fact I still feel that it has never been as big as it should have been, but this is presumably an arrogant view as it has had every chance of being recorded more often than it has been, after twenty years of high exposure in *Evita* in all its forms. The gentle, sad tune is perfect for a fifteen-year-old girl but the lyric is probably too sophisticated for the character:

> I don't expect my love affairs to last for long
> Never fool myself that my dreams will come true
> Being used to trouble I anticipate it
> But all the same I hate it
> Wouldn't you?

> Time and time again I've said that I don't care
> That I'm immune to gloom, that I'm hard through and through
> But every time it happens all my words desert me
> So anyone can hurt me
> And they do

Chris Neil sang the answering and title phrases to Barbara's beautiful lead and the overall result made us feel sure that this would be the song to give us our first significant British chart single – for all the success of *Joseph* and *Superstar* we had still

...ussing the master plan for the *Evita* album; *left to right*: Roy Featherstone (MCA-UK chief), ...d, TR and Andrew.

...d Hamilton Smith, the ebullient *Evita* engineer, mixing his one vocal line on the album ...esmanship is more than entertaining peasants' with particular care.

The three principals on the
original *Evita* album (*photogra-
phy by Snowdon*):

Left Julie Covington – the
greatest Evita who never sang
the part on stage.
Below left Colm Wilkinson –
only felt I had fully repaid th[
wonderfully gifted Irishman f[
his vocals as Che when I
successfully suggested to the
producers of *Les Miserables* [
1985 that Colm should star a[
Jean Valjean.
Below right Paul Jones – the
magnificent Manfred Mann
man and powerful Peron who[
interpretation of Dylan's 'Wi[
God On Our Side' in 1965 g[
me thinking about a Jesus/Ju[
musical idea.

Above Heartaches CC v. Bill
...ath's Gents, May 1977;
...ck row, left to right: Philip
...bo, Simon Buxton, Mic
...ad, Mike Baker, Harold
...plan, John Fingleton;
...nt row, left to right:
...thony Deal, Chris
...ooker, TR, Mike d'Abo,
...ris Cliff.

...ght Rare net practice
...ich my career figures
...ly has not paid off –
...ybe I'm batting the
...ong way round;
... everything else
...nt-handed.

The first man to sing the role of Elvis/Pharaoh in public (me), at Colet Cou[rt] School in 1968, prepares for his professional début [in] the role, at Oxford in 19[ ] (*Michael Barrett*)

Another airport, anoth[er] show: Andrew and Sa[rah] Lloyd Webber hanging around in a Reykjavik departure lounge, 197[ ]

...ve Evita rehearsals, May ...8. Hal Prince with Elaine ...e and David Essex. The ... time I enjoyed rehearsals. *...n Timbers*)

...ht With Hal, Elaine and ...rew, days before Elaine's ...ational appearance as the ...d's first stage Evita. *...n Timbers*)

Above The newly arrived Donald Alexander Hugh, showing indifference to the fact that his dad has two singles the charts, with mother and sister.

My favourite Seventies' shot of Eva (*left*) – and one of r favourites of Jane *(below)*.

ove A 1975 performance by what is now Wang and the Cheviots
was then Just Plain Smith. *From left to right*: Chris Hatt (rhythm
tar), Tim Rice (mind elsewhere), Bill Heath (worried vocals) and
vid Ballantyne (lead guitar). Twenty-four years later we have still
discovered what the sign BRAIN indicated. (*Erica Echenberg*)

ht My grandmother, by then a great-grandmother, aged eighty-
in 1977. A fount of practical wisdom, one of her top tips was
n't marry for money, but marry for love where there is money'.

ow My father and I with AYU 594 in 1977, a snip at £40 in
6, and still in the Rice garage today.

So much media attention had been given to *Evita* in the months before the show opened that this *Evening Standard* advertisement on 21 June 1978 needed just two words of explanation. Joss Ackland (Peron), Elaine Paige (Eva) and David Essex (Che). (*Ad design: Russ Eglin/Barrie James*)

not grazed the UK Top Forty after nearly ten years of trying. Eventually 'Suitcase' was to stagger to number 18, by which time 'Argentina' had sold nearly a million singles and made Number One. (Eight years later, I was to reach the very top with Barbara, with a song from *Chess* 'I Know Him So Well'.)

The next number, 'Dangerous Jade', a semi-funky march with ventures into 'Ascot Gavotte' territory, was a choral piece for the two Argentine groupings notably opposed to the rise of Eva Duarte as mistress to a military leader and infiltrator into high society, the army and the aristocracy. The soldiers note that

> She should get into her head
> She should not get out of bed
> She should know that she's not paid
> To be loud but to be laid

High society complains:

> Things have reached a pretty pass
> When someone pretty lower class
> Graceless and vulgar, uninspired
> Can be respected and admired

while Che, in journalist guise, pesters Eva about her sleeping arrangements. Che also bangs on again about his fly-killing idea, taking heart from Eva's rise:

> To see an underdog succeed
> Is the encouragement I need

'Dangerous Jade' was to get a substantial working over for the stage show, which improved it considerably (all references to insecticide excised). The first half of the piece was concluded with a seven-minute scene which alternated between Eva and Peron's bedroom and the Argentine workers' rallies which Eva manipulates and brilliantly encourages. Peron is here portrayed as the less assured of the two, wondering if they would not be better off nipping into exile rather than risk oblivion, were they to continue participation in the struggle for control of the chaotic country, but Eva is contemptuous of 'crazy defeatist talk' and of their rivals for power:

> It doesn't matter what those morons say
> Our nation's leaders are a feeble crew
> There's only twenty of them anyway
> What is twenty next to millions who
> Are looking to you?
> All you have to do is sit and wait
> Keeping out of everybody's way
> We'll—
> You'll be handed power on a plate
> When the ones who matter have their say
> And with chaos installed
> You can reluctantly agree to be called

I was delighted that Eva's Freudian slip when she says 'We'll' before correcting herself to 'You'll' always got a laugh when performed live. Peron still has his doubts:

> There again we could be foolish
> Not to quit while we're ahead
> For distance lends enchantment and that is why
> All exiles are distinguished
> More important, they're not dead
> I could find job satisfaction in Paraguay

But Eva is off and running. The scene moves seamlessly from boudoir to factory floor (easy to do on record) and Andrew's rousing anthem 'A New Argentina' in which Eva exhorts the *descamisados* (her 'shirtless ones') to rise up and give their all to Peron is a very plausible rallying cry for the deprived. His bedroom music is by contrast subtle and seductive, reprising chunks of 'I'd Be Surprisingly Good For You'. There is a fair amount of politics and history in this sequence and, if I may so, accurately researched.

The first half of our recording ended with a quiet, contemplative Eva. After Peron's last shot at backing out ('There again I could be foolish/not to quit while I'm ahead/I can see me many miles away, inactive/sipping cocktails on a terrace, taking breakfast in bed/sleeping easy, doing crosswords, it's attractive'), Eva says she 'often gets those nightmares too' which got a laugh on stage that I never anticipated, and 'sometimes it's very difficult to keep momentum if it's you that you are following'. (The latter line Jane later presented to me embroidered into a pillow as a token of affection, or possibly criticism.) But Eva's determination to get her way is her final thought in Act One:

> Would I have done what I did if I hadn't thought—
> If I hadn't known – we would take the country?

As with *Superstar*, the time restrictions imposed by the need to cram everything on to four sides of vinyl had made us write *Evita* with concise urgency to the great benefit of the work; we got on with it. The start of the second half (side three of the album) jumped ahead to Peron's inauguration as President in June 1946, over a year after the events depicted in 'A New Argentina'. Eva and Peron had got married (while the records were being changed) and all was set for her big scene, the scene that Andrew always stated he wanted to be a political 'Over The Rainbow'. Cue the biggest hit he and I ever wrote together.

Chapter Twenty-six

E va did not actually deliver any major oration on the day of Peron's inauguration but it was not long after becoming Argentina's new First Lady that she was making highly emotional speeches of the intensity we hoped to capture in 'Don't Cry For Me Argentina'. Despite Andrew's quite brilliant orchestration of Eva's major aria, as delivered from the balcony of the Casa Rosada in the heart of Buenos Aires, and Julie Covington's terrific vocal performance, this intensity was not immediately achieved. This was because of the lyric. Julie first recorded the song as 'It's Only Your Lover Returning', and when that didn't work as the first line of the chorus, some even worse titles were tried, which I have been shamed into forgetting, although I do recall one was along the lines of 'All through my reckless and wild days'.

We got more and more desperate as the delivery date for the finished recording approached. Most of the rest of the album had been put to bed but the work's most important number lacked a half way decent title. Nothing we tried worked and although the music and ninety-five per cent of the lyrics were clearly in great shape, that missing five per cent dragged the whole track down to a level of embarrassing mundanity. Part of the problem was that I kept trying to come up with a title that would make sense out of the context of the show; we did not think that the song would ever have commercial potential in its own right unless it could make sense away from the trappings of the political and dramatic story which caused it to be written in the first place. What a crass decision! It was probably the only time (honest) that I had made the mistake of caring more about a lyric's potential outside the show than its importance within it, and as a result both song and show suffered.

We had, however, already recorded the problem line earlier in *Evita* as 'Don't Cry For Me Argentina' when the voice of the dead Eva is heard by her millions of mourners, begging them not to weep because she is gone. Even beyond the grave our Eva's sincerity was in doubt as she sung that line, but there was no doubt that it was a powerful phrase that matched the melody perfectly. Andrew suggested that we reprise the line for the balcony scene, noting that if we came up with a better line after the album's release we could always change it for any subsequent stage show. As soon as Julie inserted 'Don't Cry For Me Argentina' into the scene it was transformed. We reckoned it now hadn't a hope of being a chart hit with a title that made it crystal clear it was not a love song, but it certainly kicked the entire album into a higher gear. So the world never heard:

> It's only your lover returning
> The truth is I never left you
> All through my wild days
> My mad existence
> I kept my promise
> Don't keep your distance

Yikes! A narrow escape.

We were of course wrong about the chart hit bit. The song was so successful that any thought of a re-working for stage was very quickly made ludicrously unnecessary. But because 'Don't Cry For Me Argentina' became such a massive hit beyond the confines of the show, most people have forgotten that it is first and foremost a speech within a play. It has become so well known that it is now a victim of its own success, almost a cliché. It has been slammed by many for being a string of meaningless platitudes, but that is precisely what it was meant to be in the first place. As a speech by a megalomaniac woman attempting to bamboozle half a million people, it is right on the button; it is meant to be low on content and high on emotion, just like Evita herself. That doesn't stop it from being a beautiful song, nor Eva from being an irresistible icon. If millions around the world love the song at face value, we are delighted, but maybe they have been fooled as Eva's adoring *descamisados* were.

> And as for fortune, and as for fame
> I never invited them in
> Though it seemed to the world they were all I desired
> They are illusions
> They are not the solutions they promised to be
> The answer was here all the time
> I love you and hope you love me

But above all, what really made the song beautiful was Andrew's melody and orchestral accompaniment. It is hard to hear it with fresh ears today, but its impact on first hearing was overwhelming. From the bombast of Peron, from the harsh mindless chants of the plebs in the square, emerges a ravishing mellifluousness of strings, andante, both pizzicato and flowing, a gorgeous introduction to Julie's strong but gentle vocal. The structure is light and shade, subtle and extravagant, one passage actually hummed by the choral forces. The most delicate of final reflections

> Have I said too much?
> There's nothing more I can think of to say to you
> But all you have to do is look at me
>   to know that every word is true

is followed by a thrilling, huge London Philharmonic climax. To this day, every time I see this scene performed live I dread some bored punter yelling 'Yes!' after Eva's query 'Have I said too much?' but if that has ever happened, to date I have missed it.

As soon as Eva finishes 'Don't Cry For Me Argentina', to rapturous acclaim from the mob, she lets rip with quite a different series of emotions as she crows to Peron, 'Just listen to that! The voice of Argentina! We are adored, we are loved!' She is not so loved by some of Peron's colleagues on the balcony; one has the temerity to observe that 'Statesmanship is more than entertaining peasants' (this line delivered with exquisite sub-operatic pomp by David Hamilton-Smith, which saved us a vocalist's session fee) and she snaps back, 'We shall see, little man' before returning to harangue the crowds with blatant dishonesty and volume, justifying being decked out in jewels and finery. These exchanges, which put the whole 'Don't Cry For Me' charade into a different and murkier light, are not often played on the radio after the hit single.

Next up was the new version of 'Down On The Farm', the failed Maynard Williams song about agricultural progress, now reborn as 'High Flying Adored'. This was one of the few songs in *Evita* I wrote from a personal perspective in that I was commenting on my own reactions to my success, minor though it may have been, as well as permitting Che to decry Eva's arrival at the top of the heap. Andrew said he could not agree less with my hints of disillusion at our achievements. Frankly, I was having a great time being slightly famous and fairly rich, but there was a genuine streak in me that wondered what now?

> High flying, adored
> What happens now, where do you go from here?
> For someone on top of the world
> The view's not exactly clear
> A shame you did it all at twenty-six
> There are no mysteries now
> Nothing can thrill you
> No one fulfill you . . .

But I wasn't looking for sympathy. I always liked this lyric which I thought did justice to the tune in a way 'Down On The Farm' hadn't. Some of the words don't sit perfectly on the emphases of the melody but

> Were there stars in your eyes as you crawled in at night
> From the bars, from the sidewalks
> From the gutter theatrical?

worked pretty well. Colm sang it magnificently. When he sang we believed she was 'a cross between a fantasy of the bedroom and a saint'.

'High Flying Adored' did lead to a fairly big, albeit brief, bust-up between Andrew and me when I heard one of his original orchestral ideas for the number, a kind of Adam Faith pizzicato-string effect which I criticised a little too soon after hearing it, i.e. about five seconds in. Andrew flew into a rage and I used this as an excuse to nip away to Lord's for the Test Match. This in turn led to an Andrew walk-out leaving David Land, who had come to witness the album's terrific progress, and David Hamilton-Smith with an orchestra on their hands and no producers. Somehow the basic track got laid down, and the pizzicato strings got the boot.

My relationship with Andrew certainly had a few rocky moments during the creation of *Evita* – I can recall very few during *Superstar* – but I never felt that this was the beginning of the end. Inevitably we were leading more separate lives away from the piano and studio. Wives and children, money to spend. I became less tolerant of his exaggerations and tantrums, he less so of my apparently casual approach to our partnership. But my attitude to *Evita* was never less than one of dedication; I had already lived with the project for over two years before we even entered the recording studio and as the excellence of our work together unfolded I had no intention of letting this golden opportunity to create another major work slip by. But I must have been very annoying at times in failing to show the fanatical obsession that most high achievers in show business display. I was too English and too middle class, too worried about showing that I was keen. Andrew's passion encouraged my show of indifference. My most tactless moment was having a go at *Jeeves* during one argument, accusing Andrew of wasting time on a crappy show while I was slogging away at Eva Peron research. Tactless, partly because I was right.

The next number in the show, 'Rainbow High', caused no dissent between us; the only problem was the devastating range of the vocal part for Julie. She conquered it. 'Rainbow High' is the number that Andrew in particular felt came near to grand opera, although of course that was not the way we required Julie to sing it. The couplets 'they need to adore me/so Christian Dior me' and 'That's what they call me/so Lauren Bacall me' came in for both ecstatic praise and vituperative criticism. I thought they were quite slick and well researched in that both Dior and Bacall were at their peak in 1947 and Evita beyond doubt craved the international recognition of the fashion and film stars of the day; unfortunately 'Bacall' and 'call' is not a rhyme but the same syllable twice. I only noticed that some years later but it was by then too late to switch to 'That's how they see me/so Vivien Leigh me' which was my first idea.

'Rainbow Tour' was a jolly narrative telling of Eva's exploits in Europe, when she entranced Spain but failed to repeat the impact in Italy and France, and never remotely fulfilled her ambition to take England by storm. She refused to visit England at all when the royal family were advised to tread warily as far as giving her any kind of official reception was concerned. 'Who does the King of England think he is?' yells our Evita. I slipped in a mini-tribute to *My Fair Lady* with the line 'Franco's reign in Spain should see out the Forties'.

As Evita's Rainbow Tour hit the rocks, and as the first intimations that her health was failing appeared, Andrew inserted crafty variations on earlier themes such as 'On This Night Of A Thousand Stars'. In all his works reprises of principal tunes have been his trademark, and frequently the cause of unintelligent criticism. This practice makes the whole much more than a string of tunes and can often make points that mere words cannot, such as the physical decline of a star. Mike Smith and Mike d'Abo were leading lights throughout 'Rainbow Tour'. *Evita*, incidentally, was the first recording to feature both ex-Manfred Mann vocalists Paul Jones and Mike d'Abo.

Back in Argentina, Eva changes her image, becomes harsher, as illustrated in her riposte to the hated aristocracy, 'The Actress Hasn't Learned The Lines You'd Like To Hear'. Che breaks in with yet another plea for his fly-killing project, but is dismissed as brutally as had been the aristocrats. Eva is more concerned with her Foundation, which is 'good news for Argentine flies'.

The song celebrating Eva's Foundation, sung on the album with terrific vim by Christopher Neil as the Foundation's manager, though wisely given to Che in live productions, is musically almost a straight lift from a tune featured in Carlos Pasini's *Queen Of Hearts* documentary, in turn a track on an album I found of Peronist marching songs. Andrew simply switched it to 7/8 time. Entitled 'The Money Kept Rolling In', it tells of the uses and abuses of an enterprise that by the year of Eva's death, 1952, had an income estimated to be equal to one-third of the entire Argentine national budget. Cash flowed into the Foundation in a variety of ways, usually with an element of compulsion involved. It was of course as much an exercise in public relations for the Perons as it was a charity.

> And the money kept rolling in from every side
> Eva's pretty hands reached out and they reached wide
> Now you may feel it should have been a voluntary cause
> But that's not the point my friends
> When the money keeps rolling in you don't ask how
> Think of all the people gonna see some good times now
> Eva's called the hungry to her – open up the doors!
> Never been a fund like the Foundation Eva Peron!

This was the last exuberant moment in the show. Eva's health was in a tailspin, as her progress to near sainthood in the eyes of her followers zoomed into the stratosphere. Children sing 'Santa Evita' to another variation of 'Don't Cry For Me Argentina' and Che launches into his last attacks, 'Why try to govern a country when you can become a saint?'. This is followed by the final showdown between the two principals – portrayed as a waltz, Andrew's Strauss-like melody a weird counterpart to the angry, complex argument, including a musical reprise of the 'Goodnight and Thank You' tirade, lyrics about the inevitable infidelity and cynicism of lovers replaced with lines about the inevitability of political corruption ('There is evil/ever around, fundamental/system of government quite incidental'). I knew that the couplet 'Why go bananas/chasing Nirvanas?' would raise eyebrows or a sneer, but loved it (Eva was of common stock, after all) and refused to remove it, for this album at least. The waltz was one of the few tracks we recorded outside the Olympic Studios. Andrew wanted a pure ultra-live orchestral sound and we repaired, with the Philharmonic, to the Henry Wood Hall in Trinity Church Square, a favourite haunt for classical recording managers.

Next came another musical reprise of a verse of 'Down Thru' Summer' as Eva first acknowledged her illness, 'What is the good of the strongest heart/In a body that's falling apart?' Eva's pain at recognising that the 'physical interferes' was succeeded by a final burst of insecticide-fuelled anger from Che, announcing that any fidelity to his country of birth was clearly misplaced: 'I might as well have been as loyal to El Salvador, Afghanistan, the South of France, Japan, Hong Kong!' I deliberately left Cuba off the list, hoping to make the point that his reason for ultimately signing on to Castro's 1959 revolution had nothing to do with any long-standing sympathy to that cause, but was merely the most exciting job that came his way in the next few years. Naturally this insight went completely unnoticed and on all future versions of *Evita* was regarded as surplus to requirements.

The pretty and sophisticated melody of 'She Is A Diamond' is about the tenth tune to give the lie that Andrew's score for *Evita* had only one tune that kept coming back for want of any better idea. 'Diamond' has in fact deliberate musical and phrasing echoes of 'I'd Be Surprisingly Good For You'. Paul Jones sang Peron's tender defence of his wife to his military opponents with delicate precision, as befitted an actor who was playing Hamlet in between sessions at Olympic. I was thrilled to hear that great voice of 'Pretty Flamingo' and 'Do Wah Diddy Diddy' (and of course 'With God On Our Side') get so much out of the final scenes of the recording. I had one of the lines of this song (slightly altered) engraved on to a gold medallion for Jane: 'You are the diamond in my dull grey life'. Corny but nice. The song ends with the officers twisting Peron's claim that 'she's the one who put us where we are' to 'she's the one who put you where you are'.

Peron's massive role in the story of Argentina is somewhat downplayed in *Evita* but it was never meant to be a deep analysis of either the dictator or of the nation's history during Eva's time, merely the Cinderella story of a remarkable woman's determined climb. I still feel that one New York review of the show, which stated that it 'fails completely as a history of Argentine politics', was less than fair in that such a history had not been our aim. 'Fails completely as an analysis of the French Revolution' would have been an equally reasonable criticism. However in the final scenes we attempted to deal with the last stages of the relationship with Eva and Peron, as he desperately juggles with her impending death (and her refusal to accept it), his political and military adversaries, and his country's slide into chaos. Peron has a measure of genuine concern for Eva, not entirely because he knows his fate is bound to hers. At one point he sings, 'Your little body's slowly breaking down' – forever one of David Land's favourite lyrics, which this ever-effervescent man would quote as time and decline claimed friends and colleagues over the years. The Perons are both brutal in discussion about their enemies and each other, but come to no conclusion: 'So what happens now?', a frightened reprise of the line sung by the mistress Eva expelled in the days when their affair was hot and new.

I wrote most of the lyrics for the long sequence on the album 'Dice Are Rolling' which includes 'Eva's Sonnet' before Andrew composed any music, an unusual process for us, though one or two lines in the very early scene with Magaldi had also been written that way. Consequently the music is sometimes difficult to assimilate, but the more I listened to it, the more I thought it fitted the scene perfectly. In both stage and film versions, this not obviously catchy section was considerably cut back, which led to us winning an Oscar twenty years later when most of 'Dice Are Rolling' was replaced by the conventional pop aria 'You Must Love Me',* but I do not feel any director ever improved upon the structure of the original scene. I am proud of the fact that this lengthy track on the album could have worked well without any music, as if in a play, though on the album Andrew's mixture of jagged new themes and fragments of earlier melodies was faultless.

'Eva's Sonnet' was just that, fourteen iambic five-foot lines, with a defined and definite rhyme scheme, which was mercilessly hacked down to six for the stage. The eight that went were

---

* The Oscar for best movie song can only be won by a song that débuts in a movie. Thus no songs from *Evita*'s original theatrical or record incarnations qualified when they re-appeared in Alan Parker's 1996 film version. The one new song in the film was 'You Must Love Me'. Frankly, Oscar considerations weighed as heavily as dramatic ones when it was decided to give 'Dice Are Rolling' the boot.

almost my favourite expression of Eva's determination in the whole work:

> Those shallow mean pretenders to your throne
> Will come to learn ours is the upper hand
> For I do not accept this is not known
> Already in most quarters of our land
> To face the storms so long and not capsize
> Is not the chance achievement of a fraud
> Conservatives are kings of compromise
> So if it suits them, even they'll applaud

Eva knows she is doomed. In an emotional final broadcast to her people she delivers a version of 'Don't Cry For Me Argentina' that actually makes sense and in which she actually means what she says. She declines the chance of becoming Vice-President. As she slips into terminal decline, a montage of images, people and events in her life swim in and out of her fevered mind while the nation's grief begins to build to hysterical proportions. Now it is Peron who sings 'High Flying Adored'. Eventually we are beside Eva on her deathbed and Andrew's majestic funeral tune returns with Evita's final thoughts, her lament. This was a lyric truly mucked up by all subsequent treatments.

I wanted Eva on her deathbed to end her life with very personal thoughts rather than any kind of summary of her achievements. Above all, I was sure she would have wondered why she had to die so young and why she never had a child. She sees her fate as having been determined by the choices she unknowingly made – excitement and glory in a short life, or anonymity in a full one; the love of millions of strangers, or the love of her own children. In each case she chose the former option, in each case she now regrets it.

> The choice was mine and mine completely
> I could have any prize that I desired
> I could burn with the splendour of the brightest fire
> Or else – or else I could choose time
> Remember I was very young then

And a year was forever and a day
So what use could fifty, sixty, seventy be?
I saw the lights and I was on my way
And how I lived! How I shone!
But how soon the lights were gone!

The choice was mine and no one else's
I could have the millions at my feet
Give my life to people I might never meet
Or else to children of my own
Remember I was very young then
Thought I needed the numbers on my side
Thought the more that loved me the more loved I'd be
But such things cannot be multiplied
Oh my daughter! Oh my son!
Understand what I have done!

Other than the fact that I now see that the second line should
have been 'I could have any prize I might desire' which would have
created a true rhyme with 'fire', I was as happy with these lines
as I was with any in *Evita* but somehow they never had their full
moment on stage (or film). Partly for reasons of length, and partly
because it was felt that Che should have some concluding thoughts
to the same tune, Hal cut most of Eva's second stanza, leaving just
the final two lines intact. Thus 'Oh my daughter! Oh my son!'
barely made sense. Indeed Hal told me that he had assumed all
along that Eva meant her people when she cried out to a daughter
and a son. Surely she would have then said 'daughters' and 'sons', I
thought – how could the great man get it wrong? Anyway my wish
to portray the dying megalomaniac's final moments as one of utter
despair over her childlessness never made it to any stage production, though I bet that was one of the last things on her mind.

But on the original album the Lament did what it set out to
do. And at the fag-end of that scorching summer of 1976, when
we played back the final complete mix of *Evita* to David Land
and to MCA, we felt that every other song had too. It had been
a frantic race against the clock to deliver the finished tapes to Roy
Featherstone in time for a pre-Christmas launch of the album,

but Roy's unbounded happiness with what we gave him justified the last few eighteen-hour days (and David Hamilton-Smith's sacrifice of half a holiday). We now had to switch from writing hats to promotion hats. Could we and the record company convince a record-buying public that had never heard of our dead Argentinian heroine to show interest in an expensive double album which we did not expect to inspire commercial radio play or a hit single?

Chapter Twenty-seven

We finished the *Evita* album – at around 103 minutes a quarter of an hour longer than our original *Superstar* album had been, but somehow still squeezed on to just two vinyl discs – at the end of August, emerging blinking into the Barnes daylight just as the freakishly hot summer of 1976 was showing signs of cracking up. The ten weeks or so left before the release of our enterprise in Great Britain set us even more terrifying deadlines than the recordings had; production of the cover, sleeve notes, photo sessions for all involved, promotion plans, presentation of the work to record company sales forces around the country – all these and more had to be addressed with urgency. We all therefore went off on holiday.

My break at least was not totally devoid of constructive moves towards the ultimate success of the venture, in that Jane and I went to Bermuda to stay with Robert Stigwood, now a resident of that island paradise, taking tapes of *Evita* with us. To put it mildly, we hoped Robert would like the work, for if it didn't appeal to his commercial ears it was unlikely that any other major theatrical impresario would go for it. Robert's palatial joint that occupied twenty-six acres of Bermuda (roughly equivalent to someone owning Yorkshire in the UK) was not quite ready to receive guests, or even Robert, so we were all based in his temporary HQ, rented from the government, a Bermudan stately home that doubled as a tourist attraction. During the day armies of visitors wandered around the gardens and parts of the house, which still left the nocturnal Robert plenty of space and time to operate in his normal extravagantly generous way in the evenings when the only other occupants of the beautiful grounds were thousands of noisy frogs.

Also staying with Robert at the time were Linda and Barry Gibb, and his youngest brother Andy. The Bee Gees were right back on top of the world with a slew of hits, their greatest moment of all, *Saturday Night Fever*, still in the wings. Andy Gibb, looking about fifteen but already married, talked confidently of his plans to become a solo recording star. Although Jane and I really warmed to the lad, we both felt that he was being somewhat over-optimistic as far as his plans for world domination were concerned. He was shy and innocent, awkward even. Six months later he had turned into a dynamic sex symbol, was Number One in the charts all over the world, having apparently aged five years and sprouted a hairy chest. For most of 1977 and 1978 he was almost the only artist in America to rival his brothers' massive success. The timid and charming adolescent we met became a lady-killing pop idol, clearly equipped with his fair share of the amazing Gibb legacy of talent. It is desperately sad that he was ultimately destroyed by the excesses of the music business. He played the lead in *Joseph* on Broadway towards the end of his troubled career, but I never once saw him in the role as his attendance record was disastrous; we remember him with affection and admiration.

Having one of the greatest songwriters of the day present while I introduced *Evita* to Robert added to my apprehension and I briefly considered the idea of merely playing a few highlights, whatever they were. But courage prevailed and the after-dinner gathering nobly sat through the full 103 minutes. Both Robert and Barry, not to mention the other assorted Gibbs and pals, seemed genuinely impressed. Even the frogs seemed to quieten down a bit during the playback. As one's own work can often sound so much less brilliant than previously thought when listened to in the company of others, I was very happy in that most of the twenty-three tracks came over to me as strongly as they had back in Olympic studios. Robert seemed one hundred per cent convinced that the whole shebang had huge potential and a great evening was wound up with a few Barry Gibb songs, some brand new, all good.

Back in the UK, others apart from the MCA team and David Land, who had of course heard *Evita* dozens of times at every stage of its creation, were also exposed to the tapes. The reaction from MCA's sales force, the blokes who would actually have to flog the album to the shops, and from the promotion boys, who had to convince the media that this was worth a spin, was pretty positive. Some expressed doubts about the subject matter – an unknown heroine and story – but these would probably have been the types who dismissed *Superstar* because the hero was too well known. The most valuable feedback concerned 'Don't Cry For Me Argentina'. Andrew and I still did not reckon that it had much potential as a single, but the word from many of the chaps in the field was that this was a certain chart-topper. If MCA wanted 'Argentina' to be a single, that was fine by us, but we had our doubts. Nothing from *Superstar* had been a hit on the singles charts in Britain, and *Evita*, 'Argentina' in particular, seemed too sophisticated for the regular Top Forty. But we felt we had 'Suitcase' in reserve if the first single flopped, and if we had the salesmen's enthusiasm, we would be mad to stand in their way. I began to think that maybe 'Argentina' really had hit-song potential when the composer and producer Andrew Powell, soon to enjoy mega-sales with Kate Bush and 'Wuthering Heights', rang me up out of the blue to say he had heard 'Argentina' being mastered in the studio and was certain that it would go all the way.

So with the first single heading for the presses, we devoted most of our attention to the packaging of our baby, the cover artwork and photos. This was my job – Andrew's main concern was to have a visual presentation of the album ready in time for his by now annual Sydmonton Festival, a junket that has grown massively over the years, but then a comparatively modest gathering of friends and musical associates for a weekend at his stately pile, during which he lays on a variety of entertainment, generally centred around his own most recent creation. The idea in 1976 was that the Sydmonton presentation of the album would be a dry run for the first public presentation, booked by Roy Featherstone for 9 November in the New London Theatre, at that time a house that had never had a sniff of a hit show and thus nearly always available for one-off extravaganzas. Andrew was to change the fortunes of the New London dramatically five years later when *Cats* opened there, a show now nearly into its third decade.

With the invaluable help of Carlos Pasini and his extensive collection of Peron memorabilia, I chose some striking black and white Eva photographs for the cover and booklet, which was also to contain extensive credits, a short note about the background to the story, and the entire libretto. Anton Furst, a gifted film designer friend of Carlos, came up with a simple but very effective white outer cover with a rose-cum-rainbow logo the only splash of colour. Anton's final triumph, before he took his own life in Hollywood a decade later, was to be the brilliant claustrophobic design of Gotham City for *Batman*. Carlos, Anton and I were up literally all night before the day of the Sydmonton presentation, matching every moment of the album with a succession of slides, many containing the lyrics, over 150 photographs of Eva, Argentina and other relevant visual aids. Somehow we managed to run everything to order the following day and there was not the slightest doubt that the Sydmonton audience were surprised and impressed, though it would have been difficult for any of the guests to have slagged off their host's new work while knocking back his food and drink in his home. There again, they had paid for the privilege.

Speaking at the Sydmonton dinner that evening, John Selwyn Gummer, the future Conservative cabinet minister, by now one of Andrew's closest pals, referred extremely politely to our efforts and seized upon the line 'conservatives are kings of compromise' from the final scene between Eva and Peron as the basis for much of his oration. Ironically (and annoyingly, for me at least) that was one of the lines that got the chop when Eva's Sonnet was brutally pruned for the stage.

I was keen to have photos of the main contributors to the exercise included in the package and, full of confidence and feeling like going for the top, persuaded Roy to call Lord Snowdon. To my surprise, Tony Snowdon accepted the assignment with alacrity and Colm, Paul, Julie and David Hamilton-Smith (and me) all trooped into his studio to face his celebrated and expensive shutter. Andrew was not so keen for some reason and Tony had to draw on his considerable reserves of charm and persuasive chat to convince the strangely reluctant composer to join the gallery. Eventually Andrew agreed to be snapped in his own drawing room and all went as well with his mugshot as it had with the others.

I felt at this point that Andrew was getting extremely nervous about the whole thing and was subconsciously trying to distance himself from it; perhaps memories of *Jeeves* were haunting him. The success of Sydmonton calmed him down considerably, but by no means totally, as I was to discover on 9 November. One vital move that Andrew had already made by this time, however, was to contact the king of the American musical, Hal Prince, with a view to directing *Evita* on stage.

Evita seemed to have made no impression at all upon the US end of the MCA empire, i.e. the heart of the international company. But this hardly concerned us as we worked frantically to get everything ready for the launch at the New London Theatre. Basically, the show was to be a smarter, slicker, bigger version of the Sydmonton slide show, with the visuals linked by computer to the soundtrack of the album, in turn to be broadcast over a mammoth PA system to an audience of over a thousand – music and media people, virtually everyone involved with the recording, and a large contingent of friends. All would be given a copy of the finished double LP, plus a handy information and glossy-pix package explaining a good deal more than they needed to know.

The run-through during the day went fine as far as I was concerned, but not in the view of my co-author, who was nothing less than distraught at the rehearsal. Andrew was in tears at one point, claiming that his music was being destroyed by the appalling sound, that he would not attend the launch and that the whole enterprise was a disaster. David Land earned his percentage that afternoon, convincing him otherwise. When it came to the actual performance, Andrew was as good as gold, spoke cheerfully with me to the assembled multitude at the start, and quite justifiably basked in the terrific reaction we got at the finish. We moved on to the Zanzibar round the corner and saw in my thirty-second birthday with an excess of wine and a lot of genuinely enthusiastic pals. The only bad news of the evening for me was hearing that Lilian, my devoted cleaning lady at Northumberland Place (who had refused an offer to move out of London to join us at Romeyns

Court), had died on the day of the *Evita* record première. Jane and I were not too smashed to toast her memory in the Zanzibar.

The album and the single of 'Don't Cry for Me Argentina' were both issued a week or so after our 9 November bash. We didn't have many problems with the press. Early critical reaction was pretty positive, with our loyal supporter Derek Jewell's *Sunday Times* review headed 'Simply a Masterpiece', the kind of summing-up that Andrew and I (and MCA) could live with. In fact, looking back through these initial reviews of the record, it is hard to find a bad word. I am sure there were some, but, even more so than had been the case with *Superstar*, the abuse only really arrived later, after the work's success. There seemed to be a general feeling within the record business, and from our colleagues and chums, that *Evita* was going to be a hit, but we soon worried that we were going to intrigue everyone but the public. We got a lot of column inches in the *Observer*, *Sunday Telegraph* and even the *Financial Times*, with the writers for the most part more interested in our method of work than the creation itself. Inevitably, some went on about the obscurity of the heroine. This and the fact that we were still not (quite) household names meant that we needed much more than some upmarket raves to reach the masses. What we craved was some radio play. This meant Radio One.

Commercial radio was still in its infancy, and the BBC's most popular station was the most reliable route to a hit. A string of television performances was also a good bet, but we had nil hope there with our single requiring a massive symphony orchestra for adequate impact, not to mention the fact that Ms Covington was beginning to show a marked lack of enthusiasm for the cause. Radio One had a fairly tight play-list policy, then as now, but at least back in 1976 the odd moderately adult pop single had a chance of getting on to it. However, then as now, if your record wasn't on the favoured list, then it would not be played at all on any of the programmes that mattered. With Stuart Watson of MCA, Andrew and I flogged round the country visiting the few out-of-town radio stations that existed then, plus any local TV show that would talk to us without the support of a live performance of our new release. For two or three weeks Radio One brutally refused to add the Covington single to the play-list and although many local and/or commercial stations loved it, we began to think in terms of a panic release of 'Another Suitcase'. Barbara Dickson was, after all, a known radio and record quantity.

But just when I felt sure Andrew was going to let me know what a lousy idea this *Evita* thing was (and I would have probably agreed with him), Radio One relented. Suddenly we couldn't stop hearing our song on the radio, and not just on the BBC's flagship. Furthermore, almost every time it got played, the presenter raved about it. We almost felt embarrassed by some of the praise, but not enough to ring in and complain about it. Familiarity has bred a certain amount of contempt for the song in some quarters during the subsequent decades but in its first few weeks of public life it was one of those new original records that makes nearly everything else around seem run of the mill. It was Andrew's arrangement that did it, but once that had hooked the listeners, they discovered plenty of other striking things going on within the grooves, such as subject matter, tune and Julie. And grooves they were, as singles were only available as beautiful vinyl 45s in those days. We eventually unloaded just under a million of them in the UK alone, although we only got to Number One by the skin of our teeth.

This was in part because Julie refused to promote the single. I never quite got her reasons, but it seemed to be a combination of her not wanting to perform it unless the huge studio sound could be exactly recreated, her feeling that it was misleading the public to flog one track from the whole work for fifty pence when *Evita* was something that only made sense in its entirety, and other things she had to do. She was certainly in demand then. I recall seeing her (stark naked at one point and acting very well throughout) in Tom Stoppard's *Jumpers* around this time, during which she did not seize the chance to hum a bar or two of her big hit. Andrew and I felt she could have been nobbled by the Socialist Workers Party or some leftist theatrical grouping who had convinced her that we were middle-class capitalist pigs callously exploiting the workers with cheap songs about fascists. Her first big act of non co-operation was a refusal to go on to *Top Of The Pops* when the single had just begun to show at the bottom of the charts, incidentally giving us our first ever Top Forty hit in our home country. The week after her non-appearance, 'Argentina' only went up a couple of places and we were filled with renewed gloom.

But in fact the record was unstoppable. After Christmas, the single leaped from Twenty-five to Seven and the following week to Number Two. Here it got stuck behind 'Don't Give Up On Us' by David Soul, then at the very peak of his fame as Starsky (or was it Hutch?) in the hugely popular American cop TV series. For three anxious weeks we hung in at Number Two, never selling quite enough to overtake Mr Soul. We were a little unlucky in that his single turned out to be the biggest seller of 1977, with 'Argentina' destined to be the year's Number Two, and that both came out at exactly the same time. But fortunately, David Soul's record tailed off just a little quicker than ours and we squeaked to the top slot for just seven days before Leo Sayer's greatest hit 'When I Need You' swept past us. But just as one England cricket cap makes you as much an England cricketer for the rest of your days as would a hundred, just one week at Number One in the charts was enough to ensure our membership of what was then still a pretty exclusive club – Number One hitmakers! We were thrilled.

So, I think, was Julie. She finally agreed to appear on *Top Of The Pops*, during the week of her supremacy. She didn't actually sing, but turned up in the studio to mix with the bopping masses and acknowledge the programme's tribute to her and to the song by means of a hastily patched together succession of Eva Peron newsclips and photos that accompanied the playing of the single. Andrew threw a small spur-of-the-moment party to celebrate and she even came to that. In the wake of the single, the double-LP also became a spectacular hit, rising to Number One on some charts, although stalling at four in the most official one, that of *Music Week*. It hung around in the best-sellers for most of 1977 and, not untypically for our kind of album, has sold consistently ever since. We seemed to have done what we set out to do.

In England anyway. As had been the case with *Superstar*, MCA hoped for a worldwide hit and the album and single were released almost everywhere. Andrew, David and I did go on a few enjoyable Euro-hops with Roy Featherstone but the main target abroad was of course the United States. In Europe the Julie Covington single was a fairly instant smash and the album began to do quite well in its wake. Spain, where of course most of the population knew quite a bit about Eva Peron, seemed notably interested in the entire project. Last time around, the US record company had led the way for our rock opera's international acceptance, so we had reason to hope for another fairly solid Stateside push, especially bearing in mind that this time the UK team had already delivered a hit in Europe.

The US promotional campaign for *Evita* was an absolute disaster. No one in the American record company seemed to have a clue about the whole concept, about what we were trying to do, about Eva Peron, or even much of a clue about us. The contrast between MCA in 1970 and 1977, at least as far as we were concerned, could not have been more marked. All our old US pals, such as Dick Broderick, had long departed and none of the new top bananas had been around in *Superstar* days. We lurched through a few cities, often not even being treated to first-class travel, and if we were lucky enough to be met at all at airport or station, it was usually by some harassed salesman in his beat-up station-wagon. We quickly deduced that *Evita* was not a major part of MCA's 1977 game plan.

The overall cock-up was perfectly illustrated by their release of 'Don't Cry For Me Argentina' on the label of which they billed the artist as 'Evita featuring Julie Covington', thinking that Evita was the name of some English band we had dug up to record our song. We got a little press, and once again I was surprised on trawling through the archives to see that most of it was fairly favourable. However, the reaction from radio stations from Southern California to Bangor, Maine, and all stops in between, was a big yawn and neither single nor album ever stood a chance. We became thoroughly disgruntled at MCA's treatment of us and of *Evita* and although we fired off a memo or two of serious gripes, we could see that American conquest with this one was best put on hold. They never even laid on a hooker.

Naturally we preferred being back in the good old UK, where excitement about *Evita* continued to mount. At home there was a great deal of interest in what happened now. As I had predicted, Eva Peron herself was becoming a star, with almost as many pieces about her (fashion, historical, political) appearing in all parts of the media as there were about our show. David was inundated with offers, suggestions and advice. We assumed that Robert would want to produce the show himself and fate (in the shape of the dramatic failure of the recordings in the USA) decreed that London was the obvious starting point for the theatrical presentation.

Andrew's most significant contribution to the business end of *Evita* had been to send the finished tapes of the album to Hal Prince, and all readily agreed that he would be the dream director, though surely unlikely to take the job. He was Broadway's most celebrated musical figure, currently working on *Sweeney Todd*, one of a string of Stephen Sondheim shows he had directed, all to sensational critical reaction, many to good commercial acclaim. He had staged some of the greatest Broadway shows from *West Side Story* to *Fiddler On The Roof* – why would he leave his home patch and work in London with two semi-rockers, not yet established in the theatre?

The answer was that Hal liked the work. He sent Andrew a three page response as early as 26 July 1976, after 'one hearing'.

> . . . I have tried to include everything that occurs to me, without regard for your feelings . . . overall I think it's a fascinating project. You fellows deal in *size* and I admire that. Before I get into individual scenes, numbers and lyrics, I would like to say I had a feeling (which grew) that something is missing in the second act. That *fate* intervenes and levels Evita rather than instruments of her own doing. You touch on growing disillusionment within the government, but you don't describe it theatrically. There is no confrontation in which Evita (and Peron) accelerate their own downfall. The first act is structured so well that I found myself considering eliminating the intermission, which is a cop-out, and then I realized what I was missing in the structure of the second act. It's all in number sixteen ['And The Money Kept Rolling In'] and probably should be solved there.
>
> . . . The opening is dazzling. I would like, for the stage, to use the movie theatre more organically. Not for multi-media sake, but because I see something similar to *Citizen Kane* in the piece's style and aspirations.

. . . I'm crazy about the idea of Che functioning in the piece, but I think – again for the stage – he should be much cooler, loose and cynically humorous. If he is to be strident, it should be after the waltz, after he is politicized.

The funeral is brilliant, as is Magaldi's song.

I think Che is too British. I think some of his recitative is corny, quite frankly below the rest of the material. I don't get a clear character as I do Eva and Peron and some of the minor characters. He seems a familiar rock performer. 'Listen chum, face the fact they don't like your act', and 'Which means get stuffed' also seems too British.

I don't like the way the GOU is explained. It's too easy. It interrupts, but I don't think effectively. On the other hand, I would recommend eliminating number seven ['The Lady's Got Potential'] entirely, which means that the GOU will have to be explained.

'She is a natural high'* (Isn't this an anachronism?)

I like Eva's seduction of Peron and the scene that follows with his mistress. I think it will work well on the stage.

I'm sorry, but I do not like 'Dangerous Jade'. I wish that you would excise it.

The last scene in Act One is marvellous [at that point 'On The Balcony Of The Casa Rosada' 'Don't Cry For Me Argentina'] but I don't think the aristocrats are written as ingeniously, either musically or lyrically, as they should be. I don't think they necessarily need more material but they are predictable – so I wish they were better written. It remains a question in my mind whether Evita should revert in the final speech or whether she should simply capitalize on the aria; after all the audience knows by now who she is.

. . . In 'Rainbow High' I do not like the reference to Lauren Bacall (principally because it distracts.)

* Hal must have misheard – that line never appears.

I think it's a mistake for Che to say 'I don't think she'll make it to England now'. It confuses us. Wouldn't it be clearer if we knew from Che that she eagerly awaited an invitation from Buckingham Palace, and subsequently she was snubbed? (Incidentally, I would retain the quatrain about the King of England.)

Much as I like the waltz, there are some words which I do not like. 'So why go bananas chasing Nirvanas' (I think it distracts because it is not up to quality.)

Tim, I am aware you may be offended by this, but 'So Saint Bernadette ME!' faintly embarrasses. (Again it distracts.)

In summing up, I think the style of the piece should be abrasive – simple – raw is probably a better word. Contemporary Brecht. Bold.

Best to you both, Hal

PS Tim I wish I'd met you. It might make some of these criticisms easier to take in a more personal context.

Andrew and I then rather rudely all but ignored Hal's words of wisdom, occupied as we were with the final stages of the album's launch. To be honest, I was then pretty ignorant about Hal's extraordinarily distinguished career and it never crossed my mind that we were playing fast and loose with a Broadway legend. Andrew's failure to follow up Hal Prince's obvious early interest was, I later discovered, because he briefly had become convinced that the work would be better next presented as a film. In this he was in cahoots with Ronald Neame, an old friend and the director who had made *The Odessa File*, for which Andrew had done the score back in 1973.

However I was never happy about this idea. Andrew and Ronnie Neame argued long and hard on several occasions that a stage show of *Evita* would be a grave risk, but I couldn't see that. At one point Andrew and I nearly came to blows over this. I can remember where – in the lobby of the Regency Hotel, New York, during our grisly American promotional tour. But I can't recall exactly why; maybe Andrew had more or less gone and done a deal with Ronnie – in the end, we all reverted to Plan A. Nothing against

Ronald Neame of course, but I just couldn't see *Evita*, or indeed any sung-through piece, let alone one that had signally failed to set America alight, being the next *Sound Of Music*, the last truly big movie musical at that time. Furthermore, a hit stage show was more likely to lead to a movie version than the other way around. This was to be proved true in the case of *Evita* – but not for twenty years.

By the spring of 1977, with nothing really confirmed with Robert, and with a feeling creeping in that perhaps Hal was not really interested (who could have blamed him after our apparent indifference to his notes?), we were in a somewhat confused state about the future of the work. David took us at one point to discuss *Evita* with Michael White. Michael was a theatre and film producer of major stature (*Sleuth*, *The Rocky Horror Show*, *A Chorus Line*, Monty Python movies, etc.), although he had caught a cold with Robert as a co-producer of *Joseph* at the Albery and suffered a near-fatal disease with Robert mounting *Jeeves*. Nothing really emerged from these talks, at which we expressed an interest in approaching Jim Sharman to direct, apart from a filthy row between David and Michael some time later when we terminated negotiations after it became clear that Robert was going to do the show after all.

Andrew had also been approached by Lord Harewood, director of the English National Opera, to consider *Evita* being staged at the Coliseum in true operatic mode, but this could have pushed the work into an élitist corner and almost certainly limited its appeal, however well done. We had called the work an 'opera' on the album cover, but I do not think that this was because we wanted to venture immediately into Puccini or Verdi territory. It might have been a mistake labelling *Evita* thus, laying us open to charges of pretentiousness, and risking alienating vast swathes of the record-buying public, but we had wanted to avoid the by now fatally dated handle 'rock opera' and felt that 'musical' was not strictly accurate until a live version existed. Anyway, technically *Evita* was an opera in that every word was sung.

So Lord Harewood, Michael White and Ronnie Neame missed out. Robert wondered how we could ever have doubted his passionate desire to produce *Evita* and Hal Prince, repestered, got the gig. The great man was not available for a while, so we had to pencil in summer 1978 for the London opening. This would however give us plenty of time to get everything right, although, as David Land never tired of pointing out, we had already got most things in place – the world's top musical director, a highly successful producer, a hit score and a great leading lady. Surely Julie Covington would not be able to resist?

Chapter Twenty-eight

Julie was certainly able to resist, and did so. It took a long time before we believed that she truly wanted nothing to do with the stage show of *Evita*. The album (and Julie's single) had become big UK hits at the very beginning of 1977, followed quickly by a Top Twenty entry for Barbara Dickson's 'Another Suitcase In Another Hall'. Surely by then Julie would have seen the folly of her ways – perhaps she was just playing hard to get in order to improve her deal. We worried that eighteen months down the line the country's enthusiasm for *Evita* might have long since passed, but there really seemed no serious alternative to Hal as director. Robert Stigwood appeared to be happy to wait, confident that he could keep the pot boiling until the middle of the following year, by which time the entire population would be standing in line to see the show. I was not so sure, especially after we were unable to persuade Julie Covington to play Eva Peron.

However I never lost much sleep about all this in the early days of 1977 because I was as happy as Larry with every other aspect of my existence. Life at Romeyns Court continued idyllically. On 27 March Jane gave birth to our second child, a boy. Once again she did the decent thing and kept me away from the nitty-gritty of birth, this time by calling me at home and telling me the arrival was due three hours later than it actually was. When I drove to the hospital in Oxford, expecting another spot of corridor-pacing, I found my son was already two hours old. Wanting a Scottish, but not too Scottish, name, we took a while to settle upon Donald (appropriate too in that three of my greatest heroes were called Donald – Bradman, Everly and Duck), and added Alexander and Hugh in tribute to his grandfathers, both going strong at that stage, with my father's career at last back on the rails. In 1976 he and my mother had moved to Amman, Jordan, where he had taken up a post as industrial advisor to the Ministry of Overseas Development, attached to the Embassy. They were to spend four very happy years in Jordan.

Jane and I went out there to see them and quickly realised why my parents were so enthusiastic about a still strangely underrated country as far as tourism was concerned. Jordan should be high on any traveller's wish list, but I should not have gone there with an Israeli stamp in my passport. Only my father's British Embassy connections got me in and I had to be issued with a second passport. Petra is of course the jewel in Jordan's crown, but there is so much more of the country that hosted Lawrence of Arabia's greatest military strategic triumph, the wresting of the port of Aqaba from the Ottomans at the time of the Great War. The majestic Wadi Rum, a vast, silent landscape of ancient river-beds and pastel-coloured stretches of sandy desert, where we slept under the stars ... Jerash, one of the world's best-preserved Graeco-Roman cities ... Petra itself, the unique, fabulous, breathtaking, 2000-year-old rock-carved city, the pink and salmon capital of the Nabatean Arabs ... but this is turning into a travel brochure. Jordan is also the only place where I have ever seen a dead donkey.

Which is what many in the British theatrical world saw our new show as, in the light of Julie's high-profile indifference. At one point I was instructed by my *Evita* partners to take her out to a slap-up dinner and do almost anything to lure her into the part. Jane wished me well as I set off from Romeyns Court with the feeling that I had a wife's permission to turn on whatever dazzling charm I could muster to whatever effect as long as Julie signing as Evita was a by-product. This brilliant plan got off to a faltering start when Julie turned up with an uninvited bloke to join us for dinner – the Irish actor Stephen Rea. I had booked a table for two at Leith's, not the cheapest of joints, and I could sense Mr Rea's disapproval of my extravagant lifestyle before he uttered a word, of which he produced very few during the evening. Oozing

sweaty nervousness rather than irresistible charm, I failed to bring
up the topic of the show until the very end of the meal, by which
time Stephen Rea's word count had risen to about five, plus three
grunts, as he and Julie waded through the *à la carte* and a serious
bottle or two. Finally, as I picked up the lethal tab, I blurted out
the *raison de diner*:

'Er – any chance you might like to play Evita?'

'No thanks.'

And that was it. A dismal failure that did my reputation as a
charmer, or, more likely, smooth-talking bastard, no good at all.

But in the end Julie turning down the part was the biggest single
publicity boost anyone contributed to the show from start to finish.
To start with, the press had a field day, or month, implying that
everything was going wrong. 'The Eva Peron industry has been
dealt a bitter blow . . .' opined the *Evening Standard*, and the
Daily Express plastered her final refusal over their front page with
an interview on page three revealing why she had turned down
the chance to be a 'top world star' (thus unintentionally showing
that the paper reckoned that whoever took the lead role would
become internationally famous). Their story quoted Julie under
the headline 'Why I Don't Want To Cry For Argentina' (already
that song title had become a catch phrase, a cliché) as saying she
had 'thought about the offer to play Eva Peron very seriously' but
'my attitude to work is hypercritical. I didn't want to get involved
in a long running production that would stop me from doing other
things'. We were slightly surprised that the anti-publicity freak
Julie had confessed all to the *Express* but on closer inspection,
the 'revelation' looked like an interview about her latest single
(a cover of an excellent Alice Cooper song 'Only Women Bleed')
during which she found the reporter only interested in *Evita*. The
paper announced too that Andrew was now appealing to opera
singers to try for the part!

Why did Julie turn us down? I am sure that she was telling
the truth when she spoke of concerns about long runs and of
being swamped by a show that already threatened to become
a media circus; I also think she might not have felt she was
physically capable of reproducing her album vocal gymnastics on
stage every night. And then maybe she just didn't like the piece

enough, possibly for political reasons, possibly because she now saw it as nothing more than a commercial extravaganza.

From this distance, I don't blame Julie at all, although ironically it was in no small part her talent that made the piece commercial. Even the greatest Evitas over the years have struggled to sing the show every night of the week for a long run, and most major professional productions now split the role between two actresses (not on the same night). Julie wrote a very sweet letter to Bob Swash of the Stigwood Organisation in August 1977 saying that she 'did not make the decision about Evita lightly and I will follow the production's progress and eventual success (that's without a doubt) with pride and a lot of care'. She did eventually agree to appear as Eva on stage – in Australia, in the late Eighties – but having flown 12,000 miles pulled out at the last minute. This was however simply because of her dissatisfaction with aspects of the production, a view subsequently justified when this particular revival of the work failed with a high-profile replacement. Julie ain't daft.

After the story of our rejection by Miss Covington had worn a bit thin, the press, realising that we were still going to proceed with the show, turned to a somewhat more positive 'Who will be Evita?' theme. Gradually we realised that this was a story that would do us nothing but good, as long as we found somebody talented enough in the end. The search for Evita began to match David O. Selznick's epic quest for a Scarlett O'Hara in MGM's *Gone With The Wind* – would we be able to find our Vivien Leigh?

The identity of the leading actress was of course not the only problem we faced as the battalions were assembled for *Evita* in London. Gradually the Robert Stigwood Organisation began to put together all of the many elements. Robert was in the middle of an incredible roll. Not only was he still raking in worldwide income from *Superstar* in all its forms, the Bee Gees – Stigwood-managed artists – had exploded into even bigger record stars than they had been first and second time around via their brilliant soundtrack for *Saturday Night Fever* – a Stigwood film. His record label, RSO, was not only scoring with the Brothers Gibb, with both old-timers Bee Gees and younger teen idol Andy, but with a rehabilitated Eric Clapton and our own Yvonne Elliman. Would that we had owned a part of her work in 1978. Even lesser acts, such as Player and Rick Dees, took the Stigwood logo to the top of the charts around the world and a fantastic streak for the Stigwood empire climaxed with Robert's 1978 movie version of *Grease* from which spun huge record sales via Olivia Newton-John and John Travolta.

It was amazing that Robert had time for *Evita* at all, but he had a strong team operating at his Brook Street HQ, making his own day-to-day involvement unnecessary, which was just as well. Robert had the constitution of an ox on steroids and, while burning the candle at both ends in both hemispheres, somehow kept brilliant tabs on everything. This hands-off approach meant that we were still teasing Robert two weeks after opening night that he would love the second act if he ever had time to see it – the second act of *Superstar* that is.

The executive producer of *Evita* was Bob Swash, who had somehow survived holding the same position on *Jeeves*, and he ran a tight ship. His own personal political leanings were somewhat to the left of Tony Benn, so it was ironic that he should work so hard and so well for a show with an extremely right-wing heroine and two writers who were not known for their revolutionary tendencies. Bob was ruthless in denying even the humblest actor or behind-the-scenes worker a penny more than he or she was entitled to, and his efficient dedication to the cause played a major part in the ultimate mega-success of the enterprise, a capitalist venture if ever there was one.

Robert secured the Casino Cinema in Old Compton Street for *Evita*. This fine house had started life as the Prince Edward Theatre, and then switched to being a cinema for many years, though the odd theatrical production such as a flop musical about James Dean had enjoyed or endured a limited run between the films. Bernard Delfont owned the Casino and he agreed to an absolutely essential radical refurbishment (and a reversion back to the theatre's original name). In September 1977, the opening was provisionally set for 15 June 1978. This meant that final rehearsals would begin at the end of April. The off-stage creative team gradually fell into place – the American Larry Fuller as choreographer, the British team of Timothy O'Brien and Tazeena Firth as designers of both set and costumes, David

Hersey the lighting, Anthony Bowles the principal musical director.

Hal was able to find the time on two or three occasions to nip over to London for three or four days of relentless auditions during the autumn and early winter of 1977. We saw literally hundreds of actors of enormous variation in talent and renown and although the press seemed only to be interested in who would play the title role, we were acutely aware of how difficult several other casting decisions would be. The ludicrous attention paid to the auditions even rattled the vastly experienced and normally laid-back Hal, who could not understand why banks of photographers lurked outside the stage door during auditions, snapping every young lady that emerged. Andrew and I found it annoying and distracting, but understandable because of the record's success and the Covington factor, neither of which mattered a hoot in Hal's home town. We were already getting concerned that the build-up to the show was getting out of control and that whatever the final product was like, it and, above all, the poor actress who got the part, could never live up to the hype. The prospect of another nine months of manic press attention, little of it accurate, depressed us enormously and we even contemplated employing a press agent to keep us *out* of the papers, which would have been a West End show-biz first. The show's publicist, the redoubtable Genista Streeton, had a mixed blessing of a job but securing column inches was not one of her problems.

As dozens of potential Evitas trooped across the stage we gradually whittled them down to around twenty or so, without any rock-solid feeling that within that bunch was the lady we were searching for. Every few days someone would ask whether it was worth one more try with Julie Covington. The hopefuls nearly all sang 'Don't Cry For Me Argentina', whose five-minute-plus length Andrew and I now heartily regretted. But slowly some other gaps were filled. Hal felt that the only other star of the record he was inclined to go with would be Tony Christie as Magaldi, but Tony did a Julie, doubtless feeling happier singing twenty songs a night in Sheffield rather than just one and a half in the West End. Hal thought Paul Jones too young and slim for Peron, and though moved by the vocal brilliance of Colm Wilkinson, he was visually not the Che he had in mind. The perfect Peron hove into view in the shape of the well-known and experienced Joss Ackland; the young unknown Mark Ryan was snapped up as Magaldi after a powerful audition; the even younger Siobhan McCarthy was cast as Peron's mistress after a very delicate audition.

On the money side the Stigwood empire had little difficulty in raising the finance for the show. The initial capitalisation for the show was £400,000 (it eventually went about ten per cent over budget), a hefty sum in 1977, but chicken-feed compared with the ludicrous sums musicals cost today. The top ticket price was £6 and investors were invited to punt in bundles of £500. The potential maximum weekly take at the Prince Edward was around £55,000 and weekly costs estimated at £30,000. As long as the show sold out each week, all production costs would be recouped within six months. (It did and they were.) Andrew and I were to receive 3.75 per cent of the box-office take (i.e. around £1925 per week) each until the show recouped, and then five per cent (i.e. around £2750 per week) each. This was a pretty good royalty, although twenty-five per cent of it went straight back to Robert and David as our managers. This would have been £1375 per week approximately, once we were on five per cent. By then of course the Stigwood Organisation and the paid-back investors would be sharing the £25,000 or so weekly profit. The investors got sixty per cent and the producers forty per cent – another £10,000 a week for the RSO. Everyone's income, in cash terms, kept rising throughout the eight-year run, as inflation roared onwards, raising ticket prices many times over. All these numbers would be multiplied by at least ten, maybe fifteen today.*

By the beginning of 1978, the mighty *Evita* machine was lumbering forward towards the first full company rehearsal date of 28 April, with reasonable efficiency and calm, despite the absence of one or two crucial cogs, such as the identity of the two leading performers. Eva-wise, one or two serious contenders had emerged from the late 1977 auditions, and these were asked to return for what had to be the final selection process in February. We really

---

* I managed to secure a few investment parcels for close family and friends and the final outcome for these lucky intimates was a return of investment a dozen times over, unlike the close-run thing my syndicate went through on Broadway with *Superstar*.

had seen hundreds of candidates, including several established names, but the extraordinary vocal demands of the part, not to mention the physical qualifications (not too tall, not too old, as Eva was a teenager for a fair chunk of the first act) eliminated many a lady with a respectable track record and many more without. One fairly well-known and very talented actress turned up for her first audition, word and note perfect for every song in the show, in full Eva Peron bejewelled garb and thus did us all a favour in showing that the sight of Evita on stage in all her finery would be a very exciting one. However she probably did herself no favours by revealing all her cards too soon, peaking too early. At subsequent call-backs, she seemed to have nothing new to offer, while those who began less confidently tended to grow in our estimation. Perhaps the lesson is not to be too good at the first audition.

Hal had the notion that an American actress he had worked with could be the answer to our Eva crisis, and although none of the Brits in the team were that keen to hand over the plum British-written musical role of the decade to a foreigner, let alone an unknown one, we all trooped over to Chicago to see a lady named Bonnie Schon in a Sondheim compilation show. She was young, maybe around twenty-five, a little stocky perhaps, but a good singer, technically almost perfect. We didn't say yes, we didn't say no, but Hal felt that if no one we all loved materialised in London, Bonnie would certainly be up to the job.

Obviously not totally stressed by the casting crisis, Jane and I went off to the Far East and Australia in January for three weeks, because I had been invited to participate as a Distinguished Guest at the Sydney International Theatre Arts Forum. I had longed to have an excuse to return Down Under since my *Superstar* visit in 1972, and needed little persuasion to accept the freebie air fares and hotel room. Travelling first-class has been the one extravagance I have consistently succumbed to since having a few bob. Most of the time I regard it as a necessity rather than a luxury, so I waived the modest fee offered in favour of an upgrade and we decided to stop off in Singapore and then Bali for two mini-holidays. In wildly contrasting ways, both destinations enthralled us.

In Bali we tooled around on motorbikes, my second serious

venture ever as driver of such a machine, the first being back in 1961 when I had serenely cruised into a post on Adam Diment's farm. Jane was of course a biker supreme and I soon became mildly competent. We were both mystified by the initial instructions given to us by the hirer who told us never to fuck in the middle of the road – something that we had not planned on, however romantic the Indonesian island atmosphere became. Some time later we deduced that we had misunderstood his pronunciation of the word 'park'.

I am still not quite sure exactly what the overall concept or indeed status of this Oz festival was, but our part of it was very hospitably and jovially run by a robust poet named Amy Cumpston. My fellow British Distinguished Guests were the director Wendy Toye, songwriter and record producer Norman Newell, composer Stephen Oliver and music publisher Richard Toeman. I barely knew any of them beforehand, but we all bonded (a term unknown in 1978) like leeches and spent almost the entire fortnight in each other's company, even to the extent of sharing forum time.

The original idea was that each of us would deliver a solo lecture on our particular area of theatrical expertise, but as none of us really felt we had enough of gripping interest to hold an audience's attention for more than a few minutes, and as we were enjoying each other's company so much, we asked Amy if we could pool our lecture time and all appear together five times over. This worked a treat and we built up various running gags and almost knockabout routines during our existence as a five-strong panel, answering questions and even dispensing the odd word of wisdom. Frankly, attendance was sparse, but the few were always well-informed about matters theatrical and their appreciation considerable. There were several other events vaguely connected with the Forum, such as the obligatory cruise around Sydney Harbour, and lunches and dinners at which Mr and Mrs Gough Whitlam seemed permanent fixtures. I touched base with a few of my old *Superstar* pals such as Jim Sharman and Kate Fitzpatrick and for the second time was totally won over by all things Oz, as was Jane on her début there.

For me it was a particular thrill to get to know Norman Newell, the producer of so many pop hits of my younger days, notably the

Russ Conway piano smashes, many of Shirley Bassey's power ballads and Peter and Gordon's 'World Without Love'. Norman was
also a prolific and internationally known lyric writer – 'Portrait
Of My Love' (Matt Monro), 'Romeo' (Petula Clark) and 'More'
(nearly everyone) – and a funny, gentle man. The member of the
panel I was to get to know best of all in subsequent years was the
young and hilariously outrageous opera composer Stephen Oliver,
with whom I was to write a musical in 1982–3, *Blondel*, Stephen's
one venture down-market.

I came back from Australia bristling with fitness and eager to
get back into the *Evita* fray. But the joy of being reunited with our
children at Romeyns Court on a cold, crisp Oxfordshire morning
and my excitement at getting back to work on another possible
hit were dealt a body blow within minutes of arriving home. As
per usual after a longish trip abroad, a vast quantity of mail
had accumulated during my absence, most of which did not
scream 'Open me'. But I spotted that two envelopes sported the
unmistakable hand of Alan Doggett, dated a week apart, and as I
hadn't heard a great deal from old Dogwash lately, opened them in
chronological order. The first was an amusing plea for the chance
to earn a small royalty from certain work he was still doing with his
boy choirs on *Joseph*. This not unreasonable request was rendered
academic when I read the second Doggett epistle. It was a suicide
note. In part it read:

> We all have to sail our own ship through life and this ship
> has capsized. No one could have helped, it was my destiny.
> Pray for me, my parents, family and friends. The way I
> have chosen, the way of the Greeks, though hard, is best.
> I am sorry I have not completely lived up to it.

Almost before I was absolutely certain that this was indeed
Alan's final communication David Land called, spent half a second
welcoming me home and then gave me the tragic low-down. Allegations of impropriety with young boys had apparently surfaced
(not for the first time), Alan had been arrested and charged,
whereupon he wrote a goodbye letter to several close friends and
threw himself in front of a train.

I say 'not for the first time' but I cannot believe that Alan was truly a danger, or even a minor menace, to the many boys he had worked with over the years. The only previous time in ten years that Andrew and I had come across such rumours concerning Alan, the allegations were proven to be exactly that, as the time and place of the supposed transgression clashed precisely with a recording date at which all three of us were continually present. It has been known for young boys, and more commonly their parents, to manufacture or exaggerate incidents when they know and (understandably) disapprove of a teacher's inclinations. I am certainly not saying that this was the case with the circumstances that led to Alan's awful end, or that Alan was squeaky clean throughout his musical dealings with his singers. However I suspect that there was a lot less to the cause of his tragedy than met the eye – just enough to render him incapable of facing the humiliation and shame that he knew he had brought upon himself. It was hard for me to believe that Alan, working with boys so closely for so many years, could have got away with any such behaviour for so long without being caught and hard to speak about him at his funeral, which I readily agreed to do. He played a crucial part in Andrew's and my success, was an excellent choirmaster, and was never less than a highly amusing and generous companion.

The show must go on, and frankly very few members of the by now vast *Evita* team had been particularly close to Alan in any event. I still found time for extra-curricular activities in that towards the end of 1977 I had rather pompously and overambitiously formed a record production company, Heartaches Records Ltd, with my financial friend Michael Campbell-Bowling. This was in part a reaction to Andrew's great success with his *Variations*, an instrumental work for cello and rock band written for his brother. The album of the piece had been a huge hit in the UK and one of the principal themes remains unavoidably high profile to this day as the signature tune for Melvyn Bragg's longrunning *South Bank Show* on television. I was slightly miffed by one newspaper interview Andrew gave when plugging *Variations*, during which he described me as lazy, from which I inferred that he felt he had more or less been forced to write an instrumental work as I had no inclination to come up with any new ideas.* True, I hadn't had a fourth world-beating idea for a show in the past four years, and I felt that making sure the third idea worked out should take precedence over any brand-new mega-projects, but composers never really appreciate that lyrics take longer to write than tunes and that words can rarely be transferred from one show to another if they do not work in their first incarnation. Would the lyrics of 'Don't Cry For Me Argentina' have worked in *The Lion King*? I think not, but the tune could have.

Anyway, *Variations*, complete with the odd melody from *The Likes Of Us*, was a smash in Great Britain and Heartaches Records released two pop singles. Both were by Hal Prince rejects – one Colm Wilkinson's recording of his own song 'Born To Sing' which had been chosen to represent Ireland in the Eurovision Song Contest that year, the other a weird idea of mine to rearrange a Sex Pistols song to sound like an easy-listening ballad, which appealed to Paul Jones. Colm's song was just about OK by Eurovision Standards but not a world-beater – unless he fluked a win in the actual contest. Michael Campbell-Bowling and I nipped over to Paris to cheer the Irish entry on. Colm sang with enormous gusto but was drawn to go on first and by the time the votes came in at the end of an evening that seemed to have lasted a week his gallant emoting had been long forgotten east of Dublin. Those formidable Europeans, the Israelis, won with the excruciating 'A Ba Ni Bi'. Colm's single didn't even make much noise in Ireland.

The tracks we recorded with Paul Jones were more interesting. Paul and I wrote a couple of songs together, both blues-based, called 'No Chicken' and 'Loose Change', and also recorded a cover of the wonderful Bob Dylan saga 'Lily, Rosemary And The Jack Of Hearts' which, being around ten minutes long, was probably not the wisest choice of material for a pop single in 1978. The two tracks that were clearly the most commercial were the sophisticated, beautifully orchestrated (by my old Norrie Paramor colleague, Nick Ingman) versions of two punk hits 'Pretty Vacant' by the Sex Pistols and 'Sheena Is A Punk Rocker' by the Ramones.

---

* The fact that *Variations* largely consisted of old ALW tunes or re-workings of Paganini rubbed salt into the wound. I do concede, however, that *Variations* was a wizard wheeze and a fine album.

These were released with a modicum of fanfare by Polydor, the major label lumbered with the Heartaches deal, but despite picking up a few good reviews and a little airplay, the single did not sweep all before it. I'm afraid I quickly lost interest in Heartaches Records – *Evita* was simply claiming too much time.

The search for Eva was narrowing down to the final few suspects. One petite lady who had impressed everyone more and more every time she was called back was a fireball named Elaine Paige. At her first audition she sang Paul McCartney's 'Yesterday' quite beautifully, scoring points for not giving us the seventeenth version of 'Argentina' that day. Next time she had to sing some of the *Evita* score and it was quickly obvious that the extremely testing vocal range of the part was well within her capabilities. So was her ability to hit the back row of the circle with a full, sweet and mighty sound. Could she act? What had she been in before? No one could remember, so the tone of her response to the latter question was justifiably earthily aggressive – she had served time in *Superstar* for a year. More important, she had had a major role in the John Barry-Don Black musical *Billy*, playing opposite Michael Crawford. All research we undertook re that assignment produced favourable reports about the feisty Ms Paige. Elaine was actually then going through a rather quiet period (naturally, she did not go on about this) and had recently accepted a part in *Confessions of a Plumber's Mate* (she did not drop that into the conversation either).

Elaine gradually moved all other local opposition aside. I was convinced she could be a superb Eva and was certain that her initials, E.P., were a good omen. Julie Covington, after all, had the initials of our previous leading character. Most of the rest of our side were in agreement, notably Bob Swash, who reckoned she would be extremely cheap to sign on. He was unmoved by my suggestion that his natural inclination to support the downtrodden masses should lead him to be generous with the chequebook. However, one man remained to be convinced, a bloke with considerable clout – Hal.

Hal insisted that we see Bonnie Schon again and that we should fly her over to England so that everyone could judge her up against Elaine in a final head-to-head showdown, which looked as if it could end up with arm-wrestling. The two ladies would obviously not actually sing on stage together, but our American leader was confident that the close proximity of one performance to another would clinch the deal for his countrywoman. So Robert Stigwood (or, more accurately, his show's investors) forked out for Bonnie to come to London.

Elaine and Bonnie were each booked to do their thing on the Prince Edward stage one more time, in front of a serious array of judges, all of them biased along national lines, everyone pretending that the only thing that mattered was the talent. In the final analysis this is, I guess, true but we Brits all knew that Elaine was easily up to the job and Bonnie would have to be streets and streets ahead to make us vote in her favour – that is if we had votes anyway. We didn't tell Hal this in so many words. He presumably felt the same in reverse. I was worried that Hal might simply force the issue the way he wanted it and even more worried that Andrew was not totally convinced by Elaine and might eventually go for Bonnie in deference to the infallible Broadway icon.

After both actresses had given their all, it quite genuinely seemed to me that it was no contest. Bonnie was technically fine, but seemed a little lacking in confidence, no doubt largely as a result of playing away from home. Elaine seemed to me to have a much better understanding of the complexity of the character, that Eva was not just a fascist glamour-puss, had more subtlety in her every move and inflexion, and above all had one of the most crucial Evita characteristics in spades – she was sexy. Bonnie did nothing wrong, but nothing brilliant; I felt very sorry for her struggling to do herself justice in such an alien environment. After Bonnie's performance, no one said anything for several moments. No one wanted to question Hal's judgement until Tim O'Brien, the show's designer, broke the silence with a gentle comment that Bonnie's journey was really rather a waste of money. Then we all chipped in with pro-Elaine views. I think Hal saw the writing on the wall there and then, but Andrew and I had previously agreed that in addition to the Prince Edward auditions we would see both girls, just the two of us, round Andrew's piano to make absolutely sure that the composer in particular was confident the score was not beyond the singer.

Bonnie gave a much better account of herself in Andrew's

drawing room, but so did Elaine, who charmed both of us with her humour, professionalism and a strange combination of sparky confidence and self-deprecating modesty. Bonnie was without doubt a gifted singer and actress, but not in the mould that immediately struck home with our very English sensibilities. We were pretty sure she would figure in American productions of *Evita*, if these ever happened, and could at least tell her so with clear consciences. As soon as Elaine left Andrew's flat, we called Hal to say it had to be her and Hal bowed to the inevitable. It did not strike us strongly enough at the time, but we soon realised, as *Evita* excitement, hype and anticipation exploded, that it would have been a public relations disaster for me and Andrew if this once-in-a-lifetime role had not gone to a British actress. We were so lucky in that we stumbled across the best British musical actress of her generation just when she was ready to tackle that role.

Bonnie sent us a most gracious card when she returned home, wishing us nothing but the best and telling us how much she appreciated the attention we gave her in London. It was a most charming thing for her to do and I wrote back saying, truthfully, that she had 'a magnificent voice and stage presence, but you were inevitably at a disadvantage up against British performers, when almost everyone involved had a very British view of how the show should be'.

We seemed to be heading up another serious cul-de-sac as far as the second most important part was concerned, for having rejected Colm, no remotely plausible alternative applied. It was Jane who suggested David Essex. The actor/singer who had first made his mark in *Godspell* had since gone on to become a hugely successful pop star, while still maintaining impressive acting credentials via such movies as *That'll Be the Day* and *Stardust* (both scripted by my old chum from the *Evening Standard*, Ray Connolly). Hal was not over-familiar with David's work but it took only a short meeting, at which I felt David was auditioning us, for Hal to declare that David Essex was the man for Che. David wanted to be Che, but, as an established star, he did not need the role. Bob Swash got ready for a stretch of serious negotiation with David's capitalist management.

Eventually, deals were done with both Elaine's and David's

representatives. David had a dream contract, to which his star status fully entitled him, specifying top billing and a mere five-and-a-half months' commitment to the show, which meant he would probably leave before the investors got their money back. We naturally wanted him for a year, nine months at least, but were not in a position to insist, with the opening night, now fixed for 21 June, rushing towards us at an alarming rate. David also got a percentage of the box office which must have made him the highest-paid actor in the West End at the time; he was to earn around twelve times as much per week as Elaine, who signed on for a year and at a weekly starting rate of £400. Separate press receptions were given to announce each of the two major signings – there was much more interest in who was to play Evita than Che.

Chapter Twenty-nine

There is no question that Hal Prince did a terrific job with *Evita*. He was of course, I arrogantly believe, handed a pretty good new piece to direct. While a bad director can fatally damage a good play or musical (otherwise, every production of *Hamlet* would be a success) the greatest director in the world will struggle if the basic material isn't good enough. Hal himself has had a few turkeys over the years, both before and since *Evita*, and his rare failures, such as *Grind*, a grisly show I sat through for some reason in Baltimore, were generally not his fault – apart from the fact that he made the crass error of taking on the job in the first place. But a good director can afford a *Grind* or two. His disasters are usually forgotten much more quickly than a writer's, and the move on to a new project is much easier than it is for a writer. I doubt whether any writer in the theatre, particularly in the musical theatre, has ever opened four or five major shows in a year as a director often has. Am I saying that I rate writers as a more rare and valuable breed than directors? I cannot possibly comment.

So the director's first task is to get signed up to direct a decent work, be it old or new, play or musical. As far as musicals are concerned, he then has to make sure that those who will fill the most crucial posts in the enterprise are spot on – the choreographer, the designers of sets and costumes, the performers – one major error in these three most vital areas and all will go under. There are dozens of other aspects of a production both on the business and artistic sides that are almost as important.

If the director (with or without his producer's help) gets enough of these personnel choices wrong, here too he is doomed. Next, he has to unite all the various personalities – turn a collection of rampant egomaniacs into a tightly knit team, side before self, dedicated to the success of the project. This is easier to achieve when an original album of the score has been a huge hit and every newspaper in the land is pumping up the show to be the musical landmark of its time. No one wants to rock the boat of success. Hal Prince's team was superbly chosen. Almost everyone involved was at their peak and I am inclined to think that hardly anyone involved has done anything better since. Finally, the director actually has to direct the whole shooting match, shift the actors around in decent frocks without knocking over the furniture, as has been so memorably said so many times.

As we knew from his July 1976 letter to us, Hal wanted to make a few changes to our score. First to go was the distracting sub-plot about Che the wannabe fly-killing mogul. He insisted on presenting Che as Guevara rather than as an anonymous Argentine who could have been Che Guevara but equally Che Sidebottom. Musically, he requested a replacement for the out-and-out rock number, Che's 'The Lady's Got Potential', which would automatically ditch quite a bit of the insecticide plot, with a new number for Peron. But his proposals for alterations were not drastic, and we agreed with most of them. I am sure there were plenty of musical cutbacks and switches which Andrew might not have been wild about (Hershy Kay was once again brought in to tinker with the orchestrations, but in a fairly humble capacity), just as there were one or two lyric changes which seemed annoyingly pointless to me; but only somebody very familiar with the original album would have noticed any difference between what was heard on the record and what was heard on stage.

We were quite happy to write a new song for Peron, even though my 'greatest social climber since Cinderella' line was a feature of the song it replaced. I nicked the title of Rab Butler's recent memoirs, *The Art Of the Possible*, for the new scene, the art in question being politics. Andrew came up with a creepy, polished tune of highly appropriate menace. The scene depicted Peron and his fellow officers suspiciously jostling against each other in a power struggle within the military government and was eventually quite brilliantly staged by Hal as a game of musical rocking chairs, which Peron of course won.

> One has no rules, is not precise
> One rarely acts the same way twice
> One spurns no device
> Practising the art of the possible
> One always picks the easy fight
> One praises fools, one smothers light
> One shifts left to right
> It's part of the art of the possible

Words that seem strangely appropriate in New Labour's Britain in 1999.

I enjoyed adding two extra verses to 'The Money Kept Rolling In' – now sung by Che, rather than the unimportant Foundation Director, as on the album – which enabled me to get a reference to the Perons' Swiss banking activities:

> When the money keeps rolling in what's a girl to do?
> Cream a little off the top for expenses, wouldn't you?
> But where on earth can people hide their little piece of heaven?
> Thank God for Switzerland . . .

A couple of spoken speeches for Che were inserted, one depicting the British-influenced Argentine aristocracy at play at a polo match, another a tirade against Peron as his regime collapses economically and morally. In general Hal was anxious to emphasise the murkier side of the Perons more than he felt we had done on the album and most of the lyrical changes were to this end. This process was taken a stage further a year later for Broadway – a little too far in New York, I thought, but for London the balance between the enticing glamour and the vicious ambition was just about right.

I was sorry to see Eva's Sonnet truncated to become Eva's Six-fourteenths-of-a-Sonnet, together with the loss of one or two other lines from the final lengthy bedroom scene between Peron and Eva, and I also lost the battle to keep 'Why go bananas/chasing Nirvanas?' replacing them with 'So what are my chances/of honest advances?' And of course the wrecking of the Lament, described three chapters back, was a cock-up which I should have resisted. But, by and large, Hal's suggestions did wonders for the flow of the piece and for its chances of being understood clearly by the many who still knew next to nothing of the heroine or her land.

The early meetings we had with Hal, long before the cast and indeed the backstage team were assembled, were all very exciting as we could tell that our project was in the hands of a master of his art. I cannot recall as much about the first creative get-together as I should because it took place on a hot summer's day in Andrew's Eaton Place flat and my concentration on the matter in hand was diverted by an attractive young lady on the balcony in the flat across the road sunbathing topless. Luckily the only chaps facing the window were David Land and myself, and we kept quiet about the view in case more dedicated theatricals suggested a move to the kitchen away from distractions. Tim and Tazeena's early drawings and models were superb. The only slightly worrying aspect of the very early plans was that Hal seemed determined to have three actresses playing the part of Evita, each portraying a different stage of her life. The thinking behind this was in part brought about by the fact that we had found no one capable of taking on the entire gargantuan role but it seemed to me that this would only triple our Eva casting crisis and make it hard for the audience to identify closely, pro or anti, with the leading character. Fortunately this idea soon went the way of all flesh, and like the flesh of the topless sunbather, never intruded into subsequent conferences.

When the actual rehearsals began, initially in some rooms at Cecil Sharp House near Regent's Park, with all the re-writes in place, Andrew and I were almost surplus to requirements. I went to the first full company get-together at which everybody introduced themselves to the throng before Hal gave a superb demonstration with a model of Tim and Tazeena's set about what was actually going to happen. I had a chat with David Essex and asked him who his understudy was.

'It doesn't matter,' said David. 'He won't be doing it.'

David never missed a single show and his understudy, Nigel Planer (yes, neil of *The Young Ones*) had to wait until David was long gone before he got his chance to stand in for David's successor, Gary Bond (yes, Joseph).

When I did saunter in to Cecil Sharp House, all seemed to be going like clockwork. The press attention was acute, with the *South Bank Show* hanging around doing a profile of Hal, and Ann Leslie of the *Daily Mail* one of the many journalists in almost permanent attendance. I wondered if some of the ubiquitous hacks were on the payroll. Ann Leslie was not but she wrote two massive articles, very favourable, about the run-up to opening night. Then, as now, she was one of the best journalists in the country, generally these days dealing with more momentous events than musicals. I spent the mornings of the rehearsal period back at Capital Radio. The station had offered me a temporary spell on the air, sitting in for Michael Aspel, who was taking a short break from his morning show, which enabled me to give *Evita* the odd shameless plug. Not that it needed it, as the media interest was insanely high and old worries about the final product not being able to match the hype were constantly surfacing.

As a result of the media overkill, I spent more time with Genista Streeton, our all but redundant publicist (through no fault of her own) and the head honchos of Dewynters, Robert De Wynter and Anthony Pye-Jeary, than with the dedicated company of thespians. Robert and Anthony ran the outfit that has grown staggeringly over the past two decades alongside the explosion of London-based musical theatre. With *Evita*, Dewynters' main responsibilities were the glossy brochures, merchandising (a spin-off still in its infancy in those days) and the advertising campaign. They were also dedicated to a good time and put not a foot wrong socially or professionally. Anthony had worked on *Superstar* as a common or garden publicist, in which capacity he had even managed to get my mother on to the Pete Murray show on Radio Two when she wrote a book on clubs (societies, not weapons) and it was good to see that his elevation to new responsibility, as part of a show-biz partnership on the cutting edge, made no difference whatsoever to his laid-back and boisterous approach to life and love.

The three principals were all living up to our extremely high expectations. The greatest pressure was on Elaine. This was not only because she had the largest part, but because she was the centre of attention and unused to it. Conversely, David was unused to not being the centre of attention. Not that he for one moment complained. The media are always looking for stars on the way up and David Essex having another success was hardly news. Joss seemed a little bewildered by the whole set-up as he confessed many years later in his memoirs, which revealed him not to have been quite as enthusiastic about the piece or his colleagues as we thought at the time. He believed he was the 'only actor' in the show and found the script 'facile'. I wonder why he signed on in the first place. Nonetheless he was nothing less than superb as Peron and charming to boot.

David was so accomplished and charismatic in rehearsals that he inspired one excitable female press person to write a piece stating he was the only good thing in a show that otherwise had very little going for it. As a result of this less than confidence-boosting message for the cast in general, and Elaine in particular, Hal wisely called a meeting at which he rubbished the article and emphatically stated in front of one and all that he had not worked with a female of Elaine's talent since Barbra Streisand. This was a very good move and effectively kicked the blinkered journalist's view into touch.

Promises from Hal to both Elaine and David that they would set Broadway alight soon followed and although Joss was miffed that he didn't seem to have been included in the New York package, this transatlantic confidence expressed by Hal in his two young English stars did a lot for everyone's morale. This sounded like action speaking louder than words – if Elaine and David were Broadway-bound at the behest of the great Hal Prince, then they were obviously going to take London by storm. They did, but somehow the Broadway promise was spirited away.

In rehearsal, Elaine got better and better. She sung like an angel, with tenderness, anger, power and wit, as required. Scarcely five feet tall, the source of the beautiful noise that she could generate from a tiny frame was inexplicable. I found her too good to watch sometimes, spine-tinglingly irresistible.

Before we played even once in front of a live audience I knew David's Che was all I had wanted and more. His first number, 'Oh

What A Circus', was delivered with a mastery of understatement, leaving himself plenty of places to go as the show and his story progressed. When he sung I always sensed Che's envy of Evita, his determination to outflank her, his admiration and loathing for her, his own vaulting ambition – things I hoped I had written into the part, which David brought brilliantly to the surface.

As the first preview drew nearer, even events way beyond our control seemed to be conspiring to draw attention to *Evita*. The World Cup was taking place in Argentina, which inevitably the host nation went on to win, enabling more than one imaginative sub-editor to use our show's best-known song as the banner headline on the sports pages of the national press. There was even a horse called Evita, and that won a couple of races. The fashion world, never one which has ever held me in more than the most tenuous thrall, went to town with Eva Peron-inspired collections. Cover versions of many of the numbers from the show began to crawl on to the market, nearly all at the Musak end of things, rather too many by obscure German organists and pipe bands. David Essex made by far the biggest contribution to the show in this department by recording 'Oh What A Circus' and 'High Flying Adored' as a pop single, under the outstanding production and arrangement supervision of Mike Batt. Released soon after the show opened, it was one of the biggest hits even he had had for a while.

It was an apprehensive but confident company who delivered *Evita* in public for the first time, two weeks before the official opening. We all expected plenty to go wrong, but nothing did. The reaction of the audience (and amazingly the house was not quite full as tickets were only sold or given away at the last minute in case the first preview had had to be cancelled) was so strong that at the post-mortem we all wished it had been the opening night proper. The cast had got all the way back to their dressing rooms, fags lit and bottles broken into, after what they assumed was the final, final curtain call when they realised that the audience was still cheering. They had to return for yet more instalments of a fabulous reception which, because it was not an opening night crowd of investors, relatives, party-goers and sycophants, had to be genuine. It was then we knew that, barring a totally unforeseen disaster or terrorism, we had a hit. The remaining shows between the first preview and the first night were now a frustrating holding period during which it would be difficult for things to get any better.

During the two weeks up until 21 June Andrew and I continued to be in constant media demand. I wrote an article tracing the history of the show's genesis for the *Sunday Times*, or rather gave them the foreword to a book about Evita which I had just completed. I had been approached after the record's success by a young publisher and great fan of *Evita*, Colin Webb of Elm Tree Books, to write a book about both Eva Peron and our show, which would be copiously illustrated and would include all my lyrics. I actually put considerable effort into this, somehow meeting the deadline necessary for the book to be published just as the show opened. I was helped in my research for this by the re-publication of what I consider to be the best biography of Eva Peron ever written – Mary Main's *The Woman With The Whip*. I wish I had discovered Main's work when we were working on *Evita*. Andrew added a chapter about the music. It was a new and satisfying experience to hold in my hands a book I had been responsible for, rather than a record; the book was not a spectacular success but it did lead to a lasting friendship with Colin Webb, with whom I was to establish a new publishing house, Pavilion Books, three years later. Michael Parkinson was also an investor in this venture, which ended in tears in the mid-Nineties.

An ironic result of Evitamania at this time was the emergence of several other books about (or by) the Perons; besides the Mary Main tome, some reprints of long-forgotten works, and many brand new. Whether cheapo cash-ins or allegedly serious studies, none gave our show any credit or, in some cases, even a mention. As the show's fame spread around the globe, more and more books about Evita appeared over the years and every time I would search hopefully for a word or two about *Evita* the show, surely the only reason for the renewed interest in the lady, and thus for the publication of all these books. If there was a reference to us, it was generally less than complimentary, our show dismissed as a wildly inaccurate portrayal of Eva and/or a blatantly money-making exercise. Leaving aside the facts that the show was researched in great detail and at first considered the worst musical idea anyone had had for many a moon, I was by now even more convinced that by far the best way to capture the melodramatic, almost unbelievable, glamorous and ruthlessly populist characteristics of Eva Peron was through the melodramatic, almost unbelievable, glamorous and ruthlessly populist characteristics of a musical.

Hal's show was truly spectacular, which is not the same as being vast and physically overwhelming. The actual set was often nothing more than a bare stage, Tim and Tazeena bringing the Argentina of the time to wonderful life with stunning costumes rather than lumbering mechanics, David Hersey's lighting often a set (or a floor or a wall) on its own, creeping or bounding in from any or all sides, instilling warmth, fear, triumph and doom in endless combinations. The set always served the show, rather than taking over the show (or bringing it to a complete halt), as has so often happened with my subsequent theatrical efforts. So many scenes were quite brilliantly interpreted by Hal and the designers with simple strokes of genius – the revolving doors through which Eva's lovers passed during 'Goodnight And Thank You', the rocking chairs during 'The Art Of The Possible', the bedrooms – the atmospheres within moving from sexually-charged double-bedded bliss to cold hospital-like single beds as the passion died and as the Perons clung to each other through fear of losing power rather than love.

Then there was the first act closer, 'A New Argentina', in which Hal filled the Perons' boudoir with thousands of *descamisados*, carrying placards and flaming torches in an unforgettable call to arms that all but raised the roof, and the scene on the Casa Rosada balcony itself, when Elaine made what Kurt Ganzl's *British Musical Theatre* described as

> an entrance outshining every leading lady entrance ever made. Dressed in a full, bodiced white gown, a perfect recreation of a Dior model, hair pulled back severely from her face, she is far from the little girl of the early scenes, far from the go-getting girl of the first act. She is the first lady of Argentina, and she addresses her public with calculated emotion.

How glad I was when I first saw Elaine captivate an audience with 'Don't Cry For Me Argentina' that we had not cast three women in the one part.

Then there were the small scenes, just as powerful – Peron's mistress's eviction leading to 'Another Suitcase In Another Hall' sung plaintively by Siobhan, with the entire visual back-up being one battered suitcase; Magaldi's tacky nightclub act, and Eva's final broadcast in front of one studio microphone in desperate contrast to her tirade before the hundreds of thousands who had cheered her from the Plaza de Mayo. The choreography, another aspect of musicals that tends to fill me with dread, was so well marshalled by Larry Fuller that one was hardly aware of any movement that did not seem perfectly essential to the story, be it during Eva's celebration of Buenos Aires, or the army's goose-stepping threats to Peron. The final philosophical showdown between Eva and Che as a waltz seemed the most natural interpretation of the clash that could have been devised.

And the cast matched all this. Somehow they managed to keep the adrenalin flowing throughout the two weeks of previews, including several often fairly ghastly charity gala evenings at which a good percentage of the audience was there for the party afterwards. Frenzy mounted; within all nooks and crannies of the press, within and around the Prince Edward, within and around my family and friends. I began to feel strangely immune to the excitement and distanced from the hoopla as 21 June approached, more interested in what would happen (as if I were on the outside looking in) than worried or elated about what was likely to be the biggest and most crucial night of my career. Joss, Elaine and David in turn suffered voice loss panics; the dancers seethed with revolutionary rumblings that they were being made to sing as well as dance and were not being paid as much as the singers – or was it the other way round? Andrew's emotions ran the gamut from pessimism to despair.

My only real worry at this time was getting my hands on enough first night tickets. Three days before the big night Heartaches CC played the forty-ninth match in their by now five-year history; I must have been in relaxed mode about life in general as I scored a quite staggering (for me) twenty-three and took a wicket with the only ball I bowled, leading my side to a big win over Great Haseley, the team up the road from Romeyns Court. I was also putting in quite a bit of work organising the team's first ever tour of Cornwall, which was to take place a month later. Looking back on the summer of 1978, I am not sure which event had a greater long-term effect on my life – the opening night of *Evita* or my first visit to the Duchy since schooldays, which was to lead to many other tours and holidays there and in time to a Cornish home of my own, where I am writing these words.

The big night dawned, to coin a phrase. I ran around backstage dishing out and receiving first-night presents, hugs and kisses, good-luck cards and telemessages (I think telegrams had just about had it by then), checking on the state of mind of the principals, not that I could have done anything about it had any of them had gone AWOL or doolally. They all seemed calm and ready for action, David the coolest of all. His dressing room was always an oasis of space and serenity, in part because it was the only one with any space and partly because he had a handsome hunk of a bodyguard on guard duty outside, to prevent his molestation by fans who got past the stage doorman, or even by fellow members of the cast. The hunk, whose name was John, soon became an even greater backstage object of desire than his boss. The other dressing rooms would have tested the selling powers of a Calcutta estate agent. My own first night present to the cast was surprisingly well-received – musical boxes that played 'Don't Cry For Me Argentina'. With unusual foresight I had commissioned them from a musical box store I had strolled past in New York a few months before and although I can only vouch for one example of the two dozen I ordered, it is beautifully constructed and is still going strong. Not that I play it very often.

The first night came and went; it all went extraordinarily well and the cheering at the end seemed pretty genuine. David Land recorded the applause at the end of the evening for a privately pressed vinyl single which I have played even fewer times than I have the *Evita* musical box. It does prove, however, that we had a mighty powerful and long, positive reception. The first night party was Robert Stigwood at his hospitable best on a boat; eight hundred guests packed the SS *Tattershall Castle* off the Victoria

Embankment and partied like it was 1979. My family, not least my grandmother, had a terrific time and I think I felt most enjoyment through their participation in the celebrations. Dustin Hoffman (who was renewing an intimate acquaintance with Elaine) was the star attraction for the paparazzi – along with Elaine, whose overnight success (which had taken her around fourteen years to achieve) was a media fairytale, consigning the Julie Covington drama to history.

Hal and Elaine had the best of the reviews, the first of which trickled in as the party lurched to its climax, which was to be expected, but in the main the critics were fairly kind all round. Even those who didn't like the show, or us, or even the audience as in the case of the *Financial Times* man,* conceded that something out of the ordinary had happened to British musical theatre:

DON'T CRY FOR ELAINE
SHE'S AN INSTANT SUPERSTAR

yelled the *Sun* on page one.

John Barber, in the *Telegraph*, stated that

> Two stars dominate *Evita*, the extraordinarily successful new musical ... the first is Elaine Paige. She creates a woman at once brassy, steely, tinny – and human ... The second star of *Evita* is an American, Harold Prince, the most gifted director ever to handle a British musical.

The Times went on about a 'Puccini heroine captivated by her own dream', while Arthur Thirkell in the *Daily Mirror* proclaimed that the show was 'as colourful as a building site', but what really mattered was that *Evita* was all over every paper, not just in the arts pages, but in the news pages and gossip pages. We may have had mixed reviews as a show, but as an event we were a hundred per cent hit in every paper.

---

* This was Michael Coveney, who named Hal as the real star of the evening. He particularly bashed the lyrics, but felt that neither I nor Andrew had shown signs of improvement and that the music collapsed in Act Two. Mr Coveney is currently working on an authorised biography of Andrew in which I trust his vigorous views of *Evita* will remain unsullied.

There were some terrible reviews and articles in the pipeline, such as John Elsom's view in *The Listener* that 'With Evita, Tim Rice has supported his already strong claim to be the world's worst lyricist', and Bernard Levin's horrendous (for us) outburst in the *Sunday Times** but we knew by the early hours of the morning that we had done it again. *Evita* was virtually indestructible, just as *Superstar* and *Joseph* had proven to be. Furthermore, we both genuinely felt it to be our most mature and polished work, the most original in style and content. We had well and truly overcome the tag of 'one-hit wonders' and could see no reason why we couldn't go on to become the Gilbert and Sullivan of our time. Ten hit shows at least in the next thirty years! Well, that was what we told each other after a lot of champagne on the SS *Tattershall Castle*.

How lucky can you get? Andrew and I were the acclaimed originators and creators of three incredibly successful musical works, perceived by our peers and by ourselves to be a major theatrical force with a scintillating future. I was wealthy, famous (and in 1978 I still quite liked the idea of being well known), married to a beautiful woman, father of two perfect children, living in a most wonderful home in the heart of the English countryside that I loved; my parents and grandmother around to enjoy and take pride in my good fortune. How could anything go wrong? It did, to put it mildly.

---

* Levin savaged *Evita* a few days later, describing it as 'one of the most disagreeable evenings I have ever spent in my life, in or out of the theatre', nearly ruining my cricket tour to Cornwall when I read his vitriol one Sunday morning in a West Country pavilion. I had always greatly admired him as a columnist, but went off him a bit after that.

Epilogue

I have called a (temporary, anyway) halt to my story at this point, in part because I have gone on long enough for one volume and in part because 21 June 1978 was a watershed in the professional lives of Andrew and me – and in my case, of my personal life as well. Not that I realised this at the time, but a third consecutive musical hit for our partnership meant that, from the opening night of *Evita* onwards, Andrew and I were reassessed by the British entertainment industry and public. Like us or loathe us, we were now a show biz force rather than a fluke. Maybe not quite establishment at this point, but no longer upstart outsiders.

Looking back on how we got there, which is what I have been doing in these pages, I often wonder where we went right. Obviously Andrew had a great gift for melody and I had a feel for a turn of phrase that occasionally amused or intrigued, but so did many others. Our good fortune was that we chose an unusual way of displaying our wares, at least for songwriters starting out in the mid-Sixties when everyone else wanted to be the Beatles. I did too, actually, but Andrew's ambition to write musicals, already long-established when I met him shortly after his seventeenth birthday, distracted me from my futile (and admittedly rather half-hearted) quest to be a teenage idol, and had us operating in an arena where there was less competition. This was a fantastic stroke of luck for me, but on the other hand my unconventional and thus original approach to the theatre, founded on pure ignorance, was the one missing element in his precocious armoury of musical talents.

After *Evita* things changed. Never again was I to write a show without an army of experts telling me how to do it. I even became one of those experts and that was fatal. Despite myself, I began to worry too much about the rules of the game and what critics would say. Most artists in any field create their best work in the early days of their endeavour; originality and hunger for success are two driving forces of inspiration which inevitably lose their power as time goes by. Writers become producers, and while the latter job is usually crucial to a show's success it is one less likely to be the source of something truly barrier-breaking and exciting.

I am today more convinced than ever that the only great musicals are writer-driven rather than producer- or director-driven. A great show also tends to be one that is not expected to be a hit. No one wants to interfere with a project that looks like a flop, which means that the writers will have a clear run at it. The next big thing in musicals will not emerge from the offices of any of the characters who have dominated the genre for the past twenty years – it will be totally unexpected and created by unknown writers who break all the rules that our generation made, the rules by which our generation has been eventually and inevitably stifled, creatively if not economically.

Whether we knew what we were doing or not, Andrew and I effected an important and lasting change in British musical history, and even in world musical history, as writers. After *Evita*, the producer has been king and the only major change has been in the audiences. These have been vastly increased, in traditional musical centres such as London and Broadway, and in new ones such as almost every civilised capital city in the world. This is not because the shows have got better, but because of the huge growth in air travel and communications technology.

As more tourists come to London, so the foyers of the city's theatres bubble with more and more foreign languages. This means that most of the time most of the audience won't have a clue what the words are banging on about – not an encouraging thought for lyricists. Of course with most musicals these days, this does not matter – the sheer spectacle compensates and the basic storyline is pretty obvious. Above all there is little or no spoken dialogue to confuse the non-English-speaking tourist. So, by introducing a new era of popular musicals without books, I have contributed to the downgrading of the importance of lyrics in the contemporary musical – as Homer Simpson would say: 'Doh!'

A big hit musical can now run in London for decades not years, notwithstanding the fact that not too long after opening in London or New York an identical production of the same show will be running in a dozen other countries. Producers now have the technical means (and advance promotion in the form of CDs and television) to reproduce their hits ad infinitum, or at least ad nauseam, around the globe. Merchandising worldwide has now become an effortless seam of further profit. By the end of the Eighties the biggest hits were not so much musicals as multinational corporations.

After *Evita*, Andrew and I never wrote another show together, apart from a twenty-five-minute comic oratorio by royal command in 1986. Over the past twenty years we have otherwise collaborated at the rate of around one song every decade, but even this sluggish turnover won us an Oscar in 1997. In many ways it was a pity that we didn't stay together as a writing team, but I doubt whether we would have written anything better than *Joseph*, *Superstar* or *Evita* and I might never have had the opportunity to work with Alan Menken, Stephen Oliver, Bjorn Ulvaeus, Benny Andersson and Elton John, to name but five.

The bloke who wrote '*Je ne regrette rien*' was barking up the wrong *arbre*. There are lots of things I regret, and re-living the first thirty-three years of my life in this book has all too often reminded me of them. Few, however, are concerned with work. Indeed it would be surprising if this were the case, bearing in mind how well nearly everything went for me from 1965 to 1978. But even when things got considerably less triumphant in the Eighties and Nineties, it was rarely problems with my career that got me down for long.

Inevitably, I feel that there are many aspects of my existence in the period covered by this volume to which I should have given more prominence; many people I should have written about more profusely, many I should have mentioned who do not appear here at all. I have a two-pronged defence: (a) the book is already long enough and (b) there is always part two in which to make amends.

Those not in part one who feel they have a justifiable beef about their omission, please write soonest; likewise those in part one who wish to ensure their absence from part two.

I feel I should have said more about my love of England, about my cricket team, about other sporting ventures such as my disastrous and thankfully brief stretch as a racehorse owner, about Romeyns Court and those who looked after us there – Helen Turner, Kathleen and Harold Skaife, and Mary Anderson; about one of my closest friends from childhood days, Helen Biden – but her story is really for later; and about fellow lyricists and composers who became friends, from the great Sammy Cahn to virtually the entire membership of the Society of Distinguished Songwriters; and more about my brothers and parents*. Above all, more about what I felt and thought than what I did.

But in this part of my life I didn't often stop to feel and think, I just went out and did. The confidence, arrogance and selfishness of young men in a hurry was a big part of the formula for success – so maybe I have managed to represent my early and early-ish years with some accuracy. The time for reflection was, and is, later. In this book I was too busy making it.

---

* Paul Jones wrote and sang a marvellous number on one of his late-Sixties albums entitled 'Tarzan' in which he thanked a long list of childhood heroes from Tarzan to Buddy Holly, Charlie Parker and a 'couple of older women'. I would go along with nearly everyone he mentions plus about another 400 missing from this text.

Appendix

Tim Rice Musical Creations 1965–1978

A. MUSICALS (all written with Andrew Lloyd Webber):

1. THE LIKES OF US (1965–1967)

Musical based on the life of Dr Thomas Barnardo. Book by Leslie Thomas. Never produced.

Sixteen songs recorded on demo album (never issued commercially):

TWICE IN LOVE EVERY DAY
A VERY BUSY MAN
LOVE IS HERE
STRANGE AND LOVELY SONG
THE LIKES OF US
WE'LL GET HIM
A MAN ON HIS OWN
LION HEARTED LAND
YOU CAN NEVER MAKE IT ALONE
WHERE AM I GOING
HOLD A MARCH
YOU WON'T CARE ABOUT HER ANYMORE
GOING GOING GONE
WILL THIS LAST FOREVER
A MAN OF THE WORLD
ANOTHER CUP OF TEA

There were various other songs written for the show and discarded. 'Strange and Lovely Song' was featured by vocal quartet Cantabile in their live performances in the late Eighties. Some of the tunes have resurfaced in subsequent ALW shows.

2. JOSEPH AND THE AMAZING TECHNICOLOR DREAMCOAT

Original Colet Court School version, directed by Alan Doggett (1968):

JACOB AND SONS
JOSEPH'S COAT
JOSEPH'S DREAMS
POOR POOR JOSEPH
CLOSE EVERY DOOR
POOR POOR PHARAOH
SONG OF THE KING
PHARAOH'S DREAMS EXPLAINED
STONE THE CROWS
BACK IN CANAAN (THE BROTHERS COME TO EGYPT)
WHO'S THE THIEF
JOSEPH ALL THE TIME
JACOB IN EGYPT
ANY DREAM WILL DO

Songs added for the original Decca album, produced by ALW and TR (1969):

POTIPHAR
GO GO GO JOSEPH

Songs added for the first West End production, directed by Frank Dunlop and produced by Robert Stigwood (1973):

ONE MORE ANGEL IN HEAVEN
PHARAOH STORY
GROVEL GROVEL
THOSE CANAAN DAYS
BENJAMIN CALYPSO

Versions of 'Any Dream Will Do' (Christopher) and 'Potiphar' (Mixed Bag) with altered lyrics were released in 1969. A Prologue entitled 'You Are What You Feel' was added for the 1982 Broadway production. A song entitled 'I Don't Think I'm Wanted Back At Home', originally written for *Jacob's Journey* (see below) was briefly part of the score in the early Seventies.

There have been many different recordings over the years of the entire score, and of individual songs, notably 'Any Dream Will Do'. The first cover version of this song was by Max Bygraves and was a big hit in Australia in 1970. The first single hit from the score in the UK (a Number One) was in 1991 by Jason Donovan, star that year of the revival at the London Palladium.

In 1973 ALW and TR wrote a piece entitled *Jacob's Journey* with book by Alan Simpson and Ray Galton which accompanied Joseph for a few weeks during the Albery Theatre run. The songs were:

AND DID HE NOTICE ME
SEVEN YEARS
I DON'T THINK I'M WANTED BACK AT HOME
ESAU'S SONG
JACOB'S DREAM
LIMPET IN LOVE
LABAN'S WORKERS' SONG
JACOB HAD GOD ON HIS SIDE

3. COME BACK RICHARD YOUR COUNTRY NEEDS YOU

A musical based on the story of Richard the Lionheart for schools which only received one performance, at the City of London School in 1969, directed by Alan Doggett. It never got beyond the oratorio stage. Songs:

A ROARING START
YOU CAN RELY ON KING RICHARD THE LION
ALL TOO QUIET ON THE HOME FRONT
HELP ME INTO MY ARMOUR (WHAT A DIFFERENCE A KNIGHT MAKES)
VIOLENT INTERLUDE
BERENGARIA
SALADIN DAYS
THE LION IS CAGED
COME BACK RICHARD YOUR COUNTRY NEEDS YOU
SOMEWHERE IN EUROPE
THE LEGEND OF BLONDEL (BLONDEL ON BLONDEL)
BLONDEL'S SONG
THE LEGEND OF BLONDEL PART 2
THE BALLAD OF CHALUZ (I WANT MY HANDS ON YOUR HOLD)

The title song was recorded by Tim Rice and The Webber Group and released as the A side of a single in 1969 (RCA).

4. JESUS CHRIST SUPERSTAR

Songs on the original MCA album, produced by ALW and TR (1970):

OVERTURE
HEAVEN ON THEIR MINDS
WHAT'S THE BUZZ
STRANGE THING MYSTIFYING
EVERYTHING'S ALL RIGHT
THIS JESUS MUST DIE
HOSANNA
SIMON ZEALOTES/POOR JERUSALEM
PILATE'S DREAM
THE TEMPLE
I DON'T KNOW HOW TO LOVE HIM
DAMNED FOR ALL TIME/BLOOD MONEY
THE LAST SUPPER
GETHSEMANE (I ONLY WANT TO SAY)
THE ARREST
PETER'S DENIAL
PILATE AND CHRIST
KING HEROD'S SONG
JUDAS' DEATH
TRIAL BEFORE PILATE
SUPERSTAR
THE CRUCIFIXION
JOHN 19:41

Song added for the Broadway production, directed by Tom O'Horgan, produced by Robert Stigwood (1971) and retained for all subsequent stage shows:

COULD WE START AGAIN PLEASE

'The Trial Before Pilate' and 'Hosanna' were extended considerably for the Broadway show. First London production directed by Jim Sharman, produced by Robert Stigwood (1972).

Song added for the film, directed by Norman Jewison (1973):

THEN WE ARE DECIDED

A version of 'Heaven On Their Minds' with altered lyrics was issued by Murray Head in 1970. I made some minor lyrical changes for the 1996 West End revival and cast album. There have been many different recordings of the entire score over the years, and hundreds of cover versions of individual songs, notably 'I Don't Know How to Love Him', 'Superstar' and 'Could We Start Again Please'. The first two of these songs and 'Everything's All Right' were single hits in 1971 in the US, and many other countries, but never more than minor chart items in the UK. The original album has sold at least 7 million copies to date, at one time allegedly the biggest selling British album ever recorded.

5. EVITA

Songs on the original MCA album, produced by ALW and TR (1970):

A CINEMA IN BUENOS AIRES, 1952
REQUIEM FOR EVITA
OH WHAT A CIRCUS
ON THIS NIGHT OF A THOUSAND STARS
EVA AND MAGALDI
EVA BEWARE OF THE CITY
BUENOS AIRES
GOODNIGHT AND THANK YOU
THE LADY'S GOT POTENTIAL
CHARITY CONCERT/I'D BE SURPRISINGLY GOOD FOR YOU
ANOTHER SUITCASE IN ANOTHER HALL
DANGEROUS JADE (PERON'S LATEST FLAME)
A NEW ARGENTINA
ON THE BALCONY OF THE CASA ROSADA
DON'T CRY FOR ME ARGENTINA
HIGH FLYING ADORED
RAINBOW HIGH
RAINBOW TOUR
THE ACTRESS HASN'T LEARNED THE LINES (YOU'D LIKE TO HEAR)
AND THE MONEY KEPT ROLLING IN (AND OUT)
SANTA EVITA
WALTZ FOR EVA AND CHE
SHE IS A DIAMOND
DICE ARE ROLLING/EVA'S SONNET
EVA'S FINAL BROADCAST
MONTAGE
LAMENT

Song added for the London stage production, directed by Hal Prince, produced by Robert Stigwood (1978):

THE ART OF THE POSSIBLE

'The Lady's Got Potential' was dropped for the stage show, but returned for the film, directed by Alan Parker (1996), which also included a new song 'You Must Love Me', in place of 'Dice Are Rolling/Eva's Sonnet'.

There have been several recordings of the entire score over the years and perhaps even more cover versions of individual songs, notably 'Don't Cry For Me Argentina', than of songs from *Superstar*. Other *Evita* songs to have been multi-covered include 'Oh What A Circus', 'Another Suitcase In Another Hall', 'I'd Be Surprisingly Good For You', 'High Flying Adored' and 'On This Night Of A Thousand Stars'. ('You Must Love Me' has followed suit from 1997 onwards.) 'Don't Cry For Me Argentina' is the most popular song Andrew and I ever wrote together and gave us our first Number One hit in the UK, sung by Julie Covington. However, the first US version of the song to chart was a disco version by an outfit entitled Festival who put out an entire dance album of songs from *Evita*.

Joseph, *Superstar* and *Evita* have been staged in literally dozens of countries since their first appearances, at all levels from school upwards, as often, or more often, in the late Nineties as at any other time.

6. MISCELLANEOUS

The only other theatrically performed songs Andrew and I wrote between 1965 and 1978 were three items for the revue *Hullabaloo*, directed by Frank Dunlop in the West End in 1973:

FIRST IMPRESSION/SECOND IMPRESSION/LAST IMPRESSION COUNTS
THE PEOPLE I'VE SEEN
IT'S A TRIUMPH! – CLIVE BARNES

These were, mercifully, never recorded.

As revealed in Chapter 22, we began to write a musical about Jeeves together, but I abandoned ship after writing no more than a plot outline and words for a couple of songs.

So far, so good. Now for the less glittering side of the Rice catalogue of the period under review:

B. SONGS NOT PART OF A MUSICAL SCORE:

TR lyricist unless stated; only songs that actually escaped into the public domain are listed.

1965
THAT'S MY STORY (words and music TR)
The Nightshift (Piccadilly) (single A side)

1967
DOWN THRU' SUMMER/I'LL GIVE ALL MY LOVE TO SOUTHEND (music ALW)
Ross Hannaman (Columbia) (single A and B side)

1969/PROBABLY ON THURSDAY (music ALW)
Ross Hannaman (Columbia) (single A and B side)

Danièle Noël (EP) – issued only in France:
YOU TOOK ME FOR A RIDE (Recorded as *Les Quatre Volontes*, French lyric F. Gérard)
DANIELE (lyric in French by TR)
SOMETHING TO SAY (Recorded as *Pourtant Moi Je N'ai Pas Change*, French lyric F. Gérard)
I'LL GIVE ALL MY LOVE TO SOUTHEND (Recorded as *Je N'Aimerai Plus Jamais Personne*, French lyric B. Nencioli)
Danièle Noël (French Philips) (all tracks music by ALW)

WISH YOU WOULD SHOW ME YOUR MIND (music David Paramor)
Nocturnes (Columbia) (single B side)

1968
SUDDENLY FREE (music David Paramor)
Nocturnes (Columbia) (single B side)
BELIEVE ME I WILL (music ALW)
Sacha Distel (MCA) (album track)

1969
WE WILL ROCK YOU (traditional tune)
Christopher (RCA) (single A side)
JULIET SIMPKINS (instrumental – music TR)
The Power Pack (Polydor) (single B side)
COME BACK RICHARD YOUR COUNTRY NEEDS YOU/ROLL ON OVER THE ATLANTIC (music ALW)
Tim Rice and the Webber Group (RCA) (single A and B side)
THE OPPOSITE LOCK (music Nick Ingman)
Emperor Rosko (Polydor) (single A side)

1970
SEVEN AND A HALF PER CENT SWING (music ALW)
Floating Voters (Pye) (Single B side)
GOODBYE SEATTLE (music ALW)
Paul Raven (US Decca) (single A side) – issued only in US

1972
WHAT A LINE TO GO OUT ON (music ALW)
Yvonne Elliman (Polydor) (single A side)
BAYOU FARM (words and music TR)
Huddersfield Transit Authority (Polydor) (single B side)
ONE OF THE ALL TIME GRATES (music Roger Watson)
Huddersfield Transit Authority (Polydor) (single B side)
FINALLY (THEME FROM THE FILM *GUMSHOE*) (music ALW)
Pamela Paterson (Polydor) (single A side)
BABY YOU'RE GOOD FOR ME (music ALW) (from the soundtrack of *Gumshoe*)
Roy Young (never released on record – only heard in the film)

1973
DISILLUSION ME (music ALW)
Gary Bond (Polydor) (single A side)
CHILD OF THE FIFTIES (music TR, words Jonathan Rice)
Rover (Polydor B side)

1974
CHRISTMAS DREAM (from the soundtrack of *The Odessa File*) (music ALW)
Perry Como (RCA) (single A side)
Maynard Williams (MCA) (album track)
NOTHING DIFFERENT (words and music TR)
Tim Rice (Chrysalis) (single B side)
THE PRESIDENT SONG (words and music TR)
Victor Trumper (US MCA) (single A side)

1975
Five further tracks on *Ten Songs* (album):
THE RED ROOM
TURNING
DOWN ON THE FARM
MARISA
I CAN'T GO ON (music for all songs by ALW)
Maynard Williams (MCA)

All tracks on *Barbapapa* (album):
THE BARBAPAPA FAMILY
LITTLE SHADOW
BE A THINKER
BARBALIB
THE GREATEST ANIMAL LOVER
BARBABEAU'S PAINTBOX
BARBAPAPA ROCK
EVERYTHING IS SINGING FOR BARBALALA
SEND FOR BARBABRAVO
BARBABELLE (music for all songs by Joop Stockkermans)
Ed Stewart, Cathy MacDonald and The London Boy Singers (Philips)

1976
HEY LOVE (WHAT A WAY TO SPEND THE NIGHT) (words and music TR)
Tim Rice (DJM) (single A side)

1977
MAGDALENA (music ALW)
Tony Christie (MCA) (single A side)
IT'S EASY FOR YOU (music ALW)
Elvis Presley (RCA) (album track)
THE ONLY WAY TO GO (music Marvin Hamlisch)
Bing Crosby (United Artists) (album track)

Thus, assuming my research has been accurate, from the time of my first recorded song, 'That's My Story' in March 1965, up until the opening night of *Evita* in June 1978, forty-six of my compositions or co-compositions that were not part of a theatrical score were released on record and one other was heard in a movie. Twenty-four had music by Andrew Lloyd Webber, ten by a Dutch gent I never met, seven were my own tunes (including one instrumental), two were written with David Paramor, and one tune each was contributed by Marvin Hamlisch, Roger Watson, Nick Ingman and a long departed, out of copyright, Czech composer.

None of the forty-seven can be classified as a bona fide hit, although 'Christmas Dream' (music ALW) by Perry Como did limp into the bottom of the US Hot 100. 'The Only Way To Go' (Hamlisch) did eventually appear on a moderately popular George Burns album and of course 'It's Easy For You' (ALW), by virtue of its inclusion on Elvis' last album to be issued while he was alive, was part of a best-selling package.

The only other songs in this list to have attracted further (or 'cover') recordings were 'That's My Story' which a Mexican group called the Six Kings sang in Spanish, 'Down Thru' Summer' which was recorded by two Spanish acts, thanks entirely to Enzo Hamilton, a friend of mine who was briefly an executive of EMI Barcelona; and 'We Will Rock You' by Elaine Paige as a B side in 1982.

All in all I am glad I did not rely on non-theatre songs to make a living.

C. AS RECORDING ARTIST (VOCALS):

1969 as Tim Rice and the Webber Group
COME BACK RICHARD YOUR COUNTRY NEEDS YOU/ROLL ON OVER THE ATLANTIC (RCA single)
Both TR/ALW songs

1972 as Huddersfield Transit Authority
RUNAWAY/BAYOU FARM (Polydor single)
A side the Del Shannon 1961 hit written by Shannon & Max Crook; B side TR words and music
DIFFERENT DRUM/ONE OF THE ALL TIME GRATES (Polydor single)
A side the Linda Ronstadt & Stone Poneys 1967 US hit written by Mike Nesmith; B side TR words, Roger Watson music

1973 as Rover
WINDOW THE IN DOGGIE THAT IS MUCH HOW/CHILD OF THE FIFTIES (RSO single)
A side the 1953 Patti Page/Lita Rosa hit written by Bob Merrill (sung backwards); B side TR tune (same one as 'That's My Story') Jonathan Rice lyrics

1974 as Tim Rice
NOT FADE AWAY/NOTHING DIFFERENT (Chrysalis single)

A side a Crickets B side from 1958 written by Buddy Holly & Norman Petty;
B side words and music TR

1974 as Victor Trumper
THE PRESIDENT SONG/CHILD OF THE FIFTIES (US MCA single)
A side words and music TR; B side a re-use of the Rover B side

1975 as one of the Arzenboys
BUMP ON MY HEAD (PARTS 1 & 2) (DJM single)
Both sides by Jonathan Rice and Jonathan Chuter; the Arzenboys were Bill
Heath's band, co-lead vocals TR, under a bewildering temporary name

1976 as Tim Rice
HEY LOVE (WHAT A WAY TO SPEND THE NIGHT)/HOW DO I LOOK (DJM
single)
A side words and music TR; B side by Jonathan Rice & Jonathan Chuter

N.B. 1968:
Backing vocals on Scaffold single 'Lily The Pink' (a Number One!) (Parlophone)

D. MISCELLANEOUS
RECORD PRODUCTIONS:

1966
Solo productions:
GOODBYE LITTLE GIRL/A LITTLE BIT OF LOVIN' – The Shell (Columbia
single)
A side written by Brian Henderson; B side by the Shell
SOME DAY SOON/YOU BORE ME – Murray Head & Blue Monks (Columbia
single)
Both songs written by Murray Head

1967
Produced with Bob Barratt:
DOWN THRU' SUMMER/I'LL GIVE ALL MY LOVE TO SOUTHEND – Ross
Hannaman (Columbia single)
1969/PROBABLY ON THURSDAY – Ross Hannaman (Columbia single)
Produced with ALW:
YOU TOOK ME FOR A RIDE/DANIELE/SOMETHING TO SAY/I'LL GIVE ALL MY
LOVE TO SOUTHEND – Danièle Noël EP
All 1967 songs above by ALW/TR

1968

Produced with ALW:

ALBERT/MONDAY MORNING – TALES OF JUSTINE (HMV single)
Both songs written by David Daltrey. Nearly every Tales of Justine or David Daltrey track produced by ALW/TR in 1968/69 at Abbey Road was issued on the Tenth Planet label as a vinyl only album in 1997 – worth looking for

1968–69

With Norrie Paramor, assisted on or co-produced various titles by The Scaffold, The Power Pack, Nick Ingman, Emperor Rosko, Gracious

1969

Produced with ALW:

POTIPHAR/MILLION DOLLAR BASH – The Mixed Bag (Decca single)
ROUND AND ROUND/HAVE YOU EVER BEEN IN LOVE – The Mixed Bag (Decca single)
You're My Girl I Say was the B side to Round And Round in the US
Million Dollar Bash by Bob Dylan; other songs written by the Mixed Bag, except 'Potiphar' by ALW/TR
WE WILL ROCK YOU/ANY DREAM WILL DO – Christopher (RCA single)
A side traditional Czech tune with TR lyrics; B side by ALW/TR
COME BACK RICHARD YOUR COUNTRY NEEDS YOU/ROLL ON OVER THE ATLANTIC – Tim Rice & The Webber group (RCA single)
Both songs by ALW/TR

1970

Produced with ALW:

BRIDGE OVER TROUBLE WATER/SEVEN-AND-A-HALF PERCENT SWING – (Pye single)
A side credited to Harold and Ted, written by Paul Simon, B side to Floating Voters, written by ALW/TR
Produced with ALW & Mike Leander:
GOODBYE SEATTLE – Paul Raven A side
Written by ALW/TR

1971

Produced with ALW:

PETER AND THE WOLF (Prokofiev) with Frankie Howerd and the City of London Ensemble conducted by Alan Doggett (Polydor album)

1972

Produced with ALW:

WHAT A LINE TO GO OUT ON/INTERLUDE FOR JOHNNY – Yvonne Elliman (Polydor single)
A side by ALW/TR; B side by Yvonne Elliman
YVONNE ELLIMAN – Yvonne Elliman (MCA album)
Contained just one ALW/TR song 'I Don't Know How To Love Him'
Produced with Roger Watson:
RUNAWAY/BAYOU FARM – Huddersfield Transit Authority (Polydor single)

A side by Del Shannon & Max Crook; B side by TR
DIFFERENT DRUM/ONE OF THE ALL TIME GRATES – Huddersfield Transit
Authority (Polydor single)
A side by Mike Nesmith; B side by TR/Roger Watson
SATISFIED WITH LIFE/ETERNITY'S SWEET HONEYCOMB – Vocal Refrain (Polydor
single)
A side by George M. Cohan; B side by Jonathan Chuter/Roger Watson

1973
Produced with Roger Watson:
FRESH LIVER – The Scaffold (Island album)
*All titles written by the Scaffold from which John Gorman single WPC Hodges/
I Remember issued*
Produced with ALW:
DISILLUSION ME/ANY DREAM WILL DO – Gary Bond (Polydor single)
Both songs by ALW/TR
Solo production:
WINDOW THE IN DOGGIE THAT IS MUCH HOW/CHILD OF THE FIFTIES – Rover
(RSO single)
A side written by Bob Merrill; B side by TR & Jonathan Rice

1974
Produced with ALW:
TEN SONGS – Maynard Williams (MCA album)
Six of ten songs by ALW/TR
Solo production:
LOVE ENOUGH/SILÉ – Paul Jones (Private Stock single)
A side written by Tim Moore; B side by Paul Jones

1975
Produced with Bill Heath & Co.:
BUMP ON MY HEAD (PARTS 1 & 2) – The Arzenboys (DJM single)
Both sides written by Jonathan Rice/Jonathan Chuter

1976
Produced with Andrew Powell:
HEY LOVE/HOW DO I LOOK – Tim Rice (DJM single)
A side by TR; B side by Jonathan Rice/Jonathan Chuter

1977
Produced with ALW:
MAGDALENA – Tony Christie A side
Written by ALW/TR

1978
Solo productions:
SHEENA IS A PUNK ROCKER/PRETTY VACANT – Paul Jones (RSO single)
A side written by the Ramones; B side by the Sex Pistols

BORN TO SING/SIMPLE THINGS IN LIFE – Colm Wilkinson (RSO single)
A side written by Colm Wilkinson; B side by Gordon Waller

None of the above productions were hits; you should have heard the tracks that didn't get released.

Index

437